REMAKING THE BRIT

Remaking the British Atlantic focuses on a crucial phase in the history of British-American relations: the first ten years of American Independence. These set the pattern for some years to come. On the one hand, there was to be no effective political rapprochement after rebellion and war. Mainstream British opinion was little influenced by the failure to subdue the revolt or by the emergence of a new America, for which they mostly felt disdain. What were taken to be the virtues of the British constitution were confidently reasserted and there was little inclination either to disengage from empire or to manage it in different ways. For their part, many Americans defined the new order that they were seeking to establish by their rejection of what they took to be the abuses of contemporary Britain. On the other hand, neither the trauma of war nor the failure to create harmonious political relations could prevent the re-establishment of the very close links that had spanned the pre-war Atlantic, locking people on both sides of it into close connections with one another. Many British migrants still went to America. Britain remained America's dominant trading partner. American tastes and the intellectual life of the new republic continued to be largely reflections of British tastes and ideas. America and Britain were too important for too many people in too many ways for political alienation to keep them apart.

Remaking the British Atlantic

The United States and the British Empire
after American Independence

P. J. MARSHALL

OXFORD
UNIVERSITY PRESS

OXFORD
UNIVERSITY PRESS

Great Clarendon Street, Oxford, OX2 6DP,
United Kingdom

Oxford University Press is a department of the University of Oxford.
It furthers the University's objective of excellence in research, scholarship,
and education by publishing worldwide. Oxford is a registered trade mark of
Oxford University Press in the UK and in certain other countries

Published in the United States of America by Oxford University Press
198 Madison Avenue, New York, NY 10016, United States of America

British Library Cataloguing in Publication Data
Data available

Library of Congress Cataloging in Publication Data
Data available

ISBN 978–0–19–964035–5 (Hbk.)
ISBN 978–0–19–873492–5 (Pbk.)

Preface

American independence broke apart a single British empire that had spanned the North Atlantic and set off processes of imperial remaking, which will be a principal theme in the first half of the book. The British patched up their imperial system, in doing so making, it will be argued, rather fewer changes in direction than is sometimes suggested, while the Americans took the first steps towards what they envisaged to be an entirely new continental empire, even if many influences from the British past can be detected in it. The Anglo-American war not only disrupted the British empire but it put in jeopardy transatlantic links of many kinds. Movements of people, goods, and ideas and common patterns of consumption had all tied the colonies to the British Isles. In spite of the increasing political estrangement of Britain and the thirteen colonies that culminated in war, these links had been growing progressively closer before the Revolution. The second half of the book will try to show that many of the pre-war links were quickly restored after 1783 and were to prove enduring ones for some time to come. This world of connections between communities on both sides of the ocean ensured the continuing existence of what was still a British Atlantic, even though there were now two empires rather than one.

Political alienation combined with close economic and cultural integration are thus the main themes of the book. Historians have long identified these apparently contradictory trends in the years before the Revolution. This book will explore their persistence after independence.

A longer perspective may perhaps help us to understand a little better what seems to be the central problem of the American Revolution considered in an Anglo-American context: how had the political cultures of Britons and Americans come to deviate so sharply that they eventually went to war with one another, while they remained indispensable to one another in many other respects?

I am very conscious that the British and American sides of the relationship are treated unequally. Almost all of the archival research that has gone into this book has been done in Britain and my competence in the history of the early American republic is limited. The abundance of printed sources published in the United States and the remarkable quality of the great body of historical writing about the period offer some compensation to students who stay at home, even though keeping abreast with what can only be a portion of these riches is a truly daunting task. My efforts to do so have benefited greatly not only from the British Library but also from the University of London Library and the library of the Institute of Historical Research. The last two complement one another with their extensive collections of secondary work and published documents. My debt to both of these institutions is very great. The staff of both, particularly that of the Senate House Library, have in recent years coped with exemplary ingenuity and fortitude both with constant relocations to different parts of that remarkable building and with uncertainty about their future prospects.

Friends have been most generous in giving time to read parts of this book and offering salutary criticism. Stephen Conway read the whole thing and made many helpful suggestions, for which I owe him my deepest gratitude. Richard Johnson of the University of Washington has given stalwart help with chapters where my American knowledge is most vulnerable. Robert Travers raised many valuable points. Richard Drayton, Ian McBride, Andrew O'Shaughnessy, and Jane Samson were kind enough to pass particular chapters under their expert eyes. Thanks to the kind offices of David Hancock, I was able both to do research in the great Clements Library at Ann Arbor and to talk about Lord Shelburne in a place which has long been a centre of scholarship about him. I am greatly indebted for the unstinting support which the book received at Oxford University Press from Christopher Wheeler and Stephanie Ireland and to Jeremy Langworthy for meticulous copy-editing.

Much of the material in chapter 15 first appeared in an article called 'Transatlantic Protestantism and American Independence' in *The Journal of Imperial and Commonwealth History*, XXXVI (2008), 345–62, published by the Taylor and Francis Group.

In quotations the original spelling has generally been kept, but capitalization has been modernized.

P. J. M.

Braughing, July 2011

Contents

List of Abbreviations

BL	British Library
Davies (ed.), *Documents*	K. G. Davies (ed.), *Documents of the American Revolution 1770–1783*, 21 vols. (Shannon, 1972–81)
Giunta (ed.), *Emerging Nation*	Mary A. Giunta (ed.), *The Emerging Nation: A Documentary History of the Foreign Relations of the United States under the Articles of Confederation*, 3 vols. (Washington, DC, 1996)
Parliamentary Register	J. Debrett (ed.), *The Parliamentary Register; or History of The Proceedings and Debates in the House of Commons*, 45 vols. (London, 1780–96)
TNA	The National Archives
WLCL	William L. Clements Library, University of Michigan

Introduction

I

This book deals with the crucial decade in the reordering of relations between Britain and its empire and an independent America. Its starting point is in 1781, when it became clear, especially after the battle of Yorktown, that the retention within the British empire of a substantial part of the old thirteen colonies was no longer a possibility. American independence in some form was inevitable. It ends at about 1790. Both sides had by then done much to repair the damage wrought by a long war. Expectations, widely held in Europe, that America without Britain would fragment or even collapse into anarchy had not been fulfilled. The states that had thrown off British rule had survived and had replaced their loose confederation with a tighter federal union. A process of transcontinental expansion was beginning. What Americans were calling their new empire was soon to incorporate fresh territory to the west. In August 1790 George Washington could write with cautious optimism. 'We have a good government in theory, and are carrying it pretty happily into practice . . . [P]opulation increases, land is cleared, commerce extended, manufactories introduced, and heaven smiles upon us with favourable seasons and abundant crops.'[1] On the other hand, confident expectations that Britain without America would fall into the second rank of powers had not been fulfilled either. By 1790 Britain had won diplomatic successes over France and Spain, her leading enemies in the American War, and it was obvious that she remained a powerful presence in Europe, America, and Asia. Her imperial possessions were expanding anew. Many historians have seen the 1780s as a formative decade in the creation of what they call a second British empire. Britain's economy was undergoing rapid growth. 'The country is at this moment', William Pitt told the House of Commons in April 1790, 'in a situation of prosperity far greater than at any period the most flourishing before the last war. . . . [O]ur commerce, our manufactures, our industry, our population, and our wealth' were all increasing rapidly.[2] By 1790 America and Britain had both achieved a measure of stability, even if few historians would argue that the processes that constituted the American Revolution had as yet run their course and the reverberations of the French Revolution were soon to convulse both Britain and America.

---

[1] To Rochambeau, 10 August 1790, W. W. Abbot et al. (eds), *The Papers of George Washington: Presidential Series* (Charlottesville, VA, 1987–), VI, p. 232.
[2] 19 April 1790, *Parliamentary Register*, XXVII, p. 453.

During the 1780s some elements of the Anglo-American relationship changed dramatically: others changed more slowly or even hardly at all. Political and constitutional changes were, of course, sweeping. The American states were no longer part of the British empire nor subjected to any formal British authority. Their constitutions and the new federal Constitution owed much to their British inheritance, but ostensibly they were professedly established on entirely new republican principles in direct conflict with the principles believed to be embodied in the British mixed monarchy. American pride in their new systems of government was to be matched by vehement British restatements of the virtues of the incomparable British constitution. A brisk exchange of polemics denouncing a corrupt British oligarchy or a licentious American democracy, begun during the war, was to continue after the peace.

Hopes for a post-war reconciliation that might have transcended separation and what purported to be antagonistic systems of government were soon dashed. Americans quickly diagnosed hostile British designs against them. They believed that Britain was trying to strangle their seaborne trade and subvert their union. Much of what Americans interpreted as hostility seems, however, to have been indifference and lack of concern. Having risked so much on a war to keep the colonies within the empire, Britain appeared—as Richard Price, the most consistent and fervent upholder of the American cause, noted in 1785—to have gone to the other extreme. 'During the war the cry was that our essential interests depended on keeping the colonies. Now it seems to be discover'd that they are of no use to us.'[3] His point was a fair one. Relations with the new America now came low on the scale of British post-war political calculations. Disputes, above all over commercial matters, were allowed to fester and no formal attempt was made to resolve them until the negotiations for the Jay Treaty of 1794. A continuing British imperial presence on the American continent carried the potential for fresh disputes. Britain consolidated her hold over her remaining colonies around the Gulf of St Lawrence and the Caribbean and seemed at times to be challenging American expansion both in the Northwest and in the Southwest. The conditions that made it possible for Britain and the United States to blunder into war in 1812, mutual disesteem, American resentment at what seemed to them to be Britain's insistence on its right to control their maritime trade, and a continuing British presence on the continent, were essentially put in place in the 1780s.

Under the old imperial order Anglo-American ties had involved much more than the exercise of metropolitan authority. What has been called a 'British Atlantic world', created by 'kaleidoscopic movements of people goods and ideas', had grown up loosely within the British empire.[4] People crossed the Atlantic in great numbers

---

[3] To Lansdowne, 29 October 1785, D. O. Thomas and W. Bernard Peach (eds), *The Correspondence of Richard Price*, 3 vols. (Cardiff and Durham, NC, 1983–94), II, p. 318.

[4] David Armitage and Michael J. Braddick, 'Introduction' in Armitage and Braddick (eds), *The British Atlantic World 1500–1800*, 2nd edn (Houndmills, 2009), p. 1. The concept of a British Atlantic world as expounded in this book seems to be an enlightening one. It needs, however, to be applied with the obvious reservation that involvement in the Atlantic was unequal. So long as the settlements of colonial or early national America were mainly coastal and dependent on seaborne trade,

between Britain and America and many from the British Isles migrated to live permanently in the American colonies. Economically the thirteen colonies were closely integrated into the empire by a very large volume of trade with Britain and the British West Indies. The great majority of the white population of the colonies shared a common culture with the peoples of the British Isles based on the English language, the same religious affiliations, mostly to Protestant denominations, and similar patterns of taste and consumption.

Changes in the very diverse links that had bound the old thirteen colonies into the British Atlantic world were much less cataclysmic in the immediate aftermath of the war than the constitutional separation and political alienation that put Britain and America apart and kept them apart. Constitutional independence held out the prospect for loosening other ties with Britain and for enabling America to develop economic self-sufficiency and cultural autonomy as well as to foster closer contacts with other parts of Europe. Many Americans welcomed such possibilities. Realizing this potential was, however to take a considerable time. In the meantime, British links endured. America still drew the great majority of its European immigrants from Britain and Ireland. Britain remained America's dominant trading partner. Most white American Protestants continued to be members of denominations that had originated in Britain. Culturally, the American elites in particular were still very much English men and women in their outlook and tastes, while imported British goods were consumed at all levels of white American society. The British Atlantic world seemed to be surviving without its political dimension.

The first half of this book deals with the failure of Britain and America to establish any sort of harmonious political relations after the trauma of rebellion and independence. It analyses the peace settlement that left lasting resentments on both sides and many areas of conflict unresolved. A separate chapter on the 'Politics of Trade' describes the commercial disputes that festered long after the peace, doing much to sour Anglo-American relations. Chapters 3 and 4 try to show how each side interpreted the other. The political leadership neither of a new America nor of a changing Britain professed to think well of one another. The concept of 'challenge' is used, implying that both sides stressed difference and in some degree envisaged the other as threatening their political order. This was especially the case with the Americans. Finally, chapters in the first half of the book will deal with the continuing British empire in the Atlantic, that is over Ireland and to the north and the south of the United States, in what was to become Canada and around the Caribbean. All three areas had close contacts with the United States in the movement of trade and people, but here too the British stressed difference as they generally continued to try to order their empire along lines set well before the American Revolution and to regard American influences as a threat to stability.

---

they were fully integrated into an Atlantic world. The Atlantic was very important for parts of the British Isles, notably for Ulster, for Bristol, Cork, Liverpool, and their hinterlands; for the Devonshire fishing ports; and for western Scotland. London transacted a great deal of Atlantic business. The main orientation of the greater part of Britain and much of Ireland was not, however, necessarily towards the Atlantic.

While the first half of book deals with the failure of both sides to pick up the pieces of a shattered empire, the second half will be concerned with the extent that the pre-Revolution British Atlantic world was able to survive American independence. Its first chapter will be about the transoceanic movements of people, showing how America continued to recruit most of its free immigrants from Britain. The following chapter deals with the evolution of Anglophone communities in North America that remained under British rule. An important new element among them was the so-called loyalists, who had renounced their political links with the United States but still often remained in contact with them, and with them were very much part of a continuing linked British Atlantic world. There are chapters on the recovery of Anglo-American trade, and on the survival of what are here called 'customs in common'. These varied from commitment to the same ideals of liberty guaranteed by law, similar models of polite behaviour and of fashionable décor, tastes in common in reading, and the same ways of cultivating learning in the sciences. Americans might wish, as John Adams put it, to free themselves of the 'excessive admiration of foreigners' that had been a mark of their colonial status,[5] but Britain was still seen in America as the source of much valued expertise. Despairing of Virginia's husbandry, Washington wanted to import 'a thorough bred *practical* English farmer', since 'no country has carried the improvement of land and the benefits of agriculture to greater perfection than England'.[6] Americans continued to measure their cultural achievements by British standards and sought British recognition and approval. A separate chapter will try to assess the effects of American independence on relations between Protestants on both sides of the Atlantic. Here again there was much continuity with the colonial past, although links between most denominations were weakened and America's religious life was taking distinctive forms, above all through vigorous evangelical revivals.

II

The war had sharply divided British opinion. Until 1782 a clear majority in both Houses of Parliament had been willing to vote for the war in America and there had been strong support for it in the country at large, although there seems to be no way of determining whether this was the view of a majority of the British population. Those who had supported the armed coercion of the Americans usually did so because they believed that Britain benefited greatly from empire in America through the huge volume of trade transacted with it. The thirteen colonies were a major market for British manufactured exports and great flows of commodities from America came to Britain to supply the needs of British consumers or manufacturers or to be re-exported by British merchants to Europe. Much of the

---

[5] To President of Congress, 5 September 1783, Robert J. Taylor et al. (eds), *The Papers of John Adams* (Cambridge, MA, 1977–), XV, p. 255.
[6] To G. W. Fairfax, 30 June 1785, W. W. Abbot et al. (eds), *The Papers of George Washington: Confederation Series*, 6 vols. (Charlottesville, VA, 1992–7), III, p. 89.

financial muscle that enabled Britain to maintain the world's largest navy and a considerable army was believed to be derived from colonial trade. An independent America, whose economy was no longer regulated by Britain, would, it was assumed, cease to be an asset but instead would grow into a formidable rival in commerce and shipping and a large proportion of its trade would probably go to Britain's European competitors. America's alliance with France since 1778 aroused deep apprehension for the future were it to persist. Typical fears were that 'If America (especially connected with France) becomes independent, we may possibly be allow'd to eat bread and beef in our little island; but imperial sway, national dignity, ostentation, and luxury must with our commerce be annihilated.'[7]

For those who thought that the war must be fought to a successful conclusion, there were also fundamental ideological principles at stake. In their view, the Americans were not an oppressed people rejecting the tyranny that British ministers aimed to impose on them. They were being deluded by the machinations of their power-crazed leaders into wantonly rebelling against a benevolent empire that allowed them virtually all the freedoms of the people of Britain itself and under whose benign system of economic regulation they were undoubtedly prospering. Such a rebellion was not directed against the policies of a particular government but, in the words of a Scottish divine, against 'the whole legislature of the country', that is against the British constitution. The 'too manifest aim' of those leading the revolt was, 'to ferment in the people a seditious and ungovernable spirit'.[8] A government pamphleteer wrote that the principles expounded in the Declaration of Independence were not only '*repugnant to the British constitution*. But beyond that they are subversive of every actual or imaginable kind of government.'[9] Such principles could not be allowed to prevail. The danger of the contagion spreading to other colonies, to Ireland and to Britain itself was obvious. It was often alleged that a 'republican faction' in Britain was sustaining rebellion in America. They could not be allowed to prevail either.

Failure to subdue America did not necessarily discredit the principles for which supporters of the war believed that it had been fought. They expected little from the new America and had no interest in establishing a new relationship with it beyond recovering as much of its trade as possible. In their view Britain should not make concessions to the Americans with a view to reconciliation. The Revolution emphatically did not mark the dawn of a new order of human freedom and happiness. Everything that they heard of post-war America convinced them that government was failing throughout the states and that Americans had condemned themselves to political instability and poverty. As a struggle to try to save the Americans from the consequences of their own folly or at least to quarantine the pernicious principles of the Revolution within the confines of the old thirteen

---

[7] Letter of Earl of Buckinghamshire to H. Clinton, 8 December 1781, *Historical Manuscripts Commission, Lothian MSS* (London, 1905), p. 404.

[8] George Campbell, *The Nature, Extent, and Importance of the Duty of Allegiance: A Sermon Preached at Aberdeen, 12 December 1776*, 2nd edn (Aberdeen, 1778), p. 31.

[9] [John Lind], *An Answer to the Declaration of the American Congress* (London, 1776), p. 120.

colonies, the war had been worth fighting. William Knox, an under-secretary throughout the war, was one of those who believed that if Parliament had relinquished its authority over America without a war, 'the republican disposition which is every day gaining ground in this island and in Ireland, under the masque of free thinking and philosophy, but in truth through the prevalence of infidelity and self-sufficiency' would have ensured that 'these islands would not long have retained their people or the state its power'.[10] Knox, who was unremittingly hostile to the new America, will feature prominently in this book as he enjoyed a kind of Indian summer of influence with post-war governments. His political survival is a strong indication that the mindset which had justified going to war to subdue the colonies was surviving the failure of the war.

Many who had supported the war were, however, willing to reassess old maxims about how essential possession of the thirteen colonies had been to Britain's standing as a great power. There was very little, if any, post-war repining for dominion over them. William Smith, an American loyalist who lobbied persistently on behalf of schemes of reunion with the United States, was rebuffed by all shades of opinion from George III downwards.[11] Richard Price's observation that it now seemed generally to be believed that the colonies had been 'of no use to us' was well founded. So to many it seemed. The thirteen colonies, especially the northern ones, were increasingly seen to have been anomalies within the British imperial system. They had outgrown their usefulness to the empire. They were too sprawling and too diverse to be kept within it. In a book published in the last year of the war, the political economist James Anderson argued that the interests of America and Britain had often diverged, so that the two peoples had not formed 'one compacted whole tending towards one object', but had been 'an aggregate, consisting of discordant elements' conflicting with one another.[12] American shipping and fishing competed with vital British interests and they would in time become manufacturers. It would be better to exclude them than to try to readmit them to the empire after the war. The views of a 'Mr Cochran' (presumably John Cochrane, agent of a British bank in Quebec) seem to have been characteristic of what was coming to be conventional wisdom. The Americans within the empire had been 'running away with it'. He believed that 'The severance of the empire was precisely at the best juncture. Great Britain, all her 100 millions of debt notwithstanding, is a gainer, her strength more concentrated, her navigation and marine force increased.'[13] Lord Macartney, future ambassador to China, came to believe that the British empire was 'a great deal stronger' without its American component, which had been 'too heavy for the edifice which it was thought to adorn'.[14]

---

[10] *Extra Official State Papers*, 2 vols. (London, 1789), II, pp. 22–3.

[11] See below, pp. 87–8.

[12] *The Interest of Great Britain with Regard to her American Colonies Considered* (London, 1782), pp. 35–6.

[13] William Smith Diary, 23 May 1786, L. F. S. Upton (ed.), *The Diary and Selected Papers of Chief Justice William Smith 1784–1793*, 2 vols. (Toronto, 1963–5), II, p. 95.

[14] Cited in P. J. Marshall, *The Making and Unmaking of Empires: Britain, India and America, c.1750–1783* (Oxford, 2005), p. 362.

Post-war experience, as British exports recovered their American markets, quickly seemed to confirm what Adam Smith and Josiah Tucker had been proclaiming for some years: Britain's dominant position in the trade of the colonies did not depend on exercising rule over them. The experience of the war and its immediate aftermath raised other doubts as to what had been received wisdom about the vital role of empire in America. Britain had financed what had been the most expensive war in her history without the revenues generated by American trade. The war had disrupted trade and caused hardship, but the capacity of Britain's manufacturing to capture worldwide, and especially European, markets was growing rapidly. Britain was proving that she could face the world without any imperial connections with America, which had probably been more of a liability than an advantage.

The bulk of the British political elite seem to have judged empire in terms of material costs and benefits. Once the costs could be shown to outweigh the benefits, empire over the thirteen colonies was jettisoned with relative equanimity and there seemed to be little point in trying to forge a new kind of relationship. A view of the British empire as embodying a common set of values had been much more strongly held in the colonies than in Britain itself.[15] When Benjamin Franklin described American patriots as the true loyalists, he was not necessarily being perverse.[16] Especially in the 1760s, British officials and ministers freely spoke of the American colonies and Britain as part of a single 'nation', but their purpose in using such language was usually little more than to try to persuade Americans to accept the obligations that went with belonging to the same nation, that is that they should pay the taxes voted by the Parliament which claimed to represent them.[17] Jefferson's rhetorical flourish, omitted from the Declaration of Independence, had an essential truth in it: '[W]e might have been a free and a great people together; but a communication of grandeur and of freedom it seems is below their dignity'.[18] America was to contribute to Britain's grandeur by providing resources to enable Britain to uphold her standing among the European powers, but it was not generally conceived to be a partner in it. British opinion took little account of a distinct 'colonial political culture'.[19] American views about a British imperial constitution in which colonies had customary rights established over a long period must yield to British insistence on the sovereignty of Parliament throughout the empire.

At the end of the war, a British well wisher for Anglo-American relations expressed the unreal hope that 'an *English minister*' might learn to 'treat the people of America at least as civilly as he would treat the county of York. It does not follow

---

[15] Richard Koebner, *Empire* (Cambridge, 1961), chs. 3 and 4; David Armitage, *The Ideological Origins of the British Empire* (Cambridge, 2000), ch. 7. The 'passion' of colonial America for monarchy and empire is the theme of Brendan McConville, *The King's Three Faces: The Rise and Fall of Royal America, 1688–1776* (Chapel Hill, NC, 2006).

[16] See below, p. 38.

[17] Eliga H. Gould, *The Persistence of Empire: British Political Culture in the Age of the American Revolution* (Chapel Hill, NC, 2000), pp. 116–22.

[18] Julian P. Boyd et al. (eds), *The Papers of Thomas Jefferson* (Princeton, NJ, 1950–), I, p. 427.

[19] Daniel J. Hulsebosch, *Constituting Empire: New York and the Transformation of Constitutionalism in the Atlantic World 1664–1830* (Chapel Hill, NC, 2005), p. 134.

that because we think little of these people, that they will think little of themselves.'[20] The American elites were not generally much regarded. They flocked to London in large numbers for pleasure, education and business, but they were poorly integrated into the governing structure of the empire.[21] Notoriously few sat in the British House of Commons and the capacity of colonial lobbies to influence policy declined from the mid eighteenth century.[22] American notables, especially colonial agents cultivated men in office when they came to Britain, but there is little to suggest that British politicians concerned themselves much with visiting Americans, Lord Shelburne being an obvious exception.[23] Colonial America offered the British political elite limited opportunities for profitable civil office-holding[24] and, especially after 1763, it gave them extensive chances for speculative accumulations of land to be held as absentees. The scale of the wars gave officers in the army and navy some exposure to America. A few individuals who served there, like Thomas Pownall, governor of Massachusetts from 1757 to 1759, came to identify themselves with America. After independence he saw it as '*my country*'.[25] Guy Carleton, who will feature much in this book, also committed himself deeply to British America, if very much on his own terms. The involvement of most seems, however, to have been superficial.[26] It will be theme of the second half of this book that the British Atlantic world was made up of a number of vigorous transatlantic communities, but at least on the British side there was no strong sense of an Anglo-American political community even before American independence.

By the end of the war from a British point of view the breaking of political connections began to seem positively desirable to some. At the beginning of the crisis Josiah Tucker warned that republicanism was an infection that would spread across the Atlantic. Those who were creating republican regimes in the colonies were 'paving the way for introducing a similar establishment into *Great Britain*'.[27] For him, this was one of many reasons for a separation. In the later stages of the war, it became clear that the new republican order in America could not be suppressed and that its recognition would be the price of maintaining any kind of imperial link. This raised questions about the consequences for Britain itself if that price were to be paid. Could the British constitution safely coexist with officially recognized

---

[20] Benjamin Vaughan to Shelburne, 15 November 1782, BL, Add MS 88906/1/19, f. 103.

[21] Julie Flavell, *When London Was Capital of America* (New Haven, CT, 2010).

[22] Alison Gilbert Olson, *Making the Empire Work: London and American Interest Groups 1690–1790* (Cambridge, MA, 1992).

[23] For Shelburne's American contacts, see below, pp. 34–5.

[24] 'Aside from the customs establishments and the governorships, there were only a scattering of positions in the North American colonies likely to attract any of the well connected and the hungry in Britain', Jacob M. Price, 'Who Cared about the Colonies? The Impact of the Thirteen Colonies on British Society and Politics, *circa* 1714–1775' in Bernard. Bailyn and Philip D. Morgan (eds), *Strangers Within the Realm: Cultural Margins of the First British Empire* (Chapel Hill, NC, 1991), p. 396.

[25] See below, p. 229.

[26] The chapter by Namier on the American connections of British MPs in the early 1760s, originally published in 1930, is still very suggestive: Lewis Namier, *England in the Age of the American Revolution*, 2nd edn (London, 1961), ch. IV.

[27] *An Humble Address and Earnest Appeal*, 2nd edn (Gloucester, 1775), p. 17.

republican institutions in the same empire? Would not such an American link strengthen pressure for constitutional change in Britain? Maurice Morgann, an adviser to Lord Shelburne, who believed that only 'reunion with America . . . can save England from ruin', thought that such a reunion would require a very thorough reform of Parliament to produce 'a constitution congenial with America'. He welcomed that prospect,[28] but to mainstream opinion it was an abhorrent one. A clean break with America would spare Britain 'the pain of making the sorts of legal and constitutional concessions necessary' for keeping Americans with hetero-dox political practices and beliefs within the empire.[29] As J. G. A. Pocock has put it, 'the empire was surrendered, and the stability of institutions maintained'.[30]

Those who had opposed the war had, however, insisted on the fundamental importance of the American connection to Britain and were in principle committed to reconciliation with the new America and the forging of new links. Opposition to the war had been widespread. In 1775 nearly 20,000 people signed petitions from twenty-one English boroughs and five counties urging peace and conciliation.[31] Protestant Dissenters and political radicals in urban areas were especially prominent in petitioning. In Parliament the war was opposed by a minority of MPs and peers largely drawn from the followings of the Marquis of Rockingham and of the Earl of Chatham, formerly William Pitt the elder. After his death in 1778, the Earl of Shelburne took on the leadership of Chatham's supporters. Following the defeat of the government of Lord North in March 1782, first Rockingham and then Shelburne formed the ministries which took Britain out of the war and into a peace with America.

Opponents of the war saw Americans as reluctant rebels driven to defending their rights rather than as conspirators seeking their long-term objective of inde-pendence from Britain. The rights which Americans justly saw as threatened by oppressive policies being pursued by British ministers were rights which they held in common with the people of Britain and which were in danger in Britain as well. The causes of American and British freedom were thus one and the same. 'The ministers of the present reign', wrote the radical pamphleteer John Cartwright, 'have daringly struck at your most sacred rights, have aimed through the sides of America, a deadly blow at the life of your constitution.'[32] Victory for its arms in America would leave the government free to remodel British institutions according to its supposedly authoritarian aims. 'If an arbitrary military force is to govern one part of this empire, I think and fear if it succeeds, it will not be long before the whole of this empire will be brought under a similar thraldom', wrote

---

[28] Undated paper for Shelburne, WLCL, Shelburne MSS 87: 147.

[29] Gould, *The Persistence of Empire*, p. 198.

[30] J. G. A. Pocock, '1776: The Revolution against Parliament' in *Virtue Commerce and History: Essays on Political Thought and History Chiefly in the Eighteenth Century* (Cambridge, 1985), p. 86.

[31] James E. Bradley, *Popular Politics and the American Revolution in England: Petitions, the Crown and Public Opinion* (Macon, GA, 1986) and *Religion, Revolution and English Radicalism: Nonconformity in Eighteenth-century Politics and Society* (Cambridge, 1990).

[32] *Take Your Choice* (London, 1776), pp. xxi–xxii.

Rockingham.[33] The Westminster Committee of Association resolved in 1780 that 'success in the American war would be the ruin of the liberties of both America and England'.[34] Accounts of the ruthless way in which the war was being waged and of cruelties inflicted on civilians and prisoners aroused disgust. Britain's honour was being sullied. In December 1781 Rockingham denounced the acts of 'cruelty and barbarity practised by the British troops and their savage associates [Native Americans] in blood and slaughter'.[35] Some delighted in America's eventual success. John Jebb, probably the most extreme political reformer of his age, 'had but one wish, viz. that victory and honour might rest on that cause, which in an especial manner, was the cause of justice and of freedom'. 'For the sake of America, for the sake of England, and for the sake of the species', he rejoiced in the outcome.[36] William Jones, a very earnest radical and later a judge in India, rejoiced 'as an Englishman, in the success of America'.[37] Sylas Neville, a diarist with republican views, went down to the Thames in the summer of 1783 hoping to see ships flying the 'flag of the new states which ought to fill our government with shame and regret'.[38]

Most British opponents of the war, however, contemplated American independence with heavy hearts. Their aim had been by conciliation to rebuild the empire from which what they saw as tyrannical British policies had driven the Americans. Lord Rockingham wrote in 1776 that while he dreaded the consequences of a decisive British victory, he did not want to see a decisive American one either. He hoped for a compromise settlement that would keep Americans within the empire on terms acceptable to them.[39] Even Richard Price, who saw the Revolution as the beginning of 'a new *aera* in the annals of mankind', nevertheless hoped in 1777, that '*America* may, perhaps, be still preserved and that dreadful breach healed'.[40] Nearly all self-styled friends of America, in and out of Parliament, were very reluctant to accept that Americans were irrevocably set on a course of total separation from Britain. Once the fighting had stopped, opponents of the war of all shades of opinion looked forward to a return at least to close friendship and alliance while many hoped for the restoration of some more tangible links. David Hartley, an MP who had cultivated the friendship of leading Americans, anticipated a 'reconciliation and federal union between Great-Britain and America', once

---

[33] To Manchester, 18 June 1775, cited in Frank O'Gorman, *The Rise of Party in England: The Rockingham Whigs 1760–1782* (Manchester, 1975), p. 340.

[34] Minutes of 30 November 1780, BL, Add MS 38594, ff. 5–6.

[35] 19 December. 1781, *Parliamentary Register*, VIII, p. 66.

[36] John Disney, 'Memoirs of the Life of the Author' in Disney (ed.), *The Works . . . of John Jebb*, 3 vols. (London, 1787), I, p. 188.

[37] To Lady Spencer, 26 May 1780, Garland Cannon (ed.), *The Letters of Sir William Jones*, 2 vols. (Oxford, 1980), I, p. 388.

[38] 14 August. 1783, Basil Cozens-Hardy (ed.), *The Diary of Sylas Neville, 1767–1786* (Oxford, 1950), p. 310. For him, see Caroline Robbins, *The Eighteenth-century Commonwealthman* (Cambridge, MA, 1959), pp. 361–3.

[39] To E. Burke, 13 October 1776, Thomas W. Copeland (ed.), *The Correspondence of Edmund Burke*, 10 vols. (Cambridge, 1958–78), III, ed. G. H. Guttridge, *1772–1778*, pp. 295–6.

[40] *Additional Observations on the Nature and Value of Civil Liberty; and the War with America* (London, 1777), pp. 87–9.

North had been driven from office.[41] Few opponents of the war shared Price's enthusiasm for the republican plans of government that were emerging in the American states. Many hoped that Americans might think again and revert to the British constitution and with it to a continuing constitutional connection with Britain.

Those who had opposed the war had not necessarily identified with American aspirations. Their opposition had been rooted in British concerns: the need to curb the designs of what was to them an arbitrary-minded king and ministry, and to reform the abuses that, it was believed, had kept them in power against the will of the political nation. Once American issues ceased to intrude on British politics with the ending of the war, and when it became clear that hopes for reconciliation, let alone hopes for some sort of continuing union, were in vain, most of those who had championed the American cause took little further interest in America. Only a very small minority believed that the new America was any sort of model for the future development of Britain.

What quickly became apparent was how little effect the goodwill towards America expressed during the war by parliamentary politicians, political radicals, and religious Dissenters was to have on the course of Anglo-American relations after the war. There were very powerful countervailing pressures in the opposite direction. Supporters of the war did not feel cowed or discredited. They accepted separation but were not interested in conciliation. The prospect of generous terms for the Americans would arouse much opposition. The peacemakers who had replaced Lord North were to be harried by their critics in the press and the House of Commons was to censure the peace, although its terms were still ratified. These terms were indeed generous to the Americans, but they left many issues unresolved and they had emerged from a process of acrimonious Anglo-American bargaining rather than embodying a spirit of healing reconciliation between British people on both sides of the Atlantic. There was to be little evidence of such a spirit in the years ahead.

---

[41] To C. Wyvill, 22 March 1780, C. Wyvill (ed.), *Political Papers*, 6 vols. (York, 1794–1804), III, p. 188.

PART I

TRANSATLANTIC POLITICS

1

Ending the War

I

On 25 October 1781 Lord North, head of the government that had been waging war against rebellion in America since 1775, was told of the surrender of Lord Cornwallis and some 6,000 troops at Yorktown to a combined French and American army. North was reported to have taken the news 'as he would have taken a ball in the breast' and to have exclaimed 'Oh God! It is all over.'[1] All was indeed shortly to be over for his ministry. There had been much opposition to the forcible coercion of America in the country at large, but the government could count on a considerable degree of popular support for its policies and in Parliament its majorities had remained intact. With the defeat at Yorktown, however, many MPs had evidently come to the conclusion that America could no longer be reconquered at any price that was worth paying. The House of Commons passed a resolution on 27 February 1782 forbidding the 'further prosecution of offensive war on the continent of *North America*, for the purpose of reducing the revolted colonies to obedience by force'.[2] The war on land in North America was thus effectively brought to a close. North resigned on 27 March. He was replaced by the Marquis of Rockingham as chief minister of a government committed to peace with the colonies. Negotiations for peace began almost immediately and in November 1782 the British government, headed after Rockingham's death on 1 July by Lord Shelburne, concluded a provisional peace treaty with the Americans. This was ratified in September 1783. The peace recognized the full independence of the United States of America and conceded American claims to all lands between the sea and the Mississippi from the Great Lakes in the north to Spanish Florida and Louisiana in the south. It was for Americans a triumphant peace that had given them virtually all that they could have expected. They were surely the victors and Britain had as surely been vanquished.

Many historians see the outcome of the war as a resounding British defeat with very significant consequences for Britain and its empire. Brendan Simms, for instance, gave his distinguished study of eighteenth-century war and diplomacy the title of *Three Victories and a Defeat: The Rise and Fall of the First British Empire*,

---

[1] Piers Mackesy, *The War for America 1775–1783* (London, 1964), pp. 434–5.
[2] *Journals of the House of Commons*, XXXVIII, p. 861.

1714–1783. The American War was the defeat, which he describes as 'catastroph-ic'.[3] Many others have argued that defeat destroyed a 'first' empire and forced Britain to embark on a second and altogether different one, while at home it required the exertions of the younger Pitt to bring about a 'national revival'.[4] The War of American Independence, put in a long perspective, is said not only to have 'created a new nation in the United States of America', but to have 'helped to forge a very different Great Britain'.[5] There are, however, problems in a catastrophic interpretation of Britain's undoubted defeat. An alternative verdict that 'what seemed like a disastrous defeat had cost the country very little but money and prestige' at least merits consideration.[6] Many contemporaries came to see it in that way.

Stress on the overwhelming nature of Britain's defeat tends, in the first place, to distort understanding of how the war was actually brought to an end and peace was made. Yorktown had not destroyed Britain's military capability in America. Nor was it the case that a prostrate Britain had no option but to concede terms so favourable to America. American gains in no way reflected the strength of their position at the end of the war. As the next chapter will try to show, they depended on shifts in British politics and on Britain's preoccupation with securing advantages over its European enemies, and they were bitterly resented by large sections of British opinion. This had very important consequences for post-war Anglo-American relations.

To see the ending of the American War as a total disaster for Britain may also give a misleading impression of its long-term effects on Britain. It certainly would have been fitting had the British resolved to mend their ways after waging a futile and destructive war on their former colonies. The findings of this book tend, however, to support a rather different view. They incline towards Professor Po-cock's judgement that 'the Revolution was less of a traumatic shock to the British than a display of their capacity for losing an empire without caring very deeply'.[7] Although the loss of America was severely felt immediately, leading to much national introspection and stimulating pressures for reform of the abuses assumed to have produced so grievous a failure, within a short time a sense of national crisis weakened and contemporaries began to take a less critical view of the war, often coupled with a reassessment of what Britain had actually lost by her forced relinquishment of empire over the thirteen colonies. As early as November 1783, the American Silas Deane, now in exile in London, felt that 'The loss of America is already forgotten except in some party debates and writings, and there the principal

---

[3] (London, 2007), p. 661.

[4] *William Pitt and National Revival* is the title of the first volume of J. Holland Rose's biography, published in 1912, which remained the standard account of Pitt's early years in office until it was replaced in 1969 by John Ehrman's *The Younger Pitt: The Years of Acclaim*.

[5] Linda Colley, *Britons: Forging the Nation 1707–1837* (New Haven, CT, 1992), p. 145.

[6] N. A. M. Rodger, *The Insatiable Earl: A Life of John Montagu, 4th Earl of Sandwich, 1718–1792* (London, 1993), p. 300.

[7] 'British History: A Plea for a New Subject; a Reply', *Journal of Modern History*, XLVII (1975), 627. See Richard Bourke's exegesis in 'Pocock and the Presuppositions of the New British History', *Historical Journal*, LIII (2010), 747–70.

question is, whether on the whole, it be a loss.'[8] The diarist Nathaniel Wraxall recorded in his memoirs that within a year or two, 'the American War seemed to be nearly forgotten, and to have passed into history, like the "War of Succession" or the "War of Seven Years"'. It ceased to be 'the perpetual weapon of declamation'.[9]

This book will be as much about continuities as about changes. It will, for instance, argue that there is little to suggest that British opinion recognized the future significance of the creation of the American republic or even thought that new attitudes would be appropriate towards the new America. British imperial practices did not change markedly. The experiences of the war seem to have reinforced rather than weakened the commitment of British people to what they believed to be the immutable virtues of their constitution. Only a minority saw any need for fundamental reforms. In giving thanks for peace, the king's subjects were exhorted also to thank God, who has 'blessed us above all other nations with the enjoyment of liberty, both civil and religious'. This was a characteristic expression of continuing national complacency.

The importance of the Franco-American victory at Yorktown was that it finally broke the will of the British Parliament to continue supporting a war on land. Sober Americans were, however, in no doubt that they had not defeated Britain. The British still had powerful forces on the continent and, were they so minded, they had the resources to go on fighting. Washington certainly did not believe that Yorktown would inevitably lead to the end of the war.[10] When the war was finally over, ever careful in his choice of words, he did not claim that he had defeated the British; rather they had been 'baffled in their plans of subjugating' America. He was amazed 'that such a force that Great Britain has employed for eight years in this country' could be baffled by his men, 'oftentimes half starved, always in rags and without pay'.[11] In an essay published in the bicentennial year 1976, John Shy endorsed Washington's measured judgement. Rather than claiming that the Americans won, he wrote, 'a safer more accurate statement is that they did not lose . . . [T]hey hung on long enough to discourage the British government and people'.[12]

The nature of the war changed fundamentally for Britain in its later stages. Britain's main concerns were now with fighting the French, the Spanish, and the Dutch all over the world rather than with crushing the American rebellion. The supreme test of Britain's standing in the world in the eyes of her people was her capacity to worst her great European rivals. Her failure to subjugate her rebellious colonial subjects was an undoubted humiliation, but in the last resort it was a secondary issue. The international war as well as the narrowly American war had

---

[8] To Simeon Deane, 3 November 1783, 'The Deane Papers', V, *Collections of the New York Historical Society for 1890* (New York, 1891), p. 226.

[9] H. B. Wheatley (ed.), *Memoirs of Sir Nathaniel William Wraxall 1772–1784*, 5 vols. (London, 1884), III, p. 426.

[10] John Ferling, *Almost a Miracle: The American Victory in the War of Independence* (New York, 2007), pp. 548, 551.

[11] To N. Greene, 6 February 1783, Richard K. Showman et al. (eds), *The Papers of General Nathanael Greene*, 13 vols. (Chapel Hill, NC, 1976–2002), XII, p. 420.

[12] 'The American Revolution Today' in *A People Numerous and Armed: Reflections on the Military Struggle for American Independence* (New York, 1976), p. 12.

brought defeats, but at the very end there had been a marked upturn in Britain's fortunes against the French, the Spanish, and the Dutch and some notable victories. Yorktown was in a way the last of the bad news. Good news had followed. The French had been defeated at sea in the West Indies, Gibraltar had been held against the Spanish, and the East India Company appeared to be keeping its enemies at bay. Some enthusiasts argued that if Britain fought on for another year or two she would be in a position to dictate terms to all her enemies. Most accepted, however, that peace must come as soon as possible to bring to an end what the 'Form of Prayer and Thanksgiving', issued by 'His Majesty's Special Command', called 'the late bloody, extended, and expensive war'. Realists accepted that peace could only be got at a price. So the terms of the peace treaties made more or less simultaneously with France, Spain, and the United States of America were not matter for celebration. Yet for many the price seemed excessive, above all that paid to America, deemed the weakest of Britain's enemies. In British eyes, York-town had been lost to the French navy and the French artillery, not to the Americans. Independence probably could not be have been withheld from them, but they were not entitled to all the other favours added to it.

Yet if the war had not been a catastrophic defeat, its outcome had certainly not fulfilled British hopes and expectations. The thirteen colonies had been lost and the French and Spanish had both captured a number of British colonies and threatened the British Isles with invasion. Explanations and remedies for the future were inevitably sought.

The starkest explanation was that the British people, uniquely favoured by God as the upholders of the Protestant cause in the Seven Years War, had by their sinfulness and neglect lost God's favour and were being duly chastised. The catastrophes of colonial rebellion and civil war, let alone the later dismemberment of empire, were seen as evidence of God's displeasure. The 'vindictive hand of God' was soon detected in the American upheavals. Britain was being punished for 'the vast spreading of infidelity' and for 'universal dissipation', shown most blatantly in masquerades.[13] Periodic days of national humiliation and fasting with prayers for forgiveness to be led by the clergy of the Church of England were instituted from 1776.[14] Dissenters joined in. On these and other occasions sermons were preached denouncing national sins and calling for amendment of life. George Horne, future Bishop of Norwich, asked why 'well appointed armies under able generals should have done nothing, or worse than nothing' in America? We should not blame them nor the ministers who had sent them, he urged. The explanation lay in our own 'national wickedness which has called down national calamities'. He listed 'conjugal infidelity and senseless luxury' among others.[15] The Dissenter Samuel Savage also

---

[13] 'Fidelio' in *Morning Chronicle*, 20 September 1776.

[14] There is a volume of collected fast sermons in British Library, 694 i. 9. They are discussed by Paul Langford in 'The British Clergy and the American Revolution' in E. Hellmuth (ed.), *The Transformation of Political Culture: England and Germany in the Late Eighteenth Century* (Oxford, 1990), pp. 277–83.

[15] *A Sermon Preached before the Honourable House of Commons . . . on 4 February 1780* (Oxford, 1780), pp. 13, 15.

denounced 'excessive *luxury* and *extravagance*' as well as lack of due 'subordination'. Worst of all, we were cultivating '*the atheistic principles and loose morals of the French*'.[16]

Campaigns after the war for the improvement of public morals and against vice and immorality were no doubt an attempt to win back divine favour,[17] but crimes overseas as well as depravity at home were also crying aloud for amendment. Slavery and the slave trade and the oppressions being practised in the East India Company's provinces were often included in lists of national sins for which God was meting out punishment. Granville Sharp had warned in 1776 that the involvement 'of the WHOLE BRITISH EMPIRE in slave-dealing and slave-holding...must inevitably draw down from God some tremendous *national* punishment'.[18] In his journals for 1776 John Wesley anticipated divine vengeance for the 'merciless cruelty' of the British in Bengal. 'Wilt thou not visit for these things, O Lord?'[19] Colonial rebellion and unsuccessful war seemed to confirm such premonitions. As Christopher Brown has cogently argued, 'the experience of defeat in Britain prompted more careful scrutiny of imperial institutions and practices'.[20] 'Have we navigated and conquered to save, to civilize, and to instruct; or to oppress, to plunder, and to destroy?' the Unitarian Gilbert Wakefield asked his hearers in a sermon preached after the war. 'Let INDIA and AFRICA give the answer to these questions.' They would tell of British 'barbarity,...unexampled amongst former ages and other nations...What indeed can we expect, but that other nations should be raised to punish our disobedience?'[21] Edmund Burke believed that in India 'Millions of innocent individuals had been made the victims of our indiscretion', but 'the arm of God was abroad—His righteous visitation was already begun...This great work Providence was visibly carrying on against a country, who by its crooked policy, had ripened itself for destruction.'[22] Although concerns for indigenous peoples brought within the orbit of British trade and empire were being articulated well before the American Revolution,[23] the moral self-examining provoked by the need to account for the reverses of the American War probably did much to focus these concerns into purposeful campaigns to abolish the slave trade and to bring to punishment Warren Hastings, Governor General of British India.

More secular explanations for Britain's wartimes failings were heavily influenced by expectations aroused by the Seven Years War that British success in war was part

---

[16] *National Reformation the Way to Prevent National Ruin...* (London, 1782), pp. 28–9.

[17] Arthur Burns and Joanna Innes, 'Introduction' to Burns and Innes (eds), *Rethinking the Age of Reform in Britain 1780–1850* (Cambridge, 2003), p. 9.

[18] *The Law of Liberty: or, Royal Law, by which all Mankind will certainly be Judged!* (London, 1776), p. 49.

[19] Journals, 23 February, 13 November 1776, *The Works of John Wesley*, 14 vols. (London, 1872), IV, pp. 68, 88–9.

[20] *Moral Capital: Foundations of British Abolitionism* (Chapel Hill, NC, 2006), p. 324.

[21] *A Sermon Preached at Richmond in Surry on 29th July 1784, the Day Appointed for a General Thanksgiving on Account of the Peace* (London, 1784), pp. 16–18.

[22] Speech of 30 July 1784, Paul Langford (ed.), *The Writings and Speeches of Edmund Burke* (Oxford, 1981–), V, ed. P. J. Marshall, *India: Madras and Bengal 1774–1785*, pp. 471–2.

[23] P. J. Marshall, *The Making and Unmaking of Empire: Britain, India, and America c.1750–1783* (Oxford, 2005), pp. 190–206.

of the natural order of things. In accounting for Britain's failure to prevail in the American War, the public was therefore more inclined to blame human failings than to accept that there were limitations on British naval and military capacity and that attempts to subjugate a rebellious people spread over a great land mass or to wage a global war against three formidable European enemies at once might be beyond her capacity. Britain's capacity was unbounded and the warlike spirit of her people was indomitable. 'The resources which have supported a war so distant, so various, so expensive, have been superior to the expectations of the most sanguine. Our advantages may be fairly ascribed to the strength and the spirit of the country', Lord Sheffield wrote in his very widely read *Observations on the Commerce of the American States*. Explanations must therefore be sought in the failings of Britain's leaders. For Sheffield, failures in the late war had to be attributed to 'the misconduct of individuals and the errors of parliament'.[24] Faction had prevailed. It was 'the factions within my kingdom, not the weight of my enemies', George III felt, that had forced him to accept an adverse peace.[25] John Andrews, who wrote tracts on political and historical themes, believed that the 'majority of the nation' considered that the 'dismemberment of the British empire is owing principally to that spirit of discord, which has taken possession of the leading men in this kingdom'. What he called 'party rage' had risen to 'the height of ungovernableness and indecency'.[26] Admiral Lord Hood reflected that the only hope for the British in a future war was for them to become 'once again an united and rational people'.[27]

As they had done in response to the initial failures of the Seven Years War, the British people vented their frustration by turning against their leadership. William Duff of the Church of Scotland in a sermon on the causes of 'National Prosperity and National Ruin' regarded the loss of America as a 'national misfortune' for which the immediate causes were: 'The ignorance and folly, the venality and corruption of our rulers, and the want of unanimity and vigour in their administration.'[28] Heroes worthy of the adulation bestowed on those of the Seven Years War only emerged in the closing stages of the war in the shape of Rodney, victor at the Saintes, and Eliott, defender of Gibraltar. Senior commanders had divided into factions, most blatantly in the navy. The rising politician Henry Dundas thought that there was an entirely unacceptable lack of 'discipline, subordination or sense of duty' in the highest ranks of the army and the navy. This had lost America and, unless there was reform, 'our Eastern empire and our West Indian colonies' would be lost as well.[29] To many, the peace settlements were the final proof of the turpitude of Britain's political leadership. Britain had given away far too much,

---

[24] *Observations on the Commerce of the American States with Europe and the West Indies* (London, 1783), pp. 5–6 fn.
[25] To Grantham, 21 October 1782, J. Fortescue (ed.), *The Correspondence of King George III 1760–1783*, 6 vols. (London, 1927–8), VI, p. 147.
[26] *An Essay on Republican Principles and on the Inconvenience of a Commonwealth in a Large Country or Nation* (London, 1783), pp. 88–9.
[27] Cited in Mackesy, *The War for America*, p. 516.
[28] *National Prosperity the Consequence of National Virtue; and National Ruin the Effect of National Wickedness* (Aberdeen, 1785), p. 33.
[29] To R. Rigby, 26 July 1781, National Archives of Scotland, GD 51/1/5/3.

above all to America. Lord Shelburne, the minister responsible, was told he had made a 'mad sacrifice of your own country' in his 'infatuated prodigality to America'.[30] He had 'forced on us a peace more injurious to our honour, more damning to our importance, and more deadly to our existence' than Britain's enemies could have hoped. His 'treason is so evident and so hopeless'.[31]

The failure of Britain's leaders to prosecute a successful war or to negotiate a peace which secured Britain's honour led to demands for reform. Above all, aristocratic power must be curbed. The monarchy was increasingly invoked as a check on the undue extension of aristocratic power. Reformers demanded that the lower houses in both kingdoms, instead of being manipulated by aristocratic influence, should be made accountable to a public opinion that would, it was assumed, have been able to prevent the folly of the American War and to insist on the effective prosecution of the war against Britain's natural Bourbon enemies. There were demands for administrative reform to eliminate waste and corruption, including the perquisites of aristocratic leaders, and to reduce taxes. Administrative reforms, already launched under Lord North, were to be carried forward, but parliamentary reform was shelved in both Britain and Ireland. Campaigns for reform had been limited by the wide consensus about what needed to be remedied. Failure in war had been a failure of leadership, not a national failure. The ministry of the younger Pitt hardly constituted a radical break with the past but the emergence of an apparently uncontaminated new figure was still enough to restore confidence. The loss of America ultimately 'not only failed to disrupt in any permanent way the ordinary pattern of domestic politics but arguably left the Whig regime of George III at least as secure as it had been twenty years before'.[32]

The American War quickly came to be regarded as less than a total defeat. The war, an MP said in December 1783, had been 'remarkably unfortunate to us; but still it served to place the British character for martial deeds in the highest point of view; no nation was ever involved in a more arduous a struggle; and no nation ever maintained one with so much firmness and so much valour'.[33] Some years later, William Pitt, who had opposed the war against the colonies as his father had done, felt that 'our resistance must be admired, and in our defeats we gave proofs of our greatness and almost inexhaustible resources'.[34] 'Far from thinking the last war disgraceful', wrote a newspaper columnist in 1788, 'I scruple not to assert that at no period were more gallant actions performed both by land and sea.' Through its 'great exertions' Britain had won what had proved to be a secure peace.[35] The following year an MP used the same language as Washington had done. Britain had been able to 'baffle' 'the united efforts of the three most potent states in Europe'.[36]

---

[30] 'Letter VI of Egbert to the Earl of Shelburne', *Public Advertiser*, 11 March 1783.

[31] 'Thomas Northcote to the Rt. Hon. The Earl of Shelburne', ibid. 28 February 1783.

[32] Eliga H. Gould, *The Persistence of Empire: British Political Culture in the Age of the American Revolution* (Chapel Hill, NC, 2000), p. 179.

[33] Lord Upper Ossory, 11 November 1783, *Parliamentary Register*, XII, p. 3.

[34] 12 February 1787, ibid. XXI, pp. 176–7.

[35] 'Spectator' in *London Chronicle*, 17–19 January 1788.

[36] Henry Beaufoy, 24 March 1789, *Parliamentary Register*, XXV, pp. 530–1.

II

The road from the defeat at Yorktown and even from the fall of North and the ending of offensive operations to a peace with an independent America in possession of all the territory to which it had laid claim was to be by no means a smooth one. Nor to contemporaries, not least to Washington, did arrival at that destination seem in any way inevitable. There was still much to play for between Britain and America. Most sections of British opinion might have become resigned to the inevitability of American independence in some form, but the terms on which America got its independence remained a vital issue for many. It was not even clear if and when the British would withdraw from those parts of the territory of the United States that they still held in strength. It was possible that they might remain in major American ports, encouraging disaffection and perhaps even the dismemberment of the union, while maintaining what had become a strict blockade that was crippling American overseas trade and having a very adverse effect on its economy.

The terms on which peace was made did not depend on Britain and America alone. By the time that Cornwallis surrendered, the American War had become a great international conflict. Britain had been at war since 1778 with France, with Spain from 1779, and with the Netherlands from the end of 1780. Fighting was still taking place at sea, in the West Indies, around Gibraltar, at Minorca in the Mediterranean, and in Asia. So a quick settlement with America that would enable Britain to concentrate her resources against her European enemies seemed very advantageous. The United States were, however, bound by treaty to make no peace independent of France. For many months after Yorktown America remained fully committed to the French alliance that gave it security against what many Americans suspected to be Britain's ultimate aim, that is, to reconquer them once Britain's European enemies had been worsted. Eventually, the Americans were prepared to conclude what amounted to a separate peace, but they extracted a high price for doing so. Both the international situation and their domestic political concerns pushed British ministers into paying such a price.

The resolution to end active hostilities against America on land left many unresolved problems. What was to be done with the large forces that Britain still had in the thirteen colonies, at New York, Charleston, Savannah, and Penobscot in Maine? British forces together with Native American allies also controlled much territory in the Northwest which Americans claimed. Assuming that the end of offensive operations was the preliminary to some kind of peace settlement with America, on what terms should peace be made? Was American independence to be totally without conditions? An America that was fully independent and wholly separated from Britain was desired by virtually no one in Britain. As a newspaper put it, 'The *irrevocable* independence of America is a stumbling-block to many well wishers of the truest interests of that country. They wish America to be free, i.e. to have every privilege which England enjoys— they would heal the wounded limb, but not rashly cut it off.'[37] An independent

---

[37] *London Packet*, 27–30 December 1782.

America remaining in close alliance with France to whom she might give the kind of commercial privileges and military support that Britain had once enjoyed was an intolerable prospect.

Those who had opposed the war and were to assume office in 1782 expected that a free America would accept a continuing close association with Britain. Most Americans, they thought, had never wanted independence, but had been reluctantly driven to it and to swallow what had seemed a very bitter pill for British sympathizers of America, that is, the alliance with France, by the intransigence of the North government and the horrors of the war waged against them. Once the old government had been removed and coercion had been abandoned, it was generally assumed that America would gladly resume close ties with Britain, especially over trade, that she would renounce her French connection, and that some continuing constitutional arrangement might possibly be negotiated. The most optimistic even hoped that America might ally with Britain to wage war against France. Welcoming the fall of North, the Bristol Common Council anticipated 'the blessings of peace, commerce and liberty' and saw good prospects of Britain's 'reuniting with America and once more becoming the dread and envy of the world'.[38] Edmund Burke, one of Rockingham's leading followers, told Henry Laurens that he hoped that 'fair dealing and moderation, on both sides, may bring all right, and fix things upon a new foundation' for 'the whole British nation, on both sides of the Atlantic'.[39] Charles Fox, who led the Rockingham connection in the House of Commons, sent a message to Benjamin Franklin, telling him that 'in spite of all that has happened, he and I are still of the same country'.[40]

The parliamentary politicians who had opposed the war were divided about the degree of independence that should be conceded to America. Fox thought the idea of sovereignty over America ought to be totally renounced, although he still hoped that no one would give up America without obtaining 'a substantial connection with her', even if such a connection did not involve 'any advantage whatever we shall have a right to enforce'.[41] In July 1782 he proclaimed that the independence of America was 'a just, wise, and equitable measure' which must be conferred without conditions, trusting to the 'generosity' and 'affection' of 'a brave and loyal people attached to this country by common habits and common feelings'.[42] While Fox might have been willing to accept a settlement that did not include formal recognition of some sort of continuing union between Britain and America, Lord Shelburne, who had also opposed the war and joined in a coalition with Rockingham to form a ministry in March 1782 was most emphatically not willing to concede that. In February 1782 he had announced that he would 'never consent,

---

[38] *Felix Farley's Bristol Journal*, 20 April 1782.
[39] To H. Laurens, 27 March 1782, Thomas W. Copeland (ed.), *The Correspondence of Edmund Burke*, 10 vols. (Cambridge, 1958–78), IV, ed. John A. Woods, *1778–1782*, p. 428.
[40] To T. Grenville, 21 May 1782, Duke of Buckingham and Chandos (ed.), *Memoirs of the Courts and Cabinets of King George III*, 4 vols. (London, 1853–5), I, p. 30.
[41] 28 February 1782, *Parliamentary Register*, VI, p. 342.
[42] Speech at Westminster Meeting, 17 July 1782, C. Wyvill (ed.), *Political Papers*, 6 vols. (York, 1794–1802), II, pp. 178–9.

under any possible given circumstances, to acknowledge the independency of America'.[43] His maxim that 'the sun of Great Britain' would set with American independence was to be cited against him on innumerable occasions. Although as the king's chief minister after July 1782 he was to be the architect of the eventual peace with a fully independent America, he had the most ambitiously optimistic hopes for future close relations between Britain and America of any major British politician.

Those who had supported Lord North and the waging of war had been forced to recognize that there was no alternative to accepting that most of America could never be conquered, but they insisted that American independence could not be unconditional. An independent America, left to itself, would probably remain tied to France, would challenge British commerce, particularly in the West Indies, and would develop its own navy. Precautions must be taken to prevent such future dangers. The only safe relationship with America for the future must involve some recognition of a 'justly qualified dependence on the mother country'.[44] Although unconditional independence was ultimately to be conceded, some supporters of the North ministry continued to do their utmost to limit what they saw as its adverse effects on Britain. Charles Jenkinson, who had been one of North's most effective ministers, prophesied that, were the Americans fully separated from Britain, their ports would 'every day encrease in wealth and power, a circumstance this nation should use their utmost endeavours to prevent'.[45] Effectively in control of British commercial policy under Pitt after 1784, Jenkinson was to work assiduously to limit independent America's development as a maritime power and to curb its capacity to compete with Britain.[46]

The most immediate problem facing the new ministry that took power on the fall of North was to decide what should be done with the British garrisons in American ports. Opinion was divided as to whether they should be kept there or withdrawn. Even General Conway, an inveterate opponent of the war, in proposing the motion on 27 February 1782 to end offensive operations, would not say 'a syllable of withdrawing our troops from the places which they actually held; he had not advised any such measure; and he would not advise it'.[47] To some there seemed to be a case for retaining the southern ports rather than the main base at New York. They were regarded as essential for protecting the trade of the West Indies and they would give Britain access to 'some of the most lucrative branches of the American trade'.[48] If the British troops stayed, albeit without launching offensive operations, and the Americans had no realistic prospect of getting them out,

---

[43] *Parliamentary. Register*, VIII, p. 103.
[44] Thomas Orde, 27 November 1781, ibid. V, p. 4.
[45] 22 February 1782, ibid. VI, p. 277.
[46] See ch. 5.
[47] *Parliamentary Register*, VI, pp. 313–14.
[48] John Sinclair, *Thoughts on the Naval Strength of the British Empire: Part II* (London, 1782), p. 8. William Knox was another who advocated the retention of South Carolina and Georgia (*Extra Official State Papers*, 2 vols. (London, 1789), I, p. 27).

especially after the French switched their resources to the West Indies, the war was reaching a stalemate.

The Rockingham government decided to break the stalemate by ordering the withdrawal of the garrisons. This would serve a dual purpose. On the one hand, the troops tied up in American ports could now be redeployed for campaigns against France and Spain in the West Indies and even on the Spanish American mainland, where it was believed that British intervention would incite revolts that would quickly destroy the Spanish regimes. Shelburne intended that troops taken from New York were to go with a naval escort to the River Plate and ultimately to Callao, the port of Peru, seizing the Canary Islands on their way as 'a most desirable acquisition'.[49] On the other hand, evacuation of the ports would convince the Americans that Britain now seriously intended to make peace with them. In the dispatch ordering the evacuation, Sir Guy Carleton, the new commander-in-chief at New York, was told by Lord Shelburne to do all he could 'to revive old affections and extinguish late jealousies' and to persuade the people of America to come back to Britain and reject French domination.[50] Savannah and Charleston were abandoned during 1782, but the main British force remained at New York until late in the following year and none of the grandiose plans for operations against Britain's European foes were realized.

That the troops stayed in New York was owing to the lack of transports available to take them to the West Indies, let alone to South America, but Guy Carleton was happy to keep them there for reasons of his own. Far from reducing the New York garrison, he hoped to reinforce it with troops withdrawn from Charleston and Savannah. He professed to consider that this was necessary to defend the city from possible attack, but he also believed that a strong army could play a vital role in determining the future of relations between Britain and the United States. He seems fully to have accepted that any form of coercion would be self-defeating and must not be attempted, but, fed by a great volume of reports of discontent, especially in the New England states, against the war and its burdens of taxation and economic dislocation, and of aversion to the French alliance, he had come to believe that a weak and ineffective Congress regime was on the point of collapse. A strong British presence at New York would sustain the loyalists and give encouragement to popular movements against Congress and in favour of a reunion with Britain 'on safe and generous terms'. He envisaged a settlement that would be 'perfectly pleasing to the people and useful to Great Britain'. He even foresaw the possibility of 'more fighting'. American and British arms might be joined in a common effort against France. He was later reported to have said that he was willing to incorporate the Continental Army into the royal army.[51]

[49] Shelburne to T. Townshend, 10 September 1782, WLCL, Sydney MSS, X.
[50] 4 April 1782, Davies (ed.), *Documents*, XXI, p. 54.
[51] Carleton's dispatches to Shelburne, 12 May, 17 August, to T. Townshend, 29 October 1782, TNA, CO 5/106, f. 21, Davies (ed.) *Documents*, XXI, pp. 112–13, 133–4. See also William Smith's record of Carleton's views in his diary, 17, 23 May, 2 August, 18 [October] 1782, 8 March 1783. William H. W. Sabine (ed.), *Historical Memoirs, from 26 August 1778 to 12 November 1783, of William*

British ministers chose, however, to seek a settlement with the United States through negotiations with the envoys officially appointed by Congress in Europe rather than to wait on events in America while trying to make direct contacts with those who might have views independent of Congress, as Carleton was urging and Shelburne had initially wished to do. In a dispatch of 5 June 1782 Shelburne ordered Carleton to tell Washington and Congress that Britain was willing to recognize American independence without conditions. Carleton thought that this was a premature and gravely mistaken move which had destroyed what he regarded as a reasonable prospect a reaching a locally negotiated settlement that would have brought about 'reunion' between Britain and America on terms agreeable to both.[52] He resigned his post in disgust, but in fact stayed at New York until the final evacuation in November 1783. Instead of presiding, as he had hoped, over a reconciliation between loyalists and patriots, Carleton had to devote himself to the resettlement of the loyalists in British colonies, a duty that he was to discharge with considerable distinction.

Carleton's hopes for a settlement between Britain and America, to be worked out in America under his guidance, rested on what was almost certainly an exaggerated view of the severity of America's difficulties in 1783. The authority of Congress and of those who held office under it had been seriously eroded, federal finances were in a parlous condition which the states refused to remedy, there were mutinies in the army by unpaid soldiers, taxes levied by the states were resented and in some cases being resisted, and there was acute economic dislocation accentuated by the collapse of the currency and a rigorous British blockade. Yet serious as the situation was in much of the United States at the close of the war, the individual state regimes were still firmly in control, debts were beginning to be paid off, and the army was to be pacified and eventually to be disbanded without undue turmoil. Expectations of a massive swing of opinion towards Britain and the acceptance of something short of unconditional independence were the purest delusion. Carleton himself had a much better reputation in America than any other British general due to stories of his humanity to the defeated American troops in Canada and of his refusal to use the Indians in offensive operations. Nevertheless, Britain's credit with most Americans, probably including a majority of the loyalists who had opposed the Revolution, was now at a very low ebb.[53] In areas which the British army had occupied for long, they had turned potential loyalists into patriots.[54]

Even if Carleton's expectations can easily be dismissed as having been based on misapprehensions and wishful thinking, they were important evidence of how developments in America were being interpreted in Britain. The wide

---

Smith (New York, 1971), pp. 509, 510, 541, 553. 575 and Paul H. Smith, 'Sir Guy Carleton, Peace Negotiations and the Evacuation of New York', *Canadian Historical Review*, L (1969), 245–64.

[52] Smith's Diary, 2 August 1782, Sabine (ed.), *Historical Memoirs*, pp. 541–2.

[53] For the frustration of loyalists with the British refusal to institute civilian government in New York, see Daniel J. Hulsebosch, *Constituting Empire: New York and the Transformation of Constitutionalism in the Atlantic World 1664–1830* (Chapel Hill, NC, 2005), pp. 161–7.

[54] Joseph S. Tiedemann, 'Patriots by Default: Queen's County, New York, and the British Army, 1776–1783', *William and Mary Quarterly*, 3rd ser., XLIII (1986), 35–63.

dissemination of views such as his exerted a powerful influence both in government circles and among the newspaper-reading public. British ministers got material prophesying the imminent collapse of the American union from Carleton and also directly from those in London or New York who claimed to speak for the loyalist Americans and who assiduously lobbied British ministers or senior officers.[55] Such material also appeared in abundance in the British press, some of it probably again directly supplied by loyalists, but in most cases derived from American newspapers, especially from the vigorous loyalist press that flourished in New York until it was evacuated in November 1783. 'Rivington's New York Gazette' was frequently cited as the source for the very numerous paragraphs telling British newspaper readers of the troubles that were afflicting the new United States. A 'General Idea of the State of North America', written by the prominent loyalist William Smith, was published by Rivington for consumption not only in America but in Britain, where it was intended 'to correct the design of the Rockingham party for giving up the dependency of the colonies'.[56] Paragraphs appearing in September 1782 were typical of many in the London press. An 'authentic letter from New York' reported that America could no longer pay for the war and that most people wished to be rid of 'their despotic rulers' and to return to a British connection well short of unconditional independence.[57] The *Morning Herald* thought it 'more than probable' that America would shortly lapse into civil war and that Washington, who has 'all the innate principles of Cromwell' (an allegation often repeated), and his army would throw off their obedience to Congress.[58]

The public was warned against 'the impositions of the American refugees, who daily fill the public prints with abusive paragraphs upon our officers, with tales of divisions within the American counsels, and other matters equally and notoriously false'.[59] Little, however, appeared that stated a contrary view. The volume of adverse reports in the press about conditions in the United States, going far beyond what can be directly attributed to loyalist sources, was seriously damaging to hopes of an easy return to good relations with a potentially cooperative new America entertained by the ministries that had succeeded North. A barrage of hostile newspaper comments against undue concessions to a weak and unstable America was to be kept up throughout the months of the peace negotiations. Ministers were repeatedly told that unconditional American independence would be unacceptable to the British public. 'Which of you, my generous countrymen', asked a newspaper paragraph addressed 'To the People of England', 'can lay his hand upon his heart, and sincerely wish America to be independent of Great-Britain?'[60] Nine-tenths of

[55] See, for instance, J. Galloway to E. Nepean, 13 June 1782, enclosing letters from New York showing that 'the power of Congress was never so low as at present', TNA, CO 5/8, f. 285.
[56] W. Smith's Diary, 25 September 1782, Sabine (ed.), *Historical Memoirs*, p. 552.
[57] *Morning Post*, 12 September 1782.
[58] *Morning Herald*, 26 September 1782.
[59] *A Word at Parting to the Earl of Shelburne* (London, 1782), p. 20.
[60] *Morning Herald*, 9 August 1782.

men 'of all denominations' were said to be willing to see the war last for another three years rather than to yield 'unconditional, unlimited independence'.[61]

Peace would have to be made in the face of a press deeply sceptical about the future of America and the need for concessions. The political climate was also changing against the peacemakers. In spite of having been driven from office, Lord North remained a potent force in British politics with a strong potential following in the Commons. He expressed no remorse over the war. He had done his inescapable duty. He would admit that it 'had been calamitous to the country', but 'it was the war of the people'. In fighting it he had carried out their will and the will of the House of Commons.[62] Earlier he claimed that he had embarked on the war on 'a truly English principle, and that, as an Englishman, he had a right, and it was his duty to maintain it for the purpose of supremacy, if not revenue'.[63] It is likely that this was the view of many who had supported the war until it finally seemed to be unwinnable. North still commanded the allegiance of conservative-minded men who thought that the British constitution was in danger from the reforming policies of Rockingham and Shelburne and who would resent any sell-out to America. A tumultuous reception at Manchester on 29 August 1782, when North was entertained sumptuously by 'near a hundred of the principal inhabitants' and 'the populace' drew his coach for 2 miles, was an indication of his returning popularity.[64] North made himself the patron of the loyalists, advising them on tactics to further their cause in Britain. As will be shown later, the emergence of compensation for loyalists as a major political issue would do much to turn public opinion against conciliatory terms in the peace with America.

A revival in Britain's fortunes during 1782 also stiffened resistance to any peace that seemed to be based on unwarranted concessions. Rodney's great naval victory in April 1782 at the battle of the Saintes in the West Indies aroused passionate public enthusiasm.[65] With good reason, Americans were apprehensive that the victory might harden public attitudes towards the terms of any peace with them. George III was sure that it had. '[T]he great success of Lord Rodney's engagement', he wrote, 'has again so far roused the nation that the peace which would have been acquiesced in three months ago would now be matter of complaint.'[66] The triumph of the Saintes together with other successes turned 1782 into something of a year of victories. A public that saw Britain as now in the ascendant expected much more from the peace than Shelburne eventually offered. Why, a pamphleteer asked, did we accept 'the most disgraceful peace . . . with the trumpet of victory sounding from all quarters . . . with the face of our contest entirely changed in our favor?' To make matters even worse, it was 'a peace dictated in the first instance, by the *infant,*

[61] *Morning Post*, 6 September 1782.
[62] 18 April 1785, *Parliamentary Register*, XVIII, p. 65.
[63] 15 March 1782, ibid. VI, p. 467.
[64] *Morning Herald*, 29 August 1782.
[65] Stephen Conway, '"A Joy Unknown for Years Past": The American War, Britishness and the Celebration of Rodney's Victory at the Saints', *History*, LXXXVI (2001), 180–99.
[66] To Shelburne, 1 July 1782, Fortescue (ed.), *Correspondence of George III*, VI, p. 70.

unauthoritative states of America; without the grant of a single favorable stipulation to the mother country'.[67]

By March 1782 British political opinion was no longer prepared to support a war to reconquer America or to keep in office the government of Lord North that had sustained the war. New administrations came to power committed to ending the war. This was a spectacular political revolution but an interpretation of it as a victory for public sympathy for the cause of America, which had for so long been frustrated by an obstinate king and his unrepresentative ministers, would be very questionable. Those who saw themselves as friends of America might at last be in power, but it soon became apparent that, although there was no public appetite for further war with America, there was not much enthusiasm for the recognition of a fully independent America and very little willingness for concessions to be made to it at Britain's expense. Lord Shelburne had initially shared misgivings about independence, but when he committed himself to making a generous peace with a fully independent America he was to find himself working against the grain of powerful trends in public opinion. Until peace was finally made, American opinion was generally ill-disposed towards him as well. He and those in Britain who thought like him were also to find that their credentials as friends of America were very suspect in America itself. Shelburne was to be ground between the millstones of British resentment and American intransigence.

III

Americans had been considering the terms of a settlement with Britain for some years. The terms on which they would insist emerged from much hard bargaining between various state interests in Congress with frequent interventions by the French ambassador.[68] The indispensable condition for any possible negotiation was that the British must unequivocally recognize that the United States were 'sovereign, free and independent'. What, however, was to be the territorial extent of the independent United States? There were other British territories on the North American continent which had not rebelled and which were being defended by British troops, that is Quebec, Nova Scotia, Newfoundland, Bermuda, and East and West Florida. Britain had also gained in 1763 all the lands to the west of the thirteen colonies between the mountains and the Mississippi. To prevent conflict with their Native populations, settlement in them from the existing colonies had been prohibited by a proclamation of 1763. A significant part of them had later been given to the colony of Quebec by an Act of 1774.

As early as 1776 Americans were beginning to show their imperial aspirations by designating themselves the heirs of the British Crown and laying claim to 'the

---

[67] *Consequences (Not before adverted to) That are Likely to Result from the Late Revolution of the British Empire* (London, 1783), pp. 31–2.

[68] Analysed in Jack N. Rakove, *The Beginnings of National Politics: An Interpretive History of the Continental Congress* (New York, 1979), ch. XI.

exclusive, undivided and perpetual possession' of all its continental territories.[69] Nearly all Americans seem to have agreed that it was very much in the interest of the new republic that the British presence on the North American continent should be eliminated. As soon as the fighting had begun, the Americans had tried to conquer Quebec to prevent Britain using it as a base for invading the northern states. As late as 1 May 1782 Washington set out the case for trying again to take Quebec. It was a 'capital province', whose acquisition would enable America to control the northern and western Indians and thus to secure a peaceful frontier. Left there, the British might intrigue with the new states likely to be established in the west as well as with the Indians, which was a shrewd anticipation of what was to happen.[70] The prospect of British forces maintaining a strong presence in Quebec that would be supported by a naval squadron at Halifax in Nova Scotia, was not a welcome one. American negotiators were told that to obtain the cession of Quebec and Nova Scotia was 'of the utmost importance', but that it was not to be a 'matter of ultimatum'.[71] Whatever its future status, Quebec's boundaries must be redrawn. The extension of its territory made at the expense of American colonies in the redrawing of boundaries in the 1774 Quebec Act could not possibly stand.

The British must also be made to give up all claims to western lands between the Mississippi and the mountains. The great majority of the American leadership were strongly committed to a vision of westward expansion. John Rutledge of South Carolina insisted that the war had been fought not just for the freedom of the people of the eastern states, but 'for posterity; for those who would hereafter inhabit the country beyond the mountains to the extent formerly claimed by the crown of Great Britain . . . He would continue the war for ever rather than be circumscribed in narrower bounds.'[72] Whatever the American leadership might wish, huge numbers of would-be settlers and land speculators would inevitably move west. The British could not therefore be allowed to stay. As Robert Livingston, Secretary for Foreign Affairs, put it, a continuing British presence would 'render our situation truly hazardous'. If the British stayed, the southern states, in particular, would be threatened by 'a hardy race of people inimical to them', living under alien rule and inciting disaffection against them.[73] The Spanish, however, also claimed the Floridas and lands east of the Mississippi. Their troops had already captured British West Florida. Under pressure from France, Congress was willing to waive its claims to the Floridas in favour of Spain, but it still insisted on a boundary on the Mississippi and that the river should be open to American navigation.

---

[69] J. C. A. Stagg, *Borderlines in Borderlands: James Madison and the Spanish American Frontier, 1776–1821* (New Haven, CT, 2009), p. 15.

[70] Memorandum, 1 May 1782, John C. Fitzpatrick (ed.), *The Writings of George Washington*, 39 vols. (Washington, DC, 1931–44), XXIV, pp. 197–9.

[71] Worthington C. Ford et al. (eds), *Journals of the Continental Congress*, 34 vols. (Washington, DC, 1904–37), XIV, pp. 959–60, 14 August 1779.

[72] Congress Notes of Debates, 8 August 1782, Paul H. Smith (ed.), *Letters of Delegates to Congress, 1774–1789*, 26 vols. (Washington, DC, 1976–2000), XIX, p. 45.

[73] To B. Franklin, 7 January 1782, Giunta (ed.), *Emerging Nation*, I, p. 288.

In instructions drafted in August 1779, full independence and a boundary on the Mississippi were laid down as fundamental principles without which there could be no peace. Appropriate boundary lines between the American states and Quebec and Nova Scotia were specified and the American negotiators were instructed to try to obtain guaranteed access for American ships to the fisheries around Newfoundland, although this was another issue that was not to be forced to an 'ultimatum on the present occasion'.[74] For the New England states the question of the fisheries was, however, a matter of overwhelming importance and they campaigned relentlessly for it. As colonies, they had enjoyed free access to all fishing grounds off British territory and had built up very large fishing industries, supplying the rest of North America, the West Indies, and southern Europe. Were American ships to be excluded after the war, New England's spokesmen insisted that their states would be 'depopulated and deserted' and that their people would feel that all their sacrifices in the war for liberty had left them worse off than they had been before the Revolution.[75] American attempts to claim access to the fisheries were, however, strongly opposed by France. The French ambassador feared that the Americans might 'one day be more dangerous rivals to us than the English themselves' and that the strength of the French fishing fleet, an essential source of men for the navy, would be compromised.[76]

Commissioners were appointed to undertake negotiations. In September 1779 Congress appointed John Adams to go to France where he was to act as minister plenipotentiary to negotiate treaties of peace and commerce with Britain.[77] In June 1781 Benjamin Franklin, who was already in France as American envoy to the French court, joined him. John Jay was later added, as was Henry Laurens. The commissioners were given new instructions and told that they must 'undertake nothing' without the French ministers' 'knowledge and concurrence; and ultimately to govern yourselves by their advice and opinion'.[78] When the change of government in Britain in March 1782 made serious negotiations possible, only Franklin was in Paris. Adams was in the Netherlands and Jay in Spain. During the crucial stages of the negotiations in the summer and autumn of 1782, Franklin, Adams, and Jay effectively conducted the negotiations. Unlike the British negotiators, who were able to keep in close contact with their superiors in London and to refer crucial decision to them, the American commissioners were very much on their own.

By 1782 the deepest crisis in American affairs was past. The victory at Yorktown followed by the British decision to cease offensive operations on land and their stated intention to withdraw from New York and other garrisons had greatly eased pressures. Financial and economic difficulties were, however, acute and thought to

---

[74] *Journals of the Continental Congress*, XIV, pp. 956–60.
[75] Luzerne to Vergennes, 1 January 1782, translation in Giunta (ed.), *Emerging Nation*, I, pp. 274–5.
[76] Luzerne to Vergennes, 11 January 1782, translation in ibid. I, pp. 293–4.
[77] For Adams as diplomat, see James H. Hutson, *John Adams and the Diplomacy of the American Revolution* (Lexington, KT, 1980).
[78] *Journals of the Continental Congress*, XX, p. 651, 15 June 1781.

be getting worse and, above all, the patriot elite sensed a profound popular weariness with the war and a disquieting erosion of commitment to it. Washington was typical:

> That spirit of freedom which at the commencement of this contest would have gladly sacrificed every thing to the attainment of its object has long since subsided and every selfish passion has taken its place; it is not the public interest but the private which influences the generality of mankind nor can Americans any longer boast an exception.[79]

Alexander Hamilton thought that about one-third of the population of New York state still secretly favoured the British and that the rest would accept peace on any terms, 'not from inclination to Great Britain, or disaffection to independence, but from mere supineness and avarice'.[80] America urgently needed peace. It came in the nick of time, when army committees

> demand with importunity their arrears of pay—the Treasury is empty, no adequate means of filling it presents itself—The people pant for peace—Should contributions be exacted, as they have hitherto been at the point of the sword—the consequences may be more dreadful than is at present apprehended.

A further campaign could only be waged if America's European allies would pay for it.[81]

Few Americans, however, believed that peace would come either swiftly or easily. Virtually nobody in America shared the easy optimism of so many in Britain that the fall of the North government had cleared the way to Anglo-American reconciliation. The new ministers might see themselves as friends of America, but in America they were objects of suspicion and hostility. Benjamin Rush thought that 'The United States had far less to fear from the satiated fury and gratified avarice of Lord North and his junto than from the hungry poverty and unmortified pride of the present ministry. There never existed in my opinion in any country a more formidable combination against the liberties of mankind.'[82] Washington's considered verdict was that no prospect existed 'for a speedy peace on the principles of independence'. A close reading of the parliamentary debates convinced him that

> they want to amuse us in America, whilst they attend to other parts of their empire; which being secured, they will have time and means to revert to this continent again, with hopes of success.
>
> An idea of American independence on its true principles don't appear thro' the whole debates; but an idea of reconnecting us to the British nation, by dissolving our connexion with France is too prevalent.[83]

---

[79] To J. Laurens, 10 July 1782, Fitzpatrick (ed.), *Washington Writings*, XXIV, pp. 421–2.

[80] To R. Morris, 13 August 1782, Harold C. Syrett et al. (eds), *The Papers of Alexander Hamilton*, 27 vols. (New York, 1962–87), III, p. 141.

[81] R. Livingston to B. Franklin, 6 January 1783, Leonard W. Labaree et al. (eds), *The Papers of Benjamin Franklin* (New Haven, CT, 1959–), XXXVIII, p. 553.

[82] 'On the United States Navy', [4 July 1782], L. H. Butterfield (ed.), *The Letters of Benjamin Rush*, 2 vols. (Princeton, NJ, 1951), I, p. 276.

[83] To G. Clinton, 7 May 1782, Fitzpatrick (ed.), *Washington Writings*, XXIV, p. 228.

American opinion was soon to come to a more generous view of Rockingham and in particular of Fox, but Shelburne still aroused deep suspicion, which was to persist until the terms of the peace became clear. Safely out of office, Americans would regard Shelburne as the best British minister with whom they had ever had to deal; when he became the king's chief minister in July 1782 they generally assumed that any peace process would be seriously set back.

2

Making Peace

I

The Rockingham government which had succeeded Lord North in March 1782 was keen to sound American opinion about the possibility of a settlement as soon as possible.[1] Dealing with America was the responsibility of Lord Shelburne as Secretary of State for home affairs in which the colonies were still included. By 1782 he had gained some practical experience of dealing with American problems as Secretary of State from 1766 to 1768 and acquired a range of contacts with individual Americans unusual for a British politician. One of the connections that he formed then was with the Virginian Arthur Lee. Lee, who spent much time in Britain, saw himself as a member of what he called 'the College', the group of intellectuals, including Joseph Priestley and Richard Price, which met at Bowood, Shelburne's country estate, or in his London house at Berkeley Square. During the war Lee continued to assure Shelburne of his 'perfect esteem' for him.[2] After the war, he professed his happiness to resume correspondence with 'a nobleman I so much respect and esteem'.[3] His brother Richard Henry Lee had never met Shelburne, but believed that he was 'adored in this country'.[4] Arthur Lee's political significance was past its peak by 1782, but Shelburne had long-standing contacts with a man who was to play a crucial role in the peace. Benjamin Franklin's relations with Shelburne began in 1763 and developed much further during Shelburne's period as Secretary of State. He too became a regular visitor to Bowood. Shelburne recalled how they had discussed 'the means of promoting the happiness of mankind' together.[5] The connection seems to have lapsed during the war, but

---

[1] The fullest account of the peace negotiations with a powerful, if now controversial, interpretation of Shelburne's motives is still Vincent Harlow, *The Founding of the Second British Empire 1763–1793*, 2 vols. (London, 1952–64), I, chs. VI–VIII. Recent accounts are in H. M. Scott, *British Foreign Policy in the Age of the American Revolution* (Oxford, 1990), ch. 12; Andrew Stockley, *Britain and France at the Birth of America: The European Powers and the Peace Negotiations of 1782–1783* (Exeter, 2001); and Charles R. Ritcheson, 'The Earl of Shelburne and Peace with America, 1782–1783: Vision and Reality', *International History Review*, V (1983), 322–45.

[2] Letter of 18 December 1776, J. C. Ballagh (ed.), *The Letters of Richard Henry Lee*, 2 vols. (New York, 1914), II, p. 128.

[3] Letter of 23 July 1783, Giunta (ed.), *Emerging Nation*, I, p. 896.

[4] Letter to [A. Lee], 19 May 1769, Ballagh (ed.), *Letters of Richard Henry Lee*, I, p. 35.

[5] 6 April 1782, Leonard W. Labaree et al. (eds), *The Papers of Benjamin Franklin* (New Haven, CT, 1959–), XXXVII, p. 103.

Franklin invoked his 'ancient respect for your talents and virtue' at the beginning of the peace negotiations in March 1782.[6]

Not all Americans who encountered Shelburne were beguiled by him. He was a person who aroused much mistrust which initially coloured the attitude of many Americans to him. When Shelburne returned to office in 1782, he sought out an understandably very embittered Henry Laurens, former president of Congress, who had been taken off a captured ship and confined in the Tower. Shelburne lectured him on the future of Anglo-American relations, which Laurens found hard to bear. He thought that Shelburne was a man with an entirely justified reputation for 'duplicity and dissimulation' and an 'overweening opinion', both of his own abilities and of his influence in the United States, which Laurens thought was non-existent. In as far as he could understand them, he found Shelburne's ideas completely unrealistic.[7]

As Chatham had done, Shelburne strongly opposed the armed coercion of America, but, also like Chatham, he would have no truck with any idea of American independence. In his *Observations on the Nature of Civil Liberty*, published in 1776, Richard Price inserted a passage paying high tribute to Shelburne. As Secretary of State from 1766 to 1768, he wrote, Shelburne 'without ever compromising the authority of this country' had enjoyed the 'confidence' of the colonies, 'a confidence which discovered itself by peace among themselves and duty and submission to the mother-country'.[8] A dependent relationship based on mutual confidence seems to have been Shelburne's ideal. In 1778 he propounded his alternative to offering America independence. Fighting must stop, all American grievances must be met and their rights must be guaranteed for the future. Then he was sure that, although the activists in Congress might hold out, 'the bulk of the people . . . would be easily brought to a reconciliation' and would 'come back to an alliance with this country'.[9] He believed that American independence would be a disaster, not only for Britain, whose sun would set, but for the Americans themselves. He told Henry Laurens that he had 'always regreted the independence of the United States for the sake, he said, of the inhabitants[;] he was sure they would not be so happy without as with the connexion of Great Britain'.[10] He was convinced that Americans could be made to see the error of their ways and be brought to recognize that their republican experiments were doomed to failure. A return to something like the

---

[6] Letter of 22 March 1782, ibid. XXXVII, p. 24.

[7] Laurens to Franklin, 24 June 1782, Labaree et al. (eds), *Franklin Papers*, XXXVII, p. 526; to Price, 2 September 1782, D. O. Thomas and Bernard M. Peach (eds), *The Correspondence of Richard Price*, 3 vols. (Cardiff and Durham, NC, 1983–94), II, p. 137; to Lafayette, 6 August 1782, P. M. Hamer et al. (eds), *The Papers of Henry Laurens*, 16 vols. (Columbia, SC, 1963–2003), XV, p. 548.

[8] *Observations on the Nature of Civil Liberty, on the Principles of Government, and on the Justice and Policy of the War with America* (London, 1776), p. 148.

[9] Speech of 8 April 1778, J. Almon (ed.), *The Parliamentary Register*, 18 vols. (London, 1774–80), X, p. 395. See also version of the speech in B. Vaughan to B. Franklin, 28 April 1778, Labaree et al. (eds), *Franklin Papers*, XXVI, p. 368–9.

[10] Laurens Journal, 31 March 1782, Hamer et al. (eds), *Laurens Papers*, XV, pp. 399–400.

British constitution was the only way forward for them. He told Henry Laurens that 'The constitution of Great Britain is sufficient to pervade the whole world' and that he could not see why Americans should not 'be content to be on the same footing as Ireland'.[11] He was reported to have told the House of Lords that he would welcome an opportunity to appear before Congress in person in order to persuade them that 'if their independence was signed, their liberties were gone for ever'. He thought that there were 'great numbers' in America who saw 'ruin and independence linked together'.[12] So fixated was he on his hopes that the mass of Americans were only waiting for an opportunity to turn against their leaders and to reunite with Britain, that the British commanders in New York were instructed to try to make direct contact with American opinion to spread the news of the good intentions of the new ministry. Americans should contrast their present 'dependence' on France with 'British union and all the advantages resulting from returning affection and confidence'.[13]

Shelburne sent Richard Oswald as his envoy to Paris in April 1782 in response to an exploratory letter from Franklin. Oswald was an unusual choice.[14] He was neither a diplomat nor a politician, but a merchant in his late seventies who had traded with America on a very large scale and had many American contacts who liked and admired him. Shelburne wanted a man to 'excite confidence' in the Americans and so deliberately chose the 'most intimate and respected friend' that Henry Laurens 'had in the world'.[15] Oswald's conduct of his mission came to be much criticized in Britain for being far too conciliatory to the Americans. He was to be pilloried in the press as an ally of the American rebels, 'notoriously linked with the ring leaders of that party'.[16] The Cabinet came to see him as the advocate of 'the cause of America, not of Britain'.[17] Eventually, even Shelburne turned against him.

Nevertheless, given Shelburne's initial hopes for the negotiations, which as Vincent Harlow shrewdly put it, he envisaged not so much as 'a diplomatic contest' but rather as a 'cooperative effort to heal a family breach',[18] Oswald's relations of friendship and trust with leading Americans made him an entirely appropriate choice. Oswald was to tell Franklin that he wished to deal with him not only as a personal friend but 'as a friend to England'. He assured him that Shelburne 'had the

---

[11] H. Laurens to J. Bourdieu, 10 August 1782, WLCL, Shelburne MSS, 35, f. 55.

[12] Version of speech of 10 July 1782 in Thomas Paine, *A Letter to the Earl of Shelburne*, new edn (London, 1791), pp. 7–9.

[13] Instructions to G. Carleton, 4 April 1782, Davies (ed.), *Documents*, XXI, p. 54.

[14] For an authoritative assessment of him, see Charles R. Ritcheson, 'Britain's Peacemakers 1782–1783: "To an Astonishing Degree Unfit for the Task?"' in Ronald Hoffman and Peter J. Albert (eds), *Peace and the Peacemakers: The Treaty of 1783* (Charlottesville, VA, 1986), pp. 70–100. See also David Hancock, *Citizens of the World: London Merchants and the Integration of the British Atlantic Community 1735–1785* (Cambridge, 1995), pp. 390–5.

[15] B.Vaughan to J. Monroe, 18 September 1795, Richard. B. Morris (ed.), *John Jay: The Winning of the Peace* (New York, 1980), p. 346.

[16] 'On the Peace now in Agitation', *Public Advertiser*, 5 February 1783.

[17] George III to Shelburne, 5 December 1782, J. Fortescue (ed.), *The Correspondence of King George III*, 6 vols. (1927–8), VI, p. 172.

[18] *Second British Empire*, I, p. 246.

greatest confidence in his good intentions towards our country'.[19] According to John Adams, Oswald told the Americans that Shelburne was willing to 'cede to America every thing she could reasonably wish, in order to obliterate past unkindnesses, and restore mutual friendship'.[20]

Shelburne seems to have assumed at the beginning of the negotiations that evidence of good intentions on Britain's part would get America quickly out of the war and back into good relations with Britain, which, he hoped, would not involve total separation. The details of any settlement would not then be very material. Oswald was not inclined to drive hard bargains nor on most points was he instructed to do so. Such an approach was fatally flawed. Shelburne misjudged both the determination of the Americans to accept nothing short of total independence while also extracting territorial and other concessions and the unwillingness of British opinion to yield such concessions. In time it became clear that what the Americans insisted on were regarded by large sections of British opinion as unacceptable. Increasingly aware of the strength of public hostility, Shelburne felt compelled to change tactics and to try to limit what was to be conceded. By then, however, it was too late. The Americans got most of what they wanted, while conceding nothing about any future connection with Britain. British opinion was to take its revenge on Shelburne when the House of Commons refused to endorse his peace.

II

Richard Oswald spent a week in Paris in April 1782 in which he talked at length with Franklin about Shelburne's principal objective: would the Americans agree to start negotiations for a separate peace? Franklin assured him that there was no possibility of that.[21] Shelburne's other major concern, on which he had pressed Laurens, was whether the Americans might accept 'accommodation on any terms short of independence'.[22] Oswald seems not to have thought it worth raising such a possibility, which he must have known Franklin would not have entertained for a moment. There was every indication that American opinion was utterly inflexible on unconditional independence and at this point in time on the necessity of no peace separate from France. Franklin had also shown something of American ambitions when he asked Oswald whether the British might not voluntarily relinquish Canada in the interests of future Anglo-American harmony.

Oswald's first encounter with Franklin can have left Shelburne in little doubt that an easy reconciliation was out of the question. Franklin was not going to behave like a friend of England, nor were John Adams and John Jay when they

[19] Oswald to Shelburne, 8 July 1782, Giunta (ed.), *Emerging Nation*, I, p. 453.
[20] To President of Congress, 14 December 1783, Robert J. Taylor et al. (eds), *The Papers of John Adams* (Cambridge, MA, 1977–), XV, p. 423.
[21] Oswald's Journal, 18 April 1782, Giunta (ed.), *Emerging Nation*, I, p. 345.
[22] J. Adams to Franklin, 16 April 1782, ibid. I, p. 338.

joined the negotiations. Hard diplomatic bargaining lay ahead. While the Americans were showing themselves to be intransigent, Shelburne was also becoming aware that certain British concerns would have to be safeguarded and that there were specific groups to whose interest in a settlement any government would have to pay attention. Shelburne, nevertheless, persisted with Oswald as his emissary, sending him back to Paris in early May after a briefing in which he set out his aims for peace in rather greater detail. Oswald was to tell Franklin what Shelburne had already told Laurens: he regarded the 'separation of America from Eng[lan]d' as 'a misfortune to America'. His own wish was for something that he called 'federal union', which he seems to have envisaged as a union of equals without any loss of sovereignty on either side. He recognized, however, that Americans might insist on independence. If so, a settlement would have to be reached quickly. Franklin should not be deceived by 'the cry of the country for peace and in favour of America. The country at large is in no way reconciled to independence.' If the Americans prevaricated, they might find a new government in power that would concede nothing to them. A separate paper listed concrete conditions to be met. Britain must have free trade with the whole of America without duties. Canada would not be handed over. Penobscot in Maine, which the British at present occupied, should be added to Nova Scotia. The interests of two groups were specifically mentioned. British creditors, whose debts had gone unpaid during the war and who later produced claims amounting to some £3 million, must be given means of recovering them, and, most important of all, Shelburne insisted on the need to provide for the loyalists who had sided with Britain. The Americans must restore 'the loyalists to the full enjoyment of their rights and privileges...Lord Shelburne will never give up the loyalists.'[23]

The cause of the loyalists was to cast a very long shadow over Anglo-American relations. Those who professed to represent the very diverse and deeply divided body of Americans who had taken refuge in areas held by the British army in America or fled to Britain itself had long been active. They gave themselves the title of loyalist, one obviously calculated to appeal to British sympathy, early in the conflict. To American patriots, they were usually known as 'refugees' or 'royalists' and of course as 'Tories'. Franklin thought that 'the name *loyalist* was improperly assumed by these people. *Royalists* they may perhaps be called. But the true *loyalists* were the people of America.'[24] At least one fastidious exile from Massachusetts to Britain thought that those who 'affect the pompous character of loyalists' did not gain much 'credit' by so doing. They were more properly '*runaways*'.[25] Associations of loyalists were formed in New York and later in London to try to influence the British command in America and the government at home. The self-appointed leadership of the loyalists in London, whose connections with the great mass of

[23] [28 April 1782], WLCL, Shelburne MSS, 71, p. 25; Lord Fitzmaurice, *Life of William, Earl of Shelburne*, 2 vols., 2nd edn (London, 1912), II, pp. 127–8.

[24] To F. Maseres, 26 June 1785, J. Bigelow (ed.), *The Complete Works of Benjamin Franklin*, 10 vols. (New York, 1887–8), IX, p. 133.

[25] Samuel Curwen to his wife, [31 October 1783], Andrew Oliver (ed.), *The Journal of Samuel Curwen Loyalist*, 2 vols. (New Haven, CT, 1972), II, p. 974.

those who had fled from their homes and were sheltering under the protection of the army in America were likely to have been slight, consisted of a coterie of ex-governors and a few American notables. They put their point of view in published addresses and petitions and through intensive use of the press. Throughout the war they had asserted that there was massive potential support for the British cause throughout the colonies, even if the tactics pursued by the British army had utterly failed to realize it. Joseph Galloway, the most contentious of all the loyalist leaders, had put loyalist support as high as four-fifths of the population. The failure of loyalist support to materialize on anything like this scale seemed to indicate that their spokesmen had been grossly over-optimistic and they incurred much hostility as a consequence. Opponents of the war in Britain regarded them as traitors to the cause of liberty, who had prolonged the war by deliberately misleading British commanders about the strength of their support. Sir Joseph Mawbey, MP for the county of Surrey, thought that the loyalists 'deserved the execration of every Englishman', since they 'had been the chief cause of promoting and prolonging the accursed American war'.[26]

In the closing stages of the war, loyalist spokesmen were coming to accept that peace and American independence were inevitable and that they should therefore seek to secure the best terms that they could 'for their future personal safety and restitution of our property'. In any settlement with America Britain must both insist on proper compensation for them from the American states and must allocate 'some asylum' in British territory for those who could not remain in the United States.[27] On such points they could be assured of sympathy. From the early years of the war, the British press had been flooded with accounts of the severities inflicted on enemies of the Revolution. Refugees had reached Britain and some relief was already being paid. As the war entered its last months, the problem of loyalist exiles became acute. The numbers were likely to be very much larger than had been expected. Popular demands in all the American states for retribution against traitors meant that the outlook for those who had openly identified with Britain was bleak and few were likely to go back to their homes when the British evacuated their last footholds. All shades of British opinion seem to have accepted that men who had responded to calls to oppose the revolt, especially those who had taken up arms for the king, had a cause that could not be ignored. Even opponents of the war who deplored their principles of their leaders conceded that something must be done for the mass who were being persecuted for their loyalty. Writing on behalf of the Rockingham administration, Shelburne instructed Carleton to 'take the greatest possible care' of loyalists when he withdrew from New York. From every point of view, the preference of British governments was that they should stay in America under guarantees of safety and with provisions for them to recover their property. The alternative of having to provide compensation on a massive scale was most unpalatable. Shelburne thought that it would be impossible 'to order a general

---

[26] 12 February 1783, *Morning Chronicle*, 13 February 1783.
[27] Petition to the king from New York, 10 August 1782, Davies (ed.), *Documents*, XXI, p. 99.

compensation at the public expence'.[28] The cost of such relief that was being paid was arousing concern and a commission was working to reduce it. On grounds both of Britain's own interests and of justice, it became a political necessity that as many loyalists as possible be settled back in America on terms acceptable to them. This was a point on which the Americans had to give satisfaction in any peace settlement. Otherwise, Shelburne was convinced that 'the nation would rise to do itself justice, and to recover its wounded honour'.[29]

What the Americans expected from a peace was revealed by Franklin early in July in a list of 'necessary' and 'advisable' articles, based on what the Americans had decided in 1779 and 1781. Independence, 'full and complete in every sense', the evacuation of all British troops from the territory of the old thirteen colonies, satisfactory boundaries, the limitation of Quebec's territory fixed in 1774, and fishing rights were the necessary conditions for any settlement. It would be advisable for the British to make reparation for the damage they had done to American towns, for Parliament to apologise for that damage, and for all Canada to be handed over to the United States. A commercial settlement based on free trade, a point of the utmost importance to the British, was also listed as advisable. Any compensation for the loyalists was out of the power of the commissioners appointed by Congress. It was a matter that had to be left to the states. Britain must not expect to retain any 'sort of sovereignty' but a 'federal union' might eventually be possible. Oswald was optimistic that on these terms, which he regarded as unexceptionable, 'the American quarrel' could be quickly brought to an end.[30]

For Shelburne, the king's chief minister from July 1782 and henceforward in full control of the negotiations, unconditional independence was still a sticking point. He was by now prepared to accept that it would not be possible for Britain to retain any vestige of sovereignty and would have to settle for reconciliation and for the closest future cooperation between sovereign entities. He told the House of Lords on 10 July that he would yield to 'the fatal necessity' of independence.[31] Americans could not, however, expect to get recognition of their independence without paying a price for it. In the last days of Rockingham's ministry he had persuaded the Cabinet to reverse a decision to proceed by making an unconditional grant of independence and then negotiating terms with the Americans and to agree instead that independence should be offered to the Americans as part of a peace settlement. Shelburne's insistence that independence should only be conceded in return for a peace whose terms were satisfactory to Britain was a widely shared view. 'Common sense' told the king that if Britain conceded unconditional independence at the outset, she would have no counters left with which to bargain with the Americans.[32] Thomas Orde, one of Shelburne's closest younger henchmen, found

---

[28] 5 June 1782, ibid. XXI, pp. 83–4.
[29] To R. Oswald, 21 November 1782, Giunta (ed.), *Emerging Nation*, I, p. 682.
[30] To Shelburne, 10 July 1782, ibid. I, pp. 462–4.
[31] *Parliamentary Register*, VIII, p. 366.
[32] To Shelburne, 11 July 1782, Fortescue (ed.), *Correspondence of George III*, VI, p. 81.

by conversing with several persons of weight in the City and having connections of interest in the country, that a great alarm is taken at the supposed concessions made by this country. The independence of America, *as the price of peace* might be reconcilable to the minds of many, who, even averse to the thing, are ready to acknowledge the necessities of our situation and therefore to allow the unfavorable conditions of a bargain for a good, of which we stood in need. But persons, less averse to the separation, cannot endure the idea of a voluntary, unconditional and possibly *inconsequential* dereliction of that bond, by which we maintained some controlling influence over the full exertion of American power, or at least reserved some claim of dignity to our government, which might be made use of as a consolation to our national pride.[33]

At the end of July Shelburne spelt out the British response to Franklin's requirements in a personal letter to Oswald and a set of instructions approved by the Cabinet. American independence was conceded, but it was to be part of a treaty; it could not be granted separately in advance of any other negotiations. Oswald was ordered to make certain that the Americans did not use their independence to ally with France. 'You will be particularly earnest in your attention and arguments to prevent their binding themselves under any engagement, inconsistent with the plan of *absolute and universal independence*, which is the indispensible condition of our acknowledging their independence.' The British made no response to Franklin's 'necessary' requirements about fisheries and boundaries, but they reiterated that satisfaction must be obtained for the two groups whose cause Shelburne had already pressed on Oswald. The settlement of debts to British subjects incurred by Americans before the war was 'a matter of absolute justice' and 'a restitution as well as an indemnification' must be obtained for the loyalists. Once a settlement had been reached, Shelburne hoped for 'the foundation of a new connection better adapted to the present temper and interest of the countries'. Towards this, Oswald was instructed to propose 'an unreserved system of naturalization ... between our kingdom and the American colonies'.[34]

The question of how America obtained its independence was to be resolved relatively quickly, although it required much hectic diplomacy, in which John Jay took the leading role on the American side. The peace terms, boundaries, fisheries, and compensation for debtors and for loyalists, were, on the other hand, to lead to very protracted wrangling. The terms eventually reached on most of these issues were to be highly satisfactory to the Americans but would be virulently attacked in the press and in Parliament and would leave the peace very vulnerable in Britain.

John Jay had taken a strong line on the absolute necessity of Britain's making an acknowledgement of American independence that would be separate from any treaty, but he was also intimating to Oswald and to Benjamin Vaughan, an unofficial go-between communicating with Shelburne, that were this to be done,

---

[33] To Shelburne, 26 September 1782, BL, Add MS 88906/1/17, f. 4. George Rose also told Shelburne of 'the extraordinary agitation in the City' about the possibility of American independence being conceded without any conditions (letter of 28 September 1782, BL, Add MS 88906/3/21, f. 134).

[34] Shelburne to Oswald 27 July, Instructions, 31 July 1782, Giunta (ed.), *Emerging Nation*, I, pp. 479–84.

it would 'cut the cord that ties us to France'.[35] Jay's approach to the British reflected a growing mistrust of France, which Adams, but not Franklin, fully shared. There was some foundation for their mistrust. France was totally committed to American independence as a necessary means of cutting Britain down to size from having been the maritime superpower which had cowed the world in the Seven Years War. But the aggrandizement of an independent America was not a French interest. America's ambitions for western expansion would conflict with those of Spain, France's ally, and America's demand for access to the fisheries was likely to conflict with France's own fishing interests. Deeply suspicious of France, Jay decided to try to achieve his goals through a direct deal with Britain, in spite of America's commitments to act strictly in conjunction with its ally. For the British his move meant that the prize of separating America from France that had seemed unattainable for so long was suddenly materializing. The price to be paid was an immediate acknowledgement of American independence before a treaty had been concluded. Shelburne was in no doubt that the price now had to be paid and the Cabinet agreed with him. Oswald was given a new commission that recognized the United States as an independent entity.

Oswald assumed that once America had been guaranteed its independence, the 'necessary' articles on which Franklin insisted—boundaries and fisheries—could be easily settled.[36] British ministers agreed. Oswald was authorized 'to go to the full extent of them', with the exception that the Americans should not have the right of drying their fish on British shores.[37] Oswald also seems to have believed that the problem of the loyalists, even though Shelburne had been very pressing about them, was not a serious obstacle to a final settlement. Again British ministers apparently acquiesced. Oswald was told on 1 September that as Franklin declared himself not to be empowered to make a settlement on the debts and the loyalists, Britain would not insist that those matters should be included in a treaty, but expected that the states would agree to do justice on them.[38]

By early October Oswald was confident that virtually all matters had been resolved. He forwarded articles for the final treaty drafted by John Jay and agreed with him. The boundaries were to be fixed as the Americans wished and they were to fish wherever they 'used formerly' to do. There were no provisions about debts or loyalists, but there was a clause for complete freedom of trade: 'the merchants and merchant ships of one and the other shall be received and protected like the merchants and merchant ships of the sovereign of the country' and should pay the same duties.[39] No doubt considerably to his surprise, the Cabinet rejected Oswald's draft terms and he was shortly to receive a sharp letter from Shelburne telling him that matters were far from settled. Shelburne blamed Oswald for having been much too willing to yield to the Americans on 'every point of favour or

[35] Oswald to Townshend, 17 August 1782, Vaughan to Shelburne, 24 August 1782, ibid. I, pp. 530, 542.
[36] To Shelburne, 11 July 1782, ibid. I, p. 469.
[37] T. Townshend to R. Oswald, 1 September 1782, ibid. I, p. 546.
[38] Townshend to Oswald, 1 September 1782, ibid. I, p. 546.
[39] To Townshend, [5–8] October 1782, ibid. I, pp. 598–9.

confidence'. This was 'diametrically opposite to our interests'. Questions of the boundaries, the fisheries, the debts, and the loyalists must be reopened.[40] Henry Strachey, an experienced administrator and diplomat, was sent to Paris to join with Oswald in getting better terms.

III

Shelburne had clearly come to believe that without a radical change of tack in the way that the negotiations with the Americans were going, any treaty would be overwhelmed by opposition in Britain. He was relatively sure of the king, but was less sure of his Cabinet. He was only too aware that his government would have great difficulty in commanding a majority in the House of Commons where Lord North had a considerable following. He himself was enigmatic and apparently unsure as to his own intentions, but some of his supporters were extremely hostile, especially on the American issues. Those followers of Lord Rockingham who had adhered to Charles Fox when Shelburne became chief minister were also hostile. The terms of peace with France and Spain would involve cessions which would be unpopular. Gibraltar might be given back to Spain, which would certainly provoke a great uproar. If Gibraltar was kept, Britain was likely to relinquish the Floridas and Minorca and to reduce its claims to settlements on the Central American coast for cutting mahogany and logwood. Shelburne knew that groups with interests in these places would find a voice in Parliament. Concessions would have to be made to the French in the West Indies and West Indian proprietors and merchants were not people with whom lightly to tangle. They would certainly 'make much clamour indeed'.[41] Were the Americans to have their way on what they wanted, as Oswald was advising and Shelburne and his colleagues had up to now accepted, there would be yet more public opposition and more interested groups would be outraged. Shelburne was in no doubt about the absolute necessity of getting satisfaction for the loyalists and for the creditors. If they were not assured of repayment, 'the clamour . . . will scarcely be to be withstood'.[42] He believed that to concede the American demands over borders, which involved handing over western lands indiscriminately, would be to dispose of assets that could be used to compensate loyalists. He did not, however, seem to have anticipated the ferocity with which the London fur-trade merchants would denounce the loss of Canadian lands and of the posts which they deemed vital to their trade. Continuing American access to the fisheries with their associations with Britain's naval power as a nursery of seamen, would, he well knew, certainly be a sensitive issue.

Something must urgently be done to reduce the damage, but the time available for clawing back the Americans' expectations was now very short. The terms of the various peace settlements with Britain's enemies must be fixed before Parliament

---

[40] Letter of 21 October 1782, ibid. I, pp. 620–2.
[41] Shelburne to Grantham, 28 December 1782, BL, Add MS 88906/3/11, f. 54.
[42] To Oswald, 23 October 1782, TNA, FO 97/157, f. 168.

resumed in November 1782. Both Houses would then be presented with treaties which they must accept or reject in their entirety. 'Interests and passions supported by party and different mercantile interests' could not be permitted to try to change parts of the treaties by imposing their views on matters that were not yet settled: under such conditions 'no negotiation can advance with credit to those employ'd or any reasonable prospect for the publick'.[43]

The parliamentary timetable gave an urgency to the peace negotiations, but Shelburne was in a hurry for other reasons as well. He still hoped to detach America, but his belligerence against France and Spain was evaporating and he wanted a quick peace with them too. He was worried about the ability of the armed forces to mount further campaigns and he was concerned about Britain's capacity to sustain the burdens of a prolonged war. In a letter which seems not have survived, he expressed his 'anxiety' to a correspondent who agreed with him that unless the troops overseas could be brought back 'within a few months, . . . all the oeconomy wisdom can suggest will not save us . . . This country is full of distress—bad crops, a bad harvest and poverty both of landlords and tenants.'[44] Bank stock and 3 per cent consols had sunk to a low level and the Bank of England's bullion holdings were being seriously depleted.[45] In July 1783 Francis Baring, Shelburne's chief financial adviser, told him that he could not remember 'a greater scarcity of money'. 'Under these circumstances, my Lord, what would have been the fate of the nation with the continuance of war for another year?'[46]

Shelburne's impatience to get Britain out of a war was, however, driven not only by his apprehensions about Britain's capacity to continue to wage it, but by his ambitions to use the peace to build a better world. He wanted to put Britain's relations with the United States on a new basis and he saw a chance of doing the same with France. He knew that the French minister, the Comte de Vergennes, was also looking for a quick peace and hoped that it might be possible to bring about a great shift from antagonism to cooperation with France. The emissary sent to him by Vergennes reported that he had said that France and Britain were not 'natural enemies' and that 'if we are truly in agreement, we can lay down the law to the rest of Europe'.[47]

In his instructions for renegotiated terms with the Americans, Shelburne told Oswald and Strachey that the question of boundaries and of compensation for the loyalists were linked. People who were perfectly reconciled to American independence were 'strenuous for the subject of boundaries, and of a provision for the refugees'. American demands for western land and restricted Canadian boundaries must be resisted. The loyalists could either be settled on vacant land or it could be sold and the proceeds used to compensate them. The '*honest* debts' of the creditors must be '*honestly* repaid in *honest* money', not in hopelessly depreciated Congress

[43] He expounded his views in letters to Lord Grantham, 25 December 1782, BL, Add MS 88906/3/11, ff. 47–50 and to Alleyne Fitzherbert, 21 October 1782, WLCL, Shelburne MSS, 71, p. 300.

[44] R. Jackson to Shelburne, 29 September [1782], BL, Add MS 88906/3/14, f. 61.

[45] J. H. Clapham, *The Bank of England: A History*, 2 vols. (Cambridge, 1944), I, pp. 251–5.

[46] Letter of 8 July 1783, BL, Add MS 88906/1/1, f. 44.

[47] Translation from Rayneval's notes of 18 September 1782 in Stockley, *Britain and France*, p. 100.

money. On access to the fisheries, Shelburne insisted that the Americans should not be permitted to dry their fish on the coast of Newfoundland and should be confined to what he enigmatically called 'a *drift fishery*'.[48]

Compelled to get a settlement in the limited time left before Parliament reassembled, the British negotiators were able to extract much less from the Americans than the Cabinet desired. Their greatest success was the provision that there should be 'no lawful impediment to the recovery of the full value in sterling money of all bona fide debts'. The Americans had always regarded this as a reasonable requirement and felt that repudiation of the debts would be very damaging to the future credit of the independent American states.[49] The British extracted some extension of the boundaries of Quebec and Nova Scotia beyond what the Americans had originally proposed, but the additions were certainly not on a scale for new loyalist provinces to be created either in Maine or across the Ohio, where, as Franklin put it, 'we did not chuse such neighbours'.[50] The loyalists would have to be resettled within existing British colonies. John Jay put persuasive arguments as to why the British should not concern themselves with the great swathe of territory between the mountains and the Mississippi but should be content with having a guaranteed right freely to navigate the river and thus to trade with the American settlers who would quickly occupy the new lands. He even encouraged the British to send an expedition to recover West Florida from the Spanish, whom he now feared much more than the British as an obstacle to American expansion. Exercising authority over remote western territory was not a claim to which the British were at all committed and so Jay had no difficulty in getting what he wanted. Unrestricted American access to the fisheries was, however, a much more contentious matter. When Strachey returned to London briefly in November, he was given more explicit instructions. Ostensibly to prevent disputes between British and American fishermen, the coasts on which the Americans might dry their fish were to be strictly limited and they were to be excluded from inshore fishing within three leagues of any British possession. Otherwise, the Americans were to have the 'liberty' but not the 'right' to fish in British waters. For the New England states full access to the fisheries was a vital issue, on which John Adams professed that he was prepared to continue to fight the war without French help rather than yield, above all on the inshore fishing on which the New Englanders depended.[51] Heated bargaining ended with the Americans getting nearly all that they wanted. Strachey believed that they would have broken off the whole negotiation if they had not done so.[52]

---

[48] Notes for instructions to Strachey, [20 October 1782], Giunta (ed.), *Emerging Nation*, I, p. 619; Instructions to Strachey, 20 October 1782, WLCL, Shelburne MSS, 87: 205; Shelburne to Oswald, 23 October 1782, ibid. 70, pp. 323–4.

[49] American Commissioners to R. Livingston, 14 December 1782, Giunta (ed.), *Emerging Nation*, I, p. 717.

[50] To R. Livingston, 5–[14] December 1782, Labaree et al. (eds), *Franklin Papers*, XXXVIII, p. 413.

[51] R. Oswald to H. Strachey, 9 January 1783, TNA, FO 97/157, f. 254.

[52] To T. Townshend, 29 November 1782, Giunta (ed.), *Emerging Nation*, I, p. 725.

What, if anything, the Americans would do for the loyalists was for the British the issue with the highest political charge. British ministers were in no doubt that they must have something to show Parliament and the public. Britain, Shelburne told Oswald, would not accept 'terms of *humiliation*' from the Americans of all people on a point that so much affected her honour.[53] The security of the loyalists from revenge and persecution as well as the possibility of compensation for their losses must be obtained. The Americans were unsympathetic to such demands. In any case, they insisted that it was a matter for the states under whose laws loyalists had been attainted and suffered confiscations and that they were not empowered by Congress to settle such points. If the matter was to be referred to Congress, peace would be delayed for several months and it was likely that Congress would insist on reparations from Britain for damage done to America, a stipulation that Franklin considered that America had every right to expect. The most that the British negotiators could get was a provision that Congress would 'earnestly recommend' that the states should provide for the restitution of property confiscated from exiles who had not taken up arms against the United States. Others should have permission to spend twelve months 'unmolested' in America to try to get back property confiscated from them. There were to be no further prosecutions of loyalists and no one was to suffer in 'his person, liberty or property' for what he had done in the war. Henry Strachey thought they had got more for the loyalists than could have been expected.[54] The loyalists themselves did not agree. They dismissed the terms as derisory and British public opinion generally took the same view. Events quickly nullified any expectations that loyalists would benefit from the provisions of the treaty. The states did not make restitution and loyalists could not be sure of immunity. A great upsurge of popular hatred for 'Tories' made it hazardous for exiles to return for some time and impossible for them to seek redress through the courts. Compensation would have to come in money from Britain and in land from the remaining British colonies.[55]

The American commissioners were in no doubt that the peace, for which they signed provisional articles on 29 November 1782, was a good one, fully 'consistent with the honor and interest of the United States'.[56] Apart from popular outrage that anything should be attempted for the loyalists, anxieties about how debts were to be repaid, and some scruples that America had not kept to her undertakings to

[53] Letter of 21 November 1782, ibid. I, p. 682.
[54] To E. Nepean, 29 November 1782, ibid. I, pp. 689–90.
[55] British colonial land was to be the most important source of compensation for loyalists. It has been estimated that some 40,000 land grants were made in North America (J. M. Bumsted, *The People of Canada: A Pre-Confederation History* (Toronto, 1992), p. 166). These arrangements will be described in ch. 8. Some land was distributed in the Caribbean, see ch. 9. Financial compensation was also paid by the British Treasury. This became a matter of much self-congratulation in Britain, but it affected far fewer people. It was sanctioned by Parliament in 1783 on the initiative of the Coalition government in which Lord North, who particularly championed the cause of the loyalists, was a minister. Over £3 million was paid out on the recommendation of commissioners to 2,291 claimants, mostly people who had been of some substance (Maya Jasanoff, *Liberty's Exiles: The Loss of America and the Remaking of the British Empire* (London, 2011), p. 138; Mary Beth Norton, *The British-Americans: The Loyalist Exiles in England* (London, 1974), ch. 7.
[56] To R. Livingston, 14 December 1782, Giunta (ed.), *Emerging Nation*, I, p. 717.

France, opinion in the United States enthusiastically welcomed the peace. James Madison saw it as 'the consummation of our wishes, . . . happy it may indeed be called whether we consider the immediate blessings which it confers, or the cruel distresses and embarrassments from wh[ich it] saves us'.[57] It was widely seen as the work of divine Providence. God had 'erected and established a new and extended empire in this western world' to fulfil His purposes.[58]

The British negotiators thought that they had done the best they could in extremely difficult circumstances. They had never seen calling the Americans' bluff and risking the stalling of the negotiations to be an option, given the urgency of Shelburne's timetable and the need to have a done deal before the parliamentary session. 'If this is not as good a peace as was expected, I am confident that it is the best that could have been made', Strachey wrote.[59] Shelburne received Strachey 'with great cordiality, and with great expressions of acknowledgement, little short of obligation'.[60] He presumably recognized that the peace was the best that could be got in the circumstances. He particularly prided himself on having separated America from France, a process already well under way but which was accelerated by the generosity of the terms that the Americans saw that they could get from Britain. Shelburne explained to the loyalist William Smith that having failed to prevent American independence, 'he thought it second best to gain advantages over the French by generosity to the colonies'.[61] The peace which Shelburne finally accepted was, however, far from fulfilling his earlier hopes of it. Initially, Shelburne had resisted American independence. In office as chief minister, he had come quite quickly to accept that there could be no progress towards peace unless independence was conceded, even though he insisted for as long as he could that independence should not be yielded in isolation, but must be part of a treaty settling all issues and including, he hoped, provisions for future close relations between Britain and America. He had yielded on that point too.

In place of a constitutional dependence on Britain that could not be maintained, Shelburne floated the concept of a 'federal union'. What the links of such a union might be remained somewhat shadowy. To Henry Laurens, who heard Shelburne's ideas face-to-face, they seemed to be 'for somewhat of a connection between Great Britain and America, like Platonic love', something which he 'mumbled but could not define'.[62] In 1787 Shelburne told Arthur Lee that he was hoping for 'a lasting and firm union with America, which will do honour to mankind. I need not say that by this I do not mean a legislative union; in truth, not so much an alliance, as a similarity of principle which may embrace all nations, and contribute to the

[57] To E. Randolph, 25 March 1783, Paul H. Smith (ed.), *Letters of Delegates to Congress 1774 to 1789*, 26 vols. (Washington, DC, 1976–2000), XX, p. 105.

[58] E. Dyer to J. Trumbull, 12 April 1783, ibid. XX, p. 171.

[59] To E. Nepean, 29 November 1782, Giunta (ed.), *Emerging Nation*, I, p. 690.

[60] To A. Fitzherbert, 10 December 1782, ibid. I, p. 712.

[61] Smith's diary, 2 February 1785, L. F. S. Upton (ed.), *The Diary and Selected Papers of Chief Justice William Smith 1784–1793*, 2 vols. (Toronto, 1963–5), I, p. 187.

[62] Laurens to Franklin, 24 June 1782, Labaree et al. (eds), *Franklin Papers*, XXXVII, p. 526.

happiness of all.'[63] Common citizenship was certainly included. Oswald had been instructed to propose an 'unreserved system of naturalization'.[64] During the peace negotiations, John Adams was assured that Britain wished to make 'no distinction between their people and ours, especially between the inhabitants of Canada and Nova Scotia and us'.[65]

Shelburne evidently envisaged common citizenship as an integral part of what he cared about most, complete freedom of trade, which seems for him to have been the essential underpinning of any federal union. He had long been interested in the liberalizing of international trade. For honing his ideas, he acknowledged a deep indebtedness to conversation and correspondence with the French *philosophe* André Morellet.[66] He had come to see freedom of trade as an engine for spreading peace and prosperity throughout the world. 'The systems of this statesman', wrote Benjamin Vaughan, who took on himself the role of interpreter of Shelburne's ideas, even to Shelburne himself, 'go to the abolition of wars, the promotion of agriculture, the unlimited freedom of trade, and the just freedom of man'.[67] Shelburne evidently envisaged a settlement with America based on free trade as the first instalment of this global programme. France was also to be included. A French envoy was told that 'every view should be directed to the great end of introducing liberty of commerce'.[68]

Questions relating to trade were eventually left out of the main treaty with America to be dealt with in a separate commercial treaty. They required the amendment of British acts of Parliament, a process on which Shelburne's administration embarked but could not complete before it lost office. When he came to defend the main treaty in the House of Lords, Shelburne insisted that many of its articles were based on free-trade principles.[69] He gave the Lords a general disquisition on free trade. Enlightened Europe was now shaking off 'the vile shackles of oppressive, ignorant monopoly'.[70] Britain, with its abundant capital and manufacturing, must be in the van. A new pattern of relations with the United States would develop on a basis of reciprocal free trade. As Vaughan put it, 'the plenty of American lands' promised 'a long continuation of production and consumption on their side and of supply on ours'.[71] American expansion was in

---

[63] 4 February 1787, R. H. Lee (ed.), *The Life of Arthur Lee, LLD.*, 2 vols. (Boston, 1829),. II, p. 358.

[64] See above, p. 41.

[65] To R. Livingston, 17 July 1783, Taylor et al. (eds), *Adams Papers*, XV, p. 134.

[66] For their connection, see Dorothy Medlin and Arlene P. Shy, 'Enlightened Exchange: The Correspondence of André Morellet and Lord Shelburne' in K. H. Doig and Medlin (eds), *English-French Exchanges in the Eighteenth Century* (Newcastle, 2007), pp. 34–82.

[67] To J. Monroe, 18 September 1795, Richard B. Morris (ed.), *John Jay*, II, p. 343.

[68] To Grantham, 25 December 1785, BL, Add MS 88906/3/11, f. 47.

[69] *Parliamentary Register*, XI, pp. 65–78 is the main source for Shelburne's speech of 17 February 1783. At least two newspaper reports, those in the *Morning Post*, 20 February 1783 and *Parker's General Advertiser*, 19 February 1783, contain valuable additional material. Vincent Harlow compiled an extended summary of Shelburne's speech from various sources (*Second British Empire*, I, pp. 434–43).

[70] *Parliamentary Register*, XI, p. 67.

[71] Brief for treaty, WLCL, Shelburne MSS, 87: 209.

Britain's interest. To try to cramp it would be a self-defeating policy. Benefits for Britain would flow from generosity to America. Shelburne applied free-trade principles to some of the most contentious articles of the treaty, namely western lands, the Canadian boundaries, and the fisheries. Britain had no need to rule over vast tracts of wilderness or to have exclusive monopolies over furs or fish. On the western lands he used arguments relayed to him by John Jay via Benjamin Vaughan.[72] Jay, as he was later to tell Shelburne, shared his sense that 'a perfect freedom of commerce' was an 'extension of divine benevolence'.[73] Leave the land for the Americans to settle and the trade would accrue to Britain especially as the treaty included a guarantee of free navigation of the Mississippi. In notes for his speech Shelburne coined a phrase that was to have much resonance with future historians of the British empire: 'trade not dominion' was Britain's interest in the Mississippi.[74] There can be no question that Shelburne was a devout believer in free trade, but in investing the articles about boundaries and fisheries with high principle, he was making the best of a bad job by providing a rationale for concessions that he knew would be intensely unpopular and that he had tried to retract when it was too late to do so.

The most damaging articles of all, those relating to the loyalists, could only be defended on grounds of necessity. He deplored them, but 'A part must be wounded, that the whole of the empire may not perish.'[75] In this case, Shelburne can hardly be faulted for not having given Oswald repeated injunctions that something must be obtained. The harsh reality was, however, that nothing could be done and that British public expectations that firmer negotiating would have produced different results were entirely unreal. Further guarantees, could they have been obtained, would have existed only on paper. With the notable exception of Franklin, the American elite was generally sympathetic to reconciliation and to reintegrating the loyalists. Nevertheless, Congress did not have the power to impose its will on the states and the states did not have the power to control popular fury against loyalists at the end of the war. Loyalists would have been subjected to very rough treatment had they ventured back and would not have recovered their property whatever stipulations might have been extracted for them. Reconciliation had to be left to time.

IV

On the news that the preliminaries of peace with America, France, and Spain had been signed, it was reported that 'in most of the towns of England . . . there were the greatest rejoicings; the bells were set a ringing, bonfires lit up '.[76] The rejoicing was

---

[72] Jay to R. Livingston, 17 November 1782, Giunta (ed.), *Emerging Nation*, I, p. 669
[73] Letter of 20 April 1786, BL, Add MS 88906/3/14, f. 70.
[74] WLCL, Shelburne MSS, 87: 222.
[75] *Parliamentary Register*, XI, p. 70.
[76] *London Chronicle*, 6–8 February 1783.

likely to have been over the ending of a long and costly war rather than over the terms of the peace. The commonest defence of Shelburne in the press and in Parliament was that Britain urgently needed peace, even if the terms left something to be desired. Others had got Britain into a war; Shelburne had got her a peace. The Scottish MP, Lord Fife, supported Shelburne because he thought that 'whatever is humiliating is owing to war-makers and not to peace makers'.[77] Enthusiasm for the terms that Shelburne had been able to obtain is not easy to find.

'Every call under Heaven', Shelburne told the Lords, 'urges you to stand on the footing of brethren' with the Americans.[78] In the House of Commons Thomas Townshend, speaking for the administration as Secretary of State, 'hoped to God . . . that we should continue to consider the Americans as our brethren, and give them as little reason to feel that they were not British subjects'.[79] Ministers were able to get an endorsement of their hopes for a new relationship with America from the City of London, whose address to the king hoped for a restoration of 'our commercial intercourse with our American brethren; and we beg leave to declare it to be our firm persuasion that the great commerce interest of this country and of North America, are inseparably united'. The king, with Shelburne and his colleagues 'about his chair', replied that he hoped for 'such a friendly intercourse in future, as ought to result from mutual interest and returning affection'.[80] The county of Surrey also hoped for 'cordial reconciliation and lasting friendship' with America[81] and Londonderry, the port from which so many had left for America, commended Shelburne's efforts to 'unite the interests of Britain and America . . . on which the safety, dignity and prosperity of the British empire must ultimately depend'. Londonderry hoped for a 'reunion'.[82]

Optimism about the future was, however, overwhelmed by a torrent of criticism and denunciation of the American treaty. It was almost universally accepted that American independence had to be conceded, but not on terms that were humiliating to Britain and damaging to her interests. There was no necessity to 'bury the faith and honour of England in the same grave with her commerce and grandeur. The bitter draught might still have been qualified; and something might yet have been saved.'[83] The Americans were 'unnatural revolters' and Shelburne's talk of '*natural* ties' with them 'affords not a ray of hope' for Britain.[84] There were allegations of treason in the press. Oswald was certainly an American agent and Shelburne should be put on trial.[85]

The failure to provide for the loyalists produced most hyperbole, especially from former ministers whose direction of the war had served them so badly. Lord

---

[77] To W. Ross, 18 February 1783, Alistair and Henrietta Tayler (eds), *Lord Fife to His Factor; being the Correspondence of James, 2nd Lord Fife 1729–1809* (London, 1925), p. 150.

[78] *Parliamentary Register*, XI, p. 67.

[79] Ibid. IX, p. 260.

[80] *Morning Herald*, 22, 27 February 1783.

[81] *Parker's General Advertiser*, 28 March 1783.

[82] Address of 24 October 1782, BL, Add MS 88906/7/7, f. 33.

[83] *A Letter to the Earl of Shelburne on the Peace*, 3rd edn (London, 1783), p. 12.

[84] 'Columbus', *Public Advertiser*, 1 February 1783.

[85] *A Letter to Shelburne*, p. 14; *Public Advertiser*, 10 March 1783.

Sackville (formerly Lord George Germain) thought that the clauses relating to them 'must be accursed in the sight of God and man'.[86] 'Never was the honour, the humanity, the principles, the policy of a nation so grossly abused', Lord North told the Commons.[87] The press was full of paragraphs about the loyalists, who were described as 'men and brethren who have lost their all in the cause of allegiance'.[88] A number of speakers in the Lords also took up the plight of Britain's Indian allies, for whom no provision was made in the treaty.

A very damaging campaign was directed by the British Canada merchants against the clauses relating to the boundary between British territory and the United States. They argued that by the surrender to the Americans of all the territory south of the Great Lakes together with the long-established posts there the supply of furs to Canadian ports on the St Lawrence would be completely cut off. Without the fur trade, Canada would be virtually valueless. They obtained interviews with Oswald, Thomas Townshend, the Secretary of State, and Shelburne himself. Their account of the interviews made much sport of ministers' apparent ignorance of the subject. Shelburne, they reported, told them: 'There must be some mistake—The fur trade was never meant to be given up . . . Could not you contrive to get furs from New York?' Townshend, professed 'his ignorance relative to every one of the objects of their complaint. He seemed not to know which side of the boundary line the forts lay or whether there were any forts there or no.' He explained that he had deferred to 'the great local knowledge of Mr *Oswald*'. Oswald admitted that the fur trade '*appeared* to be given away', but he assured his listeners that the Americans did not intend 'to take any ungenerous advantage of those possessions'.[89] Shelburne's political opponents of course made much of all this.

The handing over of land across the Ohio was said not only to give the fur trade to the Americans but also to make them a present of '200,000 square miles of the best lands in all America',[90] into which loyalists or others willing to become British subjects would have moved. Had Britain kept the western lands, 'the settlers on it would have been ours'. They would be 'an advance guard to us, and as a bridle to the Americans'.[91] Letting the Americans back into the fisheries was said to have 'at one stroke annihilated our navy' and thus to have 'put an end to our existence as a commercial nation'.[92] The Americans and French would train up 80,000 seamen on the fisheries. Once the Americans had created a navy, 'it will be in vain for us to try to defend any of our possessions'.[93]

The treaties with America, France, and Spain were submitted to Parliament on 17 February 1783. The Lords passed a resolution expressing their 'satisfaction' with

[86] 17 February 1783, *Parliamentary Register*, XI, p. 63.
[87] 17 February 1783, ibid. IX, p. 249.
[88] 'Egbert to the Earl of Shelburne, II', *Public Advertiser*, 12 February 1783.
[89] W. Y. W, 'Observations on the Treaty with America', *Public Advertiser*, 13 February 1783. This is one of several letters by the same hand. For Oswald's account of his meeting with the merchants, 6 February 1783, see TNA, PRO 30/8/343, f. 35.
[90] W. Y. W., 'Observations', *Public Advertiser*, 5 March 1783.
[91] A.B., 'On the Peace', ibid. 7 February 1783.
[92] 'A Country Member of Parliament', ibid. 13 February 1783.
[93] 'Piscator', ibid. 12 February 1783.

the American treaty, but the House of Commons withheld its approval for the treaties by 224 votes to 208 and passed a resolution censuring them for having made too many concessions by 207 votes to 196. Contemporaries, including Shelburne and his circle, generally believed that the American treaty was the main contested ground between the government and its opponents. The treaties with France and Spain gave relatively little ground for complaint.

A majority of the press was strongly critical of the terms obtained by the Americans.[94] Recent work on the press tends to stress its autonomy.[95] A study of the newspaper press specifically in relation to the American Revolution concludes that it was 'a reasonable barometer of literate public opinion' and 'answered primarily to market forces rather than to elite patrons with political agendas or angry mobs'.[96] There are, however, problems in using late eighteenth-century newspapers as a reliable indicator of public opinion on issues like the peace. There can be no doubt, that both the government and leaders of political connections cultivated the newspapers. It was widely believed that Shelburne's parliamentary opponents were systematically using the press to attack him and his peace. He was warned that his enemies were determined to 'write him down' and had 'set their emissaries to work to represent you in an unfavourable light in nearly every one of the news-papers'. Since nearly all 'people of all ranks form their ideas of ministers and measures from the public prints', he would be well advised to try 'to counteract the poison and malevolence of [his] enemies in these publications'.[97] A well-disposed newspaper editor offered to set up 'a *secret committee* of friends perfectly conversant in political disquisitions' and to send material 'to every town of consequence in England'.[98] Shelburne was with good reason apprehensive about the 'clamour' that lobbies as well as political opponents could raise against the peace. The Canada merchants were an obvious example of a group that placed material in the press. Whether deliberate manipulation, purposeful as it seems to have been, can account for the full scale of the press onslaught seems, though, to be doubtful. The press probably was in a general way responding to widespread disillusion with what was taken to be the appeasement of America, even if interested parties did their best to stoke up resentment.

Some commercial communities with strong American connections might share the hopes of Shelburne and those close to him for reconciliation with their American brethren, but to the mass of British opinion, which seems to have included even some of the Americans' once-staunch allies, the Protestant Dissenters,[99] the experience of the war had turned Americans into aliens who had no

---

[94] The press response is analysed in Charles R. Ritcheson, 'The London Press and the First Decade of American Independence 1783–1793', *Journal of British Studies*, II (1963), 88–109.

[95] E.g. Hannah Barker, *Newspapers, Politics and Public Opinion in Late Eighteenth-Century England* (Oxford, 1998), p. 4.

[96] Troy Bickham, *Making Headlines: The American Revolution as Seen through the British Press* (DeKalb, IL, 2009), pp. 10, 49.

[97] R. Tomlinson to Shelburne, 20 July 1782, BL, Add MS 88906/3/25, f. 49.

[98] I. Jackman to Shelburne, 28 September 1782, BL, Add MS 88906/3/14, ff. 59–60.

[99] See below, p. 298–9.

claims to favour. British national interests should be maintained against them as against any other foreign people. Lord Shelburne was judged not to have done that. George Byng, one of the MPs for Middlesex, seems to have caught something of this. He had opposed the peace because of the Canadian boundary and the fisheries. Even so, 'He had met many of his constituents in the street who said "Good God, Mr Byng, what a peace have you made!"'[100]

The House of Commons could censure treaties, but it could not reject them, since treaty-making was the prerogative of the Crown. The treaties were to be ratified essentially as they stood some months later. The House's censure, however, proved fatal for the minister responsible for the treaties. His colleagues warned him that he did not have sufficient support to give him any real chance of standing firm and trying to maintain himself in office after the adverse vote.[101] Shelburne resigned on 24 February 1783, although his administration was to stagger on for a further month. Shelburne was never to hold office again. Whether he had ever had the political support to sustain a government over any length of time seems unlikely. If he had hoped that his role as peacemaker would give him the public popularity that he had hitherto lacked, he was to be disappointed.

If the terms of the American treaty were held against him, according to Benjamin Vaughan, Shelburne retained 'all his old American sentiments and repents of nothing'.[102] Had he been able to stay in office, he certainly would have pressed on with his project for establishing free trade with America. He had approached one of his political allies, the Earl of Surrey, about going there to negotiate a commercial treaty and to stay on as ambassador 'to ratify it and adjust the terms of a federal commercial union'.[103] An American Intercourse Bill to clear the way for commercial negotiations by amending British statutes was introduced into the Commons after Shelburne's resignation. It failed to make progress and negotiations for a commercial treaty never got under way. Whether Shelburne, even if he had remained as the king's principal minister, would have had the political authority to overcome the formidable opposition that was to arise to any free trade agreement with the United States is questionable. As it turned out, there was to be no Anglo-American commercial agreement until the Jay Treaty of 1794 and no British ambassador was to go to America until 1791. 'Federal union', whatever it might have meant, was never to be on any future official British agenda.

Shelburne's aspirations for the peace do credit to his idealism. The kind of peace he desired was, however, acceptable to neither British nor American opinion. If he wanted to ensure his survival in British politics, Shelburne should from the outset have recognized this and have concentrated on extracting the best terms he could for Britain. He changed tack far too late.

---

[100] Middlesex Meeting, 5 March 1783, *Parker's General Advertiser*, 6 March 1783.
[101] John Cannon, *The Fox-North Coalition: Crisis of the Constitution 1782–4* (Cambridge, 1969), p 58.
[102] To J. Adams, 11 March 1783, Taylor et al. (eds), *Adams Papers*, XIV, p. 326.
[103] Surrey to Shelburne, 16 December 1782, BL, Add MS 88906/3/24, f. 80.

V

In April 1782, in a conversation with Oswald, Franklin mused on the distinction between 'a mere peace', concluded between nations that are 'both weary of war' and a genuine 'reconciliation'. Reconciliation, he thought, required 'reparation'. In Franklin's view reparation was due from only one side in the conflict—from the British who had wantonly waged unprovoked war. It should include such acts as the handing over Quebec and Nova Scotia, whatever their inhabitants might wish, to the United States.[104] Shelburne would have no truck with the idea of reparation, but he ardently desired reconciliation. The preamble of the peace did indeed state that its intention was to 'promise and secure . . . perpetual peace and harmony' between Britain and America. The articles that followed were, however, more appropriate to a 'mere peace' that ended a war of which both sides were weary.

The peace brought the war to an end, but it generated resentment rather than laying any basis for future reconciliation. Trade quickly revived between Britain and the United States, but on terms which without a commercial treaty caused great bitterness on the American side. The loyalist clauses were unenforceable and their obvious flouting evoked much resentment in Britain. Enforcing the provisions about debts was a very protracted business, generating many British accusations of bad faith. Which river constituted the treaty frontier between Nova Scotia, later New Brunswick, and Maine was long disputed. The northern frontier of the United States also remained unsettled as Britain, under the pretext of American failure to fulfil articles of the treaty, refused to evacuate the fur-trading posts. The seventh article stipulated that when the British forces withdrew, there should be no 'carrying away any negroes or other property of the American inhabitants'. Many African Americans whom the British commanders deemed to have guarantees of freedom left with the British evacuation. Americans saw this as a breach of faith about which there was to be much subsequent wrangling. Even as a 'mere peace', the treaty ratified in 1783 did not serve the future of Anglo-American relations well.

---

[104] Notes of a Conversation [18 April 1782], Giunta (ed.), *Emerging Nation*, I, p. 342.

3

The Challenge of Revolutionary America

I

At the beginning of the American War an MP told the House of Commons that 'it would have been better for this country that America had never been known, than that a great consolidated American empire should exist independent of Britain'.[1] In 1783 the United States of America formally became independent of Britain. Although some objected to the term, such as William Gordon, the English chaplain to the Massachusetts Congress, who wanted America to 'remain a collection of republics and not become an empire',[2] most American patriots seem to have been in no doubt that they lived in a 'rising' empire, even though it was to be an entirely new kind of empire, one dedicated to liberty. Abigail Adams looked forward to 'the new empire' becoming 'the guardian and protector of religion and liberty, of universal benevolence and phylanthropy'.[3] The concept of an American empire became common currency. This new empire posed a challenge to Britain in a number of ways.

In terms of power politics Britain had little cause for apprehension, once she could be assured that the rupture of the French alliance, that had become manifest when America entered into what was essentially a separate peace, would not be repaired and that France would not be able to dominate the trade of America. Under the Articles of Confederation the United States was a loose union of republics with a weak central executive and, once the Continental Army had been disbanded, exiguous standing military forces. Although there was a rising swell of dissatisfaction with the limited nature of federal authority, apart from those who thought like Alexander Hamilton, few Americans advocated the creation of a state in any way comparable to those of Europe. A standing army, heavy taxation, and a permanent debt would have amounted to an abnegation of the principles of the Revolution. Americans had neither the means nor the ambitions to play a major role in international rivalries. Nor did the new America have any desire to be drawn into the maelstrom of European power politics, which, as Washington put it,

---

[1] John Dyke Acland 26 October 1775, R. C. Simmons and P. D. G. Thomas (eds), *Proceedings and Debates of the British Parliaments respecting North America, 1754–1783*, 6 vols. (Millwood, NY, 1982–6), VI, p. 96.

[2] To J. Adams, 7 September 1782, 'Letters of the Reverend William Gordon: Historian of the American Revolution, 1770–1799', *Massachusetts Historical Society Proceedings*, LXIII (1929–30), 469.

[3] Diary 4 July 1784, L. H. Butterfield et al. (eds), *The Diary and Autobiography of John Adams*, 4 vols. (Cambridge, MA, 1961), III, p. 163.

played states against one another. America, he urged, should keep aloof from such concerns. She should aim to be 'respectable', ensuring that 'our independence is acknowledged, our power can be regarded, or our credit supported among foreign nations'.[4] For the next few years, at least until 1790 when the United States might have become a factor in a possible war with Spain, British diplomats could safely ignore them and did so.[5]

American concerns were focused on the North American continent. British observers were well aware that the new America viewed the surviving Spanish and British possessions on the continent with dislike and suspicion and hoped that they would ultimately be absorbed into the United States. They were also well aware of the dynamic for westward expansion of the rapidly growing and highly mobile American population, which the British had tried vainly to contain in the colonial era. American expansion seemed, however, to present no great threat to British interests in the immediate future. The United States lacked the means to evict the British from Quebec or Nova Scotia and American immigration into the British colonies was coming to be welcomed as a much-needed addition to their population rather than as a threat of subversion.[6] The westward expansion of settlement as far as the Mississippi seemed likely to be to Britain's advantage. It would result in new communities which, it was assumed, the loose union of the existing states would be incapable of incorporating. The new settlements would trade with Britain through Canada or on the Mississippi and political connections could probably be established with them. Largely unsuccessful attempts were to be made to draw such communities into the British orbit. There seems to have been no awareness of the creativity that was being shown by the Congress of the Confederation in evolving mechanisms whereby the western settlers could form their own states and be enabled to enter into union with the existing states on the eventual basis of full equality.

Commercial competition from an America no longer restrained by British economic regulations was the prospect that caused most foreboding about American independence. Rich and enterprising merchant communities had grown up in the port cities in the colonial period. The potential of the northern states to maintain extensive merchant fleets could not be doubted. Before the Revolution a high proportion of the British empire's shipping had been built in America. American ships were cheap to construct and to sail. Operating as a national mercantile marine, it was assumed that they would quickly win much of the trade of the West Indies and of the northern fisheries, and would soon compete with British shipping all over the world. During the war the American states had created a navy and great numbers of privateers had done much damage. They had all the resources needed in time to develop a powerful navy that 'will one day

---

[4] Washington circular to states, June 1784, in Don Higginbotham, *George Washington: Uniting a Nation* (Lanham, MD, 2002), pp. 117–20, and his letter to J. Warren, 7 October 1785, in W. W. Abbot et al. (eds) *The Papers of George Washington: Confederate Series*, 6 vols. (Charlotteville, VA, 1992–7), III, p. 229.

[5] In Jeremy Black's extremely thorough study of British diplomacy in the 1780s, the United States hardly features at all, *British Foreign Policy in the Age of Revolutions 1783–1793* (Cambridge, 1994).

[6] See below, pp. 159–60.

deprive us of all we possess abroad'.[7] Above all, an independent America would be able to cripple Britain by drawing off her population. '[B]urthened as we are, with an immensity of taxes, our poor and even our monied men, and most of the numberless hosts that now compose our fleets and armies,... will emigrate in crowds to the fertile regions of America.'[8] As chapter 11 will show, there was much alarm at the prospect of large-scale emigration in official circles as well as among a wider public.

Some of these forebodings had substance. There was much emigration to America, especially from Ireland and by the 1790s America had a large and highly competitive fleet of merchant ships. Even so, what was from the British point of view a largely satisfactory economic relationship of complementarity rather than competition evolved. The development of large-scale manufacturing in the United States was limited and thus it remained a growing market for British exports, while a considerable proportion of American exports of primary products continued to go to Britain or to pass through Britain. The French ambassador to the United States observed bitterly that Britain 'without making any sacrifice, without seeking the friendship of a people deprived of principles, of system, of government' still dominated American trade and the American states remained Britain's 'fertile and profitable colonies'.[9]

II

By 1775 at least, it was becoming obvious that Americans were not merely contending for independence so as to run their own affairs without any external control; they were seeking to remodel their institutions on fundamentally new principles by which liberty was to be secured under republican government. These principles were considered to be universal ones. America, Ezra Stiles of Yale wrote in his celebratory sermon on *The United States Elevated to Glory and Honour*, had fought not 'for the liberties of *America* only, but for the liberties of the world', certainly including those of England and Ireland.[10] In 1789 Washington was happy to note that 'the American Revolution, or the peculiar light of the age, seems to have opened the eyes of almost every nation in Europe; and a spirit of equal liberty appears fast to be gaining ground everywhere'.[11] To mainstream British opinion, however, the Americans were not merely rebels against properly constituted authority, who should have been brought to heel by armed force, but they were propagators of false doctrines which needed to be countered by restatements of

---

[7] 'A True Briton', *Morning Chronicle*, 24 July 1782.
[8] 'Indignant Briton' to Lord North, ibid. 7 February 1783.
[9] Moustier to Montmorin, 29 May 1788, translation in John P. Kaminski and Gaspare J. Saladino (eds), *The Documentary History of the Ratification of the Constitution: Commentaries on the Constitution, Public and Private*, 6 vols. (Washington, DC, 1981–95),VI, p. 145.
[10] 2nd edn (Worcester, MA, 1785), p. 81.
[11] To M.-G. J. de Crèvecoeur, 10 April 1789, W. W. Abbot et al. (eds), *The Papers of George Washington: Presidential Series* (Charlottesville, VA, 1987–), II, p. 44.

British constitutional verities if they were not to take root in Britain and the remaining parts of its empire. Both sides greatly exaggerated the ideological differences between them. American republicanism was deeply rooted in American interpretations of British constitutional traditions. Nevertheless, much British opinion saw the most dangerous challenge emerging from the new America as ideological. It had to be fought with ideological weapons. British concepts of liberty under a limited monarchy had to be asserted against the specious claims of republican liberty.

'Republican' in the eighteenth century was a term that conveyed various meanings. Essentially it was an ordering of a free system of government for the pursuit of virtue and the common good in which the will of the citizen body as a whole was able to prevail. A monarchy subject to law was not necessarily incompatible with a republic. In intellectual circles there was inconclusive discussion as to whether England was or was not a republic. Montesquieu thought that England 'may be justly called a republic under the form of a monarchy' and in the view of a modern scholar, England's 'famous "limited" or "mixed" monarchy was in fact a republicanized one'.[12] The radical MP John Sawbridge thought so too: 'The country was a republick with a chief magistrate at the head of it; call him king, emperor or what you would, he was no more than the chief magistrate, the executive branch of the government.'[13] John Adams believed that England was 'a monarchical republic'. A 'limited monarchy', like that of England, 'when limited by two independent branches, an aristocratical and democratic power in the constitution, may with strict propriety be called a republic'.[14] Madison, on the other hand, was sure that England was not a republic since it has 'one republican branch only, combined with an hereditary aristocracy and monarchy'. For him a republic was a government 'which derives all its powers directly or indirectly from the great body of the people'. Britain did not qualify.[15] While they might admire what they regarded as republican virtues, few in the mainstream of British politics were prepared to describe England as a republic. Too many opprobrious overtones were attached to republicanism. Above all, it was associated with popular democracy, social levelling, and the overthrow of the monarchy in the mid seventeenth century. It was in these terms that the mass of British opinion interpreted the American Revolution from its outset. The great American constitutional debates about the balancing of order and civil liberty were largely ignored or dismissed as irrelevant to what seemed to be the unfolding of events, as that was understood in Britain, that had enabled the mob or those who claimed to speak in its name to take power.

Americans in the past had also rejected republicanism. In December 1765 the South Carolina Committee of Correspondence complained that the epithet 'republican' was being maliciously applied to the colonies. 'No people in the world

---

[12] Gordon, S. Wood, *The Radicalism of the American Revolution* (New York, 1992), p. 98.
[13] 14 March 1781, *Morning Chronicle*, 15 March 1781.
[14] 'A Defence of the Constitution of Government of the United States of America' in Charles F. Adams (ed.), *The Works of John Adams*, 10 vols. (Boston, 1850–6), IV, p. 296.
[15] Federalist Papers, 39, J. R. Pole (ed.), *The Federalist* (Indianapolis, IN, 2005), p. 207.

can be more averse to republicanism than the British Americans', they insisted.[16] In 1776, however, Americans formally became republicans when they renounced their allegiance to their king. For many Americans, 'republican' far from being a term of reproach now embodied aspirations that they proudly embraced for a new political, social, and moral order. They had 'come to believe that the Revolution would mean nothing less than a reordering of eighteenth-century society and politics as they had known and despised them—a reordering that was summed up by the conception of republicanism'.[17]

Authority was now to be derived directly from the will of the people. In practice the will of the people seemed to be being asserted in ways that provided substance for British fears. The old colonial order was everywhere being replaced by conventions, congresses, and local committees claiming to embody the authority of the people. The committees, originally constituted to enforce the Articles of Association prohibiting the import and consumption of British goods proclaimed by Congress in October 1774, took control of local government and expanded their functions to economic regulation, raising resources for the war effort and above all to enforcing support for the Revolution by silencing opposition.[18] Such bodies, apparently acting without regard for the law or any authority except what they allegedly derived directly from the people, attracted much hostile attention in the British press. They seemed to represent the worst excesses of republican democracy.

In May 1776 Congress formally decreed that 'the exercise of every kind of authority under the . . . crown should be totally suppressed' and that 'all the powers of government' should now be subject to 'the authority of the people of the colonies'.[19] All the new states, with the exception of Connecticut and Rhode Island, who regarded themselves as already independent of British authority, drafted new constitutions. Although the terms 'republic' and 'democracy' were often used interchangeably, republics answerable to the supreme authority of the people were not necessarily democracies in which the people actually governed. Thomas Paine in *Common Sense* urged that all checks on the exercise of popular sovereignty should be swept away, but most of the revolutionary elite were strongly opposed to democratic government. They hoped that the people would entrust the business of government to a new aristocracy of talent and virtue rather than birth, who would pursue the public good, setting aside sectional interests, and they intended that there should be institutional checks on the uncontrolled exercise of political power even if it emanated from the people. In practice, however, power in the first wave of the new state constitutions was generally tilted towards elected bodies in which elite dominance was greatly weakened in favour of 'middling' people such as farmers, artisans, and tradesmen. Elected lower houses took control

---

[16] Cited in P. J. Marshall, 'Britain and the World in the Eighteenth Century: II, Britons and Americans', *Transactions of the Royal Historical Society*, 6th Ser., IX (1999), 12.

[17] Gordon S. Wood, *The Creation of the American Republic 1776–1787* (Chapel Hill, NC, 1969), p. 48.

[18] The committees are the main theme of T. H. Breen, *American Insurgents, American Patriots: The Revolution of the People* (New York, 2010).

[19] Wood, *Creation of the Republic*, p. 132.

of the executive and tended to usurp the independence of the courts. The Pennsylvania constitution of 1776 was the most determined move towards popular democracy. It had a single-chamber legislature elected on a very wide franchise with provisions for all acts of the legislature to be referred back to the people. The executive was entrusted not to a governor but to a rotating council. It was characterized by a 'wholesale rejection of the ideal of balanced government'.[20] Reports about the working of the early state constitutions inevitably reinforced British assumptions that American republicanism was in practice the unrestrained rule of the lower orders.

To British opinion the Americans seemed to be intent not merely on transferring power to the populace but also on levelling social distinctions in the name of equality. The Declaration of Independence, reprinted throughout the British newspaper press, proclaimed the equality of all men. State bills or declarations of rights generally began in the same way. In states where there were religious establishments there was strong pressure from those who felt themselves discriminated against for declarations of religious freedom. Virginia included in its declaration the words that 'all men are equally entitled to the free exercise of religion according to the dictates of conscience'. Similar sentiments were commonly repeated by other states, as were Virginia's provisions against a traditional aristocracy: 'exclusive or separate emoluments or privileges' could only be justified by services to the community and could not be inherited.

Within a short space of time there were movements in most American states to 'reverse the democratic tendencies of the early constitutions . . . and conversely to strengthen the magisterial power', that is to create balanced constitutions according to what were both the classical British and intellectual republican notions of government, in which the executive would be largely separate from the legislature. The independence of the courts were also to be safeguarded. Such principles were enacted in the New York constitution of 1777 and those of Massachusetts of 1780 and New Hampshire of 1784. There were strong pressures to revise the Pennsylvania constitution which eventually produced a new one in 1790.[21] The later constitutions seem, however, to have done little to shift British stereotypes that continued to equate American republicanism with the breakdown of ordered government and the tyranny of the mob. Constitutional developments in America seem to have received little serious attention, at least until the Constitutional Convention of 1787. The London Quaker John Fothergill, who thought that the 1780 Massachusetts 'frame of government . . . appears near perfection', wrote that the 'general ignorance that prevails here of your abilities, intentions and resources, is inconceivable'.[22]

---

[20] Jack Rackove, *Revolutionaries: A New History of the Invention of America* (New York, 2010), p. 184.
[21] Wood, *Creation of the Republic*, ch. XI, quotation on p. 437.
[22] 'To a gentleman of Massachusetts', 20 October 1780, *The American Museum*, IV (1788), 378.

III

There is little to suggest that the mass of British opponents of the war felt any enthusiasm for the new political programmes being unveiled across the Atlantic, let alone envisaging them as a viable alternative to British constitutional arrangements, even if these were in need of reform. The Newcastle Philosophical Society seems to have been something of an exception when it carried by two votes a motion in 1776 that a republic was to be preferred to a limited monarchy.[23] What most appear to have wanted was an end to the war that they detested and the restoration of good relations with the colonies, who would, they hoped, again enjoy the benefits of the British constitution within the empire on terms which would satisfy their justified grievances.

There were, however, individuals who paid close attention to what was happening in the new states and approved of what they knew of it.[24] The Earl of Abingdon, a consistent supporter of radical causes, quoted the example of the Massachusetts draft constitution at some length in arguing for the affinity of the new American constitutions with Britain's: 'They are founded on original compact, and so is ours.'[25] Thomas Day, the radical-minded author, thought that the principles upon which 'the little nursling republics in America' were established were 'certainly the most generous and noble, which were ever made the foundation of a state'.[26] William Jones, another literary radical, thought 'the form of government, which the American states have established, manly, sensible, rational, and as perfectly adapted to them, as long as they continue virtuous'.[27] Richard Price did most of all to present the new order in America in a favourable light to British audiences. In 1776 he published *Observations on the Nature of Civil Liberty, the Principles of Government, and the Justice and Policy of the War with America*. This sold in great quantities, going through at least fifteen editions in 1776 alone, including 'a small and cheap' one to be had for one guinea per hundred copies.[28] In 1777 Price published *Additional Observations on the Nature and Value of Civil Liberty and the War with America*, dedicated to the City of London who had awarded him its Freedom. The two were reissued in 1778 with additional material as *Two Tracts on Civil Liberty, the War with America and the Finances of the Kingdom*. Price's *Observations* stimulated many refutations and much polemical

---

[23] Jenny Uglow, *Nature's Engraver: A Life of Thomas Bewick* (London, 2006), p. 85.
[24] Colin Bonwick, *English Radicals and the American Revolution* (Chapel Hill, NC, 1977) is the standard treatment. His conclusion that British radicals in the 1770s and 1780s were not generally much engaged with American republicanism as a system of government (p. 259) is supported by the findings of this book. For a different view, see Arthur Sheps, 'The American Revolution and the Transformation of English Republicanism', *Historical Reflections/Réflexions historiques*, II (1975).
[25] *Thoughts on the Letter of Edmund Burke, Esq.; to the Sheriffs of Bristol on the Affairs of America* (Oxford, 1777), p. 41.
[26] To H. Laurens, 5 January 1783, Philip M. Hamer et al. (eds), *The Papers of Henry Laurens*, 16 vols. (Columbia, SC, 1968–2003), XVI, p. 121.
[27] To Lady Spencer, 26 May 1780, Garland Cannon (ed.), *The Letters of Sir William Jones*, 2 vols. (Oxford, 1980), I, p. 388.
[28] Advertisement in *General Evening Post*, 4–6 April 1776.

abuse was heaped on their author. In the fevered atmosphere of the early years of the American War he was frequently denounced as an 'incendiary' and a danger to public order. After the war, Price published his *Observations on the Importance of the American Revolution and the Means of Making it a Benefit to the World* (1784), probably the strongest endorsement of what the Americans had achieved to appear in Britain.

Price's 1776 tract tried to establish the principle that all men had the right to self-government, 'a right derived from the Author of Nature only'. Self-government required the 'fair and equal representation of all that are governed'.[29] A 'civil society or state' on the same principle had a right to govern itself 'by laws of its own making'. The American colonies were in his view separate civil societies (John Cartwright had already called all the British colonies in the Americas 'independent nations'),[30] and so any authority that the British Parliament attempted to exercise over them without their consent was illegitimate. Price hoped for the survival of the British empire, but its only basis could be as an alliance between equals, perhaps kept together by a common monarch and a Great Council.[31] The constitutions that were being put in place across the Atlantic seemed in the abstract to him to be much preferable to the institutions of Britain in their present corrupted state. He rejoiced in what appeared to be the establishment of complete freedom of worship, as did many other British Dissenters. Price had high hopes of the new America. He saw 'A new aera in future annals, and a new opening in human affairs beginning among the descendants of *Englishmen*, in a new world;—a rising empire, extended over an immense continent, without BISHOPS,—without NOBLES,—and without KINGS. *O the depth of the wisdom of God! How unsearchable are His judgements!*' In America 'every subject of human enquiry shall be open to free discussion, and the friends of liberty, in every quarter of the globe, find a safe retreat from civil and spiritual tyranny'.[32] An earlier anonymous pamphlet had struck something of the same almost millennial note of expectation about America. 'From this continent, doubtless in due time, civil and religious liberty, light and knowledge, will spread over all the nations of the world.'[33] In his 1784 *Observations* Price saw the Revolution as probably the most important event in world history since the coming of Christianity. America had 'forms of government more equitable and more liberal than any that the world has yet known'. Its influence must spread round the world, including to Britain.[34] By 1787 he saw 'a general fermentation', spreading from America through Europe. The 'minds of men are becoming more enlightened, and the silly despots of the world are likely to be forced to respect human rights', if they hoped to retain their power.[35]

---

[29] *Observations on Civil Liberty*, p. 39.
[30] *American Independence the Interest and Glory of Great Britain* (London, 1775), p. 21.
[31] *Observations on Civil Liberty*, p. 28.
[32] *Two Tracts*, pp. xv–xvi, p. 103.
[33] *The Case Stated, on Philosophical Ground, between Great Britain and her Colonies* (London, 1777), p. 103.
[34] *Observations on the Importance of the American Revolution*, p. 2.
[35] To Franklin, 26 September 1787, D. O. Thomas and W. Bernard Peach (eds), *The Correspondence of Richard Price*, 3 vols. (Cardiff and Durham, NC, 1983–94), III, p. 149.

Price, however, expressed some reservations, not always well received by his American friends, in his *Observations on the Importance of the American Revolution*. He was concerned about lack of unity, the possible growth of inequality and luxury through overseas trade and especially about the survival of slavery. The barrage of adverse comment about post-war America later evidently shook even him. He feared that he had been 'too hasty and sanguine' in what he had written about America.[36] At all times Price was careful not to appear to be an advocate of a British republic. He thought that the health of a republic depended on the virtue of a body of roughly equal citizens. This might be the case in the new American states, assumed to be largely populated by yeomen farmers, but there was too much social inequality in Britain, 'too much of the high and the low', for a republic to be practical there.[37] He was later to be more positive about 'our own constitution of government'. It was 'better adapted than any other to this country, and in theory excellent &c.'.[38] William Jones, often thought of as republican before he accepted a royal appointment in India, was also wary of the term. America for him was the *'land of virtue and liberty'*,[39] but he was 'no more a *republican* than a *Mahomedan* or *Gentoo* . . . I have ever formed my opinion from what appeared to me, on the calmest inquiry, the true spirit of our constitution.'[40] It was not until the 1790s, and then largely due to Thomas Paine's advocacy of America as an alternative model of a representative democracy to France in the second part of *Rights of Man*, that America was put 'firmly on the agenda for the radical cause' in Britain.[41]

Most parliamentary politicians who opposed the war seem to have deplored the constitutional experiments on which the Americans had embarked. Their future lay in a return to the fold of the British constitution and in British protection from the internal conflicts and the external threats that would inevitably arise from their weak federation, so contrary to contemporary British predilection for a strong unitary sovereignty. Lord Shelburne had tried to convince Henry Laurens of this. Edmund Burke had accepted in his great speech on Conciliation in 1775 that colonial governments had become 'popular in a high degree; some are merely popular', but he still believed that the colonies would maintain their 'interest in the British constitution' so long as 'you have the wisdom to keep the sovereign authority of this country as the sanctuary of liberty'.[42] When it became clear that Americans had embarked on making their own constitutions, he advised them against 'Untried forms of government'. 'That very liberty, which you so justly prize

[36] To J. Jay, 25 November 1786, ibid. III, p. 89.

[37] *Observations on the Importance of the American Revolution*, p. 72 fn.

[38] To W. Smith, 1 March 1790, Thomas and Peach (eds), *Price Correspondence*, III, p. 273.

[39] To B. Franklin, 5 August 1782, Leonard W. Labaree et al. (eds), *The Papers of Benjamin Franklin* (New Haven, CT, 1959–), XXXVII, p. 704.

[40] To L. Kenyon, 27 January 1783, Cannon (ed.), *Letters of Sir William Jones*, II, p. 601.

[41] Mark Philp, 'The Role of America in the "Debate on France" 1791–5: Thomas Paine's Insertion', *Utilitas*, V (1993), 230.

[42] Speech on Conciliation, 22 March 1775, Paul Langford (ed.), *The Writings and Speeches of Edmund Burke* (Oxford 1981–), III, ed. Warren M. Elofson and John A. Woods, *Party and Parliament and the American War 1774–1780*, pp. 121, 164.

above all things, originated here; and it may be very doubtful, whether without being constantly fed from the original fountain it can be at all perpetuated and preserved in its native purity and perfection . . . England has been great and happy under the present limited monarchy . . . None but England can communicate to you the benefits of such a constitution.'[43] After the war, Burke on at least one occasion surprised those with whom he was conversing by 'the disparaging, and even contemptuous terms' in which he spoke of Americans. He expressed his continuing anxieties about their future, fearing that the union would break up.[44] The drafting of the Constitution somewhat allayed his fears and in his 'Fourth Letter on a Regicide Peace' of 1795 he looked forward to an alliance 'upon the bottom of mutual interest and ancient affection'.[45] Briefly in office under the coalition with Lord North in 1783, Fox greatly disappointed Americans by his failure to give them the kind of commercial settlement that they had expected.[46] In London, John Adams found he had no rapport with the old Whig opponents of the war, such as Burke and Fox, who showed him 'nothing but ceremony'. He preferred the company of Lord Mansfield, whom Americans had regarded as one of their most inveterate enemies.[47] At the end of his embassy he was still complaining of 'dry decency and cold civility' of the opposition politicians.[48] He lamented that no MPs, either in government or in opposition, could be induced to talk about America. They had 'wholly forgotten that such a place as America ever existed'.[49]

The American War was a powerful stimulus to movements for reform throughout Britain and Ireland. Most of those who had led the opposition to the war were convinced that it was only the corruption of Britain's present constitutional practices that had prevented them from stopping it. They demanded reform of the public finances to end extravagance and political corruption, an end to abuses in the electoral system, and changes in the distribution of parliamentary seats. The programmes that the reformers propounded showed little if any regard to the new order that was evolving in America. It is possible to find some acknowledgements of the relevance of American examples in the debates in 1790 on the repeal of the Test and Corporation Acts that discriminated against Protestant Dissenters,[50] but it is very hard to find any such thing in those on the reform of Parliament. Virtually all plans of reform, such as the bills for a limited redistribution of seats introduced by William Pitt in the British House of Commons in 1782, 1783, and 1785, were

---

[43] 'Address to the Colonists', [January 1777], ibid. 283.

[44] Thomas Somerville, *My Own Life and Times 1741–1814* (Edinburgh, 1861), p. 222; F. P. Loch, *Edmund Burke*, 2 vols. (Oxford, 1998–2006), II, p. 55.

[45] Langford (ed.), *Burke Writings and Speeches*, IX, ed. R. B. McDowell, *The Revolutionary War and Ireland*, p. 80.

[46] See below, p. 110.

[47] Diary 15 November 1783, Butterfield (ed.), *Adams Diary*, III, p. 150; Letter to President of Congress, 14 December 1783, Robert J. Taylor et al. (eds), *The Papers of John Adams* (Cambridge MA., 1977–), XV, p. 423.

[48] To J. Jay, 14 February 1788, Adams (ed.), *Adams Works*, VIII, p. 475.

[49] A. Adams to I. Smith, 12 March 1787, L. H. Butterfield et al. (eds), *Adams Family Correspondence* (Cambridge, MA, 1963–), VIII, p. 9.

[50] See, for instance, Fox's comment that 'universal toleration' brought 'no disadvantage to the government of the states', 2 March 1790, *Parliamentary Register*, XXVII, pp. 146–7.

concerned with restoring an ancient constitution by purging it of recent abuses, not with adopting new models. In introducing his resolutions on 7 May 1783 Pitt warned against 'a spirit of speculation' or schemes 'founded on visionary and impractical ideas of reform'. Their task was not to 'innovate', but 'to renew and invigorate'.[51] Radical reformers also couched their programmes in terms of constitutional renewal. For John Cartwright annual parliaments and entitlement to vote according to personality rather than property, were not innovations; they were '*the ancient practice of the constitution*' going back to the Saxon past.[52] American republicans, particularly Jefferson, felt reverence for the Saxon past too.[53] They could not, however, accept as did the Society for Constitutional Information, which Cartwright actively promoted, that a 'hereditary sovereignty and nobility' were 'essential parts of the constitution'.[54]

Committees to urge reforms of abuses in the very narrow and oligarchic Scottish electoral system met from 1782 to 1785. In calling a General Convention the Scottish burghs were said to be following the example of the Americans.[55] The Lord Justice Clerk of Scotland was concerned that the principles underlying 'the revolt of the American colonies, and the late revolution in Ireland' were infecting the minds of 'inconsiderate men' in Scotland.[56] Petitions for reform of the parliamentary franchises, however, made no progress.[57]

Movements for parliamentary reform were much stronger in Ireland than in Scotland. William Drennan, the future United Irishman, found Scottish attempts to organize volunteer paramilitary corps, 'rude and imperfect sketches' of the Irish originals, for which he blamed 'the immeasurable distance that takes place between the gentry and the commonality' in Scotland by comparison presumably with the situation in Protestant Ireland.[58] For some of the Irish Volunteers, who had done much to force the British government to concede the legislative independence of the Irish parliament in 1782, and for militant groups in Belfast and Dublin, the independence of an unreformed Irish parliament meant no more than 'the transference of arbitrary power from despotism abroad to aristocracy at home'. A Grand National Convention and a Congress met between 1783 and 1785 to formulate demands, which in spite of the use of American concepts of popular organization, were mostly very moderate ones. They were rejected by parliament and the Irish

[51] Ibid. IX, pp. 690–1.

[52] *Take Your Choice!* (London, 1776), pp. xxiv, 15, 22.

[53] Colin Kidd, *British Identities before Nationalism: Ethnicity and Nationhood in the Atlantic World 1600–1800* (Cambridge, 1999), pp. 277–8.

[54] Second Address to the Public for the Society of Constitutional Information, C. Wyvill (ed.), *Political Papers*, 6 vols. (York, 1794–1804), II, pp. 500, 503.

[55] *Public Advertiser*, 18 February 1784.

[56] T. Miller to North 14 April 1783, TNA, WO 1/684, ff. 144–6; to Sydney 19 July 1784, TNA, HO 102/2, ff. 120–1.

[57] James Vance, 'Constitutional Radicalism in Scotland and Ireland in the Era of the American Revolution, c.1760–1784', University of Aberdeen PhD thesis, 1998; John Cannon, *Parliamentary Reform 1640–1832* (Cambridge, 1973), pp. 107–14.

[58] To S. McTier, [17] September 1782, Jean Agnew (ed.), *The Drennan-McTier Letters 1776–1793* (Dublin, 1998), p. 61.

government, although alarmed by popular disturbances that accompanied the petitioning, had little difficulty in containing the movement.[59]

IV

Although many British people had opposed the war, there was a great body of opinion that was outraged by the American revolt and believed that it must be suppressed. For such people the political doctrines that the Americans were espousing were pernicious. This had to be demonstrated in order to rally opposition in America and to refute those like Richard Price who were using them to subvert order at home. In Britain the American Revolution inspired far more affirmations of British constitutional arrangements than critiques of them.

Defences of the British empire and of the British constitution poured from the press in Britain in the early years of the war. They were written by American loyalist opponents of the Revolution and by a great variety of British people. They appeared in newspapers and pamphlets. Some publications were written with the encouragement of the government. Authors, it would seem, usually wrote in expectation of reward rather than for contracted payments. Pamphlets written on such terms included James Macpherson's *The Rights of Great Britain Asserted against the Claims of the American Colonies*, which Lord North thought 'the best defence of the American War',[60] and John Lind's *An Answer to the Declaration of the American Congress*, both published in 1776. Samuel Johnson's *Taxation No Tyranny* of 1775 was also a commissioned work, although Johnson said that he 'neither asked nor received from government any reward whatsoever'. John Vardill is a well-documented case of one who wrote enthusiastically against the Revolution and was rewarded for doing so. He had been Professor of Natural Law and Languages at King's College, New York. To one of his admirers he was 'the Pope, Milton, Adison and Swift of our continent'.[61] In 1772 he published a pamphlet against John Witherspoon. He came to Britain in 1775 for ordination into the Anglican church and remained there doing various 'secret services' for the government and publishing pamphlets and a numerous articles, above all in the *Morning Post*, throughout the war. His reward was to be given the appointment, which he could never take up, of Regius Professor of Divinity at King's College and to receive a payment of £500.[62]

If the North administration certainly tried to influence opinion, assertions by opponents of the war that most adverse comment on America came from what Burke called the 'vermin of court reporters' suborned by the government seem,

[59] See below, pp. 143–6.

[60] Note to George III, [26 March 1782], which sets out the rewards given to Macpherson, 'a very able and laborious writer in favour of government' (J. Fortescue (ed.), *The Correspondence of King George III, 1760–1783*, 6 vols. (London 1927–8), V, p. 414.

[61] J. Maunsell to J. Toler, 20 December 1783, TNA, A 13/105, f. 241.

[62] Vardill supported his claims for compensation as a loyalist with many testimonials and abundant specimens of his writing, see TNA, A 13/54, 13/67 and especially 13/105.

however, to have been well wide of the mark. Many men and some women wrote unprompted on their own initiative because they disliked what they understood to be happening in America and saw it as a threat to Britain. This seems to have been true of the well-known, such as John Wesley and Josiah Tucker, whose independence Burke unwisely impugned,[63] as well as a host of anonymous contributors. Thirty published replies have been found to Price's *Observations on Civil Liberty*. Only a few of them can have owed anything to government sponsorship.[64]

American patriots tended indiscriminately to call their enemies 'Tories'. Most American loyalist writers, the Anglican clergymen Myles Cooper and Jonathan Boucher being exceptions,[65] as well as the mass of British opponents of the Revolution, again with exceptions like Johnson and John Shebbeare, were probably not Tories in any meaningful sense of the term.[66] Charles Jenkinson, one of John Vardill's patrons, insisted that in defending 'the cause of this country' Vardill had deduced 'his chief arguments from the principles of the British constitution as settled at the Revolution'.[67] Josiah Tucker drew a distinction between 'those of republican principles', who 'dignify themselves by the name of WHIGS' and 'the genuine *constitutional Whigs* of this kingdom'.[68] Most who wrote against the Revolution would have called themselves 'genuine constitutional Whigs', albeit somewhat conservative ones. They accepted that government arose from the original consent of the people and that its aim was to maintain their liberty and their due rights. Liberty did not, however, depend on the exercise of unfettered popular choice in which the views of every individual were equal. That was the heresy being propagated both by Richard Price and in the Declaration of Independence, with which Lind specifically engaged. The doctrines of both were denounced as being 'subversive' of government.[69] 'Americus' was asked in a dialogue with 'Britannicus': 'Must every one do just what is right in their own eyes on pretence, that if he does not, self-government will be destroyed and slavery

---

[63] Speech on American Taxation, 19 April 1774, Langford (ed.), *Burke Speeches and Writings*, II, ed. Langford, *Party, Parliament, and the American Crisis, 1766–1774*, p. 446.

[64] D. O. Thomas, John Stephens and P. A. L. Jones, *A Bibliography of the Works of Richard Price* (Aldershot, 1993), pp. 56, 170–7.

[65] Cooper preached divine right. For Boucher's rejection of ideas of compact or government by consent, see Anne Y. Zimmer, *Jonathan Boucher: Loyalist in Exile* (Detroit, MI, 1978), pp. 280–1. J. C. D. Clark, however, includes him with other 'Anglican loyalists' in the category of defenders of 'the principles of 1688' (*The Language of Liberty 1660–1832: Political Discourse and Social Dynamics in the Anglo-American World* (Cambridge, 1994), pp. 8–9).

[66] For Whigs and Tories, see Margaret E. Avery, 'Toryism in the Age of the American Revolution: John Lind and John Shebbeare', *Historical Studies*, XVIII (1978), 24–36; Paul Langford, 'Old Whigs, Old Tories and the American Revolution', *Journal of Imperial and Commonwealth History*, VIII (1980), 106–30; James E. Bradley, 'The Anglican Pulpit, the Social Order and the Resurgence of Toryism during the American Revolution', *Albion*, XXI (1989), 361–86; Nigel Aston, 'Archbishop Markham and Political Preaching in Wartime England, 1776–1777' in Robert D. Cornwall and William Gibson (eds), *Religion, Politics and Dissent* (Farnham, 2010), pp. 185–217.

[67] To Loyalist Commissioners, 12 November 1784, TNA, AO 13/105, f. 318.

[68] *An Humble Address and Earnest Appeal*, 2nd edn (Gloucester, 1775), p. 17.

[69] [John Lind], *An Answer to the Declaration of the American Congress* (London, 1776), p. 120; John Shebbeare, *An Essay on the Origin, Progress and Establishment of National Society* (London, 1776), p. 91.

established?'[70] Such sentiments were the road to tyranny as factions and demago-
gues, claiming to speak in the name of the people, would impose their will on the
populace as a whole without any restraint. True liberty was preserved under
governments in which the mass voluntarily submitted themselves to the guidance
of the few who had the capacity to rule, in which the exercise of power was checked
by the separation between king, lords, and commons, and between legislature,
executive, and judiciary. Justice was not a matter of popular whim but was
administered according to established laws by an independent judiciary. A subject
was not entitled to take issue with the government whenever what he believed to be
his natural rights had been violated, but only when, while 'paying *due obedience* to
the established laws of his country, he is not protected in his established rights'.[71]
Liberty, according to the much admired Swiss commentator John Louis De Lolme,
consisted much less in actively participating in politics than in living in a country
where the laws were equal for all and justice was properly administered. British
liberty depended more on juries and a free press than on voting for Parliament.[72]
This is what the American patriots had rejected and what incendiaries like Price
were encouraging Britain to reject too. Americans, as Tucker put it, were subjecting
'every degree of magistracy and government to the perpetual controul and caprice
of the mob'.[73] Should 'the republican party now prevail' in Britain, there would be
'a general wreck of private property, and *crush* of subordination'.[74]

The republics that the Americans were setting up, for all their claims that checks
and balances were built into their new constitutions, would inevitably degenerate
into unrestrained popular democracy. Ancient and modern history equally showed
that this was so. De Lolme contrasted contemporary Britain with the Roman
Republic, much to the advantage of Britain. His strictures on ancient republics as
unstable and bound to end in anarchy or tyranny could easily be applied to
America. In the 1784 edition of a book first published in 1775 he noted that
'several articles of English liberty already appear impracticable to be preserved in the
new American Commonwealths'.[75]

Those who professed to speak for the American loyalists wanted none of this.[76]
As early as 1774 Boston loyalists had 'seen, with great grief and concern, the
distressing effect of a dissolution of all government, whereby our lives, liberties
and properties are rendered precarious, and no longer under the protection of the
law'.[77] Loyalists rejected American independence since they did not believe that

[70] John Martin, *Familiar Dialogues between Americus and Britannicus* (London, 1776), pp. 19–20.
[71] [Lind], *An Answer*, p. 128.
[72] David Lieberman, 'The Mixed Constitution and the Common Law' in Mark Goldie and Robert
Wockler (eds), *The Cambridge History of Eighteenth-Century Political Thought* (Cambridge, 2006),
pp. 330–1.
[73] *A Letter to Edmund Burke Esq . . .* , p. 14.
[74] *An Humble Address and Earnest Appeal*, p. 46.
[75] John Louis De Lolme, *The Constitution of England*, ed. David Lieberman (Indianapolis, IN,
2007), p. 16.
[76] For the initial loyalist critique of the Revolution, see Janice Potter, *The Liberty We Seek: Loyalist
Ideology in Colonial New York and Massachusetts* (Cambridge, MA, 1983).
[77] Carole Berkin, *Jonathan Sewall: The Odyssey of an American Loyalist* (New York, 1974), p. 107.

Americans were a separate people. The colonies were communities within the empire with rights and privileges of their own derived from the British constitution. Most loyalists accepted that the British Parliament, in taxing America, and in its punitive measures of 1774, had violated these rights and privileges, but that was no justification for armed resistance and for dismantling the security which only the empire could provide. For loyalists there had to be a supreme authority within the British empire, which could only be the British Parliament. Only within the empire could Americans be assured of the benefits of the British constitution. The alternative was the lawless anarchy which the Revolution was unleashing. 'We are attached to a monarchical form of government; . . . we are wedded to the British constitution; . . . we think the colonies can never be so happy or so free, as in a state of connection with Great Britain and Ireland, as part of the empire.'[78]

Abundant evidence of the abuses being committed as self-appointed committees and associations established their control over the new states in the name of the people was presented in the British press. Anglican clergy, among the first to seek exile in Britain, brought accounts of violence and brutality with which their churches were closed. To enforce non-importation agreements, members of the self-appointed patriot committees broke into houses and seized property indiscriminately. Oaths of loyalty to the new order were said to be enforced by cruel punishment of the refractory. Imprisonment, tarring and feathering, riding on a rail, even, according to Lind, 'googging', that is 'a way of tearing the eyes out of the sockets',[79] were all used. Samuel Seabury, a New York Anglican, denounced 'Anarchy and confusion, violence and oppression'. Americans were being made 'the most abject slaves . . . If I must be enslaved, let it be by a KING at least, not by a parcel of lawless upstart committee-men. If I must be devoured, let me be devoured by the jaws of a lion, and not gnawed to death by rats and vermin.'[80]

Provisions for religious freedom in state bills of rights were denounced as hypocritical.[81] The New England Congregationalists were alleged to be the driving force behind the Revolution as their ancestors had been of the Puritan Revolution in seventeenth-century England. Like them, they had seized power in order to demolish the Church of England, which is 'as much persecuted by American Republican fanatics at this time, as it was in the days of Oliver in Britain'.[82] For good measure they also resumed persecuting the Quakers, some of whom were said to have been hanged for refusing to use paper currency.[83] The Virginia Declaration proclaimed 'That the freedom of the press is one of the greatest bulwarks of liberty and can never be restrained but by despotic governments'. Criticism of the new

---

[78] Address of the Loyalists to the King, Parliament and People of Great Britain, n.d., TNA, CO 5/82, f. 236.

[79] *An Answer to the Declaration*, p. 100 fn.

[80] *Free Thoughts on the Proceedings of the Continental Congress* (Philadelphia, 1774), p. 36.

[81] *Hypocrisy Unmasked. Or a Short Account of the Religious Complaints of our American Colonists* (London, 1776).

[82] *Morning Chronicle*, 10 October 1776.

[83] *General Evening Post*, 9–12 November 1776.

order was, however, suppressed and those who published such material were forced to flee.[84]

V

Adverse verdicts on developments in America, established in the early years of the war, were to have a long life. They were to be reinforced by material published in Britain after the war which was almost unanimous in depicting economic and social disruption, popular discontent and failures of government at every level in the new America. There were numerous prophecies that the union would disintegrate into smaller groupings or that the individual states would break away. It was likely that Americans would seek reincorporation into the British empire as a solution to their problems. Conventional maxims that republics were by their nature unstable and required exceptional conditions to survive seemed to be abundantly vindicated. Americans might complain with some justice that their critics with their obsession with a strong central power were 'inconceivably ignorant of whatever relates to the practice of a free government',[85] but the Confederation seemed to be weak to the point of powerlessness, while the states were lapsing into popular democracies.

British understanding of conditions in postwar America were summed up by a letter in the *Morning Chronicle*: 'The United States are at present under the least controul of any civilized nation in the world.' Congress was powerless and not only the assemblies in the individual states 'but every town and district regard themselves as independent'.[86] The American example seemed clearly to reinforce conventional wisdom against republican government. In *An Essay on Republican Principles and on the Inconvenience of a Commonwealth in a Large Country and Nation*, John Andrews, a writer of tracts on history and politics, came to the conclusion that 'a great and opulent nation can never be well and peaceably governed under the form of a republic'. Britain alone had preserved 'the real and true original of substantial freedom', which was based on a combination of 'royalty and liberty'.[87] William Smith, the loyalist, recorded a conversation with the Secretary of State, Lord Sydney:

> We accorded perfectly in our ideas of the impossibility of being happy under a republic. He said it was the ruin of Rome and other great states, and therefore excessively absurd for large countries to set out with that form of government. He mentioned Holland as no bigger than a hat and going to ruin, and spoke of Americans as looking down upon all Europe as a trifle for extent, and yet about to repeat the folly.[88]

[84] 'The Case of Mr James Rivington', *Public Advertiser*, 12 November 1776.

[85] See William Short to James Madison, 24 October, 21 December 1787, William T. Hutchinson et al. (eds), *The Papers of James Madison* (Chicago and Charlottesville, VA, 1962-), X, pp. 221, 343.

[86] *Public Advertiser*, 7 August 1783.

[87] (London, 1783), pp. 81, 84.

[88] Diary, 23 October 1784, L. F. S. Upton (ed.), *The Diary and Selected Papers of Chief Justice William Smith 1784–1793*, 2 vols. (Toronto, 1963–5), I, p. 153.

Comparisons between Britain and the Netherlands, almost invariably to the latter's disadvantage, were very characteristic of eighteenth-century Britain. 'The gentlemen who are so particularly attached to the *republican* form of government' were urged to 'turn their attention to the present situation in Holland'. 'Holland is little more than a great trading company, having much industry, craft, cunning, an impoverished revenue, little strength and less spirit.'[89] The predicament of the Netherlands in 1787—when factional rivalry enabled France on the one side and Prussia and Britain on the other to intervene in her domestic affairs—seemed to be an object lesson of the perils of weak republics. The monarchical republic of Poland was another, as Americans anxious about the designs upon them of rival European powers, were well aware.[90]

Recent developments in Britain seemed to offer an unequivocal vindication of the balance of powers on which the British mixed monarchy and therefore British liberty were thought to rest. The threat to balanced government in America was perceived to come from popular democracy. In Britain and Ireland in the prolonged political crisis at the end of the American War the balance now seemed to be threatened by an ambitious aristocracy who dominated unreformed parliaments. They were imposing their choice of ministers on the king and thus bringing the executive under the control of the legislature.

By the late eighteenth century the balance of powers in the British constitution had in reality become largely a myth, albeit a still potent one. It was the king's prerogative to choose ministers, but it was a well-established convention that he should appoint ministers who were able to command a majority in the House of Commons and so the executive was in reality passing under the control of the legislature. For the leaders of parties in the House openly to dictate who should be minister to the king could, however, be represented as an unconstitutional usurpation of his right of choice. In March 1782 the king was compelled to appoint Rockingham. In July 1782 Fox and his colleagues tried to choose Rockingham's successor, thus, according to the erudite Lord Shelburne, bringing down George III to the level of 'the King of the Mahrattas who had nothing of sovereignty but the name'.[91] When Shelburne was defeated in February 1783 the king had, much against his will, to accept a coalition government formed by what to many seemed to be the unprincipled alliance of men who had opposed and sustained the American War, that is of Fox and Lord North. The Coalition's India Bill was seen as the final outrage. The administration of the British dominions in India was to be taken from the East India Company, on the grounds that they had proved themselves to be incapable of ruling India justly, and was to be assumed by nominees of the House of Commons. 'Vesting the influence of that great commercial company in a few aristocratical persons', Christopher Wyvill of the Yorkshire

---

[89] *Morning Herald*, 4 January 1783.
[90] B. Harrison to Washington, 8 January 1784, W. W. Abbot et al. (ed), *The Papers of George Washington: Confederation Series*, 6 vols. (Charlottesville, VA, 1992–7), I, pp. 22–3.
[91] Cited in Richard Pares, *King George III and the Politicians* (Oxford, 1953), p 122. For the classic account of these controversies, see pp. 120–36.

Association of reformers thought, would mean that 'a new power would have been created unknown to the constitution and utterly subversive of it; an aristocracy would have been formed, which, aided by the treasury of Bengal, would have been willing to degrade the crown to the ground, and trample also the rights and privileges of the people under their feet'.[92] The king struck back, dismissing the Coalition in December 1783 for a government formed by Pitt, which was able to win a majority at the ensuing general election in the following year. This dubious manoeuvre was widely acclaimed as proof that liberty was safe under Britain's balanced constitution; the monarchy could frustrate aristocratic ambition and thus protect the people's rights. The Merchants and Traders of the City of London assured the king that they would support 'such legal exercises' of his prerogative 'as may be necessary to secure stability to your government and security to your people'.[93] In February 1784 Pitt was given the Freedom of the City of London for his support of 'the legal prerogatives of the crown *and* the constitutional rights of the people'. A large concourse demonstrated their loyalty to the Crown. Among the toasts drunk, was 'May this free constitution continue unimpaired to the end of time.'[94] Far from shaking confidence in the verities of the British constitution, the American challenge had reinforced it.

VI

In October 1786 British ministers were advised by their consul at New York that 'Mobs, tumults and bodies of men in arms are on tip toe in various parts of the country.' Not only was the authority of Congress nullified but that of the states was held in 'contempt and disregard'. He concluded that 'general confusion will take place before any permanent government can be established in this unhappy country'.[95] William Grenville told the House of Commons in March 1787 that 'at present it was so difficult to decide whether the United States of America were under one government, whether they consisted of many discordant governments, or whether they were under no government at all'.[96] By then, however, news of a Convention assembled in Philadelphia to propose reforms of the union was reaching Britain. Sending ministers a copy of the draft Constitution, Phineas Bond, the consul at Philadelphia, commented that it seemed that 'the sober and discreet part of the community approve the plan in its present form'. He thought that 'when due consideration is paid to the democratic temper of the times it is perhaps in the best shape in which it could be handed forth to the people'.[97] Between 30 October and

[92] Yorkshire Meeting, 10 February 1785, Wyvill (ed.), *Political Papers*, IV. 368.
[93] *Public Advertiser*, 30 January and 14 February 1784.
[94] Ibid. 1 March 1784; Linda Colley, 'The Apotheosis of George III: Loyalty, Royalty and the British Nation 1760–1820', *Past and Present*, CII (1984), 104.
[95] J. Temple to Carmarthen, 4 October 1786, TNA, FO 4/4, f. 325.
[96] 14 March 1787, *Parliamentary Register*, XXI, p. 428.
[97] To Carmarthen, 20 September 1787, TNA, FO 4/5, f. 257; copy of Constitution, ibid. ff. 259–61.

2 November 1787 the draft Constitution appeared in at least six British news-papers.[98] Radical friends of America actively disseminated it.[99] Printers brought out separate editions of it and, such was the demand, found them profitable.[100]

Bond's guardedly favourable verdict on the proposed Constitution was to be echoed by British ministers. John Adams correctly surmised that by now the British government no longer believed that American divisions were to its advantage. It wanted to negotiate with an effective federal administration, above all on commercial matters.[101] This would be greatly preferable to trying to deal with individual states that pursued their own tariff policies and claimed the right to fix their own terms on which British debts might or might not be settled. The Committee of the Privy Council for trade welcomed the powers to be given to Congress, who would, they were sure, act in commercial matters 'upon a large scale in support of a more extensive and general interest', than had the states, which were dominated by the concerns of particular groups.[102] The Foreign Secretary, Lord Carmarthen, told Adams that he had read the Constitution with pleasure. 'It is very well drawn up.'[103] Pitt was more guarded. 'The American Constitution resembled ours neither in church nor state; he most sincerely wished it had, in affording equal security for liberty and happiness in the subject.'[104]

Both press coverage and accounts of British opinion relayed to America were generally favourable. A young American, Thomas Lee Shippen, who was studying law in London, wrote that 'The people here extol [it] as the master piece of policy and the Convention as a Roman Senate—We stand six inches higher at least than we did.' The British lawyers whom he met seemed to believe that America had 'from having as they conceived no government at all adopted the best that human [infirmities] allowed to exist upon earth'.[105] 'Florus', writing in the *Public Adver-tiser* was effusive in his praise and went so far as to see it as 'an improvement on the great model of government in England'.[106] That Washington, who had been a cult figure in Britain since the war,[107] was to be the first president under the Constitution was widely applauded. Praise was, however, usually heaped on the Constitution in Britain because Americans were assumed at last to have seen the light: 'After trying every utopian scheme suggested by ancient or modern

---

[98] Kaminski and Saladino (eds), *Commentaries on the Constitution: Public and Private*, II, p. 460.

[99] T. B. Hollis to J. Willard, 30 January 1788, 'Joseph Willard Letters', *Proceedings of the Massachusetts Historical Society*, LXIII (1909–10), 628.

[100] *Maryland Journal*, 16 May 1788, Kaminski and Saladino (eds), *Commentaries on the Constitution*, VI, p. 22.

[101] To J. Jay, 14 February 1788, Adams (ed.), *Adams Works*, VIII, p. 476.

[102] Report of 28 January 1791, TNA, FO 4/9, f. 121.

[103] Adams to J. Jay, 14 February 1788, Adams (ed.), *Adams Works*, VIII, p. 475.

[104] 2 March 1790, *Parliamentary Register*, XXVII, pp. 162–3. See also his speech on the Canada Bill, 8 April 1791, ibid. XXIX, p. 76.

[105] To W. Shippen, 6 November 1787, Kaminski and Saladino (eds), *Commentaries on the Constitution*, II, pp. 462–3.

[106] 'On the new American Constitution', *Public Advertiser*, 6 November 1787.

[107] Troy Bickham, *Making Headlines: The American Revolution as Seen through the British Press* (DeKalb, IL, 2009), ch. 7.

republicans . . . , the most enlightened of their people have adopted for their general superintending government, a system, which in many of its striking features, bears a strong resemblance and affinity to that of their parent country.'[108] The rising Federalist Fisher Ames was reported to have said that the Convention had 'copied greatly' from British models wherever possible. He added for good measure: 'It is glorious for Great Britain that all the polished nations of the world are endeavouring to introduce her form of government in some form or other.'[109] A correspondent in Paris told James Madison that the British there 'exult much' at seeing that Americans 'begin to consider themselves under the necessity of approximating toward the *British Constitution*'.[110]

Those British people who identified most closely with the cause of America were reported to be divided about the Constitution. Washington was told that 'all the friends of liberty in Great Britain highly approve the constitution and ardently wish its adoption'.[111] Richard Price, who had been pressing for some time for a stronger federal authority, rejoiced at its ratification.[112] There were, however, doubters who shared the misgivings of the Constitution's American opponents. Indeed it was said that 'the greater part of the true Whigs, the liberty men of England, are opposed to the form of government that has been proposed'. A specific example was George Staunton, who had already served throughout the empire with his patron Lord Macartney and was to go with him to China. He had been seeking out Americans, going to their coffee houses and reading American newspapers.[113] In his opinion the Americans were throwing away 'the gift of heaven' in abandoning the system of government under the Confederation.[114]

In the long run British opinion seems to have accepted that the Constitution had given the United States a viable and stable system of government. A republic might be a far less desirable arrangement than a mixed monarchy, but the Americans had shown that it was a form of government that could be adapted to large territories as well as to small states and that republics would not inevitably lapse into anarchy or tyranny. In defending Thomas Paine in December 1793, Thomas Erskine, an advanced Whig, commended the 'sacred regard to property' and to 'all the rights of the individual' observed in America. There is 'less to deplore and more to admire in the institutions of America, than that in any other country under heaven'.[115] In 1799 Pitt hoped that the French republic might evolve towards 'the mixed or

---

[108] *Public Advertiser*, 21 May 1789.
[109] Conversation with G. Beckwith in Dorchester to W. Grenville, 25 September 1790, *Report on Canadian Archives for 1890* (Ottawa, 1891), p. 151.
[110] W. Short to J. Madison, 21 December 1787, Hutchinson et al. (eds), *Madison Papers*, X, p. 343.
[111] Letter of H. Knox, 25 May 1788, Abbot et al. (eds), *Washington Papers: Confederation Series*, VI, p. 291.
[112] To B. Franklin, [5–10 January 1789], Thomas and Peach (eds), *Price Correspondence*, III, p. 194.
[113] A. Adams to I. Smith, 16 July 1787, Butterfield et al. (eds), *Adams Family Correspondence*, VIII, p. 86.
[114] T. L. Shippen to W. Shippen, 20 November 1787, Kaminski and Saladino (eds), *Commentaries on the Constitution*, II, p. 468.
[115] Philp, 'The Role of America', *Utilitas*, V, p. 231.

moderate plan of government on the model of the American'.[116] The manner in which the Americans conducted their politics and the quality of their leadership, especially after the decline of the Federalists, was, on the other hand, for long to be regarded as deplorable in British political circles; a British minister dismissed the Jefferson administration of 1801as a '*mob government*'.[117] Nevertheless, the survival of the union was now at least taken for granted by all shades of opinion.

---

[116] Jennifer Mori, *William Pitt and French Revolution 1785–1795* (New York, 1997), p. 282.

[117] W. Grenville cited in Bradford Perkins, *The First Rapprochement: England and the United States 1795–1805* (Philadelphia, 1955), p. 19.

4

The Challenge of Great Britain

I

The previous chapter tried to show how the main stream of British opinion saw the American republic with its apparently unstable politics and disunited states as a model to be avoided rather than to be emulated. For American patriots the incompetence and brutality with which Britain had waged war on them showed how far she had fallen from her previous greatness. She had become a model of what those who were creating a new republic must avoid. The corruption that had brought Britain low could prove contagious and to curb its insidious threat strict republicans urged America to insulate itself as far as possible from British influences.

While it may have been relatively easy for most British people to ignore or to dismiss the new America, for even the most committed republicans in the United States wholly to repudiate Britain and to cut themselves off from her influence was virtually impossible. It would require a renunciation of the past that would be very difficult indeed for any American over a certain age. For the generation that had grown up in war, knowing Britain only as an enemy, it was still likely to remain a potent presence in their lives. Within a very few years from the ending of the war, no one could doubt that Britain remained a formidable world power with a dynamic economy. Although many Americans still saw Britain as hostile and a potential danger to them, as the second half of this book will try to show, British influences remained very strong in the years immediately after independence. Americans continued to buy British goods, read British books, emulate British politeness, and seek British recognition for their artistic and scientific achievements. The range of possible attitudes to Britain can be exemplified in two hugely documented cases. Alexander Hamilton has been described as an Anglophile, who believed that America had much to learn from Britain. Thomas Jefferson was a self-confessed Anglophobe, who saw British influence as a dire threat to the republic.

For most Americans, the experience of war is likely to have been crucial in shaping how they saw Britain. It was never the official doctrine of the British army that the people of the thirteen colonies were to be treated indiscriminately as rebels on whom unrestrained warfare could be waged. In as far as military imperatives allowed, civilians were to be spared the full rigour of war and encouraged to come back into allegiance to the Crown. By the standard of continental European wars the damage done by the British army to the civilian population may have been limited. In retrospect an officer believed that had British commanders used 'the mildest methods of European warfare, which every military author directs and every general practises', such as burning hostile villages and living off the country, the outcome of the war would have been very different.[1] Even so, for many Americans the war was still a searing experience whose legacy was a bitter hatred for Britain. A number of towns were burnt as acts of policy; buildings, livestock, and supplies were often requisitioned; and prisoners were treated atrociously. Whatever senior British officers might intend, they could not stop their own men from plundering on a massive scale.[2] Nor apparently could the British control their allies: the Hessians were regarded as even worse plunderers than the British; loyalist regiments and militia could exact severe retribution on their patriot enemies; and many lurid accounts were given of the ways in which Native peoples treated those who fell into their hands.

The legacy of hatred for Britain left by the war seems to have varied in different parts of the continent, no doubt in the main due to the intensity with which the war had been waged there. It was very strong in the south. In South Carolina the British invasion of 1780 set off what amounted to a civil war and resentment was deep and lasting. The British were said to have behaved there in 'a more brutal and more *ungentlemanly* fashion' than 'even the Prussians did in Saxony'.[3] David Ramsay was determined to establish the record for posterity in his *The History of the Revolution of South-Carolina from a British Province to an Independent State* published in 1785. The progress of the British troops was 'marked with blood, and with deeds so atrocious as reflected disgrace on their arms'. Ramsay wrote of officially sanctioned plundering to make a joint stock for the profit of officers.[4] One documented episode in this plundering was the seizure and shipping off of the bells of St Michael's Anglican Church in Charleston as the booty of the Royal Artillery.[5] A member of Congress who had served as a surgeon recalled seeing 'the enemy hang up our people in dozens' and 'destroy with the bayonet multitudes of crippled men and men who had surrendered'.[6] Henry Laurens had his plantation

---

[1] [J. G. Simcoe], *Remarks on the Travels of the Marquis de Chastellux in North America* (London, 1787), p. 64.

[2] Stephen Conway, '"The Great Mischief Complain'd of": Reflections on the Misconduct of British Soldiers in the Revolutionary War', *William and Mary Quarterly*, 3rd ser., XLVII (1990), 370–90.

[3] B. Vaughan to Shelburne, 15 November 1782, BL, Add MS 88906/1/19, f. 102.

[4] *The History of the Revolution of South-Carolina from a British Province to an Independent State*, 2 vols. (Trenton, NJ, 1785), II, pp. 66, 156.

[5] When citizens of Charleston failed to raise the required ransom, the bells were shipped off to London against the explicit orders of the commander-in-chief, Guy Carleton (P. Traille to Brig. Martin, 29 January 1783, TNA, CO 5/108, ff. 176–7). For the way in which the bells eventually found their way back to Charleston, see H. Laurens to Chapman and Mears, 16 July 1783, Philip M. Hamer et al. (eds), *The Papers of Henry Laurens*, 16 vols. (Columbia, SC, 1968–2003), XVI, p. 238 and fn.

[6] H. Williamson to T. Rushton, 21 June 1783, Paul H. Smith (ed.), *Letters of Delegates to Congress, 1774–1789*, 26 vols. (Washington, DC, 1976–98), XX, p. 353.

ravaged, even including the burning of his books, by 'those savages called British officers and soldiers'.[7]

Post-war Virginia also harboured a strong sense of grievance against Britain. Virginia whites had been outraged by the willingness of their last royal governor, Lord Dunmore, to arm slaves. Norfolk was attacked in 1776 and burnt in 1779. In 1781 Cornwallis's army invaded Virginia from the south. Maryland was largely spared, but New Jersey was badly damaged. The state was thought to have 'suffered extremely by the war, much more in proportion than any other'.[8] There was much plundering by the British army as it swept through New Jersey in 1776. After the army withdrew, loyalists and patriots fought a series of local civil wars and loyalist raids from areas under British control terrorized the eastern counties of the state.[9] The New York and Pennsylvania frontiers were another scene of bloody fighting which moved the 'American Farmer', Hector St John Crèvecoeur, to ask why must this 'great nation . . . , which looks towards the universal monarchy of trade, of industry, of riches, of power, . . . strew our poor frontiers with the carcasses of her friends, with the wrecks of our insignificant villages'.[10]

To British opinion, New England seemed to have been the seed-bed of the Revolution. But by 1790 a British emissary was told that the northern states were showing 'a degree of moderation and good sense' towards Britain by comparison with the south.[11] The war had started in New England but, once Burgoyne's invasion had failed, there had not been much fighting there since 1776, apart from the battles for control of Rhode Island or the devastating raids which the British launched against coastal towns in Connecticut. The disruption of seaborne trade had hit the merchants of New England badly, but by the end of the war 'The people of New England' were said to be 'as much at ease as tho' the millennium was come . . . They are building houses and barns, liveing in ease and plenty. They are even luxurious.'[12] Their commercial interests pulled the New England ports back into the British orbit after 1783 and kept them there up to the War of 1812. The town of New York, where the British had been in occupation from 1776 to 1783, seemed to strict republicans quickly to have become a bridgehead for reviving British influence. New York was 'steeped in Anglicism', James Madison wrote in

---

[7] To E. Bridgen, 29 August 1782 and to J. Delagaye, 6 June 1783, Hamer et al. (eds), *Laurens Papers*, XV, p. 601, XVI, pp. 208–9.

[8] J. F. D. Smythe, *A Tour through the United States of America*, 2 vols. (London, 1784), II, p. 401.

[9] David J. Fowler, '"Loyalty is now Bleeding in New Jersey": Motivations and Mentalities of the Disaffected' in Joseph S. Tiedemann et al. (eds), *The Other Loyalists: Ordinary People, Royalists and the Revolution in the Middle Colonies* (Albany, NY, 2009), pp. 45–77.

[10] *Letters from an American Farmer* (Oxford, 1997), p. 197.

[11] Conversation between George Beckwith and William Samuel Johnson in Dorchester to W. Grenville, 27 May 1790, *Report on Canadian Archives for 1890* (Ottawa, 1891), p. 136.

[12] J. Wadsworth to N. Greene, 10 July 1782, Richard K Showman et al. (eds) *The Papers of General Nathanael Greene*, 13 vols. (Chapel Hill, NC, 1976–2003), XI, p. 429. For a much less optimistic assessment of the effect of the war on Connecticut, see Richard Buel, *Dear Liberty: Connecticut's Mobilization for the Revolutionary War* (Middleton, CT, 1980).

1789.[13] The British consul there annually celebrated the king's birthday with an assemblage of Anglo-American notables.[14]

The attitude towards Britain of individual members of America's political leadership is likely to have been shaped by their experiences of the war and by the concerns of their state. The extent to which they remained committed to America's French alliance or sought a British counterpoise to French influence could be an important consideration. Age and experience were also thought to be significant. There were hopes in Britain for a speedy reconciliation through the good offices of those Americans who had spent time in the mother country before the war or who had been closely involved with the business of empire. Shelburne's appointment as peace negotiator of Richard Oswald, a man with many close contacts in the pre-war Anglo-American world, is a clear sign of such hopes. They were, however, usually to be disappointed. There certainly had been many Americans who had cared for Britain and for the British empire as they wished it to be. For most of those once they became patriots that lay in the past. Benjamin Franklin for a considerable period of his life had been deeply committed to the British empire and had high ideals for it, but in the last years before the war, 'his emotional separation from England was final and complete'.[15] After the war he was reported still to be 'censuring the warlike turn of England, and the disposition of its people to look down upon other nations' as well as dilating on 'the cruelties of our people in America'.[16] He thanked God that 'we now have less connection with the affairs of these people'.[17] Henry Laurens had spent much time in Britain and, according to Edmund Burke he 'carried his love to this country even to doting; for he had sent his children to receive their education in it, and to learn to love this country'.[18] He suffered much in the war. He himself was captured at sea and confined in the Tower of London, his eldest son was killed in action and his property in South Carolina was laid waste. Washington had never crossed the Atlantic, but he had served with distinction in the Seven Years War. His military experience with the British seems, however, to have been less happy than his later warm comradeship with French officers like Lafayette or Rochambeau. After the war he was reputed to be always suspicious of British intentions. It was thought that he 'in his heart leans to France, his obligation to that court he can never forget'.[19]

After 1783, the shaping of American policy towards the outside world was increasingly passing to a younger generation who had not previously crossed the

---

[13] To T. Jefferson, 9 May 1789, William T. Hutchinson et al. (eds), *The Papers of James Madison* (Chicago and Charlottesville, VA, 1962-), XII, p. 143.

[14] J. Temple to Carmarthen, 4 June 1788, TNA, FO 4/6, f. 152.

[15] Gordon S. Wood, *The Americanization of Benjamin Franklin* (New York, 2004), p. 151.

[16] B. Vaughan to Shelburne, 16 February 1783, BL, Add MS 88906/1/19, f. 169.

[17] To H. Laurens, 12 February 1784, J. Bigelow (ed.), *The Complete Works of Benjamin Franklin*, 10 vols. (New York, 1887–8), VIII, p. 449.

[18] 17 December 1781, *Parliamentary Register*, V, p. 186. For the Laurens family in England, see Julie Flavell, *When London was Capital of America* (New Haven, CT, 2010).

[19] W. S. Johnson's conversation with G. Beckwith in Dorchester to W. Grenville, 27 May 1790, *Canadian Archives Report for 1890*, p. 139.

Atlantic and for whom the emotional pull of Britain was likely to be weak. In the case of John Jay, Richard Oswald concluded that it was non-existent when he met him at the peace negotiations. Jay told him that people 'all over that continent were totally alienated from G[reat] B[ritain], so that they detested the very name of an Englishman'. Oswald reflected that although he had never been to Britain, Jay had 'lived till now as an English subject'; yet he is 'as much alienated from any particular regard for England, as if he had never heard of it in his life'.[20] In fact, Jay, who had become deeply suspicious of the French, was to prove a person with whom the British would have little difficulty in doing business both at the peace settlement and in negotiating the treaty of 1794 that bears his name.

Much to his vexation, British ministers showed little interest in doing business with John Adams when he was ambassador to Britain from 1785 to 1788. This seems to have been an unhappy period in his life. Although he had a high reverence for the British constitution, he was repelled by British political culture and could make no effective contacts with those who participated in it. Britain's 'royal family,' he fulminated, 'its administration and its opposition are all such as will never seduce an American mind from his duty. He will only be shocked at the sight, and confirmed in his natural principles and native feelings.'[21] Nevertheless, Adams still had a strong sense of America as English. 'The Americans are indeed Englishmen and will continue such in language and sentiments and manners, whether they are allowed to be friends or compelled to be enemies of those other Englishmen who inhabit those islands Great Britain and Ireland.'[22] His aversion to France was even stronger than Jay's and he had a hard-headed sense of Britain's place in America's interests.[23] American independence might 'depress England too much and elevate the House of Bourbon too high'. In which case Britain and America might have to combine to curb 'such absolute monarchies and ambitious nations'.[24]

Alexander Hamilton had settled in New York from a childhood in the West Indies and had fought in the Continental Army. Unlike many other Americans, he did not see contemporary Britain as a corrupted society fallen from greatness. As the 'leading maritime and industrial nation of the world', he thought that Britain was the model of what America must strive to become.[25] He admired not just the idealized British constitution of balanced powers but the way in which it worked in contemporary practice. Like Hume, whose work much interested him, he accepted the need for practices that most of his contemporaries denounced as corrupt. It was

---

[20] Minutes of Conversation 7 August 1782 in Oswald to T. Townshend, 17 August 1782, TNA, FO 97/157, ff. 59, 66.

[21] To J. Jay, 8 May 1787, Giunta (ed.), *Emerging Nation*, III, p. 495.

[22] To M. R. Morris, 2 March 1786, ibid. III, p. 112.

[23] James H. Hutson, *John Adams and the Diplomacy of the American Revolution* (Lexington, KT, 1980).

[24] Diary, 20 May 1783, L. H. Butterfield et al. (eds), *Diary and Autobiography of John Adams*, 4 vols. (Cambridge, MA), III, p. 122.

[25] Gerald Stourzh, *Alexander Hamilton and the Idea of Republican Government* (Stanford, CA, 1970), p. 7.

necessary that the king should have the means to win support for his administration in the House of Commons. Monarchy on the British pattern provided a strong executive in a way that 'republican principles' could not do. He strongly endorsed the verdict of Jacques Necker, the French financier, that Britain had 'the only government in the world "which unites public strength with individual security"'.[26] In his view, America should try to emulate Britain's system of public debt, its powerful professionalized armed forces and its manufacturing industry, which were all anathema to strict republicans. Hamilton's aim was for America to evolve into a great power that would be master of its own destiny, but for the immediate future he considered that the United States had no alternative but to cooperate closely with Britain.

Thomas Jefferson and James Madison were not well disposed towards Britain, in part at least for reasons that were characteristic of Virginians. They regarded the pre-war relationship between the usually Scottish merchants and Virginia planters as an exploitative one and were determined that Britain's grip on Virginia's economy should not be re-established. They were also outraged at the behaviour of the British army in Virginia in the closing stages of the war. The way that Britain had fought the war proved for Jefferson that 'The sun of her glory is fast descending to the horizon. Her philosophy has crossed the channel, her freedom the Atlantic, and herself seems passing to that awful dissolution, whose issue is not given human foresight to scan.'[27] Britain came to embody for both Jefferson and Madison a most dangerous threat to the republican future of the whole United States. They and those who thought like them waged an ideological war against British principles which was the counterpart of the ideological war being waged in Britain against republican principles. Americans must break away from the cultural 'vassalage', as Jefferson called it, of Britain and British influences must be kept at arm's length.[28] British sympathizers would form a fifth column trying to undermine the republic, as would British goods and British money. Jefferson came to dislike the British collectively. He believed that they were 'the only nation on earth who wished us ill from the bottom of their souls';[29] he reciprocated what he supposed to be their aversion. He drew a contrast for Abigail Adams between 'the polite, self-denying, feeling, hospitable, goodhumoured' French and the 'rich, proud, hectoring, swearing, squibbing, carnivorous animals' that she lived among in Britain.[30] 'Of all the nations on earth they require to be treated with the most hauteur. They require to be kicked into common good manners.'[31]

[26] Speech of 18 June 1787 reported by Madison, Harold C. Syrett et al. (eds), *The Papers of Alexander Hamilton*, 27 vols. (New York, 1962–87), IV, pp. 192–3.
[27] *Notes on the State of Virginia*, ed. William Peden (Chapel Hill, NC, 1955), p. 65.
[28] To T. Pleasants, 8 May 1786, Boyd et al. (eds), *Jefferson Papers*, IX, p. 472.
[29] To W. Carmichael, 15 December 1787, ibid. XII, p. 424.
[30] Letter of 21 June 1785, ibid. VIII, p. 239.
[31] To W. Smith, 28 September 1787, ibid. XII, p. 193.

II

Whatever their personal feelings about Britain might be, there was general agreement among American political opinion about the kind of relationship with Britain that should emerge after the war. America was now free to trade wherever she wished, but Britain would inevitably be a major trading partner, even if she no longer had the privileges that she had enjoyed as ruler of the empire, and her colonies, especially the West Indies, were a vital outlet for American exports. In return for giving Britain free access to American markets, Americans expected to be readmitted to their old position within the British system with full access to Britain and her colonies and free participation in the carrying trade of the empire.[32] It was confidently anticipated that a commercial treaty which had been shelved during the negotiations for the main treaty would shortly be signed.

An independent America would be a full member of the international state system, receiving and sending ambassadors and negotiating treaties. Americans aimed to be 'respectable in the world', a much-used phrase. Washington was concerned that America establish 'a national character' and that it 'be considered on a respectable footing by the powers of Europe'.[33] Americans especially wished to be respected by Britain and hoped to establish satisfactory working relations with her. Adams hoped that America would 'live in friendship with this country and have no other contention but in reciprocal good offices'.[34]

Within a very short time from the signing of the peace Britain seemed to be acting in a way that indicated that Americans' desire for normal relations was not being reciprocated. Negotiations for a commercial treaty foundered and attempts by the Americans to revive them got nowhere. Instead, Britain unilaterally imposed its own version of commercial relations with the United States by an Order in Council of 2 July 1783 by which American participation in the trade of the empire was considerably restricted. Britain received John Adams as American minister in 1785, but no British minister was sent to the United States until 1791. Britain delayed withdrawing from posts along the Canadian frontier with the United States, which she was bound to do by the peace treaty.

Americans sought explanations for this, to them, irrational hostility. Some of their explanations had a degree of plausibility, but most were highly implausible. The king was almost invariably given most blame. Jefferson considered that since George III's accession in 1760 British policy had been uniformly hostile to America except for the brief interlude in which Shelburne had made peace.[35] Adams, who sometimes saw signs of liberal views towards America in Pitt, believed that they were checked by the king, by hard-line ministers, many of whom had supported the

---

[32] See below, pp. 98–101.
[33] To J. McHenry, 22 August 1787, W. W. Abbot et al. (eds), *The Papers of George Washington: Confederation Series*, 6 vols. (Charlottesville, VA, 1992–7), III p. 197.
[34] To M. R. Morris, 2 March 1786, Giunta (ed.), *Emerging Nation*, III, p. 113.
[35] To J. Jay, 23 April 1786, Boyd et al. (eds), *Jefferson Papers*, IX, p. 402.

American War, and by the influence of the loyalists mediated through them.[36] Loyalist plots featured very prominently in most attempted explanations of British policies.

Emphasis on the king was misconceived. While George III was not likely to be well disposed to his former subjects, he did his best to be gracious when he encountered Adams and there is no evidence at all to suggest that he in any way tried to direct policy against the United States. Nor does there seem to be any foundation for theories about loyalist plots. The commercial restrictions were indeed the work of men ill disposed towards America,[37] but most British politicians probably did not feel any marked hostility to the republic, although they had little interest in it and felt no incentive to go out of their way to cultivate good relations with it. Once trade had recovered without a treaty, no vital British interest was involved. America could be safely ignored. Such lack of interest was an affront to American sensibilities. As one astute interpretation puts it, the British were, 'at the very center of our universe' and yet 'they did not really care about us, not half enough!...How could any American imagine that his country, friendly or unfriendly, could be of such small consequence, could occupy the British mind so little?'[38]

What Americans interpreted as official hostility towards the United States seemed to them to reflect that of a wider British public. Americans travelling in Britain soon began to report that British opinion was not sympathetically disposed towards the new America. In 1784 John Witherspoon, president of the College of New Jersey, and Joseph Reed, former general and Pennsylvania delegate to Congress, crossed the Atlantic to try to raise funds for the war-damaged college at Princeton.[39] Reed warned that Americans had flattered themselves 'too much in the belief of returning cordiality, and also indulged too much vanity in supposing that our conduct in the war and final success, have created sentiments of respect and esteem. It is not so.' Americans were still thought of as rebels.[40] Witherspoon agreed. 'The disposition of the people in this country is very far from what my friends who pressed the voyage upon me, expected.' In Scotland he found 'the better sort of people' to be 'even more set against America' than in England, although 'the common sort [were] much more favourable to it'.[41] John Adams reported that America 'has no party at present in her favor. All parties on the contrary have committed against her.'[42] 'The popular pulse seems to beat high

[36] Letter to J. Jay, 4 November 1785, Charles F. Adams (ed.), *The Works of John Adams*, 10 vols. (Boston, 1850–6), VIII, p. 336.
[37] See below, pp. 106–7.
[38] Stanley Elkins and Eric McKitrick, *The Age of Federalism: The Early American Republic, 1788–1800* (New York, 1993), p. 414.
[39] See below, pp. 308–9.
[40] To N, Greene, 12 February 1784, William B. Reed, *The Life and Correspondence of Joseph Reed*, 2 vols. (Philadelphia, 1847), II, p. 403.
[41] To G. Washington, 7 June 1784, Abbot et al. (eds), *Washington Papers: Confederation Series*, I, p. 430.
[42] To J. Jay, 30 August 1785, Adams (ed.), *Adams Works*, VIII, p. 313.

against America.'[43] His wife agreed. '[N]othing respecting America nor any body or any thing from America, is esteemed or respected in this country excepting by a very few individuals. I think the sooner we get out of the country the better.'[44] Other American observers of the British scene were in no doubt that hostility to America was a genuinely popular cause among a people whose overweening pride, they thought, made it impossible for them to accept their defeat with good grace. William Short, Jefferson's private secretary, wrote that 'all ranks of people from the crown to the shop-keeper may be considered to be in a state of war with whatever is American'.[45] What Jefferson wrote about Britain from Paris, where he was ambassador from 1785 to 1789, was very much the same as what Adams was telling Congress. He spent a short period in London in 1786 as joint commissioner with Adams to negotiate treaties in Europe. He described a bruising dinner encounter with 'a ministerial party' at which he was told that even were America to ask to be readmitted to the empire, Britain would not want her back: 'I think it was the sentiments of the company and of the nation.'[46] His visit convinced him that British hostility to America was 'much more deeply rooted at present than during the war'.[47]

As a realistic assessment of British views and policies, the reports of the Adamses or Jefferson or other patriotic Americans have obvious limitations. They were coloured by their extreme sensitivity to any apparent failure of 'respect' to the new republic, by the narrowness of their contacts on most occasions—the Adamses professed only to be comfortable in the company of radical Dissenters like John Jebb or Richard Price, who no doubt told them what they wanted to hear—and by the rigidity to which they were committed to the self-evident truths on which the republic was founded. This meant that they largely reiterated maxims about the hostility of a corrupt and degenerate Britain which had been formulated well before the outbreak of the war. A man like John Adams, who, for all his intellectual power, was so little capable of recognizing values other than his own or of crossing cultural boundaries was of limited practical use as minister abroad. On his first visit to London in 1783 he was 'introduced to the great politicians at their desire', but he did not find them 'sufficiently well disposed to spend much time in that way'.[48]

Americans complained bitterly, and with good cause, that the British press was hostile to the new America.[49] During the war, newspapers opposing the policies of the North government had generally been sympathetic to the American cause; after 1783 America ceased to be an issue in British politics and so no newspaper had any incentive to write favourably about it and few did. Abigail Adams wrote of the 'base

[43] To J. Jay, 19 July 1785, ibid. VIII, p. 282.
[44] Abigail Adams to J. Q. Adams, 22 July 1786, L. H. Butterfield et al. (eds) *Adams Family Correspondence* (Cambridge, MA, 1963–), VII, p. 284.
[45] To J. Madison, 12 May 1787, Hutchinson et al. (eds), *Madison Papers*, IX, p. 475.
[46] Letter to R. H. Lee, 22 April 1786, Giunta (ed.), *Emerging Nation*, III, p. 159.
[47] To J. Page, 4 May 1786, Boyd et al. (eds), *Jefferson Papers*, IX, p. 446.
[48] To C. Dumas, 28 November 1783, Taylor et al. (eds), *Adams Papers*, XV, p. 379.
[49] For a survey of press attitudes, see Charles R. Ritcheson, 'The London Press and the First Decade of American Independence 1783–1793', *Journal of British Studies*, II (1963), 88–109.

falsehoods, and billingsgate of hireling scribblers or the envenomed pen of refugees'.[50] Her husband agreed that 'The people are deceived by numberless falsehoods industriously circulated by the gazettes and in conversation.'[51] British newspapers were much read on the continent of Europe and to Americans they had an adverse effect on opinion there as well. Thanks to the British press, it was believed throughout Europe 'that there is nothing but distress, disorder and discontent in America'.[52] Americans, as was their wont, detected conspiracies against them. Various explanations were offered for the hostility of the press. The loyalists were of course blamed for this and for much else. Abigail Adams assumed the voice of Milton to describe how loyalists viewed the America from which they had been justly expelled 'with a malice and envy which the arch fiend felt when he beheld the glory of the new world, and like him they wish to destroy the happiness of its inhabitants'.[53] Jefferson, like many other Americans, believed that the press wrote against America at the command of the British government. He had formed an elaborate theory that ministers had a 'standing army of newswriters', whose task was to belittle America in order to reconcile the British public to its loss: 'This is essential to the repose, perhaps even to the safety of the King and his ministers.' He also believed that depicting America in an unfavourable light was part of a campaign against emigration.[54]

Jefferson's British correspondent David Hartley urged him to take a more relaxed view about the British press. 'Every one writes and prints what he thinks proper, and whatever may suit either his passion or his interest.'[55] Hartley was essentially right. There is no evidence of any government attempt to influence the press against America, and it is hard to imagine that they could have had any motive for doing so. Any influence that the loyalists had was likely to have been very small indeed. Even so, Americans had real grounds for concern about the hostility of the British press. The terms in which British newspapers dealt with America seem to reflect not the views of government or of loyalists, but of a wide public opinion. They indicate the continuing lack of public sympathy with America, which had become manifest in the unpopularity of the peace settlement. Appeals for generosity and reconciliation had then fallen on deaf ears and both the minister and his peace had been reviled. There was still no strong desire for reconciliation. New grievances had been added to old ones. Americans had always been regarded as cavalier about paying their debts; their stalling on paying off pre-war debts and the huge new debts that they had incurred immediately after the war were held against them. Richard Price, writing in a newspaper as 'Lover of Humanity' in April 1787 tried to counter 'the animosity and resentment of some disappointed men among

[50] To C. Tufts, 18 August 1785, Butterfield et al. (eds), *Adams Family Correspondence*, VI, p. 283
[51] To J. Jay, 19 July 1785, Adams (ed.), *Adams Works*, VIII, p. 282.
[52] W. Short to E. Carrington, 3 November 1786, Boyd et al. (eds), *Jefferson Papers*, XI, p. 50 fn.
[53] To M. Cranch, 28 April 1787, Butterfield, et al. (eds), *Adams Family Correspondence*, VIII, p. 29.
[54] To D. K. van Hogendorp, 13 October 1785, Boyd et al. (eds), *Jefferson Papers*, VIII, p. 632.
[55] Letter of 5 October 1785, ibid. VIII, p. 587.

us against the inhabitants of the United States'. He published a letter from Benjamin Rush extolling the progress of arts and learning. This provoked indignant replies from 'A Hater of Incendiaries', who dismissed as 'empty delusion' descriptions of Americans as 'a happy and flourishing people'.[56] In the colonial period, large sums in charitable donations had crossed the Atlantic from Britain to America, above all for the endowment of colleges. After the war, the flow dried up.[57] An attempt was, however, made to raise money in England for the victims of a fire in Boston on 20 April 1787 which had destroyed the Hollis Street church and a number of private dwellings. The 'humane and benevolent', who were not 'diverted by the trifling differences of political opinions' were invited to subscribe. This again produced a sharp response. Should people who were guilty of 'misrepresentation, cruel injustice and every species of barbarity . . . be fed and supported at the expence of the people they endeavoured to destroy?' The indomitable Richard Price, no doubt unaware that his name was likely to deter many other possible donors, appeared in a thin published list of subscribers.[58]

In general the Americans were certainly right in complaining that the new republic was not respected, either in the press or in public debate. The common British view was that the Revolution had been a failure. No stable political order had been established and the union was highly likely to disintegrate. That was what was to be expected of republican experiments in government. Although Abigail Adams had stories of Americans who in British company tried to 'secreat their country and pass themselves for natives to avoid being insulted',[59] it seems unlikely that the mass of Americans with less sensitive political antennae than Adams or Jefferson experienced much if any overt hostility, although they would probably have to take a great deal of ignorance and much prejudice about their country in good part. Young William Dunlap was warned that if he ventured into the sticks (to Stamford in Lincolnshire), 'the people will expect to see a black or a copper-coloured Indian at least'.[60]

III

American opinion remained for some years deeply apprehensive about Britain's intentions towards them. Realists were in little doubt that Britain would not again resort to all-out war. Washington was sure that 'the British Cabinet wish to recover the United States to a dependence on that government, yet I can scarcely think that they ever expect to see it realized'. He thought that Britain faced too many troubles

---

[56] *Morning Chronicle*, 23, 26, 30 April, 4, 14 May 1787.
[57] See below, pp. 308–9.
[58] *Public Advertiser*, 24 July, 3 August 1787.
[59] To E. Shaw, 15 September 1785, Butterfield et al. (eds), *Adams Family Correspondence*, VI, p. 362.
[60] *The History of the Rise and Progress of the Arts of Design in the United States*, 2 vols. in 3 (New York, 1834, repr. 1969), I, p. 263.

in Ireland and was in financially too weak a state to risk another war.[61] Madison agreed with this analysis. Unusually, he was sceptical about Britain's 'hostile designs' and pointed out that Britain's 'disregard' for the terms of the treaty could at least be accounted for by American failures to observe their obligations on the debts and other matters.[62] Others were not so sure that Britain might not attack. William Smith, John Adams's secretary, thought that Britain might embark on a maritime war with America with a view to supporting the loyalists and to separating the western lands.[63] There were fears that, if Britain went to war with France, America might be drawn in as France's ally, which would give Britain an excuse to attack her. Adams, who periodically prophesied war, thought the British were aiming 'at recovering back the western lands, at taking away our fisheries, and at the total ruin of our navigation, at least'.[64]

It was generally supposed that Britain would take every opportunity to encourage disaffection within the United States, perhaps with the ultimate aim of their peaceful reincorporation into the British empire. Washington argued that America had little to fear from British attempts at subversion if she put her affairs in order: 'her prospects of success must diminish as our population encreases and the governments become more consistent—without the last of which indeed, any thing may be apprehended'. At present, though, 'our affairs are under wretched management'.[65] Others agreed with him that the troubles of the Confederation were giving Britain her chance to intervene. They feared that there was a fifth column of closet loyalists waiting for their moment. Might not the American republic soon end in a royalist restoration as the English one had done? Samuel Adams reflected the anxieties of the period:

> Should we not guard against British intrigues and factions? Her emissaries under the guise of merchants, repenting refugees, schoolmasters and other characters, unless care is taken may effect another and fatal revolution. The Commonwealth of England lasted twelve years and the exiled King was restored with all the rage and madness of royalty![66]

In British governing circles there was absolutely no intention of going to war with America, no interest in any project of reunion and no inclination to incite instability in the United States, which seemed in any case to need little encouragement. 'Reunion' was the particular project of William Smith, a very prominent figure in pre-revolutionary New York politics, who had taken refuge with the British army. To Americans he was the archetype of a loyalist schemer and they attributed to him, as to other loyalists, an influence that he never possessed. He had been at odds with

[61] To J. Reed, 11 August 1784, Abbot et al. (eds), *Washington Papers: Confederation Series*, II, p. 29.
[62] To J. Monroe, 8 January 1785, Hutchinson et al. (eds) *Madison Papers*, VIII, p. 220.
[63] To J. Jay, 24 August 1786, Giunta (ed.), *Emerging Nation*, III, p. 274.
[64] To J. Jay, 30 November 1787, Adams (ed.), *Adams Works*, VIII, p. 463.
[65] To Reed, 11 August 1784, Abbot et al. (eds), *Washington Papers: Confederation Series*, II, pp. 29–30.
[66] To R. H. Lee, 22 December 1784, H. A. Cushing (ed.), *The Writings of Samuel Adams*, 4 vols. (New York, 1904–8), IV, p. 312.

most other loyalists in believing that the future lay not in the military defeat of the Revolution but in peaceful reconciliation. He attached himself to Sir Guy Carleton in New York city and seems to have persuaded him to adopt some of his views. As commander-in-chief in 1782–3 Carleton had hoped to be able to bring about a reconciliation, and evidently continued to believe for some time that, in spite of American independence, this might still be possible. With the evacuation of New York, Smith went to Britain, where he was an indefatigable lobbyist for his plans for reunion. Even modified to hopes for 'communion' between Britain and the United States, which he interpreted as 'a sway' over them, he got very little encouragement. He heard at second hand that 'Mr Pitt will not like to hear of recovering America', although 'he is full for anglifying Canada'. Lord Sydney, the Secretary of State, told him that he believed that the king 'did not wish a reunion more than his ministers and the nation at large'. Richard Sheridan, a member of the Whig opposition, said that he 'wished never to see a reunion'.[67] Lord Shelburne was interested in some sort of reunion, although William Smith's brother reported even him as saying 'God forbid that we should have America back. We can command all the good they can do us.'[68]

In 1786, when Carleton, now Lord Dorchester, became governor of Quebec with wider authority as nominal governor of the other colonies and commander-in-chief of British North America, Smith went with him as Chief Justice of Quebec. Smith hoped that Dorchester would again be able to take up the role of negotiator of an Anglo-American reconciliation. He looked forward to his being on hand to turn to advantage the new revolution that 'the miseries of America would infallibly quicken and bring forward to its maturity'.[69] Before his departure, Smith spoke freely of his hopes. Abigail Adams reported that he confidently expected that he should live 'to see America sue to Britain for protection and to be received again by it'.[70] He had told ministers of his hopes that Britain would be able to 'mould the affairs of America to her interest'.[71] Dorchester's appointment was viewed in the United States as an indication of a more interventionist British policy. He was 'known to be penetrating and judicious and the people are in the habits of thinking favourably of him', while Smith's hopes of reunion were assumed to be the policy of the British government.[72] Alexander Hamilton speculated that Britain might hope to 'see in this country a counterpart of the restoration of Charles II' and that Dorchester's 'splendid title of viceroy' might be intended to give him authority beyond the British colonies.[73] There were many rumours of contacts between Shays's rebellion in Massachusetts in 1786 and the British in Canada. Washington

---

[67] Diary 24 March, 22 May 1785, 23 April 1786, L. F. S. Upton (ed.), *The Diary and Selected Papers of Chief Justice William Smith 1784–1793*, 2 vols. (Toronto, 1963–5), I, p. 232; II, pp. 69, 77.
[68] Diary, 25 January 1785, ibid. I, p. 185.
[69] Diary, 13 June 1786, ibid. II, pp. 105–6.
[70] To M. Cranch, 28 April 1787, Butterfield et al. (eds), *Adams Family Correspondence*, VIII, pp. 29–30.
[71] Diary, 16 April 1785, Upton (ed.), *Smith Diary*, I, p. 216.
[72] E. Carrington to E. Randolph, 8 December 1786, Smith (ed.), *Letters of Delegates*, XXIV, p. 45.
[73] Speech in New York Assembly, 28 March 1787, Syrett et al. (eds), *Hamilton Papers*, IV, p. 135.

believed that Britain would try to take advantage of the outbreak of the disturbances 'with a view to distracting our governments, and promoting divisions' and
suspected that Dorchester had been sent to Quebec 'for that purpose'.[74] There were
other rumours of plots to install a British prince as king of America. Washington
was dismayed at accounts that 'even respectable characters speak of a monarchy as a
form of government without horror'.[75] Dorchester heard such reports too and
passed them on to London. He thought America ripe for change. In his opinion
there was not 'a gentleman in the states from New Hampshire to Georgia who does
not view the present government with contempt . . . and who is not desirous of
changing it for a monarchy'. He had no expectation of anything significant coming
from the Philadelphia Convention. A 'most powerful delegation' might soon be
sent from America to London. Ministers treated his information with reserve.[76]
Rumours about Dorchester's intentions are more indicative of Americans' sense of
insecurity in 1786 and 1787 than of any designs by the British government.

By contrast, American concerns about the British being 'very busy on our
frontiers' had some real substance.[77] During the war those who were trying to
establish a separate state of Vermont had been in contact with the British in
Quebec. Such contacts continued throughout the 1780s. The British also took
an interest in the new settlements forming in the western lands between the
mountains and the Mississippi. It was British policy to develop trade with new
entities such as Kentucky and to encourage them to maintain their autonomy from
the United States.[78]

For zealous republicans, British subversion could take more oblique forms than
encouraging political disaffection or secession movements, although ultimately they
were linked. The great imports of British luxury goods that followed the ending of
the war, made possible by the huge extension of credit by British merchants, was
seen as a serious threat to the ideals of the new America. A people corrupted by
luxury would turn to monarchy. Samuel Adams was dismayed at the number of
Massachusetts citizens who were 'imitating the Britons in every idle amusement or
expensive foppery, which it is in their power to invent for the destruction of a
young country . . . You would be surprised to see the equipage, the furniture and
expensive living of too many.'[79] Benjamin Rush, anxious to promote Philadelphia's
claims to be the national capital, denounced New York as 'the *sink* of British
manners and politics'. He thought that at least a third of its population were
'American citizens with British hearts'. 'Think, sir,' he urged John Adams, 'of the
influence of light tea-parties, music parties &c. &c. upon the manners of the rulers

---

[74] To H. Knox, 26 December 1786, Abbot et al. (eds), *Washington Papers: Confederation Series*, IV,
p. 483.
[75] To J. Jay, 15 August 1786, ibid. IV, p. 213.
[76] Dorchester to Sydney, 10 April 1787, TNA, CO 42/50, ff. 94–5; Sydney's reply, 14 September
1787, TNA, CO 42/51, f. 44.
[77] N. Dane to T. Dwight, 12 March 1787, Smith (ed.), *Letters of Delegates*, XXIV, p. 141.
[78] See below, pp. 161–3.
[79] To J. Adams, 2 July 1785, Cushing (ed.), *Samuel Adams Writings*, IV, p. 315.

of a great republic.'[80] Jefferson was already seeing British imports as the chains that tied American to Britain. Extravagance was for him 'a more baneful evil than Toryism was during the war'.[81] 'Every shipment, every consignment, every commission', James Madison was later to write, extended British influence. 'Thus it is, that our country is penetrated to its remotest corners with a foreign poison, vitiating the American sentiment, recolonizing the American character, and duping us into the politics of a foreign nation.'[82] Britain seemed to be pursuing a coordinated policy. By 'introducing luxury, draining our money, impairing public credit, and destroying public spirit' Britain had shown that 'she will be systematical in aiming at our destruction'.[83]

IV

Americans regarded the Britain that seemed to them so unremittingly hostile as dangerous and unpredictable. Her large professional army and navy, backed by her capacity to extract heavy taxes from her people and to run up an immense national debt made her dangerous. Her vast manufacturing capacity enabled her to assail American virtue through a flood of exported luxury items. That her government was not effectively accountable even to an unrepresentative House of Commons, let alone to an informed and virtuous public opinion, but was conducted by opaque political intrigues between the king, his favourites, and corrupt and self-seeking political elite made her unpredictable. Americans prided themselves that none of these things could be attributed to them.

Most Americans were wary of standing armed forces, hoping to rely instead on a militia drawn from the people for whatever military needs the republic might have. Americans had resisted British taxation and were grudging in the taxes they allowed the states to raise or in their response to federal requests for funds. For strict republicans, public debt was noxious because it encouraged speculation by moneyed men and even foreign intervention. By the end of the war the states and Congress had incurred very large debts. In the face of considerable opposition, Hamilton in 1790 combined state and Congressional debts into a single funded public debt under the administration of the federal Treasury. Although Hamilton believed that a properly funded permanent public debt was 'a national blessing', rather than a threat to the republic,[84] he was going against accepted republican principles. Washington thought that loans should only be raised on 'critical

---

[80] To J. Adams, 19 March, 4 June 1789, L. H. Butterfield (ed.), *The Letters of Benjamin Rush*, 2 vols. (Princeton, NJ, 1951), I, pp. 506, 513.

[81] To J. Page, 4 May 1786, Boyd et al. (eds), *Jefferson Papers*, IX, p. 445.

[82] Cited in Peter S. Onuf, *Jefferson's Empire: The Language of American Nationhood* (Charlottesville, VA, 2000), p. 91.

[83] A. Campbell to J. Madison, 28 October 1785, Hutchinson et al. (eds), *Madison Papers*, VIII, p. 383.

[84] Report on the Public Credit [9 January 1790], Syrett et al. (eds), *Hamilton Papers*, VI, p. 106.

occasions' and that they should be paid off as soon as possible.[85] Projects to develop manufacturing in America were generally regarded by the political elite as laudable and much to be encouraged. Washington wrote in 1789 with pride of the manufacturing improvements of the last few years.[86] Jefferson had taken a close interest in British manufacturing during his brief trip in 1786. He found much to admire, especially the use of steam engines. He conceded that 'the mechanical arts in London are carried to a wonderful perfection'.[87] Yet there was little enthusiasm for American manufactures to develop in the way and on the scale that Britain's had done. It was generally accepted that agriculture with the mass of the population farming their own land must be the future for America for a long time to come. Yeomen farmers were the proper foundation for sustaining a republic. They, according to Jefferson, were 'the most vigorous, the most independent, the most virtuous, and they are tied to their country and wedded to its liberty and interests by the most lasting bonds'.[88] When people 'get piled upon one another in large cities, as in Europe, they will become corrupt, as in Europe'.[89] For 'general operations of manufacture', he wrote in his *Notes on the State of Virginia*, 'let our work-shops remain in Europe'. Madison agreed that a subdivision of landed property to create small holdings was socially very desirable. In 'populous' European countries with unequal landownership people were forced into manufacturing 'superfluities'.[90] Franklin's view had long been that Britain was able to export cheap manufactures in such quantities because a grossly unequal society kept its labouring population in poverty. He believed that America should be wary of encouraging manufacturing on a large scale and thus producing an impoverished proletariat.[91]

Post-war American assessments of Britain's constitution and system of government were largely repetitions of stereotypes formed well before the outbreak of the Revolution. British corruption was still being denounced in terms derived from the opponents of Robert Walpole.[92] The British constitution as expounded by Montesquieu, De Lolme, or Blackstone was generally much respected and even revered. It was commended at the 1787 Convention, but most speakers pointed out that America's much more egalitarian social structure and what James Wilson called 'the whole genius of the people of America' required something different.[93] Franklin

---

[85] To Jefferson, 31 August 1788, Abbot et al. (eds), *Washington Papers: Confederation Series*, VI, p. 493.

[86] E. g. letters to Jefferson, 13 February and to Sir E. Newneham, 2 March 1789, W. W. Abbot, et al. (eds), *The Papers of George Washington: Presidential Series* (Charlottesville, VA, 1987–), I, pp. 299–300, 355.

[87] To C. Thomson, 22 April, to J. Page, 4 May 1786, Boyd et al. (eds), *Jefferson Papers*, IX, pp. 400, 445.

[88] To J. Jay, 23 August 1785, ibid. VIII, p. 426.

[89] To J. Madison, 20 December 1787, ibid. XII, p. 442.

[90] To Jefferson, 19 June 1786, ibid. IX, p. 660.

[91] Drew R. McCoy, *The Elusive Republic: Political Economy in Jeffersonian America* (Chapel Hill, NC, 1980), pp. 49–65.

[92] Bernard Bailyn, *The Ideological Origins of the American Revolution* (Cambridge, MA, 1967) is the classic exposition, see especially ch. IV, 'The Logic of Rebellion'.

[93] 7 June 1787, Max Farrand (ed.), *The Records of the Federal Convention of 1787*, 4 vols. (New Haven, CT, 1937), I, p. 153.

conceded that 'in its present circumstances' what he called 'a mixed form of government' was best for Britain.[94] In 1784, however, he wrote that 'The disorders of that government, whose constitution has been so much praised, are come to a height that threatens some violent convulsion' and he doubted whether the programmes being advocated for parliamentary reform would stave off the crisis. Reform required 'more public spirit and virtue, . . . more perhaps than can now be found in a nation so long corrupted'.[95] For Franklin, the root of the British malady was the huge inflation of public service by 'the enormous salaries, emoluments and patronage of great offices'. This produced factional struggles for the fruits of office.[96] He had been saying such things at least since 1775,[97] and he was to repeat them on many occasions. Lesser men denounced British corruption in time-honoured ways. Under 'royal guidance', the British are 'buried in bribery and corruption and laugh patriotism and public virtue out of countenance'.[98] American visitors after the war, as they had been in colonial times, were struck by the degradation and criminality of the British poor, especially those that they observed in London. Franklin thought that more thefts were committed in Britain than in all the rest of Europe put together, which he attributed at least in part to 'the deficiency of morality in your national government'.[99] 'Here', according to David Humphreys, the aspiring poet who served as Washington's aide, 'man from want, depravity, and despair wars against humanity. It seems to me in passing the streets, eagerness and distrust are often painted on the countenances of the multitude. This is a nation from whose morals and connections, the United States are happily separated.'[100] Adams agreed and drew the conclusion that 'American liberty' depended on the 'faith, honour and justice in the minds of their common citizens'. This had made the Revolution possible, but it was not to be found 'in the common people of Europe'.[101]

Immediately after 1783, with two years of ministerial instability, with a national debt that had risen during the war from £127 million to £243 million, with an estimated deficit of at least £2 million for 1784 and with a people said to be 'so loaded with taxes as to be hardly able to subsist',[102] it was relatively easy to portray Britain as being on her last legs. With the ascendancy of Pitt, even though most Americans still continued to depict Britain in the 1780s as they conceived it to have been in the age of Sir Robert Walpole, some seem to have recognized that Britain was undergoing rapid change of which they needed to take account.

---

[94] To J. Wright, 4 November 1789, Bigelow (ed.), *Franklin Works*, X, p. 161.
[95] To J. Shipley, 17 March 1783, Labaree, et al. (eds), *Franklin Papers*, XXXIX, p. 350.
[96] To H. Laurens, 12 February 1784, Bigelow (ed.), *Franklin Works*, VIII, pp. 448–9.
[97] Bailyn, *Ideological Origins*, p. 136.
[98] W. S. Smith to R. King, 1 January [1788], Charles R. King (ed.), *The Life and Correspondence of Rufus King*, 6 vols. (New York, 1894–9), I, p. 309.
[99] To B. Vaughan, 14 March 1785. Bigelow (ed.), *Franklin Works*, IX, pp. 84–5.
[100] To T. Jefferson, 2 November 1790, F. L. Humphreys, *The Life and Times of David Humphreys*, 2 vols. (New York, 1917), II, pp. 57–8.
[101] To J. Jay, 23 September 1787, Giunta (ed.), *Emerging Nation*, III, p. 592.
[102] E. Gerry to J. Adams, 8 November 1785, Smith (ed.), *Letters of Delegates*, XXIII, p. 9.

The 1780s have been described as 'a unique decade' in eighteenth-century British history, in which 'a wide variety of "reform" and "improvement" campaigns', concerned with public health, prisons, the criminal law, slavery, and the slave trade, 'commanded support across a broad front' in Britain.[103] Movements for reform in Britain were very similar to those in American cities like Philadelphia.[104] To many of his contemporaries, Pitt seemed to be the embodiment of aspirations for improvement. He has been described as cornering 'the market in political virtue', standing among other things for 'public service, incorruptibility, rational government and a balance between interests'.[105] In 1787 Christopher Wyvill of the Yorkshire Association told him that under his administration 'the prosperity of the country has been advanced with a rapidity beyond all expectation; . . . and government has been steadily conducted on the principles of virtuous oeconomy'.[106] By 1789 British public finances were in surplus and the average price of 3 per cent consols had risen to £80 from £54 in 1784.[107] In European politics, Britain was no longer isolated and it was clear that she was gaining an ascendancy over France even before the outbreak of the French Revolution. Accounts of Britain's pre-eminence in Europe and of the flourishing state of her finances were appearing in the American press.[108]

Most Americans dismissed Pitt as yet another cover for the king's machinations against them, but some took note of these changes, albeit with scepticism about whether they could be lasting. Washington doubted whether 'the affairs of that nation, could long go on in the same prosperous train. . . . [T]he paper bubble will one day burst.'[109] 'The surplus of revenue so long ostentatiously displayed to the public', was 'but an artificial deception', for Adams.[110] Jefferson was sceptical too. He anticipated that bankruptcies in London would soon produce 'the general conflagration of all their paper'.[111] But he tried to inform himself about systems of public finance and conceded the strengths of the British system. Although he disapproved of extensive public borrowing, he thought that America should follow British models to maintain its credit for emergencies such as war.[112]

By 1790 it was no longer possible for Americans in Britain to remain dismissive about the changes taking place there. From London David Humphreys wrote that:

---

[103] Arthur Burns and Joanna Innes, 'Introduction', Burns and Innes (eds), *Rethinking the Age of Reform in Britain 1780–1850* (Cambridge, 2003), p. 10.

[104] Sarah Knott, *Sensibility and the American Revolution* (Chapel Hill, NC, 2009), pp. 222–38.

[105] Boyd Hilton, *A Mad, Bad, and Dangerous People? England 1783–1846* (Oxford, 2006), p. 194; see also Jennifer Mori, 'The Political Theory of William Pitt the Younger', *History*, LXXXIII (1998), 234–48.

[106] To Pitt, 29 July 1787, C. Wyvill (ed.), *Political Papers*, 6 vols. (York, 1794–1804), IV, p. 33.

[107] T. S. Ashton, *An Economic History of England: The 18th Century* (London, 1955), p. 251.

[108] E.g. 'British State of Politics for May 1788', *The American Museum*, IV (1788), 173.

[109] To Lafayette, 25 April to [1 May] 1788, Abbot et al. (eds), *Washington Papers: Confederation Series*, VI, pp. 242–3.

[110] To J. Jay, 23 September 1787, Giunta (ed.), *Emerging Nation*, III, p. 592.

[111] To E. Carrington, 27 May 1788, Boyd et al. (eds) *Jefferson Papers*, XIII, p. 209.

[112] To Washington, 2 May 1788, Abbot et al. (eds), *Washington Papers: Confederation Series*: VI, pp. 254–5.

notwithstanding the enormous national debt and the heavy burdens which the people at large are compelled to bear; yet the resource of credit and the influx of money, have crowded all the public and private banks with specie and embarrassed the great money holders to determine how to dispose of it . . . It is visible to every eye that prodigious sums have been recently laid out on buildings and improvements. I believe nearly as many house have been built in this city within a year past as the city of Philadelphia contains. This is the effect of a vast current which has run in favour of this country and stagnated here.[113]

If Britain was indeed driving forward at a rapid pace, then there might be lessons for America to be learnt from William Pitt's Britain. Alexander Hamilton certainly thought so. He admired Pitt, describing him to Washington as having 'a great mind'.[114] It has even been suggested that he saw Pitt as some kind of role model.[115] The great financier William Bingham told him of the success of Pitt's recent reforms in public finance.[116] In drafting his major reports of 1790 and 1791, laying out a programme for the new federal government, on the Public Credit, on a National Bank, and on Manufactures, Hamilton drew extensively on British precedents and practice. The British experience decisively proved that a funded public debt would be beneficial.[117] Britain was the prime example of 'the height to which every species of industry has grown up' through 'the force of monied capital'.[118] As all his contemporaries did, he recognized the primacy of agriculture for the new America, but he was prepared to go much further than most in giving the federal state a role in encouraging large-scale manufacturing on the British model. He greatly admired British cotton mills, 'attended chiefly by women and children'. 'The prodigious affect of such a machine is easily perceived.'[119]

Hamilton was an Anglophile and aimed at a rapprochement with Britain. In 1789 he told a British contact that he had 'always preferred a connexion' with Britain than with 'any other country'.[120] It has been argued that by then he had revived 'federative schemes' for joining Britain and America that he had first conceived in 1776.[121] British emissaries communicated easily with him and found that he had a 'just and liberal way of thinking'.[122] Yet whatever may have been the emotional pull that he felt towards Britain, his search for better relations with the British rested on a calculated assessment of America's interests For the immediate future, American federal finance depended on duties from British trade and British hostility could do America great damage. The state-building and

---

[113] To T. Jefferson, 28 October 1790, Humphreys (ed.), *Life of Humphreys*, II, p. 45.

[114] Letter of 30 September 1790, Syrett et al. (eds), *Hamilton Papers*, VII, p. 84.

[115] Elkins and McKitrick, *Age of Federalism*, p. 227.

[116] To Hamilton, [25 November 1789], Syrett et al. (eds), *Hamilton Papers*, V, pp. 540–5.

[117] Report on the Public Credit, ibid. VI, p. 72.

[118] Report on Manufactures, ibid. X, p. 281.

[119] Report on Manufactures, ibid. X, p. 252.

[120] Conversation with G. Beckwith in Dorchester to W. Grenville, 25 October 1789, ibid. V, p. 483.

[121] John L. Harper, *American Machiavelli: Alexander Hamilton and the Origins of U. S. Foreign Policy* (Cambridge, 2004), p. 48.

[122] Ron Chernow, *Alexander Hamilton* (New York, 2004), p. 394.

economy-building which his projects were intended to bring about would ultimately free America from British dependence.

With the passing of time some wartime resentments seem to have declined. In 1789 David Hartley, a long-standing British friend of America and a perennial optimist, told John Jay that 'All memory of hostilities is abated in this country towards America.' He urged that the United States should reciprocate by sending official congratulations to George III on his recovery from what was taken to be his madness, a request which Jay politely parried.[123] Hamilton assured Washington in 1790 that there was still 'a considerable proportion of those who were firm friends to the Revolution who retain prepossessions in favour of Englishmen'.[124] Events were, however, soon to overwhelm whatever chances there may have been for a general return of good feelings.

The French Revolution and the subsequent war between Britain and Revolutionary France subjected Anglo-American relations to severe strains. The federal government proclaimed its neutrality in the war, but much American opinion was strongly pro-French and anti-British. The Pitt regime, whatever its previous reforming credentials, came to be seen as repressing its own population and allying with European despotisms in crushing liberty elsewhere. It seemed to be trampling on America's status as a sovereign state in its high-handed seizures of American ships trading with its French enemy. Citizen Genet, the French Republic's ambassador to America in 1793 won considerable popular support for his schemes for launching operations against Britain from American soil. The Washington administration's efforts to defuse a crisis in British relations by negotiations leading to the Jay Treaty of 1794 were highly unpopular. The treaty was denounced for sacrificing American interests to Britain and a vigorous campaign was mounted to try to prevent its being ratified. The French Republic also tried to nullify the treaty by grossly heavy-handed tactics, involving large seizures of American ships and repulsing with humiliation diplomatic efforts to settle differences. For a year or two popular resentment was directed against France as the two republics entered into an undeclared war at sea.

Aversion to Britain had, however, become a defining feature of the rivalry between Republicans and Federalists that was coming to dominate America's politics, which were 'bound up to an extraordinary degree with its foreign relations'.[125] The Anglophilia of which Republicans like Jefferson and Madison accused Federalists to them embodied values which they feared and detested. Those who sought accommodation with Britain were, in their view, betraying the republic. The 'Anglomen' were monarchists, lovers of hierarchy, exponents of a standing army, and of a strong centralized state which exercised power by winning support through corruption. They had, Jefferson wrote in 1797, 'bound the interests of this country entirely to the will of another', so that 'it is impossible

---

[123] Hartley to Jay, August 1789, Jay to Hartley, 14 December 1789, Henry P. Johnston (ed.), *The Correspondence and Public Papers of John Jay*, 4 vols. (New York, 1890–3), III, pp. 375–6, 382–3.
[124] Letter of 15 September 1790, Syrett et al. (eds), *Hamilton Papers*, VII, p. 50.
[125] Elkins and McKitrick, *Age of Federalism*, p. 664.

for us to say that we stand on independent ground'.[126] When later in power, Jefferson could swallow his aversion to the extent of being willing to cooperate with Britain against France over Louisiana. Practical cooperation and a willingness on both sides to settle differences marked the years from the Jay Treaty to 1805, which have been called 'the first rapprochement'.[127] Yet if they accepted the necessity of doing business with the British, this did not mean that Jeffersonian Republicans liked them or wished to emulate them. Those who voted the Federalists out of power in 1800 'sought affirmation of their values in the celebration of what was distinctly American in their eyes. To them America's departure from English norms had enormous appeal.'[128] From 1805 dealings with the British became increasingly fraught, culminating in 1812 in a new Anglo-American war.

[126] To E. Gerry, 13 May 1797, Boyd et al. (eds), *Jefferson Papers*, XXIX, p. 363.

[127] Bradford Perkins, *The First Rapprochement: England and the United States 1795–1805* (Philadelphia, 1955).

[128] Joyce Appleby, *Inheriting the Revolution: The First Generation of Americans* (Cambridge, MA, 2000), pp. 248–9.

5

The Politics of Trade

The trade of the North American colonies had been regulated from Britain from the early days of settlement. The purpose of these regulations was to maximize the contribution that the colonies made to the wealth and power of Britain and the empire as a whole and to restrict the direct participation in their trade of Britain's European competitors. Some of the most valuable commodities which the colonies produced could only be exported to Britain in the first instance and most of their imports were routed through Britain. The production of some items deemed to be of particular importance to the British economy was encouraged by bounties while some manufacturing processes that might have competed with British industries were prohibited. Partly as a result of regulations but even more as a consequence of Britain's economic dominance in the world, the colonial economies were closely linked to Britain at the outbreak of the Revolution. There was American resentment against British economic dominance, but in general the colonies had prospered greatly and the bulk of the white population enjoyed a very high standard of living in eighteenth-century terms.

From the moment that they declared independence Americans began to plan a new commercial order without the exclusive privileges that Britain had enjoyed. They would open their markets to any country that was prepared to do the same for them and would export their commodities throughout the world. They fully recognized that Britain would continue to be a very major trading partner, but trade must be on mutually agreed terms, settled by a negotiated treaty, not by rules laid down by Britain. Within a few months of conceding American independence, however, Britain showed that it was not interested in a commercial treaty and that it intended unilaterally to lay down new rules for Anglo-American commerce. These granted favours to America but also imposed restrictions on some branches of American trade with the British empire which Americans regarded as hostile and extremely damaging to them.

The new British regulations to a degree that is hard to ascertain probably did exacerbate the economic difficulties that America faced after the war, but Americans took much higher ground in their outraged denunciations. They saw them as an assault on the ideals on which the republic was founded and even as an attempt to nullify American independence. The economy of an independent America was, it seemed, still to be subordinated to Britain. British commercial policy was denounced as 'more injurious to these states' than the Stamp Act or the war had been, and as calculated 'to make us ten times more the slaves of Britain, than we were before the war'.[1] Washington believed that 'the proudest and most potent people on earth' were trying 'to prevent us from becoming a great, a respectable and commercial nation'.[2]

Americans had anticipated that they would 'lead the world into a revolution in free trade'.[3] Many of the elite shared the Enlightenment faith in free trade as a panacea, which would, in Richard Henry Lee's words, diffuse 'benefits and communication between the human species in different parts of the world'.[4] Even someone so deeply immersed in the practical business of getting rich as the great financier, merchant, and speculator Robert Morris believed that 'if all governments were to agree that commerce should be as free as air I believe they would then place it on the most advantageous footing for every country and for all mankind'.[5] As a first step, treaties were to be negotiated with any country willing to give the new republic reciprocal and equal advantages. The American commissioners in the negotiations with Britain during 1782 offered to include clauses guaranteeing reciprocity under which British and American merchants would enjoy equal rights and privileges in one another's countries. The Shelburne administration that made the peace was entirely sympathetic to such a project but felt themselves unable to include commercial clauses which would involve the amendment of British Navigation Acts, a matter that must be referred to Parliament. With the fall of Shelburne, the moment passed. No commercial treaty between Britain and the United States was in fact to be concluded until 1794. The two countries were left, as Jefferson put it, 'to scramble for the future as well as they can; to regulate their commerce by duties and prohibitions and perhaps by canons [*sic*] and mortars'.[6]

There was vigorous debate in America about the kind of commercial relations with Britain that would be desirable. Both the extent of American independence and the character of the American people were thought to be at stake. An independent America must be free of the stranglehold which British merchant capital was alleged to have exerted over parts of the colonial economy. America should seek to grow out of her old role, as Jefferson put it, of being 'useful labourers to furnish [Europe] with raw materials' and 'unimportant consumers of her manufactures and productions'.[7] While she would inevitably remain for the immediate future a predominantly agricultural society, she must seek to develop a more diversified economy. Above all, America must be free to develop a strong maritime marine of its own. In *The Federalist* no. 11 Hamilton warned that the

---

[1] 'Reflections on British Policy with Regard to America', *The American Museum*, II (1787), 291.

[2] To E. Newenham, 29 August 1788, W. W. Abbot et al. (eds), *The Papers of George Washington: Confederation Series*, 6 vols. (Charlottesville, VA, 1992–7), VI, p. 487.

[3] Drew R. McCoy, *The Elusive Republic: Political Economy in Jeffersonian America* (Chapel Hill, NC, 1980), p. 76.

[4] To T. Jefferson, 16 May 1785, Julian P. Boyd et al. (eds), *The Papers of Thomas Jefferson* (Princeton, NJ, 1950–), VIII, p. 154.

[5] To J. Jay, 27 November 1783, E. James Ferguson et al. (eds), *The Papers of Robert Morris* (Pittsburgh, PA, 1973–), VIII, p. 785.

[6] To D. Ross, 8 May 1786, Boyd et al. (eds), *Jefferson Papers*, IX, p. 475.

[7] To E. Pendleton, 18 December 1783, ibid. VI, p. 387.

Europeans would do their best to deprive us 'as far as possible of an ACTIVE COMMERCE in our own bottoms'. By doing this they would hope to clip the wings 'by which we might soar to a dangerous greatness'.[8] In the second edition of his sermon *The United States elevated to Glory and Honour*, Ezra Stiles, president of Yale, exulted that 'Navigation will carry the American flag around the globe itself; . . . and illumine the world with TRUTH and LIBERTY.'[9] The arrival of the first American ship in China in 1784 assumed great importance as a symbol of America's maritime aspirations. Richard Henry Lee saw the China voyage as 'proof of American enterprise' that will 'probably mortify as much as it will injure our old oppressors the British'.[10] John Adams insisted 'We must and will rival the English in the cod and whale fisheries; in the carrying trade of Italy, in the East India trade—in the African trade, in all other trades.'[11] The British must certainly not be allowed to dominate America's carrying trade. This was a serious economic issue. Earnings from shipping and the sale of ships within the British empire had made an important contribution to the colonies' balance of payments. But shipping was valued for more than the economic returns it brought. America's standing as a nation was at stake. James Monroe was concerned that without their own shipping the American states' 'national consequence must decline, their merchants become only the agents and retailers of foreign powers'.[12] A New York newspaper of 1785 put it more dramatically: 'We will sink to the same state with the coasts of Africa or India, where the whole trade is in the hands of foreigners—where foreigners are every thing and the natives nothing'.[13] In 1789 James Madison reflected that British dominance of American seaborne trade since the war had 'very nearly defeated the object of our independence'.[14]

However desirable free trade might be in principle, many Americans quickly came to believe that they must be able to regulate their trade in order to protect vital American economic interests from European, and above all from British, dominance. They became what has been called 'republican mercantilists'.[15] Madison was an early exponent of such views. In any commercial treaty with Britain, Virginia should 'reserve her right as unfettered as possible over her own commerce', so as to bring about a 'thorough emancipation' from the 'monopoly which formerly tyrannized over it'.[16] The European powers protected their national merchant marine as the basis of a national navy through their navigation acts. The new America must

---

[8] J. R. Pole (ed.), *The Federalist* (Indianapolis, IN, 2005), p. 55.

[9] (Worcester, MA, 1785), pp. 88–9.

[10] To [S. Adams], 20 May 1785, J. C. Ballagh (ed.), *The Letters of Richard Henry Lee*, 2 vols. (New York, 1911–14), II, p. 360.

[11] To R. Cranch, 11 March 1786, L. H. Butterfield et al. (eds), *Adams Family Correspondence* (Cambridge, MA, 1963–), VII, pp. 85–6.

[12] Report to Congress, 28 March 1785, cited in John E. Crowley, *The Privileges of Independence: Neomercantilism and the American Revolution* (Baltimore, MD, 1993), p. 108.

[13] Cited in Cathy D. Matson and Peter S. Onuf, *A Union of Interests: Political and Economic Thought in Revolutionary America* (Lawrence, KS, 1990), p. 69.

[14] Speech in House, 4 May 1789, William T. Hutchinson et al. (eds), *The Papers of James Madison* (Chicago and Charlottesville, VA, 1962–), XII, p. 126.

[15] Crowley, *Privileges of Independence*, p. xii.

[16] To E. Randolph, 20 May 1783, Hutchinson et al. (eds), *Madison Papers*, VII, p. 61.

do the same, if she was to become a naval power.'The necessity of naval protection to external or maritime commerce, and the conduciveness of that species of commerce to the prosperity of a navy, are points too manifest to require a particular elucidation', Hamilton wrote in *The Federalist*.[17]

Free access to the British West Indies was the principal American interest in any commercial settlement with Britain. 'Our natural share of the West Indian trade, is all that is now wanting to complete the plan of happiness and prosperity of our country', Adams wrote in July 1783.[18] Britain was not, however, prepared to concede this. Under the new regulations, certain commodities could be exported from America to the British West Indies, but they must be carried in British ships. Before the outbreak of war the American colonies had developed a very large trade with the West Indies in their own ships. Roughly half the ships clearing into or out of the port of New York before the Revolution were trading with the West Indies.[19] Underlying American determination to recover the trade of the British West Indies was a sense that the American continent was the natural sphere for the commercial expansion of the United States. In John Jay's opinion, 'we should constantly look forward to a commercial intercourse with all the ports and places on the American continent and American islands to whomsoever belonging'.[20] For Jefferson, the United States had a 'natural right of trading with our neighbors' and would sooner or later force open the markets of 'those placed on the same continent with us and who wish nothing better'.[21]

After independence the American political elite was much less interested in what they called the 'direct' transatlantic trade between the American states and the British Isles. They hoped to diversify transatlantic trade away from British dominance. American exports would go to other markets and manufactured imports would be obtained from other sources. Gouverneur Morris believed that 'the flood of commerce' which had poured into Britain was 'now seeking different channels'. Britain was becoming 'a lesser market for our produce than almost any other nation'.[22] The French were an obvious but generally disappointing alternative to Britain. Thomas Jefferson assiduously worked to build up French commercial connections during his embassy in Paris with little result. More realistically, Robert Morris expected the Dutch to become America's main trading partner.[23] Large quantities of Virginia tobacco and Carolina rice were indeed to be exported via the Netherlands.

---

[17] Pole (ed.), *Federalist*, p. 59.

[18] To R. Livingston, 16 July 1783, Robert J. Taylor et al. (eds), *The Papers of John Adams* (Cambridge, MA, 1977–), XV, p. 124.

[19] Cathy D. Matson, *Merchants and Empire: Trading in Colonial New York* (Baltimore, MD, 1998), p. 184.

[20] To R. Morris, 12 September 1783, Ferguson et al. (eds), *Morris Papers*, VIII, p. 507.

[21] To Washington, 4 [December 1788], W. W. Abbot et al. (eds), *The Papers of George Washington Papers: Presidential Series* (Charlottesville, VA, 1987–), I, p. 152.

[22] To N. Gorham, 28 January 1784, Ferguson et al. (eds), *Morris Papers*, IX, p. 75.

[23] To J. Jay, 27 November 1783, ibid. VIII, p. 786.

Jefferson called the 'direct trade' with Britain 'a ruinous one for ourselves'.[24] By this he meant much more than the inescapable fact that America, as in the colonial period, was likely to have a heavy adverse balance of commodity trade with Britain, importing manufactured goods whose value would be very much greater than America's exports to Britain. For Jefferson to an extreme degree and to many of his contemporaries to lesser degrees, imports from Britain were a source of moral corruption, threatening to undermine the virtue of the republic. British imports were denounced for indulging American consumers' taste for luxuries that were inimical to the austere frugality that was the hallmark of a republican citizen. To make matters worse, the liberal credit which the British offered lured Americans into debt. Jefferson was already beginning to see commerce with Britain as a form of neo-colonialism, a concept that he and Madison were to develop fully in the 1790s. British goods brought on British credit 'are the actual links', Jefferson wrote, 'which hold us whether we will or no to Great Britain. There is a great reformation necessary to our manners and our commerce.'[25] Washington thought that any curtailing of credit 'will probably turn out to our advantage'.[26] America, he thought, should 'maintain something like a war of posts, against the invasion of luxury, dissipation and corruption' from overseas.[27]

American objectives in resuming commercial relations with Britain after the war were thus to accord to Britain a place in American trade, no longer as master but as one of a number of trading partners, bound by agreements of reciprocal advantages, which would give the Americans full access to the British empire, especially to the West Indies; direct transatlantic trade would be resumed on what Americans hoped would be a somewhat reduced scale, as links were developed with other European countries. Most Americans felt that such objectives would not be difficult to obtain since they believed that their trade was of the utmost importance to Britain, who would pay any price to retain as much of it as possible. That American trade was the principal prop of the British economy and therefore of her military and naval power had been the fervent belief of colonial Americans. They had confidently anticipated that if the colonies broke off trade with Britain they could bring her to her knees. Many British people had concurred. Notwithstanding the experiences of the war, such beliefs were still uncritically accepted by Americans who assumed that the balance of power between the European states depended on their access to American trade. If Britain recovered her old dominant position in American trade, she would be able to assert her hegemony over her rivals.[28] To break this dominance was the reason that France had made war on Britain. On the other hand, were Britain to be excluded from American trade 'it would be her ruin, it would destroy her credit, dry away her revenues, suppress her manufactures, bring down

[24] To T. Pleasants, 8 May 1786, Boyd et al. (eds), *Jefferson Papers*, IX, p. 472.
[25] To N. Tracy, 17 August 1785, ibid. VIII, p. 399.
[26] To Lafayette, 29 January 1789, Abbot et al. (eds), *Washington Papers: Presidential Series*, I, pp. 263–4.
[27] Undelivered Inaugural Address [April 1789], ibid. II, p. 172.
[28] James H. Hutson, 'Early American Diplomacy: A Reappraisal' in L. S. Kaplan (ed.), *The American Revolution and 'A Candid World'* (Kent, OH, 1977), pp. 52–4.

her naval force and half depopulate her kingdom', according to John Adams.[29] Britain therefore had no realistic alternative to agreeing to the reasonable terms America would offer in order to recover an appropriate share in this immensely valuable trade. Her refusal to negotiate terms seemed to indicate that her rulers were driven by irrational motives of revenge rather than calm calculations of self interest. Realistic advice, like that from London of Jeremiah Wadsworth, who had made a great fortune out of supplying the Continental Army, that Americans were 'fools' to suppose that British would not pursue their own interest or that they 'can't do without us and that we can bring them to do what we please by scolding', had little effect.[30] The sense that in her power to impose embargoes on British trade America had the ultimate weapon to bring Britain to heel endured at least until the War of 1812.

The restoration of commercial relations was indeed a major British objective in any peace settlement with America. Lord Shelburne professed to be as committed an adherent to doctrines of free trade and to reciprocal treaties as any of the American elite. He would have offered the Americans terms which would have been generally to their satisfaction. He had a political agenda as well. He hoped that commercial concessions would be a way of softening the consequences of American independence and preserving some kind of continuing close association or even a 'federal union'.[31] Other opinions less favourable to American views and more sceptical of the overwhelming importance of American trade were, however, beginning to be heard in Parliament, in the press and in pamphlets, of which by far the most influential was Lord Sheffield's *Observations on the Commerce of the American States*, first published in 1783 and reissued in the following year in a greatly expanded version.

There was virtual unanimity in Britain on the desirability of reviving the direct transatlantic trade to the fullest possible extent. Britain should strive to remain the entrepôt for the distribution of American commodities throughout Europe and she should re-establish her dominance of the American market for manufactured goods. Beyond that, however, those who thought like Lord Sheffield insisted that Britain had other interests that did not coincide with America's and on which she should not yield. The interest that Britain must protect at all costs was precisely the one which many Americans also wished to protect—shipping. Some argued that even under British rule colonial American shipping had been allowed to grow to the extent that it damaged Britain's own shipping industry. Independence gave Britain the chance to reverse this situation. Deprived of the one-third of its pre-war merchant marine which had been American, Britain must develop its own re-sources of ships and seamen to compensate. This meant excluding the Americans from participation in British imperial trades where their competition would damage

---

[29] To E. Jenings, 18 April 1782, Taylor et al. (eds), *Adams Papers*, XIV, p. 421.

[30] Letter to G. Morris, 6 April 1784, Ferguson et al. (eds), *Morris Papers*, IX, p. 233.

[31] He had invoked this concept in the negotiations for the main treaty and evidently saw it as the ultimate objective of a commercial treaty, see J. Pownall to Shelburne, 2 February 1783, TNA, PRO 30/8/343, f. 25.

the British shipping industry. By far the most important of such trades was that between the West Indies and North America, which the Americans valued so highly. By a Proclamation of July 1783 the United States was permitted to supply the British West Indies with a list of commodities that were essential to the islands' prosperity, but they could only be carried in British ships. Similar principles were applied to trade with Newfoundland, whose fisheries had been extensively supplied from the American colonies, and with the other remaining British North American colonies: only British ships could bring in American commodities.

Underlying the Proclamation of July 1783 and other restrictions on American commercial access to the British empire were certain assumptions that the Americans easily detected and generally regarded as hostile and derogatory. In the first place, Sheffield insisted that Americans were either British subjects or they were foreigners. Hopes, such as those of Shelburne, for some kind of privileged status for them through a continuing association with Britain were quite unreal and would be very damaging to Britain could they be realized. 'By asserting their independence', Sheffield concluded, 'the Americans have renounced the privileges as well as the duties of British subjects.' America had become 'a foreign country' and must be treated as such.[32] Those were also the sentiments of William Knox, now out of office but the self-confessed architect of the 1783 Proclamation. Americans had been given a choice as to whether they wished to remain within the empire or to secede from it. They had chosen to secede, so they were aliens no longer entitled to British commercial privileges.[33] Most of the American leadership had no desire whatsoever for the kind of continuing political association that Shelburne envisaged, but the apparent brusqueness with which they seemed to be dismissed as aliens who were to be denied any continuation of the commercial privileges within the empire which they greatly valued, deeply rankled with them. Secondly, Sheffield and his allies argued that there was no point in negotiating with the Americans or trying to devise a commercial treaty with them to settle new terms. Since Congress had no authority over trade under the Articles of Confederation, thirteen separate treaties would have to be arranged, which would be an impossible task. Instead of negotiating, Britain should therefore unilaterally impose its own terms. This might seem to be a hazardous process as it laid Britain open to retaliation, but this was not a prospect to be feared since the American states would be incapable of combining behind any coherent action to impose retaliatory duties. According to Sheffield, even 'the most strenuous Americans' admitted that.[34] Finally, there seemed to be the clear supposition that even if defending British shipping interests might be putting American trade as a whole at risk, the value of that trade had probably been exaggerated in the past and could now be coolly reassessed.

---

[32] *Observations on the Commerce of the American States with Europe and the West Indies* (London, 1783), p. 2.

[33] To J. Robertson, 6 February 1782, *Historical Manuscripts Commission: Various MSS*, VI, *Knox MSS* (London, 1909), pp. 182–3.

[34] To North, 3 November 1783, BL, Add MS 61863, f. 135.

John Adams reported 'a contempt for the American commerce' in British political circles.[35] He constantly heard that trade with America was 'of no importance'.[36] George Chalmers, a loyalist exile from Maryland who found government employment in Britain, was an example of an extreme sceptic about the value of American trade. 'We favoured and encouraged our colony commerce; we debilitated other branches of traffic, by withdrawing capital and investing it in our plantation trade; till the extent of our colony commerce became a deplorable evil.'[37] 'Europe has been long wild and extravagant in looking towards America for everything', Lord Sheffield thought.[38] Comments to the same effect appeared in the press. 'What are those mighty benefits of American commerce that so much noise is made about?' asked a newspaper at the end of the war.[39] Another prophesied that revived American trade would prove to be 'another South Sea Bubble' and concluded that 'if we had all their trade, it would contribute little to make Britain a great and powerful nation'.[40] Adam Smith's considered verdict was that he felt 'little anxiety about what becomes of the American commerce. By an equality of treatment to all nations, we might soon open a commerce with the neighbouring nations of Europe infinitely more advantageous than that of so distant a country as America.'[41] This was a logical conclusion from the argument in *The Wealth of Nations* that 'distant employments' tend to be 'less advantageous to the country' than nearer ones. Francis Baring, a great international merchant and financier, elaborated the argument further. American commerce was undoubtedly of major importance, but he believed that, were the volume of British trade with the United States and with a number of European countries more or less equal, the European trade was to be preferred. Money was not be tied up for long periods in it. European payments could be expected in from three to nine months time; American payments would only be made after twelve months at the earliest with 'an extension of credit ad infinitum'.[42] More robust commentators, like Josiah Tucker, repeated the opinion, widely held in British commercial circles, that not only did Americans expect long credit but that they were notoriously bad payers. They 'bought *English* merchandise when they knew they were not able and *never intended* to pay for them ... The bad debts of the *Americans* to this country, long before the present disturbances, were great beyond imagination.'[43]

---

[35] To J. Jay, 19 July 1785, Charles F. Adams (ed.), *The Works of John Adams*, 10 vols. (Boston, 1850–6), VIII, p. 281.

[36] To M. R. Morris, 2 March 1786, Giunta (ed.), *Emerging Nation*, III, p. 114.

[37] *Opinions on Interesting Subjects of Public Law and Commercial Policy; Arising from American Independence* (London, 1784), p. 120.

[38] *Observations on the Commerce of the American States*, new edn (London, 1784), p. 272.

[39] *Public Advertiser*, 15 April 1783.

[40] *Morning Chronicle*, 22 August 1783.

[41] To W. Eden, 15 December 1783, E. C. Mossner and I. S. Ross (eds), *The Correspondence of Adam Smith* (Oxford, 1987), p. 271.

[42] 'Thoughts upon a Commercial Treaty with America', prepared for Lord Shelburne, 23 February 1784, BL, Add MS 88906/1/3, f. 52.

[43] *Cui Bono*, 3rd edn (London, 1782), p. 76.

The experience of war had done much to shake old beliefs that the connection with America was essential to Britain's wealth and therefore to her naval and military power. Loss of most of the American market had not brought Britain to her knees. In the last years of the war Britain had held off a powerful coalition of enemies without an American contribution. 'The resources which have supported a war, so distant, so various, so expensive', Lord Sheffield wrote, 'have been superior to the expectation of the most sanguine. Our advantages may be ascribed to the strength and the spirit of this country.'[44] The most obvious evidence of Britain's economic strength was the continuing expansion of her manufacturing capacity. Silas Deane, once a leading figure in Congress but now a disgraced exile, believed that British people felt that they 'could do quite as well without us as we can without them' and saw no need for 'any more advances towards our ancient intercourse and friendship'. Even during the war he thought that the output of British manufactures was as high 'as at any former period', and he believed that it had 'greatly increased since the peace'.[45] By 1785, John Adams reported, the British could claim that 'the progress of fine arts in this kingdom has given their manufacturers a taste and skill, and to their productions an elegance, cheapness and utility, so superior to any others, that the demands for their merchandise from all parts of Europe is greater than ever'. Their capacity to sell goods all over the world 'disposes them to think little of American commerce'.[46] In 1787 an MP compared the former 'monopoly of America to an annuity upon an uncertain ill administered fund', while he welcomed the great increase in trade with France, to be expected after the commercial treaty of 1786, as 'a fee simple, with prompt and constant payment'.[47]

Scepticism about the supreme importance of the American market had some substance for the immediate post-war period. In the 1780s trade with America was relatively less dominant than it had been or was to be again. In the years 1784–6 the value of British exports to Europe was almost double the value of exports to the United States. From the 1790s, however, the importance of American trade to Britain was to grow markedly with the increasing disruption of European trade by war and with the rapid growth in the United States of a white population enjoying rising living standards and producing large agricultural surpluses available for export, which eventually included a great new staple, raw cotton. In the years 1794–6 the value of exports to America comfortably exceeded the value of exports to Europe.[48] The short-lived decline in the relative importance of American trade helped to smooth the way for those who wished to pursue agendas of restricting American access to the British empire in the name of imperial self-sufficiency and naval power. Powerful and articulate lobbies of American and West Indian merchants opposed them, but they had little success.

[44] *Observations on American Commerce*, pp. 5–6 fn.
[45] To Simeon Deane, 20 October 1783, 'The Deane Papers', *Collections of the Connecticut Historical Society*, XXIII (1930), 193.
[46] To J. Jay, 19 July 1785, Adams (ed.), *Adams Works*, VIII, p. 281.
[47] Frederick Montagu, 23 January 1787, *Parliamentary Register*, XXI, p. 5.
[48] Ralph Davis, *The Industrial Revolution in British Overseas Trade* (Leicester, 1979), p. 94.

Americans recognized that the British were obsessed with shipping and naval power, but some of them detected aims that went beyond a drive for national security and believed that they were actively seeking to damage the new America and to retard its growth. John Adams, as minister in London, was easily convinced of sinister designs against America. He thought the British aim was not 'so much the increase in their own wealth, ships and sailors, as the diminution of ours. A jealousy of our naval power is the true motive, the real passion which actuates them.'[49] 'The designs of ruining, if they can, our carrying trade, and annihilating all our navigation and seamen is too apparent.'[50] Resentment at supposed British hostility led to popular demonstrations in Boston and in Charleston, where a Marine Anti-Britannic Society took to the streets to voice its displeasure at the activities of British merchants. Belief in unremitting British hostility to the new America in the years after the war became, in Charles Ritcheson's phrase, 'a classic piece of national history', cherished by future generations, which in his fine study of the *Aftermath of Revolution* he convincingly cuts down to size.[51]

Ritcheson's case that British policy-making at the highest levels was unlikely to have been motivated by conscious hostility to the United States, even if there was not much goodwill, and that commercial restrictions were aimed primarily to protect British interests rather than to damage American ones seems irrefutable. American beliefs in British conspiracies against them were characteristic of the years leading up to the Revolution. Nevertheless, they now had some substance. Influential people who worked to shape British commercial policy towards America in the 1780s through writing pamphlets, lobbying ministers, or appearing as witnesses before a new Committee of the Privy Council for colonies and commerce in its hearings on American trade in 1784, were indubitably committed to rather more than the rebuilding of British overseas trade and shipping. To put it mildly, they were not friends of the new America. William Knox, author of the 1783 Proclamation and one of the committee's key witnesses, had been closely associated with coercive policies and the waging of the war and had lost land in America. He was a man of rancorous political hatreds against those who had opposed the war, above all against Lord Shelburne. He professed to take pride in measures which he hoped would strangle 'the navigation and maritime importance' of the United States at birth.[52] Charles Jenkinson, later Lord Hawkesbury, who chaired the new Committee of the Privy Council from 1784 and directed British commercial policy in the early years of Pitt's administration, had been totally committed to the war. He had spoken in 1782 of the need to do everything possible to curb the growth of American ports if America became independent.[53] Vincent Harlow, who greatly admired his work in encouraging British exports and shipping, described Jenkinson

[49] To J. Jay, 6 August 1785, Adams (ed.), *Adams Works*, VIII, p. 291.
[50] To T. Jefferson, 18 July 1785, Boyd et al. (eds), *Jefferson Papers*, VIII, p. 302.
[51] *Aftermath of Revolution: British Policy Towards the United States 1783–1795* (Dallas, TX, 1969), p. vii.
[52] To Walsingham, 20 August 1786, WLCL, Knox MSS, 7: 38.
[53] See above, p. 24.

as 'implacable and vindictive' towards America.[54] George Chalmers, clerk to the Committee of the Privy Council and pamphleteer, was a forced exile from Maryland. Thomas Irving provided Sheffield with 'all the authentic accounts' which he published in his pamphlet[55] and was star witness to the Committee of the Privy Council in 1784. He had been Inspector General of Imports and Exports in America, which gave him an unrivalled knowledge of colonial trade. At Boston he had twice been manhandled by mobs for his attempts to undermine American non-importation. He had been put in a revolutionary jail before he fled to Britain from his last official post in South Carolina.[56] He believed that keeping the Americans out of the West Indies would prevent their breaking away from their dependence on British credit through developing a trade in sugar to Europe.[57] He struck Gouverneur Morris when he met him in 1790 as still very 'decidedly opposed to America'.[58] Brook Watson, another witness before the committee, was self-appointed '*champion of the remaining colonies*' in North America against any concessions to the United States at their expense.[59] He became agent for New Brunswick and was much involved in the trade of the remaining British colonies; about a quarter of the trade with Quebec was reputed to be in his hands.[60] He thought that 'The United States have made themselves aliens', and he was 'clearly of the opinion it is for the interest of Great Britain to keep them so'.[61] Lord Sheffield was probably more detached and it seems unlikely that he wrote at the behest of anyone else. He was, however, part of the circle around Lord North and he was in particularly close contact on commercial matters with William Eden, who led the parliamentary attack on concessions to America.[62] For such people, impairing the growth of post-revolutionary America was a welcome concomitant to the strengthening of Britain.

II

In the last days of his administration Shelburne was considering the terms of a commercial treaty with America. He had consulted John Pownall, a very experienced official in the old Board of Trade, about what would be needed to form 'a federal union founded on the basis of mutual convenience and reciprocal

---

[54] *The Founding of the Second British Empire 1763–1793*, 2 vols. (London, 1952–64), II, p. 236.

[55] Walsingham to Sydney, 15 March 1784, WLCL, Sydney MSS, XI.

[56] See his memorial, TNA, AO 13/130, ff. 21–6. On him, see John J. McCusker, 'Colonial Civil Servant and Counter-revolutionary: Thomas Irving (1738?–1800) in Boston, Charleston and London', *Perspectives in American History*, XII (1979).

[57] Evidence, 16 April 1784, BL, Add MS 38388, f. 96.

[58] Diary, 9 April 1790, A. C. Morris (ed.), *Diary and Letters of Gouverneur Morris*, 2 vols. (London, 1889), I, p. 315.

[59] Cited in Ann Gorman Condon, *The Envy of the American States: The Loyalist Dream for New Brunswick* (Fredericton, NB, 1984), p. 61 fn.

[60] Entry on him by L. F. S. Upton, *Dictionary of Canadian Biography* (Toronto, 1983), V, p. 843.

[61] Evidence, 20 March 1784, BL, Add MS 38388, f. 35.

[62] See Eden's letters to him in BL, Add MS 45728.

advantage'.[63] Following Pownall's advice, a bill was prepared for 'the Provisional Establishment and Regulation of Trade' between Britain and America pending the signing of a commercial treaty. To 'evince the disposition of *Great Britain* to be on terms of the most perfect amity with the said United States of *America*, and in confidence of a like friendly disposition on the part of the said United States', the wartime prohibitions were to be scrapped at once. American goods would be allowed into Britain paying the same duties as British-owned goods and American ships might carry cargoes to the remaining British colonies, including the West Indies, and take their commodities back to the United States.[64] In the last days of the Shelburne administration William Pitt took charge of the bill in the House of Commons. Americans in London were critical of it. Only if its provisions were enlarged, William Lee warned Pitt, would it be interpreted as indicating the government's good intentions 'to bind the two countries for ever together in an indissoluble bond of mutual interest'.[65] Sadly for the Americans and for their well-wishers, the Shelburne government was on the point of giving way to a new one, to be formed by the coalition between Charles Fox and Lord North. Furthermore, debates in the House of Commons were revealing hostility to the bill. Objections were focusing on what concerned the Americans most, namely access for the their ships to the West Indies. Pitt's bill had apparently prompted Sheffield's *Observations*. Sheffield's points were taken up most vociferously by William Eden, a former member of the North administration. American shipping would take over the West Indian trade to 'the absolute destruction of our navy', he feared, since 600 British merchant ships would be displaced. 'He supposed that his national pride must sink with the sinking pride of the nation; but he was not yet brought so low as to be reconciled to the modern plan of gratuitous and endless concessions.'[66] The great merchant and banker Sir Robert Herries also spoke against giving the Americans the carrying trade to and from the West Indies.[67] A press campaign was mounted against the bill. 'An Old Merchant' saw in it 'the loss of our seamen, the decay of our shipping, the utter extinction of the Irish linen and provision trade, the destruction of our manufactures and the ruin of our navy'.[68] The bill went into committee and two amended versions were produced. On 2 April 1783, however, the Fox–North Coalition finally took office. On 9 April Charles Fox, now the minister responsible for relations with America, urged that further consideration of the bill be postponed. His intention was that negotiations should be conducted with the American commissioners in Paris and that further legislation should be based on the terms of a treaty.[69] In the meanwhile, a brief bill immediately to open 'intercourse between

[63] J. Pownall to Shelburne, 2 February 1783, TNA, PRO 30/8/343, f. 25.

[64] Sheila Lambert (ed.), *House of Commons Sessional Papers of the Eighteenth Century*, 145 vols. (Wilmington, DE, 1975), XXXV, pp. 71–4.

[65] 14 March 1783, W. C. Ford (ed.), *Letters of William Lee*, 3 vols. (New York, 1891), III, p. 936.

[66] 7 March 1783, *Parliamentary Register*, IX, pp. 433, 436.

[67] 11 March 1783, ibid. IX, p. 482.

[68] *Public Advertiser*, 15 March 1783.

[69] 9 April 1783, *Parliamentary Register*, IX, pp. 600, 601.

Great Britain and the United States of America' by removing the wartime prohibitions passed uncontested.[70]

Although Pitt's bill was lost, Americans were not discouraged. They regarded Fox, who had advocated unequivocal recognition of their independence in the past, as a firm ally. Henry Laurens, who was in London, was optimistic. Fox asked him whether the American commissioners were authorized to negotiate an agreement 'upon terms of reciprocity without delay'. He knew that David Hartley, the new British negotiator sent to Paris, was favourable to the Americans. He understood that Fox told Hartley that he wished for a treaty 'for the mutual admission of ships and merchandise free from any new duty or imposition'.[71] Orders in Council were issued aimed at restoring the direct trade between Britain and America on terms which were very favourable to the Americans. American raw materials could be imported into British ports on the same terms as those coming from the remaining British colonies and without paying alien duties. An important exception to protect British whale fisheries was, however, later made for fish and whale oil, which had to pay prohibitive foreign duties on coming into Britain. Certain American manufactures, notably naval stores, pearl ash, potash, and indigo, were also given privileged status. American tobacco was permitted to be landed in Britain at the old rates.[72] In subsequent Anglo-American controversy, much was to be made on the British side of the undoubted generosity of these terms, which put the Americans on a more favourable footing than any other foreign country enjoyed. On the issue of the utmost importance to the Americans the Cabinet had agreed that in any negotiated settlement the Americans should be allowed to bring their own produce to the British West Indies in their own ships.[73] On 2 July, however, an Order in Council was issued to which Americans took the strongest exception. It stated that American timber and provisions, with the important exceptions of fish and salted meat, could be imported into the West Indies and that certain items of West Indian produce could go to America, but in both cases only in 'British-built ships, owned by his Majesty's subjects, and navigated according to law'.[74] American ships were to be excluded. Laurens's immediate reaction was that 'it was an insult upon a free people'.[75] This was to be the view of most of the American leadership. Although the negotiations in Paris between Hartley and the American commissioners were to go on for a time, their fate was sealed.

[70] 23 Geo. III, c. 26.

[71] Laurens to R. R. Livingston, 5 April 1783, Philip M. Hamer et al. (eds), *The Papers of Henry Laurens*, 16 vols. (Columbia, SC, 1968–2003), XVI, pp. 175–6.

[72] Orders of 14 May, 6 June, 26 December 1783 in *London Gazette*, 13–17 May, 3–7 June, 23–7 December 1783.

[73] Cabinet minute, 8 April 1783, J. Fortescue (ed.), *Correspondence of King George III*, 6 vols. (London, 1927–8), VI, p. 349.

[74] *London Gazette*, 1–5 July 1783.

[75] To J. Mathews, 9 March 1784, Hamer et al. (eds), *Laurens Papers*, XVI, p. 412.

The Order in Council was the handiwork of William Knox, issued, he was assured, 'exactly as you drew it'.[76] He was called in by Lord North and later boasted that he had prevailed 'against the opposition of Mr Fox and Mr Burke and thereby saved the navigation and maritime importance of this country and strangled in their birth that of the United States'.[77] Why Fox allowed a political opponent, deeply implicated in the policies that had led to war, to take over the direction of matters that lay within his office as Secretary of State is puzzling. An attempted explanation was offered by Richard Champion, an old friend and confidant of Edmund Burke, who was close to events and would have gone as the first British Consul General to America if policies had not been changed. In a somewhat circumlocutory way, Champion suggested that Fox could not bring himself to give sufficient application to the subject and yielded to Knox's supposed expertise. Beyond that, although he was convinced that 'the Whig leaders in the administration' sincerely wanted 'a mutually beneficial treaty', Champion thought that they were fearful, with good reason as events were to show, of George III and believed that favours to America might precipitate a royal coup against the Coalition. They therefore went along with Knox's policies as a temporary measure, hoping to reverse them in the future.[78] That Fox hoped that the exclusion of American ships from the West Indies would be subject to later revision is confirmed by reported conversations with Henry Laurens. He said that the question would be resolved in the commercial treaty. He added that 'he had no objection to opening the West India trade to the Americans but there were many parties to please'.[79] In 1790 he was still telling a visiting American that he thought that 'we should be permitted to trade in our own bottoms' with the British West Indies.[80]

The Coalition ministry was only to last a few more months. It was succeeded in December 1783 by the administration of the younger Pitt. There were to be no further negotiations towards a commercial treaty for some years. John Adams took up his appointment as the first American minister to Britain in February 1785, but he was unable to persuade British ministers to settle commercial issues with him. The view of Sheffield and his friends that negotiations aiming at a commercial treaty with a disunited America were neither practical nor necessary seems to have become the accepted wisdom for several years.

Petitions against the proclamation of 2 July 1783 from West Indian interests, who considered that American food and American timber delivered in cheap American ships were essential to the islands' welfare, were submitted to a new Committee of the Privy Council with responsibility for trade and plantations under the chairmanship of Charles Jenkinson. It considered the matter for three months before reporting on 31 May 1784. The report fully endorsed the policy of the

---

[76] Sheffield to Knox, 3 July 1783, WLCL, Knox MSS, 7: 8.

[77] To Walsingham, 20 August 1786, ibid. 7: 38.

[78] *Comparative Reflections on the Past and Present Political, Commercial, and Civil State of Great Britain* (London, 1787), pp. 84–103.

[79] Laurens to American Ministers, 9 August 1783, Hamer et al. (eds), *Laurens Papers*, XVI, p. 251. Fox said the same in his instructions to Hartley (Harlow, *Second British Empire*, I, p. 462).

[80] Morris (ed.), *Diary and Letters of Gouverneur Morris*, I, p. 317.

Proclamation of 2 July 1783. In Richard Henry Lee's view, the committee had thereby endorsed 'the silly, malign commercial restraints upon our trade with their West India islands, that are to be found in Sheffield's book'.[81] Thomas Irving seems to have been the formative influence on the committee, much of his evidence about the necessity of keeping the Americans out of the West Indian carrying trade in order to build up British shipping and of the capacity of British ships to meet the needs of the West Indies being substantially reproduced in its report.[82] There were hopes that the report might not become government policy. Pitt's biographer considers it unlikely that the report was 'the kind of response he had in mind', even if he may not have been fully committed to the principles of the bill that had been entrusted to him by Shelburne.[83] Henry Laurens thought Pitt to be 'well disposed' to the American point of view.[84] Francis Baring, who was in close contact with Richard Atkinson, organizer of the West Indian campaign against the Proclamation and a man who had done much to bring Pitt into office, heard that Pitt 'wishes to parry as much as possible the report'. Small American ships would at least be allowed into the West Indies.[85] Laurens heard much the same.[86] The West Indians were apparently given assurances of relief on the very day that Pitt moved that the existing regulations remain unchanged.[87] After repeated renewals, they were to be made permanent in a statute of 1788. Whatever their personal views may have been, Pitt and his colleagues presumably felt little inclination to challenge the recommendations made by a committee set up by the administration. The Proclamation of July 1783 appeared to be winning popular endorsement and the post-war expansion of Britain's merchant marine could more or less plausibly be attributed to it. When questioned by Adams, Pitt replied that Britain's aim was to strengthen its own shipping not to weaken that of America. 'He said we could not think hard of them for encouraging their own shipwrights, their manufacturers of ships and their own whale fishery.'[88]

The report gave no countenance to long-held fears about the consequences of American independence, that is the development of a manufacturing capacity to challenge that of Britain. In the committee's view, 'The excellency of the manufactures of Great Britain, aided by the credit at which they can be sold will force a vent through every obstacle that can be opposed to them.'[89] Informed opinion generally considered that any development of a large-scale manufacturing capacity in America was a remote possibility. Suspicions of supposed American designs to 'seduce' British artisans and filch machinery were, however, rife. The *London Gazette* published in February 1784 a threatening reminder of the penalties

[81] To J. Madison, 20 November 1784, Hutchinson et al. (eds), *Madison Papers*, VIII, p. 145–6.
[82] BL, Add MS 38388, ff. 68–72, 92–9.
[83] John Ehrman, *The Younger Pitt: The Years of Acclaim* (London, 1969), p. 335.
[84] To J. Jervais, 24 April 1784, Hamer et al. (eds), *Laurens Papers*, XVI, p. 441.
[85] To Shelburne, 25 May 1784, BL, Add MS 88906/1/1, f. 131.
[86] To T. Mifflin, 24 April 1784, Hamer et al. (eds), *Laurens Papers*, XVI, p. 442.
[87] Baring to Shelburne, 28 July 1784, BL, Add MS 88906/1/1, f. 146.
[88] To J. Jay, 25 August 1785, Adams (ed.), *Adams Works*, VIII, p. 307.
[89] BL, Add MS 38388, f. 153.

under two existing acts to which anyone who was 'in any ways concerned or instrumental in the sending or enticing of artificers or manufacturers out of this kingdom' was liable.[90] Penalties on the shipping out of artisans or machinery for the manufacture of iron or steel were strengthened by an Act of 1785, which was angrily denounced by John Adams as yet more evidence of British determination to shackle the growth of the United States.[91] The development of manufacturing in America was monitored by British consuls. In 1789 the consul at Philadelphia reported that 'many useful domestic' manufactures had been established, but that few items 'which require art, labour and expence' were being produced. It would take 'a series of centuries' for the United States to become a major industrial power. Care should, however, be taken to prevent the 'decoying [of] useful artificers' or the export of machinery.[92] Another consul wrote that American woollen cloth was now up to the standard of the English second grade, that basic metal goods were widely made and that glass and paper manufacturing were established.[93] When the Committee of the Privy Council reported again on Anglo-American trade in 1791 it found samples of American cotton goods submitted to it sadly wanting and still remained unconvinced that Britain had anything to fear from American manufactures 'at least for a long course of years'.[94]

The Proclamation of 2 July 1783 was the linchpin of the policy of protecting British shipping, but it was supplemented by measures excluding American shipping from other parts of the empire in addition to the West Indies. The supply of Newfoundland was an important issue. The growing community of British fishing people who increasingly resided there permanently had before the Revolution drawn most of what they consumed from the thirteen colonies, above all from New England. The Committee of the Privy Council considered that they could not reasonably be deprived of food and timber from the United States but that these must now come to them exclusively in British ships. Their report was embodied in a statute of 1785. From 1788 the import of American supplies in British ships required a special licence from the governor. Quebec and Nova Scotia had also imported much of their food from the thirteen colonies. The strategists of a self-sufficient empire assumed that the two colonies would soon be able not only to feed themselves but to begin to replace the United States as the chief supplier of the British West Indies with food and timber. The 1784 report had confidently predicted this, but it proved to be at best a distant prospect. In the immediate aftermath of the war and with the influx of some 30,000 loyalists, the governor of Nova Scotia felt that he had no alternative to legalizing the import of 'fresh provisions' from New England.[95] In 1785 the Committee of the Privy Council ordered that they only be admitted in British ships. This became the rule for the new colony of New Brunswick almost from its establishment. From 1788

---

[90] *London Gazette*, 7–10 February 1784.
[91] To J. Jay, 28 August 1785, Giunta (ed.), *Emerging Nation*, II, p. 776.
[92] P. Bond to Leeds, 16 November 1789, TNA, FO 4/8, ff. 154–8.
[93] J. Temple to Leeds, 23 September 1789, TNA, FO 4/7, ff. 203–4.
[94] Report of 28 January 1791, TNA, FO 4/9, f. 128.
[95] J. Parr to Sydney, 29 September 1784, TNA, CO 217/56, ff. 234–5.

American imports for both colonies in British ships also required a governor's licence. The situation of Quebec was complicated by a long land frontier with the United States across which the movement of goods could not be controlled. All trade between the United States and Quebec by sea was forbidden but overland trade was permitted, except for the export of furs from British territory.[96]

The effective enforcement of regulations to keep American ships out of British colonial trades either in the West Indies or in the northern colonies depended on customs officials being able to distinguish American ships from British ones. This was in fact extremely difficult. Ships were often owned by Anglo-American partnerships and by holding double sets of papers they could be made to appear to be either British or American as the law of either country might require.[97] It proved to be virtually impossible to distinguish British from American seamen. The American correspondent of a British minister wrote exultantly:

> We are the compleatest and most enterprizing merchants this side of the equator, no laws you can pass or the severest restrictions you can establish, can restrain us, we have now British ships, British registers, British certificates, British oaths authenticated with British seals, British subjects with certificates of their birth, British Mediterranean passes, and names on their sterns.

He readily admitted that he was 'part owner of one of these vessels that trade between [New York] and your islands'.[98] Jenkinson, who had heard that 'thirty pounds were publicly advertised for a British register in the American newspapers' was determined to take action against the 'astonishing ... impositions ... practised by the American shippers'.[99] Action took the form of a new Navigation Act passed in 1786. New systems of registration and documentation were to be enforced so that 'the entire merchant marine of the empire' was 'brought under scrutiny in order that all concealed aliens might be extruded and trading privileges effectively confined to ships built as well as owned by British subjects'.[100] John Adams commented sourly that 'Mr Jenkinson, an old friend of the British empire, is still at his labours', spreading 'poverty, weakness and ruin'.[101] Whether Jenkinson's regulations could succeed in disrupting the ingenious arrangements that British and American merchants had devised to overcome the effects of the sundering of the British empire seems, however, to be unlikely. There were to be many reports of continuing evasions.

The restrictions laid on American trade with British possessions, especially with the West Indies, seem to have been genuinely popular in Britain. One of Shelburne's contacts 'scarce met one man used to trade' who was willing to give up the West Indian carrying trade, 'the bigotry in favour of the Navigation Act being with

---

[96] On the trade with the United States of the British North American colonies, see Gerald S. Graham, *Sea Power and British North America 1783–1820* (Cambridge, MA, 1941).

[97] P. Bond to Carmarthen, 21 February 1787, TNA, FO 4/5, f. 52.

[98] P. A[llaire] to G. Yonge, 6 December 1784, TNA, FO 4/4, f. 387.

[99] 15 February 1785, *Parliamentary Register*, XVII, p. 172.

[100] Harlow, *Second British Empire*, II, p. 267.

[101] To J. Bowdoin, 9 May 1786, Giunta (ed.), *Emerging Nation*, III, p. 164.

such *universal*'.[102] Jenkinson was told by a correspondent from the tobacco port of Whitehaven that: 'To prevent [American] ships from admission into the British islands and colonies is indubitably the cornerstone on which the commerce of this country must build.'[103] Nevertheless, the policy of restriction had opponents. As was of course fully expected, West Indian planters and merchants were outraged by having, as they saw it, the great damage done to them by the war compounded by the imposition of excessively high prices for the American food and timber that were essential to them. They argued that British shipping could not possibly maintain the volume of imports that they needed and that the use of large and expensive British ships would force the prices even higher. Members of the West India Committee in Britain put their case in Parliament, in interviews with ministers, and in a barrage of pamphlets. The committee insisted that 'Nothing but the unlimited permission of navigation by American ships between the American dominions and the sugar colonies can permanently support the true interest of this country.'[104] The assemblies in the islands were even more forthright. The Antigua assembly called the Proclamation of 2 July 1783 'a measure replete with mischief and pregnant with our future ruin'.[105]

Some Americans hoped if the states took retaliatory measures, a revival of 'the spirit which dictated the non importation agreement' against British merchandise of the 1760s and 1770s would lead to mass boycotting of imports through British ships. This would revive 'the idea of national honor and glory', inciting America to rely 'on her own ships and mariners',[106] or it would at least induce British merchants trading to America to put pressure on the government to modify the restrictions. Jefferson exulted that actions against British trade in Massachusetts had 'produced a sensation among the God-dem-mees'.[107] The situation in the 1780s was, however, entirely different from what it had been during the Revolution. Congress did not have the power to make commercial policy and popular pressure on the individual states to take action against the British was patchy as was the response of the states. Willingness to renounce British goods imported on British ships did not become a mark of political virtue as it had been in the past. Seven middle and New England states did, however, impose discriminatory tonnage duties against British ships and tariffs were laid by some states on imported foreign manufactures, which of course fell most heavily on Britain. Such actions were resented in Britain. The committee of British merchants trading with America complained in 1787 that their effects 'begin to be severely felt'.[108] There was, however, no concerted pressure in Britain either for retaliatory duties on American shipping or for any relaxation of the exclusion of American shipping from British

[102] B. Vaughan to Shelburne, 4 January 1784, BL, Add MS 88906/1/20, f. 16.

[103] S. Martin, 24 February 1786, BL, Add MS 38219, f. 30.

[104] Minutes of 27 February 1784, TNA, BT 6/84, f. 109.

[105] Address of 9 October 1783, ibid. f. 139.

[106] R. King to J. Adams, 2 November 1785, Paul H. Smith (ed.), *Letters of Delegates to Congress, 1774–1789*, 26 vols. (Washington DC, 1976–2000), XXII, p. 715

[107] To N. Tracy, 17 August 1785, Boyd et al. (eds), *Jefferson Papers*, VIII, p. 398–9.

[108] Memorial of 30 March 1787, TNA, BT, 6/20, f. 422.

colonies, an issue on which the West Indian merchants were left to fight alone. The repayment of American debts owing from before the war was, it would seem, for British merchants a much more important issue. On that they campaigned persistently.

Even if there was no organized public opposition to imposing restrictions on American trade, the new policies still had their critics. Adam Smith's view was that trade between the independent United States and the British colonies should 'go on as before'. Any 'interruption or restraint of commerce' would hurt the British colonies more than it would hurt the Americans.[109] Francis Baring considered that a pamphlet written to counter Sheffield by Richard Champion was 'much nearer the truth' than Sheffield's book.[110] Champion's pamphlet was based on the assumption that 'the grandeur of our empire' had been founded on the old commercial connection with America and that Britain's future grandeur required that connection to be restored as fully as might be possible. Belief that the United States must be treated as a foreign country 'probably proceeds from a deeply rooted systematic animosity' and any design to force America to submit to British regulations was mere 'infatuation'. On the vital issue of shipping, Britain needed American ships. 'We cannot preserve our carrying trade' without them; Britain did not have enough of its own. Britain should incorporate American ships into its system rather than exclude them.[111] In a manuscript paper of 'Observations' Champion elaborated his views. American-built ships, part-owned by British merchants with British crews should be treated as British. With 'a very little encouragement' to the Americans, 'we should have the advantage of colonies and of their increasing wealth without the expence of maintaining them'.[112] Francis Baring agreed with Champion on many points. In his view, what was needed to restore Britain's trade were 'the most liberal and manly exertions, . . . instead of which the proposed regulations would disgrace a haberdasher or even a custom house clerk'.[113] He mistakenly believed that British ships could be built at much the same price as American ones and in any case, even more mistakenly, he assumed that the American states were too poor to sustain large mercantile marines. No 'sober experienced merchant', he believed, could envisage American dominance in Europe's carrying trade.[114] Little was therefore to be feared from competition from American shipping and he saw no great harm in giving their ships access to the British West Indies, although their trade with the fisheries should be restricted as far as possible.

---

[109] To W. Eden, 15 December 1783, Mossner and Ross (eds), *Correspondence of Adam Smith*, p. 271.
[110] To Shelburne, 12 June 1784, BL, Add MS 88906/1/1, f. 137.
[111] *Considerations on the Present Situation of Great Britain and of the United States of America with a View to their Future Commercial Connexions*, 2nd edn (London, 1784), pp. v, 20, 173, 190.
[112] 'Observations on American Independence', March 1784, BL, Add MS 59238, ff. 35–7.
[113] To Shelburne, 18 May 1784, BL, Add MS 88906/1/1, f. 127.
[114] 'Thoughts upon a Commercial Treaty', 25 February 1784, BL, Add MS 88906/113, ff. 49–52. Baring also explained his views on American trade to Shelburne in a letter of 30 May 1784, BL, Add MS 88906/1/1, ff. 133–4.

Sheffield, Knox, Jenkinson, and their acolytes, however, captured the making of policy in the 1780s. Whether, viewed from Britain's point of view, their policies were salutary measures necessary to restore British shipping or were largely unnecessary irritants to American sensitivities is an issue that has divided historians as much as it divided contemporaries. Charles Ritcheson believed that what he calls the 'hard-headed empirical men' who produced the measures 'served their nation well'.[115] That his 'empirical men' seem to have been as ideologically driven in their own way as any American, does not necessarily invalidate his case. As chapter 13 will show, British merchant shipping did indeed grow rapidly, even if this growth may not have owed much to the regulations against the Americans. On the other hand, Vincent Harlow, a historian not much inclined to wear liberal sentiments on his sleeve, considered that the regulations did damage 'out of all proportion to the mercantile gain' and that 'from this false start friction between Britain and the United States would grow and spread and lead on in due course to the war of 1812'.[116] Harlow's ultimate conclusion was close to that of Richard Champion. Britain needed American shipping and could incorporate it into an imperial system that was moving towards free trade.

In the short term, the fears of Lord Sheffield and those who thought like him that America would become a dangerous maritime rival to Britain seem to have been vindicated. From the 1790s the volume of American shipping increased very greatly and its relative cheapness offered formidable competition to British shipping. When officially given the chance under conditions of European war after 1794, the Americans completely took over the supply of the West Indies and shipped much foreign West Indian sugar to Europe. British sugar interests complained bitterly of lost markets. In the face of American competition, the exports of the British North American colonies languished. They lost most of their trade in supplying the West Indies and the war greatly diminished their exports of fish to Europe, while, as neutrals, the American fisheries flourished.[117] From 1807 vigorous countermeasures were taken to exclude the Americans from British imperial trades. Nevertheless, in the long run Champion was probably vindicated. A strong American merchant marine proved to be an advantage to Britain. American shipping performed valuable services for Britain during the wars. Much British trade in American ships passed as neutral and the British army in Spain was largely sustained by American supplies brought in American ships. After 1815 there was much less conflict between American trade and British interests. Both during and after the wars, 'a close relationship' developed 'between the prosperity of Britain and of American sea-borne trade'. The great bulk of the

---

[115] *Aftermath of Revolution*, p. 17.

[116] *Second British Empire*, I, p. 487.

[117] François Crouzet, 'America and the Crisis of the British Imperial Economy, 1803–1807' in John J. McCusker and Kenneth Morgan (eds), *The Early Modern Atlantic Economy* (Cambridge, 2000), pp. 278–315. See also Crouzet, 'Variations on the North Atlantic Triangle from York-town to Waterloo' in Crouzet, *Britain Ascendant: Comparative Studies in Franco-British Economic History* (Cambridge, 1990), pp. 318–40.

huge quantities of British manufactured exports to the United States were carried in American shipping. America's capacity to pay for these goods depended to a large extent on the earnings of her shipping and on the returns from her trade with Europe.[118] Champion's and Shelburne's visions of the future of Anglo-American trade ultimately proved to be prescient.

---

[118] Crouzet, 'America and the Crisis of the British Imperial Economy', pp. 306–7.

6

Imperial Frameworks

I

British opinion seems to have become reconciled relatively easily to the loss of the thirteen colonies as, at least in retrospect, the advantages of dominion over them came to be seen as a questionable proposition. Yet at the moment that independence was formally conceded few doubted the magnitude of what that involved. American independence would, George III was sure, 'anihilate the rank in which the British empire stands among the European states'.[1] The loss of America, a pamphleteer wrote, had sunk Britain's 'consequence among the nations' and had 'severed her from the noblest continent that ever formed an appendage of empire'.[2] Even Lord Shelburne, who professed to doubt the value of territorial empire, believed that Britain was parting with 'the grand source of wealth, industry and power'.[3] Most gloomy prophecies at the end of the war assumed that the loss of the thirteen colonies would begin an unravelling of Britain's imperial network, much of which, most obviously Ireland, the West Indian plantations, and the north Atlantic fisheries, was closely linked to them.

The loss of the thirteen colonies prompted questions as to what would be the future of empire without them. Some commentators took a fatalistic view. Their the loss seemed to be yet another illustration of widely held maxims about the transitory nature of empires, including that of the British. Over-expansion was their inevitable fate. Driven by an irresistible urge for expansion, empires outgrew their capacity effectively to govern outlying provinces which eventually threw off their rule. It was another maxim, notably propounded by David Hume, that the empires of free peoples, such as the British, were likely to be particularly transitory because free people were especially prone to oppress their subjects. 'What is there so beneficial to mankind in mighty empires, as to make us regret, on principles of impartial justice and general humanity, the diminution of our own?' asked Richard Watson, the mildly radical Bishop of Llandaff, in a sermon to the House of Lords at the end of the American War. 'When by conquest or colonization they become so large, that all the parts of them cannot equally participate in the benefit of civil

---

[1] To North, 21 January 1782, J. Fortescue (ed.), *The Correspondence of King George III*, 6 vols. (London, 1927–8), V, p. 334–5.
[2] *Remarks upon the Report of a Peace in Consequence of Mr Secretary Townshend's Letter to the Lord Mayor of London*, 2nd edn (London, 1783), pp. 5–6.
[3] To A. Fitzherbert, 20 December 1782, WLCL, Shelburne MSS, 71 p. 352.

union, it is the extreme of folly to expect, that the parts which are oppressed should wish for the continuance of that union.' The empire of a free people must 'from its very nature be limited in its extent'. Britain must accept her inescapable fate without seeking compensation in aggrandizement in India or any other part of the world. But the British, stripped of colonies, could still expect to remain 'a great and powerful people, though fallen from the summit of greatness which is seldom productive of virtue'.[4]

If colonies were, as the American case had shown, always likely to be transitory possessions, and if, as Adam Smith and Josiah Tucker, had been arguing for some years, the balance sheet of colonies was likely to show loss rather than profit, was the unravelling of empire not a prospect to be welcomed rather than dreaded? Tucker certainly thought that it was. Any attempt to settle colonies 'for the sake of monopolizing, or exclusive trade', he wrote in 1783, was 'the arrantest cheat, and self-deception, which poor short-sighted mortals ever put on themselves'.[5] The remaining colonies should be got rid of forthwith. The experience of the American War could be interpreted as clear evidence that colonial trade was not indispensable to Britain's greatness. Serious disruptions to oceanic trade caused hardship but they had not crippled the British economy as a whole. Nor had the loss of colonies seriously impaired the British government's ability to borrow huge sums of money with which to wage war. It was 'not territorial dominion that forms the basis of the credit of England', a newspaper commented.[6] Lord Hawke, son of the great admiral, told the House of Lords that the 'commerce and naval power of this country, are not founded on the sands of America but they are raised on the solid rock of national situation, national industry and national courage'.[7] After the war comparisons were made of the benefits of trans-oceanic trades as opposed to what might be the more advantageous short-haul European ones.

Questions were also asked about the proper balance for Britain between global and European diplomatic and military commitments. In the wars of the mid eighteenth century, supported by continental allies who had fought France in Europe, Britain had been able to maintain a naval superiority which had given her great victories. In spite of what contemporaries regarded as Britain's extraordinary resilience in holding her foes at bay in the closing stages of the American War, much had clearly gone wrong. In a letter of 1786, William Knox analysed these failings in terms which most historians would probably now endorse. Britain had lost her naval supremacy to France and Spain for a long period and she had fought the war without a continental ally. It was now high time, he argued, to bring to an end 'the delusion' that Britain could be 'the supreme maritime power' on its own. To remedy this situation he urged that Britain should stop assuming that France and Spain were irreconcilable enemies and try to come to terms with them. If that

---

[4] *A Sermon Preached before the Lords Spiritual and Temporal...*, *on Friday, 30 January 1784* (London, 1784), pp. 17, 20.

[5] *Four Letters on Important National Subjects Addressed to the Right Honourable Earl of Shelburne* (Gloucester, 1783), p. 10.

[6] *Morning Herald*, 8 August 1782.

[7] 5 December 1782, *Parliamentary Register*, XI, p. 9.

strategy failed, Britain should seek other European allies. He urged an approach to Russia.[8] Knox was by no means alone in being willing to seek better relations with the Bourbon powers and in his conviction that Britain needed continental allies. The lesson that Britain had unduly neglected Europe in the years before the Revolution and had paid a price for that neglect in the war seemed undeniable to contemporaries. After the war, little progress was made in bringing about a reconciliation with the Bourbon powers, beyond the free-trade treaty of 1786 with France, but Britain was able to gain a continental ally in Prussia.

If a turning towards Europe both in trade and defence was a legacy of the American Revolution, this did not, however, mean that there was a turn away from empire in British economic, diplomatic or military preoccupations. In the later eighteenth century few contemporaries saw empire or Europe as competing alternatives. If Britain was to pursue a more active European policy, seeking allies to whom subsidies might have to be paid, deploying squadrons in European waters, and even committing her own troops on the continent, it was firmly believed that she must nurture the financial resources which made such things possible. In spite of some doubts raised by the American War, these were still presumed to come from her maritime trade in which empire played so large a part. The wealth generated by the West Indies and by India was needed to sustain whatever European strategies Britain might develop after 1783. Knox was in no doubt about that. 'Foreign commerce I consider as the great means of political strength and the peculiar source of that branch of it which consists in a naval force.'[9] There could be no cutting back of the resources committed for the defence of empire. British ministers were soon to write of India in terms that their predecessors had used about America. In India 'perhaps the future existence of Great Britain as an independent, at any rate as a respectable power' was at stake, one commented in 1784.[10] In the war against Revolutionary France, massive resources were to be devoted to campaigns in the West Indies and terrible losses of men were to be incurred. This was justified by the maxim propounded by Henry Dundas that 'Great Britain can at no time propose to maintain an extensive and complicated war, but by destroying the colonial resources of our enemies and adding proportionately to our commercial resources, which are, and must ever be, the sole basis of our maritime strength.'[11]

The loss of the thirteen colonies may have brought to the surface some doubts about Britain's role as a worldwide imperial power, but there were few advocates of total withdrawal from empire. The Enlightenment critique of empire as economically counter-productive and as based on oppression that was bound to provoke rebellion and the independence of colonies might have its adherents in British intellectual circles, but it was nearly always applied to calls for the reform of the

---

[8] To W. Eden, 7 January 1786, WLCL, Knox MSS, 7: 26.
[9] To W. Eden, 7 January 1786, WLCL, Knox MSS, 7: 26.
[10] Carmarthen to Dorset, 9 July 1784, TNA, FO 27/12, f. 149.
[11] Henry Dundas in 1799, cited in Michael Duffy, *Soldiers, Sugar and Seapower: The British Expeditions to the West Indies and the War against Revolutionary France* (Oxford, 1987), p. 371.

empire rather than for abolishing it.[12] This was generally the view even with those who had been most critical of the American War. At a meeting of the electors of Westminster in March 1783 John Jebb, an ultra political radical opposed to empire in principle, who 'rejoiced' at America's separation,[13] proclaimed that he welcomed every loss of territory as a result of the war since it diminished 'the scope of despotism and tyranny'. He was answered by Charles Fox, one of the fiercest parliamentary critics of the war, who insisted that retreat from empire was not the necessary consequence of the loss of America. It was 'much more for the interests of the country, to amend a bad system, or repeal an improvident act,[14] than to abandon extensive territories'. He condemned Shelburne's peace for having made concessions 'in all quarters of the globe beyond all precedents'.[15] As Foreign Secretary under Rockingham, Fox had hoped to bargain the independence of America with France in return for the retention of the rest of Britain's colonial possessions as they had been at their fullest extent at the end of the Seven Years War.

Well before the ending of the war and in the peace settlements that followed it, Britain's rulers had made it manifest that they had every intention of retaining a worldwide empire and had given clear indications as to where their imperial priorities now lay. Ireland was the highest priority, even though the British position there had been gravely weakened in the last years of the American War. Then Ireland had been stripped of troops to fight overseas to the point that no effective resistance could be mounted against the huge body of Volunteers who seized the opportunity both to defend Ireland from foreign invasion and to enable Irish politicians to extract concessions from Britain with a thinly veiled threat of force. In what was seen as amounting to a bloodless revolution, the Irish parliament had forced British recognition in 1782 of the nominal legislative independence of Ireland. Far from passively accepting a new relationship with Ireland, post-war British policies were, however, to be devoted to limiting any effective weakening of Britain's hold over Ireland.

In the later stages of war, resources were poured into the West Indies and India. It is from the East and the West Indies, George III later wrote, that Britain was 'to expect any chance of putting this country into any flourishing state' after the loss of America.[16] As early as 1778, a British diplomat was urging that the army should evacuate North America in order to 'fall upon St Domingo, Martinico, Cuba, and force a free trade in the Gulph of Mexico, the straight road to the gold and silver mines, the sugar islands, and the revolt of the Spanish settlements'. 'Our

---

[12] On enlightened thought and empire, see Jennifer Pitts, *A Turn to Empire: The Rise of Imperial Liberalism in Britain and France* (Princeton, NJ, 2005) and Anthony Pagden, *Lords of All the World: Ideologies of Empire in Spain, Britain and France c.1500- c.1800* (New Haven, CT, 1995).

[13] Conversation with William Smith, Smith's Diary, 27 October 1784, L. F. S. Upton (ed.), *The Diary and Selected Papers of Chief Justice William Smith 1784–1793*, 2 vols. (Toronto, 1963–5), I, p. 156.

[14] He was referring to the Quebec Act of 1774 that Jebb had cited as a prime instance of 'despotism and tyranny'.

[15] Report of meeting on 7 March 1783, *Parker's General Advertiser*, 8 March 1783.

[16] To Shelburne, 14 September 1782, Fortescue (ed.), *Correspondence of George III*, VI, p. 126.

Presbyterian colonies will be more than compensated for', he added.[17] When the mainland of North America and the West Indies came into competition for military resources after France joined in the war, the higher priority was given to the West Indies and troops were diverted there from America. A large part of the Royal Navy was operating in the Caribbean by the end of the war. There was virtual unanimity that Jamaica was the most valuable of all British possessions and must be defended at all costs. The great naval victory of the Saintes in 1782 ensured that it would not be lost. The case for the smaller islands was made at the end of the war by Sir Charles Middleton, the reforming Comptroller of the Navy. St Kitts, recently conquered by the French, was 'in more than metaphor a mine of gold'. He considered the 'West Indies trade' to be 'not only a great nursery of seamen, but by the immense revenue arising from its produce, a great support of the navy'.[18] The British position in India must also be retained. In the later stages of the war, Henry Dundas, who was later to make India the centre-piece of his career in public life, argued that it was now becoming 'the chief seat of war'. He asked whether 'the stores and treasure of this country would be best bestowed there, or upon inland skirmishes in the woods of America'. India, he considered, had become 'our last resource'.[19] The British naval squadron in Asian waters was strengthened and ten royal regiments were eventually deployed in India to reinforce the East India Company's own army.

In the peace negotiations Lord Shelburne offered very generous terms to the Americans, but he did his utmost to restrict French gains in the West Indies and in India. He succeeded in recovering all those British islands that had been taken by the French, with the exception of Tobago, given up to get them out of Dominica. The main Bahamas settlement was restored to Britain by Spain. Shelburne contemplated deals with the Spanish that would have given Britain large gains in the Caribbean. Puerto Rico as well as the retention of the Floridas with French islands thrown in, might be the price of surrendering Gibraltar, even though the heroics of the defence of the Rock meant that such an exchange would provoke tumultuous popular opposition. The king believed that such a deal would have been 'highly advantageous to this kingdom'.[20] He would 'wish to have as much possession in the West Indies as possible'.[21] In the peace negotiations the French tried to extract grants of territory around their Indian settlements. Shelburne stubbornly resisted such propositions, restricting cessions to barely significant levels. He was happy to concede full commercial access to India to the French, but he would not permit them to acquire territory on any scale that might enable them to challenge British political supremacy.[22]

[17] H. Elliot to W. Eden, 28 March 1778, cited in Adrian J. Pearce, *British Trade with Spanish America 1763–1808* (Liverpool, 2007), p. 78.

[18] To Shelburne, 27 August 1782, BL, Add MS 88906/3/16, f. 135.

[19] To C. Jenkinson, 10, 27 August 1781, BL, Add MS 38192, ff. 14, 16.

[20] To Shelburne, 21 November 1782 Fortescue (ed.), *Correspondence of George III*, VI, p. 159.

[21] To Shelburne, 11 December 1782, ibid. VI, p. 183.

[22] Vincent T. Harlow, *The Founding of the Second British Empire, 1763 to 1793*, 2 vols. (London, 1952–64), I, pp. 367–8.

The commitments affirmed in the later stages of the war and in the peace negotiations were to be enduring ones. Ireland, the West Indies, and India were the main concerns of the post-war British empire. The remaining British North American colonies, defended at great cost during the war and the haven for a large migration of loyalist refugees, became an additional commitment that could not be evaded, although, apart from the Newfoundland fisheries, the scale of their contribution to Britain's wealth and power for the foreseeable future seemed likely to be a very limited one.

Even without dominion over the thirteen colonies, the Atlantic retained its dominant position in Britain's assessment of her worldwide interests after the war. Separate chapters will be devoted to the main components of Britain's Atlantic empire: Ireland, the West Indies together with projects for penetrating Spanish territory around the Caribbean and the Gulf of Mexico, and the remaining North American colonies.

If not yet seen as displacing the Atlantic, Britain's stake in Asia was playing an increasing part in her geopolitical calculations. By the early 1770s most of those in the mainstream of British political life had come to accept that Britain was irrevocably committed to an Indian empire.[23] The great volume of trade with India and China and the possession of valuable provinces—above all, of Bengal—from which the Company was able to collect huge sums in taxation, envisaged by contemporaries as a 'tribute', were seen as inextricably linked. The American War, in which Britain's Indian possessions were successfully defended, was further confirmation of the importance of Indian empire. Not only 'the profits on trade', but also 'the fortunes of individuals, remitted from India and placed in our funds and in circulation' were said to have played a crucial role in the financing of the war.[24] 'Certain it is', a pamphleteer wrote, 'that the encrease of duties and the general influx of wealth arising from our connection with India have proved a principal support of this country under the calamities it has of late years experienced, by sustaining the funds, supplying the defective circulation, and preventing such a depreciation of our land as would carry with it both private and public ruin.'[25]

Empire involved great liabilities. A hugely expensive army had to be maintained in India and the Company was prone to waging costly wars which undermined its financial stability. But the potential advantages of empire were too great to be renounced. Were the British to abandon their territorial possessions, the conventional view was that they would merely hand over to 'our natural enemies... advantages in that part of the world infinitely too important and too disadvantageous to us to be permitted'.[26]

[23] P. J. Marshall, *The Making and Unmaking of Empires: Britain, India and America c.1750–1783* (Oxford, 2005), pp. 199–200.

[24] A. Macaulay to Lewisham, 8 February 1783, *Historical Manuscripts Commission: Dartmouth MSS*, 3 vols. (London, 1887–96), III, p. 260.

[25] Cited in H. V. Bowen, *The Business of Empire: The East India Company and Imperial Britain, 1756–1833* (Cambridge, 2006), p. 41.

[26] Lord John Cavendish, 28 April 1783, *Parliamentary Register*, IX, p. 672.

Questions as to whether Britain would find compensation in India, where empire had been successfully defended in the war, for her losses in America and whether her ambitions after 1783 might undergo what historians have come to call 'a swing to the East', that is towards Asia and away from the Atlantic, were being freely discussed.[27] Some confident claims were made in the press about the future role of India. With the loss of America likely, it was thought, to entail the eventual loss of the West Indies, Asia was said to be 'the sole remaining source of our commerce and grandeur'.[28] India was 'in every instant rising in political and commercial consequence to Great Britain'. Properly governed, it 'bids fair to be a counterpoise to the western world'.[29] In the debate on his India Act of 1784 William Pitt said that the national importance of India had 'increased in proportion to the losses suffered by the dismemberment of other great possessions'.[30] Francis Baring, who was both a director of the East India Company and much concerned with American trade, had 'a variety of plans' in mind for India 'to improve a commerce fully sufficient to indemnify this country for the loss she has sustained from America'.[31]

Many, on the other hand, viewed the future prospects for empire in India with apprehension. The extent to which some Indian states with their armies trained and equipped in European ways were becoming formidable enemies was recognized. The British had wantonly provoked them to war and it was probable that in the near future they would seek 'to vindicate their own natural rights and to expel the Europeans for ever from their coasts'.[32] In discussing the likely direction of British policy after the war and of its consequences for America, James Monroe, later president of the United States, reflected something of contemporary doubts about Britain's future in India. He thought that it was unlikely that India would become the main focus of Britain's imperial ambitions. A huge indigenous population 'with but little attachment to the parent country' was a source of weakness. 'Will any eastern arrangement encrease the fleet or add to the army but to guard itself? . . . I am therefore of opinion that the court of London will still turn her attention to this continent in every consideration that she may have in view to add to or to increase her national strength.'[33]

By the last years of the war, there was almost universal agreement that if the British empire in India was to survive for any length of time, the East India Company and its government in India must be reformed and made more account-able to the British state and ultimately to Parliament. Reforms enacted in 1773 to

---

[27] This phrase was coined by Vincent Harlow. He meant by it 'a diversion of interest and enterprise from the Western World to the potentialities of Asia and Africa', which he detected throughout the later eighteenth century, not just after the loss of the American colonies (*Founding of the Second British Empire*, I, p. 62).

[28] *Public Advertiser*, 21 January 1783.

[29] Letter VI of 'Egbert' to the Earl of Shelburne, *Public Advertiser*, 11 March 1783.

[30] *Parliamentary Register*, XVI, p. 1.

[31] To Shelburne, 20 November 1783, BL, Add MS 88906/1/1, f. 91.

[32] 'National Affairs', *English Review*, II (1783), 239.

[33] To R. H. Lee, February 1784, Paul H. Smith (ed.), *Letters of Delegates to Congress, 1774–1789*, 26 vols. (Washington, DC, 1976–2000), XXI, pp. 394–5.

give the state a stake in the management of Indian affairs appeared to have been inadequate. State control must be strengthened so that a new order could be established which would enforce rigorous economy in India, prevent abuses, and, above all, strictly prohibit those wars against Indian powers which had brought the Company to bankruptcy. The Company must live within its means and at peace with its neighbours. Its corrupt and self-serving employees must be disciplined. A reformed Company would, it was hoped, generate great surpluses of wealth that could be transferred to Britain through its trade.

Within a very short time doubts about India's capacity to contribute to Britain's national strength were being allayed. The Company appeared to have been brought under effective state regulation. This was a highly contentious matter, since placing great new resources at the disposal of the executive was deemed to pose a dire threat to the balance of the constitution. In 1783 and 1784 three bills for the regulation of the Company failed in Parliament before a second bill introduced by William Pitt in 1784 was enacted. This became the basis for a stable system of Indian government. A department of state, called the Board of Control, was able to exercise an effective supervision over the East India Company on Indian issues deemed to be of national importance. The Company's role became that of a partner in the Asian empire as a subordinate part of the British state. A Governor General, the nominee of the national government, with increased powers was intended to exercise effective authority over Indian administration, cutting its costs and purging it of corruption. The permanent commitment of royal regiments and naval ships to India to supplement the Company's own forces seemed to have ensured the future security of British India.

Commercially the Company appeared to be flourishing. Rising tea sales, greatly boosted by the Commutation Act of 1784, which cut out smugglers by a drastic reduction of duties, made the China trade highly profitable. With the ending of the war in India and with five years of peace before the next one, the Company's operations in Bengal showed a surplus, part of which was invested in increased cargoes, mostly of textiles, shipped to Britain. The exchequer was receiving more than £1 million a year in customs on the Company's imports.[34]

The Pitt government made optimistic claims about improvements in India and the profits accruing to Britain. In March 1786 Pitt described the Company as being 'in a most flourishing way; their resources increasing, their credit rising, and their expenditure retrenched'. India would soon be contributing 'to the relief of this country'.[35] A year later, Henry Dundas, the minister responsible for Indian affairs, asserted that 'the provinces belonging to the British empire were now the most flourishing of any in India'. He urged that 'the possessions in India' should be 'properly considered as they ought to be, as the brightest jewel in the British diadem'.[36] Foreign observers seem to have accepted such assessments. Lafayette believed that India had become 'an immense, amazing source of wealth and power'

---

[34] F[rancis] R[ussell], *A Short History of the East India Company* (London, 1793), p. 30.
[35] 22 March 1786, *Parliamentary Register*, XIX, p. 435.
[36] 7 March 1787, ibid. XXII, pp. 263, 265.

for Britain.[37] Washington was warned by a young American in London that the subordination of the Company to the government meant that the Crown had gained a separate army and a revenue of £7 millions independent of Parliament. This did not bode well for America.[38]

Contemporaries generally envisaged the contributions to Britain of empire in the Atlantic and Asian worlds as fundamentally different.[39] They saw the Atlantic as a world of free trade and virtually free land, open to all and yielding bulk shipments of commodities to and from Britain. India, by contrast, was closed to all except the Company which dealt in a limited range of luxuries. By the 1780s, however, the two worlds, never as separate as was supposed, could be seen to be converging. The Atlantic world still affected the lives of far more British people—there was, for instance, no Indian equivalent of the mass emigration across the Atlantic—but the rewards of India were being diffused well beyond a privileged minority of metro-politan shareholders, dealers in high value goods, and returned 'nabobs'. As Huw Bowen's work has amply demonstrated, British India, including the great China trade that it underpinned, was being integrated into Britain's economy and British society at many points.[40] If India was not yet the mass market for British exports and the major source of raw materials that it was to become by the 1830s, exports of British manufactures and metals to Asia were growing significantly, while the value of imports of Asian tea and textiles approximated to that of imported West Indian sugar and other plantation crops. There were far more people from the British Isles earning their living from the American trades and on the huge volume of shipping that traversed the Atlantic than those that did so from Asian trade or on the relatively few East India Company ships, but the numbers in employments gener-ated by India were not inconsiderable.[41]

If empire in India and trade with other parts of Asia seemed now to be secure and there was much optimism that they would make an increasing contribution to Britain's wealth and power, most indicators still pointed to the overwhelming importance of the Atlantic world which had been little affected by the loss of the thirteen colonies. The new America remained economically tied to Britain, as the immediate revival of post-war exports to the United States demonstrated. Most opinion in the 1780s and 1790s would still have had no hesitation in identifying the West Indies as Britain's most important imperial possession. Huge commit-ments of troops were to be made in the Caribbean in the war with Revolutionary France. A shift in British priorities from west to east still lay in the future, although by the end of the eighteenth century such a shift was becoming a realistic prospect.

---

[37] To Washington, 6 February 1786, W. W. Abbot et al. (eds), *The Papers of George Washington: Confederation Series*, 6 vols. (Charlottesville, VA, 1992–7), III, p. 544.
[38] J. Trumbull to Washington, 20 June 1788 and Washington's reply, 20 July 1788, ibid. VI, pp. 346, 389.
[39] For an illuminating account of contemporary perceptions of difference, see Emma Rothschild, 'The Atlantic Worlds of David Hume' in Bernard Bailyn and Patricia L. Denault (eds), *Soundings in Atlantic History; Latent Structures and Intellectual Currents 1500–1830* (Cambridge, MA, 2009), pp. 437–43.
[40] Bowen, *Business of Empire*, especially, ch. 9.
[41] Ibid. pp. 271–2.

II

The loss of the thirteen colonies was followed not by a turning away from empire but rather by the reassertion of imperial priorities in Ireland, the Caribbean, and India and the acceptance of new ones in British North America. In all these areas continuities with the pre-Revolutionary past were to be strong in the 1780s. Yet the American Revolution undoubtedly had some influence both on the pattern of future British imperial expansion and on the practice of imperial governance.

The obvious lesson from the loss of America seemed to be that colonies settled by British people in temperate parts of the globe would in due course seek independence and that they were in any case, in the long run, undesirable possessions. They stimulated emigration which weakened Britain and in time would develop economies that competed with British interests rather than complementing them. The migration of the loyalists into Nova Scotia and Quebec meant that the British empire would still include substantial colonies of European settlement, but should not such colonies be avoided elsewhere in the future? Going further, might it not be desirable to avoid new colonial possessions of any sort which would involve expensive commitments to rule and defend them as British India undoubtedly did? Should not Britain concentrate on using the strength of her economy to open up worldwide trading opportunities with a minimum of territorial possessions? In the language developed by later historians, should not Britain shift from a formal empire of rule to an informal one of trade and influence?

Such strategies certainly appealed to ministers like Lord Shelburne or William Pitt, who were well versed in the maxims of political economy. Under Pitt, attempts were indeed made to establish new trades, backed by naval power and the acquisition of strategic bases, rather than by the large-scale deployment of military force in conquests or by any extensive migrations of British people. Much attention was given to commercial opportunities in Spanish and Portuguese America and in the new western territory being settled from the United States, but most new initiatives were launched in the east, that is in eastern Asia and the Pacific. Lord Shelburne had plans for an embassy to China and one of his advisers was trying to interest him in trade with Japan and Korea.[42] Under Pitt, Lord Macartney was sent on an embassy to China in a vain attempt to negotiate improved commercial access. British trade infiltrated into the Indonesian archipelago and new bases were established on the Malay coast. The settling of the penal colony at Botany Bay in 1788 is generally now seen as part of British commercial penetration of the Pacific. Trading contacts were established along the north-west Pacific coast where Britain's right to trade was asserted by the threat of war against Spain in 1790.

Vincent Harlow examined these schemes and initiatives with massive authority in his two-volume *The Founding of the Second British Empire*. He saw them as marking a fundamental shift in British imperial strategies away from an Atlantic

---

[42] J. Blankett to Shelburne, 8 December 1782 and 27 January 1783, BL, Add MS 88906/1/5, ff. 114, 120.

empire of colonies of white settlement and commercial regulation to a worldwide one of free trade and bases, mostly focused in the east. For him these were the first steps in the creation of a second British empire. This transformation began, in his view, in the 1760s. He did not invest American independence with particular significance in this process, but attributed great importance to the Pitt administration's determination from 1784 to apply itself to 'the great task of repairing and developing the national economy by promoting trade expansion in new Continents'. What was most striking, he thought, about Pitt was that his government took the lead in promoting and directing expansion rather than responding to the initiatives of private groups or individuals.[43] Alan Frost has recently described the Pitt administration as the first British government to think on 'a global scale', above all in 'the creation of a great triangular commerce spanning the Pacific'.[44] That the Pitt government was actively engaged, as Harlow put it, in the search for 'new markets and sources of primary materials in distant continents' has been fully proven.[45]

Whether these attempts to diversify Britain's overseas trade amounted to a radical shift in imperial priorities that can be regarded as the founding of a new type of empire in place of that lost in America, seems, however, to be questionable. By comparison with the imperatives of maintaining Britain's position in Ireland, the West Indies, and India, as well as consolidating the British North American settlements, enterprises in search of new markets were inevitably of secondary importance.

In Britain's main imperial commitments continuities with the pre-Revolutionary past are clear. Although it had attained legislative independence, Ireland, as the next chapter will try to show, would continue to be managed in the more interventionist ways developed by Lord Townshend as Lord Lieutenant from 1767 to 1772. The most obvious lesson to be learnt from the American catastrophe was surely that coercion of white populations was unlikely to succeed. Yet armed coercion of Ireland was being urged in 1783 by no less a person than the Duke of Portland, a Whig of the purest pedigree who had been totally opposed to the American War.[46] The wars in which it had been engaged had raised severe doubts about the fitness of the East India Company for an imperial role, but it was not to be replaced as a ruling power by the British state. Post-war legislation was limited to increasing the supervisory role of the national government, following the model established by Lord North in 1773.[47] The British empire as a whole was still to be marked by economic regulation. The East India Company kept its monopoly, West Indian sugar was assured of a protected British market and protection against American competition in imperial trade was extended to British shipping. Most

---

[43] *Founding of the Second British Empire*, II, pp. 227–8.
[44] *The Global Reach of Empire: Britain's Maritime Expansion in the Indian and Pacific Oceans 1764–1815* (Carlton, Victoria, 2003), pp. 8–9, 177–80.
[45] Harlow, *Founding of the Second British Empire*, II, p. 226.
[46] See below, p. 142.
[47] The continuity between Pitt's India Act of 1784 and North's Regulating Act of 1773 is well brought out by Bowen, *Business of Empire*, p. 73.

assessments of the failure of government in the thirteen colonies agreed that the colonial executives which were intended to carry out imperial policies had lost their powers to elected assemblies excessively responsive to popular pressure. This had made the thirteen colonies ungovernable. The balance must be restored by strengthening in the remaining colonies the other elements in the British mixed monarchy, the power of aristocracy, and the authority of the governors who represented the Crown. White communities continued, however, after 1783 to enjoy pre-revolutionary systems of representative government in the West Indies and Nova Scotia and even in the newly established colony of New Brunswick. It was not until 1791 that an attempt was made to balance popular assemblies with stronger second chambers and executives in the two Canadas, created out of the old colony of Quebec.

Attempts to introduce radical reforms into the British imperial system, as in the Shelburne administration's bill to admit American shipping into imperial trade, Fox's bill of 1783 for replacing the East India Company with a parliamentary commission, Pitt's proposed remodelling of Anglo-Irish relations in his Propositions of 1785, or the initial assault on the slave trade, all failed. The strength of established interests and long-held doctrines about trade and empire defeated them. As Lord Shelburne had found in making peace with America, pressure groups were extremely adept at raising 'clamour' about imperial issues and late eighteenth-century governments were rarely willing to face them down. Much that seems like colonial policy to later historians was little more than responses to outside pressure.

The loss of the American colonies was an important stage in the changing ethnic composition of the British empire which had begun in 1763. Victory in the Seven Years War had brought new peoples under British rule; new British subjects were thought to require new systems of governance. If Catholic Irish, African slaves, and numerous other peoples were left out of the account, the empire of the earlier eighteenth century could be described as formed by Anglophone, Protestant communities who could expect to be accorded the rights claimed by Englishmen everywhere, including elected representative government and the rights guaranteed by the common law. Victory in the Seven Years War brought considerable populations of French origin in Quebec and Grenada under British rule, while Britain had assumed a degree of responsibility for Native Americans in the great extent of western lands ceded by France, for Caribs in newly acquired West Indian islands, for Africans in a new colony of Senegambia, and above all for millions of Indians who had become effectively the subjects of the East India Company in Bengal after 1765.

The American War produced further changes in the ethnic composition of the empire. It did not lead to the incorporation of new peoples by conquest, but as the largely Anglophone white American population became independent, it shifted the ethnic balance of the empire still further away from the dominance of peoples of British origin. As chapter 10 will try to show, it also raised in an acute form issues about the treatment of non-European peoples, as large numbers of Native and African Americans allied themselves with the British and many sought refuge after the war in British colonies with some former slaves ending up in Britain itself. American independence at the same time took what had become the largest body of enslaved black people out of the empire,[48] leaving, as has recently been pointed out, the British West Indian slave system much more vulnerable on its own to attack by the metropolitan enemies of slavery without allies in the old southern mainland colonies.[49]

British imperial rule changed in character with the changing ethnic composition of the empire.[50] The old model of English law and British institutions of government was deemed to be inappropriate for non-British populations. New systems should be devised that took account of their different traditions and beliefs. In practice, rule became increasingly authoritarian as the proportion of imperial subjects regarded as entitled to the rights of Englishmen declined; but it also became increasingly paternalist and, in its own eyes at least, marked by humanitarian impulses towards non-European peoples. The British empire accepted religious pluralism, extending toleration not only to Catholics and Protestant Dissenters, but also to non-Christian religions. While not conceding political rights to many of its new subjects, the empire tried to respond benevolently and with even-handed justice to what it deemed to be the various needs of Indian peasants, of those Native Americans who had moved into Canada, of refugees from American slavery, and even of the slaves within the British empire. Concerns that the British empire should be seen by the world as an 'empire of righteousness' in its treatment of its non-European subjects pre-dated the American Revolution. The abuses of the slave trade and slavery, of the East India Company's rule and of the dispossession of the Carib peoples of the West Indies had all been condemned.[51] The American War, however, heightened public awareness of the plight of slaves and of Native Americans, while sermons calling for national repentance dwelt on the connection between the misfortunes of the war and divine displeasure at the unrighteousness of Britain's treatment of native peoples. The American War was thus a powerful stimulus to campaigns in the 1780s, on a scale dwarfing anything in the past, to bring righteousness to the British empire, such as those against the slave trade or for calling Warren Hastings to account.

III

By the mid nineteenth century the configuration of the British empire had changed very greatly from what it had been in the first half of the eighteenth century. Britain's main imperial concerns were now around the Indian Ocean, the China

---

[48] Philip D. Morgan, 'The Black Experience in the British Empire, 1680–1810' in P. J. Marshall (ed.), *Oxford History of the British Empire*, II, *The Eighteenth Century* (Oxford, 1998), p. 466.

[49] Christopher L. Brown, *Moral Capital: Foundations of British Abolitionism* (Chapel Hill, NC, 2006), pp. 455–61.

[50] See for instance, Eliga H. Gould, *The Persistence of Empire: British Political Culture in the Age of the American Revolution* (Chapel Hill, NC, 2000), pp. 208–14; Maya Jasanoff, *Liberty's Exiles: The Loss of America and the Remaking of the British Empire* (New York, 2011), ch. 4. My own writing has also tried to engage with this theme, e.g. 'Britain and the World in the Eighteenth Century: IV, The Turning Outwards of Britain', *Transactions of the Royal Historical Society*, 6th ser., XI (2001), 1–15.

[51] Marshall, *Making and Unmaking*, ch. 6.

Sea, and the western Pacific rather than the Atlantic. Commercial regulation had given way to free trade. The disproportion in numbers between non-European subjects of the empire ruled under various systems of more or less authoritarian governance and those of British origin enjoying degrees of local self-government had become very large. British commercial and manufacturing prowess, backed by naval power, meant that many parts of the world that were not subjected to any system of British rule could nevertheless be said to have been incorporated into a British informal empire. Evidence of change in some of these directions is unmistakable during the 1780s. If there had as yet been no fundamental shift of priorities from west to east, the China trade was growing greatly in importance and India was being given an increasingly prominent place in British calculations. British government there was coming to be a source of pride rather than of embarrassment. What was later to be a very well-worn cliché, 'the brightest jewel in the crown', was already gaining currency. The Pitt government sponsored the search for distant markets with a new sense of purpose. The dispatch of the First Fleet to found a new settlement in New South Wales was a remarkable and unprecedented exercise of long-range global power. British opinion was beginning to align itself against slavery throughout the world. Yet even allowing for these portents of the future, it is still difficult to see either the loss of the American colonies or the years that followed as crucial turning points in the working out of long-term changes. Whatever the political economists might propound, or the failure of empire in America might suggest, Britain's rulers were in no doubt that certain imperial possessions were a vital source of wealth and power. They continued to persist with strategies already in place before the American upheavals in order to maintain their hold on what they deemed to be the most important ones.

IV

While the development of the British empire after 1783 generally followed lines that had been set before the American Revolution, an empire was coming into being on the North American continent that professed to mark a complete break with the subordination of the old British empire. This was the American empire being created by a vast movement of people out of the original thirteen colonies. It proclaimed itself to be an empire of liberty, whose members were not subjects of an imperial power but were full and equal citizens of a single political community. Nevertheless, British imperial practices were an inheritance from which Americans found it difficult to free themselves. In devising new institutions, British precedents were readily to hand and Americans tended to turn to them. So much so that a historian has described the Northwest Ordinance of 1787, which became the blueprint for the new empire, as providing for 'a fully centralized, nondemocratic form of colonial government modeled after the pre-revolutionary British system'.[52]

---

[52] Jack B. Eblen, *The First and Second United States Empires: Governors and Territorial Government, 1784–1912* (Pittsburgh, PA, 1968), p. 317.

With the ending of the war, migrants poured out of old settled areas where population pressure was producing increasing subdivision of holdings and limiting access to land and were moving into previously thinly settled parts of existing states and into areas nominally claimed by the new states but hardly settled at all. A British emissary for the governor of Quebec was told that 'The emigration to Kentucké and . . . beyond the Ohio . . . have exceeded the bounds of credibility . . . The spirit of removing from the seaboard states does not subside, particularly from New England, whose enterprizing people, checked in their commercial pursuits, turn with wonderful facility to this tempting though remote country'.[53] By the time of the first United States census in 1790 over 100,000 people had moved into lands claimed by Virginia and North Carolina which were soon to become the new states of Kentucky and Tennessee. Rather smaller numbers were also going beyond the Ohio River into the Northwest Territory where state claims had been surrendered to enable the Congress of the United States of America to create a new national domain under its direct authority. In the Southwest, Georgia's enormous claims were being filled by westward migration into more or less autonomous frontier communities. Others were moving down the Mississippi into territory claimed by Spain. By 1785 more than 75,000 people were estimated to be living on new settled lands in the Southwest.[54]

These great movements of people compelled the new America to begin to give practical effect to the designs of a continental destiny which it had staked out in its insistence at the peace negotiations that it must inherit from the British Crown all lands east of the Mississippi and up to the Great Lakes. The west must be ordered as quickly as possible. The demand for land by huge numbers of new settlers offered an escape from their dire financial problems for both the states and the national government. Creditors, above all disbanded soldiers, could be bought off with grants on new land and the return on sales of land would, it was hoped, restore governments to solvency. Beyond such immediate imperatives, both the scale and the unregulated nature of the mass migration posed very serious problems for the future of the republic. Migratory movements that passed beyond the effective control of either state or federal governments had a strong tendency to try to create autonomous entities of their own. A series of 'self-governing communities and self-proclaimed independent states sprang up like mushrooms throughout the back-country'.[55] Fragmented and quasi-independent western societies were a prospect viewed with dismay by many in the established states. They would be an obstacle to the westward march of the Unites States, and the settlers might well conspire with the British and the Spanish to block it altogether. A lawless west would be a negation of the ordered liberty that the Revolution had claimed to establish. Its inhabitants would, easterners feared, become as savage as the Indians among whom

---

[53] 'Opinions and Observations of Different Persons' in Dorchester to Sydney, 14 October 1788, *Canadian Archives Report for 1890* (Ottawa, 1891), p. 103.
[54] A. P. Whitaker, *The Spanish-American Frontier 1783–1795*, repr. (Lincoln, NB, 1969), p. 26.
[55] Eric Hinderaker, *Elusive Empires: Constructing Colonialism in the Ohio Valley 1673–1800* (Cambridge, 1997), pp. 246–7.

they lived. They would certainly involve the union and state governments in wars with the Indians which they lacked the resources to fight. In conditions of disorder a proper use of the land for commercial agriculture to link the west with the east would be impossible. Without agricultural development a system of land sales could hardly function.[56] The people who were moving to the west must therefore be integrated into the republic. As James Madison put it, they could not remain 'distinct societies'; they were 'an expansion of the same society' as the existing states, 'bone of our bones, and flesh of our flesh'.[57]

A mechanism for the integration and ordering of the western settlements emerged from Congress in the 1780s 'with surprising dispatch and effectiveness',[58] principally through an ordinance for their territorial government of 1784, the land ordinance of 1785 and the Northwest Ordinance of 1787. In settling people on the land, the objectives of Congress were similar to those of the British colonial administrations. The evils to be avoided were either indiscriminate squatting by vagrant settlers, who would do nothing to improve the land, or the amassing of great accumulations for speculative purposes by people who had no intention of cultivating or improving it themselves. Small farmers were to be given secure ownership and an incentive to improve. The land was to be surveyed and laid out in townships with individual lots demarcated according to a grid system. Neither Congress nor the states could afford the bounty of free land offered by the British to loyalists, so land had to be bought.

The orderly settlement of western lands was, however, an elusive objective, especially in areas outside Congress's direct control. Neither mass squatting by migrants nor great accumulations of land by those who wished to profit by its resale could be prevented. Large landlords won a 'stranglehold' over the land in Kentucky, where by 1792 two-thirds of the adult male residents owned no land, being either squatters or tenants. On the famed blue-grass land a gentry were already living with their slaves in the manner of the tidewater gentry of Virginia from where most of them had come.[59] The pattern of settlement in Tennessee was roughly similar. Across the Ohio in the national Northwest Territory ideals of a landowning yeomanry had to be modified. Individual purchasers came forward slowly and the federal government felt that it had no alternative but to raise money by sales of large tracts to companies who undertook to provide settlers. Land speculators and land companies were able to obtain 'ownership rights to most of the unimproved western lands'.[60]

---

[56] Peter S. Onuf, *Statehood and Union: A History of the Northwest Ordinance* (Bloomington, IN, 1987), ch. 1 and 'Liberty, Development, and Union: Visions of the West in the 1780s', *William and Mary Quarterly*, 3rd ser., XLIII (1986), 179–213.

[57] To Lafayette, 12 March 1785, William T. Hutchinson et al. (eds), *The Papers of James Madison* (Chicago, 1962-),VIII. 251.

[58] Andrew R. L. Cayton and Peter S. Onuf, *The Midwest and the Nation: Rethinking the History of an American Region* (Bloomington and Indianapolis, IN, 1990), p. 4.

[59] Stephen Aron, *How the West was Lost: The Transformation of Kentucky from Daniel Boone to Henry Clay* (Baltimore, MD, 1986).

[60] Allan Kulikoff, *From British Peasants to Colonial American Farmers* (Chapel Hill, NC, 2000), p. 286.

For the long-term future government of the new settlements Congress committed itself to an ultimate objective for its colonies entirely different from those of the British ones. Territories under its direct rule would in due course become full member states of the union. Congress laid down the principle in 1780 that western land should be divided up into 'distinct republican states, which shall become members of the federal union, and have the same rights of sovereignty, freedom and independence, as the other states'.[61] The ideal of an empire of equal republican members bound in a consensual union particularly reflected Thomas Jefferson's aspirations for what the British empire should have been.[62]

Nevertheless, opinion in the established states became increasingly convinced that effective settlement of the west required firm control in its early stages. Were the settlers to be left to their own devices they would misuse the great landed resources that they claimed and probably lapse into anarchy. In the initial arrangements for governing the national Northwest Territory, models of what the British empire had actually been were followed for what James Monroe explicitly called a 'colonial' government.[63] The Northwest Ordinance provided for a federally appointed governor, secretary, and judges. Laws were at first to be promulgated by the governor and the judges. When the adult male population of the Northwest Territory reached 5,000 there was to be an assembly elected on a high property franchise. With further population increase, new 'states and permanent government[s]' would be set up and they would gain 'admission to a share of the federal councils on an equal footing with the original states, at as early periods as may be consistent with the general interest'.[64]

American colonies were thus destined to become parts of the metropolitan whole; British colonies remained external dependencies. The full integration of the colonies into British political life through representation in a single imperial parliament was rarely advocated at this time in Britain.[65] Different assumptions underlay the differing destinies for American and British colonies. The assumption underlying the doctrine of the eventual transformation of the American western settlements into states was Madison's insistence that they were in no way distinct societies. They were part of a homogeneous American population all of whom subscribed, as the Northwest Ordinance put it, to the same 'fundamental principles of civil and religious liberty'. In *The Federalist* no. 2, John Jay wrote: 'Providence has been pleased to give this one connected country, to one united people, a people descended from the same ancestors, speaking the same language, professing the same religion, attached to the same principles of government'.[66] The homogeneity

---

[61] Cited in Eblen, *First and Second United States Empires*, p. 20.

[62] Peter S. Onuf, *Jefferson's Empire: The Language of American Nationhood* (Charlottesville, 2000).

[63] Andrew R. L. Cayton, *The Frontier Republic: Ideology and Politics in the Ohio Country, 1780–1825* (Kent, OH, 1986), p. 22.

[64] Text in Onuf, *Statehood and Union*, p. 62.

[65] For later debates, see Miles Taylor, 'Empire and Parliamentary Reform: The 1832 Reform Act Revisited' in Arthur Burns and Joanna Innes (eds), *Rethinking the Age of Reform: Britain 1780–1850* (Cambridge, 2003), pp. 295–311.

[66] J. R. Pole (ed.), *The Federalist* (Indianapolis, IN, 2005), p. 6.

of the population of the new American republic, even if, as was almost invariably done, Native peoples and African Americans were excluded, was of course a fiction. To start with, Jay's ancestors had been French. It was, however, a very serviceable fiction.

The British generally did not invoke such fictions. Few ultimately believed that the diverse inhabitants of a worldwide British empire constituted a single people, 'bone of our bones, and flesh of our flesh'. Whether many people in Britain had believed this when much of the population of the empire was relatively homoge-neous, consisting of people of British origins and cherishing British beliefs, 'Protes-tant, commercial, maritime and free',[67] is a moot point. The great expansion of the empire in the mid eighteenth century to include, among others, peoples of French origin as well as millions of Indians living in the East India Company's provinces made any such belief wholly untenable. By the 1780s British people were taking some pride in ruling over a diverse empire of different peoples, recognizing different entitlements and respecting different traditions. In their view, they dealt justly with those like Native Americans or Africans whom they considered that the Americans excluded and oppressed. The contrast between an empire of uniform liberty and one of diversity and difference was a gross over-simplification, but it was to be an enduring one in Anglo-American self-perceptions.

In the 1780s, however, people living on both sides of the North American international boundary were living in not dissimilar empires. Both empires saw themselves as great landlords. British provisions for distributing land were probably more generous than any American ones. The provisions for the first stages of government in the Northwest Ordinance had real similarities with the Quebec Act of 1774, so detested by British Americans, under which Quebec was governed until 1791. In both the governor ruled without an elected body. Far from being uniformly settled by Anglophone republicans, the Ordinance accepted diversity, recognizing that the Northwest Territory included 'French and Canadian inhabi-tants', who, like the French of Quebec, were permitted to keep their own 'laws and customs' concerning property.[68]

---

[67] David Armitage, *The Ideological Origins of the British Empire* (Cambridge, 2000), p. 173.
[68] Northwest Ordinance, sec. 2; Onuf, *Statehood and Union*, p. 60

7

Ireland

I

In 1785 William Pitt told the House of Commons that Great Britain and Ireland were 'now the only considerable members . . . in what yet remained of our reduced and shattered empire'. There ought to be 'no object more impressive on the feelings of the House', than how to maintain the Anglo-Irish connection.[1] In the House of Lords, Lord Townshend, a former Lord Lieutenant of Ireland, spoke of the contribution that Ireland made to the British empire through 'her sailors and provisions in time of war, her consumption of our exports in time of peace, the manhood, intrepidity and perseverance, aids which a voluptuous empire always required and could not exist without. Let them recollect, for a moment, what Rome was when she lost her provinces and hardy allies.'[2] Few would have disagreed with him either about the nature or the extent of Ireland's contribution. Ireland provided a great many troops and sailors, Catholics as well as Protestants now being openly recruited. By the end of the century, the Irish proportion of the whole British army amounted to some 30 per cent. A major part of the peacetime army, over 15,000 men, was paid for by Ireland.[3] Many of the men who worked on the Newfoundland fisheries were drawn from Ireland. Irish provisions fed the Royal Navy and were a main source of supply to the West Indies and Newfoundland. Anglo-Irish trade was growing rapidly. As the destination of more than 15 per cent of all British exports in 1781 and more than 10 per cent in 1791, Ireland was an important market for British coal and manufactured goods, as well as for re-exports of tropical commodities shipped via Britain. In return she exported great quantities of linen and beef, butter and other food stuffs to Britain.[4] Even though British manufacturers still asked for protection from Irish competition, official British discourse now dismissed the past 'system of cruel and abominable restraint' on Ireland's economy, as Pitt called it, as being contrary to 'the real prosperity and strength of the empire'. Irish poverty damaged Britain's interests, which were best served by the growth of an Irish economy that should be as closely integrated as

---

[1] 12 May 1785, *Parliamentary Register*, XVIII, p. 266.
[2] 18 July 1785, ibid. XVIII, p. 113.
[3] Alan J. Guy, 'The Irish Military Establishment 1660–1776' in Thomas Bartlett and Keith Jeffrey (eds), *A Military History of Ireland* (Cambridge, 1996), pp. 229–30.
[4] Figures in L. M. Cullen, *Anglo-Irish Trade 1660–1800* (New York, 1968), pp. 45–7.

possible with that of Britain.[5] 'While the interests of the two kingdoms were mutual and the prosperity of Ireland added to the strength, the power and the glory of the empire, it mattered not', Charles Jenkinson thought, 'where the manufactures were carried on.'[6] Henry Dundas agreed. The Pitt administration wished, he said, to 'cement and consolidate the interests of both countries; so that an addition to the opulence of the one, would be also an acquisition to the other'.[7]

Too much was at stake for Britain to be able to contemplate an Ireland detached from Britain, still less a hostile Ireland. Adam Smith could coolly assess the case for American separation; neither he nor virtually anyone else in Britain could envisage Irish separation. He was one of many who saw the best future for Ireland in eventual union with Britain.[8] The worst scenario was for a wartime French or Spanish invasion which, it was feared, was likely to be supported by the mass disaffection of the Catholic population. In 1779 the threat of such an attack aroused acute anxiety since the garrison of regular troops had been much reduced to serve overseas. It was ostensibly to counter invasion threats that a great Volunteer force was raised in Ireland. The Volunteers quickly developed political ambitions. Their remaining in arms for some years after the ending of the war was a matter of great concern in Britain. They might become the means by which those hostile to the British connection could win power in Ireland. In a moment of despondency in November 1783, Charles Fox, then Secretary of State, believed that in such a situation 'Ireland is irretrievably lost *for ever*'. The choice would be between 'a total separation, or *civil war*'. Either would be catastrophic for Britain. 'The thought of this country receiving her final stroke of annihilation in my administration, is more than I am able to bear.'[9]

Were the British regime to lose control, some kind of civil war was a more likely denouement in Ireland than the transfer of power to an independent regime as in America. Developments in Ireland had obvious similarities to those in the thirteen colonies. Both Ireland and the thirteen colonies came under pressure from British centralizing policies in the 1760s.[10] A vigorous Irish patriot movement had emerged which, like the American patriots up to 1775, was determined to resist these pressures and assert Ireland's constitutional equality with Britain under a common Crown. Disorder could take similar forms. In the early 1780s the Irish government was very alarmed about rioting, tarring and feathering, and boycotting of British goods in Dublin. Belfast in 1782 was said to be 'a perfect Boston' and to outdo it in the 'treason' spoken there.[11] Yet there were crucial differences which

---

[5] 22 February 1785, *Parliamentary Register*, XVII, p. 249. See also Pitt to Rutland, 6 January 1785, *Correspondence between the Right Honble William Pitt and Charles Duke of Rutland, . . . 1781–1787* (London, 1842), p. 60.

[6] 22 July 1785, *Parliamentary Register*, XVIII, p. 570.

[7] 27 May 1785, ibid. XVIII, p. 430.

[8] *Wealth of Nations*, Bk. V, ch. III.

[9] To J. Burgoyne, 7 November 1783, Henry Grattan (ed.), *Memoirs of the Life and Times of the Rt. Hon. Henry Grattan*, 5 vols. (London, 1839–46), III, pp. 113–15.

[10] This theme is developed in Martyn J. Powell, *Britain and Ireland in the Eighteenth-century Crisis of Empire* (Houndmills, 2003).

[11] Pembroke to Carmarthen, [2–11 August 1782], Lord Herbert (ed.), *Pembroke Papers (1780–1794)* (London, 1950), p. 203.

made anything like an American outcome unlikely in Ireland. In the first place, total separation from Britain or the creation of a republic, let alone an alliance with the Bourbon powers, were right outside virtually all patriot agendas. Rather than independence, the Irish patriots wanted to secure what they considered to be their rightful position within the British empire. Secondly, while the aims of the American patriot elite and of the politicized activists among the mass of the white population had enough in common to sustain what, setting aside many loyalists and even more who were uncommitted, amounted to something like a united front against Britain, the leadership of the Irish patriot elite was far from secure. The objectives of the Irish patriot leaders and those of the politically involved middling Protestant people, let alone of the Catholic mass, probably only coincided in 1779 and in 1782. At other times they were sharply divided. The rank and file of those who enlisted in the Volunteers, that is small farmers and urban tradesmen, often in the north Presbyterians, developed more extreme programmes than most of their usually Church of Ireland officers would countenance. Moreover, Ireland was prone to both rural and urban disturbances which threatened not only the British regime but the aristocrats, gentry, and urban elite who led the patriots. 'Every decade between the 1760s and the Great Famine of the 1840s saw at least one major outbreak of rural unrest.'[12] Within a few years of their triumph in securing legislative independence for Ireland in 1782, the Irish patriot leaders were beginning to lose much of their zeal for reform. They faced hard questions as to whether the main danger to Ireland's liberties as they interpreted them came from British intrusions or from the threat of popular insurrection. In February 1784 the Lord Lieutenant reported that 'the influence which fear of what is passing out of doors has on the minds of almost every person of property and understanding' meant that 'the principle of supporting English government prevails over any other'.[13]

Even after the defeat of 1782, British government remained a potent force in Ireland in ways that it had never been in colonial America, The Lord Lieutenant and his Chief Secretary were a much more formidable presence than any colonial American governor had been. They acted directly on behalf of British ministers and had resources of rewards and patronage far beyond any colonial executive. Although the Irish House of Commons gained greatly in prestige and competence after 1782—the practice of annual sessions, for instance, became firmly established— its electorate remained very narrow, by contrast with the widespread participation of white males in electing American assemblies, and so the executive's powers of management were not significantly diminished by legislative independence. Irish legislation was still sent to the British Privy Council. In the last resort, the Lord Lieutenant had a powerful army at his command and the full resources of Britain were close to hand.

---

[12] Ian McBride, *Eighteenth-century Ireland: The Isle of Slaves* (Dublin, 2009), p. 315. For recent assessments of rural discontent with differing interpretations, see ibid. ch. 9 and S. J. Connolly, *Divided Kingdom: Ireland 1680–1800* (Oxford, 2008), pp. 286–305.
[13] Rutland to Sydney, 27 February 1784, TNA, HO 100/12, ff. 126–7.

In early 1782 the Irish government did lose control for some months. Deprived of much of its army, it was faced by what seemed to be an almost universal demand for an end to Ireland's constitutional subordination. Backed by perhaps as many as 80,000 enrolled in the Volunteers, these demands were swept through the Irish parliament by Henry Grattan and other patriot orators.

It fell to the Rockingham administration, which had just replaced that of Lord North, to try to deal with these demands. Leading members of the new government had contacts with the Irish patriots. Lord Charlemont, the great patron of the Volunteers, was a close friend of Rockingham and corresponded with Edmund Burke. Other grandees of the party had Irish estates and Irish connections by marriage. The Rockinghams saw themselves as friends of Ireland in the same sense that they thought of themselves as friends of America. Both Ireland and America had, in Edmund Burke's view, been victims of British ministerial designs to 'destroy every thing like liberty in the dependencies of this kingdom'.[14] On taking office in March 1782, the Rockinghams hoped that they would have the cordial support of the Irish patriots. 'Why should not the Whigs (I mean in principle not in name) unite in every part of the empire to establish their principles so firmly that no future faction shall be able to destroy them?' Fox asked Charlemont.[15] Hopes that Irish patriots would put their trust in the good intentions of their self-styled British friends proved to be almost as illusory as hopes that American patriots would be guided by these same friends. Like the Americans, the Irish were suspicious of the professions of those who succeeded Lord North. Neither Lord Charlemont nor Grattan would take office in a new Irish administration. For Grattan the funda-mental obstacle to any alliance of British and Irish Whigs in office on both sides of the Irish Sea was that it could not be a genuine alliance of equals. 'Office in Ireland' was in his view 'different from office in England; *it was not a situation held for Ireland, but held for an English government, often in collision with, and frequently hostile to Ireland*'.[16] Charlemont was warned that the Rockingham government was unlikely to give the Irish all that they wanted.[17] This was certainly true. What the Irish wanted was unconditional legislative independence. Whereas Fox at least professed that he would have conceded unconditional independence to the Americans and condemned Shelburne for trying to impose conditions on them, he thought that too much was at stake in Ireland not to insist on conditions in return for legislative independence. Britain, he believed, should not give away everything without an agreement or treaty that would secure her 'from further demands, and at the same time to have some clear understanding with respect to what we are to expect from Ireland, in return for the protection and assistance which she receives

---

[14] To C. O'Hara, 7 January 1776, T. W. Copeland (ed.), *The Correspondence of Edmund Burke*, 10 vols. (Cambridge, 1958–70), vol. III, ed. G. H. Guttridge, *1774–1778*, p. 245.

[15] Letter of 4 April 1782, *Historical Manuscripts Commission: Charlemont MSS*, 2 vols. (London 1891–4), I, p. 57.

[16] Grattan (ed.), *Memoirs of Grattan*, II, pp. 224–5.

[17] E. Malone to Charlemont, 9 April 1782, *Historical Manuscripts Commission: Charlemont MSS*, I, p. 400.

from those fleets which cost us such enormous sums, and her nothing'.[18] He was particularly concerned that Ireland should not claim the right to conduct its own foreign policy and to pursue its own commercial objectives independent of and perhaps to the disadvantage of Britain. This seems to have been the view of all the leading members of the Rockingham government. Burke believed that a 'clear and solid settlement' between Britain and Ireland required much more than just the concession of legislative independence by Britain.[19] Rockingham asked Charlemont to postpone putting the question to the Irish parliament in order to give time for further consideration, but Charlemont refused. The 'people', he replied, would never recede from an immediate 'parliamentary declaration of right'.[20] The Duke of Portland, the Rockinghams' newly arrived Lord Lieutenant, warned them that popular 'heats' and 'passions' were so inflamed that there was no alternative to concession. Ireland must be made 'independent of the legislature of Great Britain with respect to the interior government of this country' immediately.[21]

On 16 April 1782 with great panache Grattan moved an address in the Irish House of Commons that Ireland was a distinct kingdom for which the king, as king of Ireland, and the Irish lords and commons alone had the right to make law. The Declaratory Act of the British Parliament of 1720 asserting its legislative supremacy must therefore be repealed and Poynings' Law must be amended so that the Privy Council no longer had the power to suppress or alter Irish bills. The British government saw no alternative but to comply. On 17 May both British Houses of Parliament resolved that the Declaratory Act of 1720 be repealed and the king gave his consent to the Irish parliament's amending Poynings' Law. On 17 May, however, both houses of the British Parliament had also resolved that the connection between Britain and Ireland should be 'established by mutual consent upon a solid and permanent footing'. No progress was made on this. Portland had already reported 'a great reluctance on the part of the leading men of this country and almost a determination not to enter into any treaty'.[22] Neither he nor his immediate successors felt able to engage in serious negotiations for one. Instead they had to cope with what British ministers had feared, that is further Irish demands which implied that the 1782 settlement was not a final one as they had profoundly hoped. The patriots split and Henry Flood took the lead in insisting that for Britain simply to repeal the Declaratory Act was not enough. The British Parliament should pass an Act formally renouncing its powers over Ireland and specifically denying the

---

[18] To R. Fitzpatrick, 28 April 1782, Lord John Russell (ed.), *Memorials and Correspondence of Charles James Fox*, 4 vols. (London, 1853–7), I, p. 411.

[19] To J. Hely Hutchinson, [post 9 April 1782], Copeland (ed.), *Burke Correspondence*, vol. IV, ed. A. Woods, *1778–1782*, p. 440. Burke later made it clear that he disliked Irish legislative independence, but his feelings in 1782 are poorly documented. They may well have had a rather different basis to those of his colleagues. Conor Cruise O'Brien's conjecture that he was unwilling to entrust Irish Catholics to the unfettered power of a Protestant Irish parliament seems likely (*The Great Melody: A Thematic Biography of Edmund Burke* (London, 1992), pp. 243–4).

[20] Rockingham to Charlemont, 9 April, Charlemont to Rockingham, 16 April 1782, *Historical Manuscripts Commission: Charlemont MSS*, I, pp. 54, 55–6.

[21] To Shelburne, 16 April 1782, TNA, HO 100/1, ff. 74–9.

[22] To Shelburne, 24 April 1782, ibid. f. 134.

right of British courts to hear appeals from Ireland. The new Lord Lieutenant recommended compliance in the interests of maintaining public order. British ministers reluctantly agreed. Lord Shelburne, now prime minister, had hoped that far from Britain making further concessions, Ireland should now acknowledge 'the superintending power and supremacy to be where nature has placed it in *precise* and *unambiguous* terms'.[23] After a meeting with him in London, the Irish Chief Secretary concluded that, 'As far as one can separate Lord Shelburne's intentions from his verbiage and professions, I think I can see a strong disposition to resist the least tendency towards any further concession', and, if he saw the chance of doing so, 'I should think him more inclined to lessen than to extend' the gains made by Ireland.[24] What was known as the Recognition Bill, confirming Ireland's legislative and judicial independence, was, however, passed without dissent in the British Parliament in April 1783.

Fox had proclaimed that with the fall of North a new era of imperial government would begin: Whigs in Britain and Ireland and, he hoped, America would cooperate in an empire based on freedom under 'a plan of broad, just, liberal politics'.[25] '[A]s a Whig', the Duke of Portland told Lord Northington, his successor as Lord Lieutenant, 'I shall ever attribute the misfortunes and declension of the empire to the sinister policy, which adopted the measure of breaking and levelling those bulwarks of public character.' There should be a return to Whig government throughout the empire. Unfortunately, he had to recognize that neither in Britain nor in Ireland was there a single Whig party capable of sustaining an administration. Governments had to be coalitions and these coalitions were likely in both countries to extend beyond the boundaries of acceptable Whigs (his coalition with Lord North was a remarkable extension of the boundaries of the acceptable).[26] The Chief Secretary in 1783, Thomas Pelham, reported that 'ideas of party' or of 'Whig principles' were little understood in Ireland. 'Abilities in this country are at market and must be purchased for the use of government.'[27] Nevertheless, as a step towards Whig government, Portland when he had been Lord Lieutenant had given offices to some patriots and dismissed some of the old supporters of the Irish administration. In June 1783 Lord Northington, appointed Lord Lieutenant by the Fox–North Coalition, tried to strengthen his administration by inviting Charlemont and Grattan to serve on the Privy Council.[28]

Experience quickly taught the Rockinghams that for Britain to try to govern Ireland through the support that the Irish patriots might be expected to give a Whig Lord Lieutenant was impractical. British Whigs and Irish patriots claimed that British and Irish interests were perfectly reconcilable by those who sincerely sought

[23] To Portland, 9 June 1782, TNA, HO 100/2, f. 36.
[24] W. Grenville to Temple, 2 December 1782, Duke of Buckingham and Chandos (ed.), *Memoirs of the Courts and Cabinets of George the Third*, 4 vols. (London, 1853–5), I, p. 76.
[25] Speech at Westminster Meeting, 17 July 1782, C. Wyvill (ed.), *Political Papers*, 6 vols. (York, 1794–1804), II, p. 180.
[26] To Northington, 18 September 1783, BL, Add MS 38716, f. 102.
[27] Draft of letter to Portland, 24 October 1783, BL, Add MS 33100, f. 373.
[28] To North, 26 June 1783, TNA, HO 100/9 f. 181.

the common good of the empire on generous Whig principles. In reality, because of the importance of Ireland to Britain, British Whigs insisted that there were fundamental British interests that were sacrosanct and they feared that on these the support of Irish patriots could not be relied upon. They were particularly wary of Grattan. Both Portland and Fox professed to think well of him, but Portland feared that he had a craving for 'popularity', the besetting sin of the Irish patriots, that made him support dangerous measures. In Fox's view, having received so many concessions in 1782, Grattan was bound to deliver 'the Irish part of the bargain, which was nothing more than to be satisfied'. Whatever patriots might wish, it was imperative that the Irish government should stand firm against further pressures. Demands were being made for the reform of the Irish parliament. For both Fox and Portland this was out of the question. Portland urged that the army should be used 'in defence of the people's rights' to disperse a national convention advocating parliamentary reform and to arrest its leaders. The continued existence of the Volunteers as an unofficial military force making increasingly radical political demands was now intolerable. In Fox's view, if they were allowed to continue 'all is gone, and our connexion with Ireland is worse than none at all'. At a time of serious economic hardship, particularly among the Dublin artisans, there were demands for the Irish parliament to enact protecting duties on British imports. This could not be allowed. 'In all commercial cases', Portland insisted, 'it would be best to consider Ireland as a member of Great Britain . . . Ireland ought not to have the advantage of England at foreign markets, nor even the exclusive benefit of her own to the prejudice of the British manufactury.' The Lord Lieutenant must not, Fox insisted, lobby for further concessions to Ireland. Previous concessions were 'so ample that no further ones are necessary'. British opinion would be outraged by annual demands for 'something new for the sake of pleasing Ireland'.[29] Lord Charlemont specifically had Fox and Portland in mind when he reflected that 'a Whig in London will still be esteemed an excellent Whig, though he governs Ireland upon the principles of the most positive Toryism'.[30]

If patriots could not be relied upon to sustain essential British interests, even a self-consciously Whig Lord Lieutenant would have to seek support elsewhere. Thomas Pelham, Chief Secretary in 1783, conceded that in the past 'very improper means have been used' by previous administrations to enlist support, but he was still sure that it is 'in the interest of every party in England to encourage the supporters of English government in Ireland' whatever their nominal political affiliations might be.[31] Portland accepted that no Lord Lieutenant could rely solely on Irish patriots, but he urged Northington to ally with 'such a corps as would be a check upon the profligate and be a corresponding source of strength to such an administration as we should always wish to see in this country'.[32] The unpalatable

---

[29] Portland to Northington, 18 September 1783, BL, Add MS 38716, ff. 100–7; Fox to Northington, 1 November 1783, Grattan (ed.), *Memoirs of Grattan*, III, pp. 108, 111.
[30] 'Memoirs of his Political Life', *Historical Manuscripts Commission: Charlemont MSS*, I, p. 136.
[31] To Portland, n.d., BL, Add MS 33100, f. 433.
[32] Letter of 18 September 1783, BL, Add MS 38716, f. 103.

truth, however, was that unless a British government was prepared to put its control over the Irish political system at risk, which the British Whigs certainly were not, there was no real alternative to relying on the old system of management through rewards and inducements and to employing men of administrative capacity who had served previous Lords Lieutenant. Lord Temple, Shelburne's choice as Lord Lieutenant thought that the people whom Portland had introduced weakened government by their 'want of knowledge and habits of office and the thirst for popularity which pervaded them all'. He placed his reliance on men of experience.[33] Lord Northington, appointed by Fox's influence within the Fox–North Coalition, also turned to '"men of business" . . . who could be depended upon to put the necessity of the Anglo-Irish connection above personal popularity'.[34] He came to the conclusion that the government of Ireland should not be based on British 'distinctions of party'.[35] He had evidently found the ideal of a Whig empire of equality between its members incompatible with maintaining British supremacy in Ireland and seems to have had no doubt which he must choose.

II

After the passing of the Recognition Act, the British government succeeded in reasserting control over the Irish political system. The Lord Lieutenant was able to work with experienced Irish politicians of administrative ability, who cooperated with him to maintain the British connection and 'the preservation of the existing gentry-dominated social order', while trying to bring about material improvement in the condition of Ireland.[36] Although the Lord Lieutenant was generally successful in containing parliamentary opposition, in the next few years he had to face serious challenges from demands for reforms from outside the Irish parliament far more radical than those yielded in 1782. These challenges came from violent outbreaks of discontent in Dublin, from brooding disaffection in Belfast, and from serious disturbances in parts of the countryside. From 1783 to 1785 the Dublin government felt itself at times to be under siege.

For many Irish political activists, legislative independence without reform of the Irish House of Commons would be a barren achievement. It would be 'but the transference of arbitrary power from despotism abroad to aristocracy at home'.[37] The campaigns for reform of the Irish parliament that were launched in 1783 and continued into the following year were initially seen by British ministers as a crisis that threatened the Anglo-Irish connection and might require military action to

---

[33] Letter to George III, 23 March 1783, Duke of Buckingham and Chandos (ed.), *Courts and Cabinets*, I, p. 197.

[34] James Kelly, *Henry Flood: Patriots and Politics in Eighteenth-Century Ireland* (Dublin, 1998), p. 368.

[35] To Sydney, 25 January 1784, TNA, HO 100/12, f. 64.

[36] David Dickson, *New Foundations: Ireland 1660–1800*, 2nd edn (Dublin, 2000), p. 175.

[37] [W. Drennan], *Letters of Orellana, An Irish Helot to the Seven Northern Counties* (Dublin, 1785), p. 19.

quell. Superficially, they might seem to be Ireland's re-enactment of events in America 1775–6. The initiative was taken by unofficial bodies demanding reforms in the name of 'the people'. Delegates were summoned to a Grand National Convention in 1783 and later to a Congress. The reforming manifestos that caused British ministers most concern, those of the Freemen, Freeholders, and Inhabitants of Dublin of 7 June 1784[38] and of the Inhabitants of Belfast of 17 July 1784,[39] refused to recognize the authority of a totally corrupt Irish parliament and demanded that the king dissolve it. The dominant role being played in these campaigns by the Volunteers seemed to be a particularly threatening aspect. Programmes for reform were formulated at their meetings. The implication that legally constituted authority was being overawed by bodies of armed men seemed clear. In Dublin the lead was later being taken by artisans and tradespeople with Catholic involvement. They were described by the Lord Lieutenant as 'desperate and violent men'.[40]

Throughout the campaigns the Americans were invoked as an example of a people who had won their liberty. 'What is the difference between an Irishman and a freeman?' William Drennan, later a prominent United Irishman, asked. 'Not less than three thousand miles.'[41] The summoning of a 'Congress' had obvious American resonances as did the language of the Dublin meeting with its call to restore 'those rights to which we are entitled by the laws of God and nature'.[42] Americans took a sympathetic interest. Ezra Stiles fondly believed that, following America's example, 'by *open systematical measures, committees of correspondence* and the *military discipline* of an armed people, *Ireland* has become gloriously independent of *England*'.[43] More realistically, others recognized Ireland's continuing subordination. George Washington, who kept up a correspondence with Sir Edward Newenham, the radical Irish MP, congratulated him in 1785 on the defeat of Pitt's Irish Propositions, which he saw as 'the British administration's interfering with [Ireland's] manufactures, fettering its commerce, restraining the liberties of its subjects'.[44] Significant American influences are, however, hard to detect in the campaign for parliamentary reform. The Irish government feared French but not American subversion. The Chief Secretary did not believe that American agents were actively fomenting disaffection: 'Their hands are full on that continent.'[45] He and his colleagues were, on the other hand, obsessed with supposed French plots.

The programme of the Irish reformers has been realistically described as 'an overspill from the contemporary reforming rhetoric in Great Britain',[46] rather than

---

[38] TNA, PRO 30/8/323, ff. 160–6, 172–4.

[39] TNA, HO 100/14, ff. 66–9.

[40] Jacqueline Hill, *From Patriots to Unionists: Dublin Civic Politics and Irish Protestant Patriotism, 1660–1840* (Oxford, 1997), pp. 176–9; Rutland to Sydney, 7 July 1784, TNA, HO 100/13, f. 187.

[41] *Letters of Orellana*, p. 12.

[42] TNA, PRO 30/8/323, f. 166.

[43] *The United States elevated to Glory and Honour. A Sermon*, 2nd edn (Worcester, MA, 1785), p. 82.

[44] Letter of 25 November 1785, W. W. Abbot et al. (eds), *The Papers of George Washington: Confederation Series*, 6 vols. (Charlottesville, VA, 1992–7), III, p. 386.

[45] T. Orde to W. Pitt, 31 August 1784, TNA, PRO 30/8/329, f. 126.

[46] R. E. Foster, *Modern Ireland 1660–1972* (London, 1988), p. 255.

a re-enactment of events in America. The advice of British reformers, including William Pitt, was sought rather than that of Americans, apart from Franklin. There was no overt discussion of separation from Britain in even the most radical manifestos. For the Volunteers, Ireland was a 'sovereign independent state', but it was united with Britain on 'a basis of equal liberty'.[47] An ancient constitution, the inheritance of both Britain and Ireland, was to be restored from the usurpations of an aristocratic oligarchy by limiting the duration of parliaments, redistributing seats, a moderate extension of the franchise, and the exclusion of placemen. This would restore the Irish commons to their proper place in a balanced constitution with the Lords and the Crown.[48] Even the Belfast memorial of 17 July 1784 whose claims—that 'no government can be permanent that is not frequently reduced to first principles' and that 'in the native energy of the people rests under Providence the authority and power to effectuate redress'—alarmed British ministers, accepted that 'the just prerogatives' of the Crown, 'the privileges of the Lords' and the 'inherent rights of the people' were equally necessary to the constitution.[49] William Drennan considered that what was at stake in the reform campaign was whether Ireland is to continue an '*oligarchy* or to become a limited monarchy'.[50] In the event, the reform campaign was contained without much difficulty for the government. Some leading patriots took no part in it and the movement split over votes for Catholics, a proposition to which the great majority of reformers were opposed. Henry Flood presented proposals from the Grand National Convention, which the House of Commons first declined to receive and then rejected by 159 votes to 85. The Congress met from October 1784 into 1785. John Jebb, unusual among British radicals for taking a close interest in what was happening across the Irish Sea, looked to Ireland 'with prophetic expectation'.[51] It was, however, poorly attended and the government were able to 'turn it and its proceedings into ridicule' through the press.[52] The American reformers had swept aside the established legislatures in most states. Like the British reformers, the Irish reformers tried to make their case for reform to their parliament and implicitly abided by its refusal to countenance what they wanted.

The Duke of Rutland, Pitt's Lord Lieutenant, was in no doubt that parliamentary reform must be defeated at any cost. He cannot have been encouraged by the charges made against the existing House of Commons in the reformers' petitions. It had failed to protect Irish manufacturing and squandered Irish taxes on 'an enormous military establishment' and on 'places and pensions that insult our poverty'.[53] A reformed Irish House of Commons, Rutland thought, would become

[47] *Proceedings Relative to the Ulster Assembly of Volunteer Delegates* (Belfast, 1783), pp. 4, 21.
[48] The total commitment of Irish reformers to restoring historic rights within the British constitution is the theme of James Vance's thesis, 'Constitutional Radicalism in Scotland and Ireland in the Era of the American Revolution, *c.* 1760–1789', University of Aberdeen PhD, 1998.
[49] TNA, HO 100/14, f. 66.
[50] *Letters of Orellana*, pp. 39–40.
[51] To G. Washington, 4 June 1785, Abbot et al. (eds), *Washington Papers: Confederation Series*, III, p. 38.
[52] Orde to Pitt, 6 November 1784, TNA, PRO, 30/8/329, f. 184.
[53] Tipperary Freeholders' Petition, 19 August 1784, TNA, HO 100/14, f. 110.

unmanageable. 'I do not see how quiet and good government could exist under any more popular mode.'[54] For British ministers the question was embarrassing. To any would-be reformer, the way in which the Irish House of Commons was elected was indefensible. Pitt personally sponsored measures for the reform of the British Parliament in 1783 and 1785 and believed that the Irish parliament ought to be reformed as well. 'I think that the government can never be carried on to any good purpose by a majority *in parliament alone*, if that parliament becomes generally and lastingly unpopular. We may keep the parliament but lose the people.'[55] He hoped for 'a *prudent and temperate reform of parliament*', which would 'unite the Protestant interest in *excluding Catholics from any share in the representation or the government of the country*'.[56] Yet, as Lord Camden, the Lord President, put it, 'their corrupt parliament is the only means we have left to preserve the union between the two countries'.[57] Although Pitt felt that 'the substance' of parliamentary reform' could not be 'finally resisted with prudence or with credit',[58] the Cabinet decided to instruct the Lord Lieutenant to let matters lie for the moment while testing opinion.[59] Britain chose to keep the Irish parliament and run the not very acute risk of losing the Protestant people; the Catholics only entered into British calculations as people who must be kept out of politics.

The launching of reform programmes coincided with outbreaks of disorder. Bad harvests in 1782 and 1783 were causing widespread hardship. In Dublin the effect of high food prices was exacerbated by the problems of the textile workers in certain Liberties within the city, who were losing their employment in a serious recession.[60] They were described as 'a jealous, restless and impatient set of men . . . and who are but too ready to attribute all their distress to the power and superiority of the English'.[61] They had reason for so doing since they faced stiff competition from British cloth made even more competitive by generous credit. They organized non-importation agreements and campaigned for protective duties against British imports. When the Irish parliament rejected such duties in April 1784, serious rioting broke out. A crowd forced its way into the House of Commons and was dispersed by troops. 'We are really in a very disagreeable situation with respect to disorder', the Chief Secretary lamented. 'These accursed manufacturers pent up in a vile suburb of the city are brooding mischief upon the instigation, no doubt, of more considerable people.'[62] The government was concerned at reports that the Volunteers in Dublin were recruiting from much lower social strata and that Catholics

---

[54] To Pitt, 16 June 1784, *Pitt–Rutland Correspondence*, p. 16.
[55] To Orde, 19 September 1784, Lord Ashbourne (ed.), *Pitt: Some Chapters of his Life and Times*, 2nd edn (London, 1898), p. 89.
[56] To Rutland, 7 October 1784, *Pitt–Rutland Correspondence*, p. 40.
[57] To Grafton, 13 August 1784, W. R. Anson (ed.), *The Autobiography and Political Correspondence of Augustus Henry, 3rd Duke of Grafton* (London, 1898), p. 391.
[58] To Rutland, 14 December 1784, *Pitt–Rutland Correspondence*, p. 49.
[59] Cabinet Minute 10 January 1785, A. Aspinall (ed.), *Later Correspondence of George III*, 5 vols. (Cambridge, 1962–70), I, pp. 126–7; Sydney to Rutland, 11 January 1785, TNA, HO 100/16, ff. 5–7.
[60] Hill, *From Patriots to Unionists*, p. 173.
[61] Portland to Shelburne, 18 May 1782, TNA, HO 100/1, ff. 268–9.
[62] T. Orde to E. Nepean, 13 April 1784, TNA, HO 100/12, f. 287.

artisans were forming their own Liberty companies.[63] Two more regiments were moved into Dublin.

Ulster had developed closer connections with America, above all through a huge volume of emigration, than any other part of the British Isles. Many had been sympathetic to the revolutionary cause and continued to be so. In Belfast in 1787 when a toast was drunk to Lord Rawdon's 'glorious' victory at Camden in South Carolina at an entertainment for the Lord Lieutenant, Rawdon, who had raised an Irish loyalist regiment in America, was himself embarrassed and 'mentioned his distress upon it from his knowledge of the Belfast people' and their feelings for America.[64] Belfast was said in 1784 to have 'ever been infected with disloyalty and is so still'.[65] At a Volunteer review, men paraded with axes, said to be 'aimed at the king'.[66] Belfast newspapers seemed to the government to spout sedition. When the Lord Lieutenant toured Ulster in 1787, he commented that the province was full of Dissenters, who are 'in a general way very factious—great levellers and republicans'. Most 'Dissenting ministers' were, he found, 'very seditious'. Nevertheless, he concluded that the 'once factious province' was now in 'a state of loyalty'.[67] By then the government's attention was overwhelmingly focused on what it took to be the threat from the Catholics.

The government identified rural turbulence in the south with the revival of earlier Whiteboy movements. What were now more usually called the 'Rightboys' were especially active from 1785 to 1788.[68] The tithes of the established church were their chief grievance but they also objected to what they regarded as excessive dues collected by Catholic priests and the Catholic hierarchy was very hostile to them. Large numbers, including some Protestant gentry, were enlisted in movements to enforce acceptable rates. The army was deployed against them. By October the Lord Lieutenant believed that the army was now in control. Although modern research stresses that there was 'little serious violence',[69] he thought that large parts of southern Ireland had been in 'a state little less than war' and he was still anxious for the future.[70] Disturbances were to continue for some months.

The extent of disorder prompted members of the Irish administration to look for some underlying cause beyond particular manifestations of discontent. Some came to the conclusion that they were facing an upsurge of Catholic sedition. During the American War the government had received pledges of loyalty and support from

[63] Hill, *From Patriots to Unionists*, p. 177.

[64] M. McTier to W. Drennan, n.d. [1787], Jean Agnew (ed.), *Drennan-McTier Letters*, I, *1776–1793* (Dublin, 1998), p. 273.

[65] E. Cooke to E. Nepean, 30 October 1784, TNA, HO 100/14, f. 209.

[66] Hillsborough to Rutland, 15 July 1784, *Historical Manuscripts Commission: Rutland MSS*, 4 vols. (London, 1888–1905), III, p. 124.

[67] To Sydney, 5 August 1787, ibid. III, p. 403. On his reception in Belfast, see Journal of Tour of North of Ireland, 3 July, 3 August 1787, ibid. III, p. 421.

[68] J. S. Donnelly, 'The Rightboy Movement 1785–8', *Studia Hibernica*, XVII–XVIII (1977–8), 120–202.

[69] Ibid. p. 181.

[70] Rutland to Sydney, 27 October 1786, *Historical Manuscripts Commission: Rutland MSS*, III, p. 352.

the Catholic elite and Catholics been extensively recruited into the army.[71] To reward and consolidate supposed Catholic loyalty, the British government had encouraged the passing of an Irish Act in 1778 that removed some of the restrictions on Catholic landownership. In the euphoria generated by the sense of a united Ireland winning its emancipation in 1782, the Irish parliament also offered rewards to Catholics by an Act further dismantling the penal laws. Catholics were no longer discriminated against economically and they generally had freedom of worship, but they were still politically excluded: from some professions, from office, from juries, and from voting. The Irish government expected that Catholics would be satisfied with what they had been given and would make no further claims, but there were indications that this was not so. The old leaders who had supported the government were believed now to want more and in any case no longer to be in control. The 'lower order of their priests', especially those educated abroad, were reported to be 'the writers and instigators of sedition and revolt'.[72] Members of a Catholic Committee were said to be claiming 'nothing less than a general participation in the rights of citizens'.[73] There was pressure to give Catholics the right to vote. 'The whole Roman Catholic body' was said to be 'engaged in the cause of their elective rights'.[74] Presbyterians were reported to be combining with Catholics in demanding extensions of the franchise.[75] Catholic influences were detected behind the Dublin disturbances of 1784. The ultimate aim of extremists like the leader of the Dublin radicals and future United Irishman, James Napper Tandy, was said to be 'a separation from England and the establishment of the Roman Catholic religion'.[76] 'The language of the Papists is insolent to the last degree' and 'they are in possession of several of the news papers'.[77] The most inflammatory articles in the Dublin press were said to be written by Catholic priests.[78] Matthew Carey's *Volunteer Journal* was openly calling for the separation of Ireland and England. Under prosecution, Carey escaped to Philadelphia, becoming probably the first Irish political exile to the new United States. Many unsubstantiated stories circulated about correspondence with France and of the activities of French agents. The most sensational rumours concerned the Earl of Bristol, who was also the Church of

---

[71] On Catholic relations with the government, see Thomas Bartlett, *The Fall and Rise of the Irish Nation: The Catholic Question 1690–1830* (Dublin, 1992). The loyalty of the mass of Catholics to the government has been questioned by Vincent Morley, *Irish Opinion and the American Revolution 1760–1783* (Cambridge, 2002).

[72] Orde to Shelburne, 30 August 1784, BL, Add MS 88906/1/17, ff. 130–1.

[73] Sydney to Rutland, 26 September 1784, *Historical Manuscripts Commission: Rutland MSS*, III, p. 140.

[74] Mornington to W. Grenville, 23 November 1783, *Historical Manuscripts Commission: Fortescue MSS*, 10 vols. (London, 1892–1927), I, p. 224. In reality, those who claimed to represent Catholics were deeply divided on the wisdom of pressing for the vote, see James Kelly, 'The Parliamentary Reform Movement of the 1780s and the Catholic Question', *Archivium Hibernicum*, XLIII (1988), 95–118.

[75] Orde to Rutland, 17, 24 June 1784, *Historical Manuscripts Commission: Rutland MSS*, III, p. 110, 113.

[76] Rutland to Sydney, 26 August 1784, TNA, HO 100/14, ff. 87–8.

[77] Mornington to W. Grenville, 3 October 1784, *Historical Manuscripts Commission: Fortescue MSS*, I, p. 238.

[78] Orde to Nepean, 30 April 1784, TNA, HO 100/13, f. 8.

Ireland Bishop of Derry. He was said to be raising a regiment and to be importing arms for them.[79] Alarmist predictions flourished. The future Marquis Wellesley thought 'the time is not far distant when all men of property must unite to save their possessions and the constitution'.[80] The Church of Ireland Bishop of Clogher anticipated that 'The island must be fought for in a much shorter time than is commonly imagined.'[81]

The Irish government's fears of concerted Catholic plotting were almost certainly greatly exaggerated. Nevertheless, they seem to have been the pretext for a marked hardening of official policy towards Catholics.[82] Even the Catholic peers and gentry with whom the government was accustomed to deal were now regarded with suspicion. In crude terms, the Duke of Rutland and his Chief Secretary, Thomas Orde, were willing to 'play the Catholic card', in ways already advocated by the Duke of Portland,[83] in order to unite Protestants behind the government.[84] Rutland took comfort that Protestant reformers were coming to be alarmed 'at the pretensions of the Catholics and for that very reason would stop very short of the extreme speculative notions of universal suffrage'.[85] Orde, who has been credited with giving official currency to the term, argued that maintaining the 'Protestant ascendancy', rather than just the 'Protestant interest', was essential to the security of British government in Ireland.[86] There must be no more concessions to Catholics, he argued. 'The ascendancy of Protestants' must be established with 'more firmness and security . . . not only in privileges but in all acquirements and endowments. The strength and perpetuity of the connection with Great Britain most materially depend upon the success of these precautions.'[87] Pitt agreed that 'too much pains cannot be taken to encourage the salutary jealousy of the designs of the Catholics which begins to show itself. . . . The Protestant interest must be the bond of union between Ireland and this country.'[88]

---

[79] Rutland to Sydney, *c.* 24 March 1784, *Historical Manuscripts Commission: Rutland MSS*, III, p. 84.

[80] Mornington to W. Grenville, 23 November 1783, *Historical Manuscripts Commission: Fortescue MSS*, I, p. 224.

[81] To Buckinghamshire 7 November 1783, *Historical Manuscripts Commission: Lothian MSS* (London, 1905), p. 422.

[82] Kelly, 'Parliamentary Reform Movement', pp. 108–12; Bartlett, *Fall and Rise of the Irish Nation*, pp. 108–16.

[83] He thought it desirable that the 'jealousies' of 'the inferior orders of Protestants' should be 'raised sufficiently to represent to them the real views and designs of the Catholicks' (to T. Pelham, 27 October 1783, BL, Add MS 33100, f. 283).

[84] Thomas Bartlett, '"A People Made Rather for Copies than Originals": The Anglo-Irish 1760–1800', *International History Review*, XII (1990), 21.

[85] To Pitt, 7 October [1784], *Pitt–Rutland Correspondence*, pp. 46–7.

[86] James Kelly, 'The Genesis of "Protestant Ascendancy": The Rightboy Disturbances of the 1780s and their Impact upon Protestant Opinion' in Gerard O'Brien (ed.), *Politics, Parliament and People: Essays in Eighteenth-century Irish History* (Dublin, 1988), pp. 120–6.

[87] To Pitt, 17 February 1787, TNA, PRO 30/8/329, f. 295.

[88] To Orde, 25 September 1784, Ashbourne (ed.), *Pitt*, p. 94.

III

The distance which it chose to keep from Catholics was one of a number of ways in which the Irish government sought to strengthen its position after the upheavals of the early 1780s. With the defeat of Pitt's proposals by the British Parliament in 1785, British ministers ceased to press for parliamentary reform in Ireland. Acts were passed to control the press, to reform the Dublin police—creating a 'salaried, armed and uniformed body, under the control of the state'[89]—and to try to strengthen the rural police. Supposedly authoritarian trends in the government of Ireland were condemned by John Jebb, who saw Ireland as 'a faithful mirror' of 'the real maxims' of Pitt's government,[90] and also (with a convenient lapse of memory about what he and his friends had been advocating a short time before) by Charles Fox.[91]

While there was a hardening of official attitudes towards disaffection and a determination to resist any further constitutional concessions, neither British ministers nor Irish politicians were opposed to reforms that might bring about material improvement in Ireland. '"Improvement", one of the great buzzwords of the eighteenth century, was the new "civility"; adding fresh moral force to the attempts of the Anglican elite to drag their underdeveloped, priest-ridden land into the eighteenth century.'[92] On the British side, there was a sense of urgency about this. Ireland could not be left as it was. Much was at stake. On the one hand, the condition of Ireland seemed to be too dangerous to be left unchanged, but, on the other, every effort should be made to try to harness its burgeoning economy towards making an even greater contribution to Britain's wealth and power. A number of leading British politicians gave their attention to schemes for Irish improvement. Lord Shelburne, a great Irish landowner, especially in the south-west, was prominent among them. He has been described as being 'at once dismayed and exhilarated' by what he saw on his estates in Kerry.[93] William Grenville, younger brother of the then Lord Lieutenant, Lord Temple, reported a conversation in December 1782 with Shelburne when he was the prime minister. Grenville told him that the mass of the population 'are really oppressed and miserable to a degree that I had not at all conceived till I went into the country'. Shelburne replied that the remedy lay in 'an extended commerce and the wisdom of internal regulations', which Grenville thought an inadequate response.[94] Someone with Shelburne's doctrinaire commitment to free trade naturally saw 'extended commerce' as the recipe for Ireland's improvement, but it was a belief fully shared by others, including Pitt, as he was to show in 1785. As a general principle, Shelburne was opposed to 'any line of high government' intervention. The Irish administration

---

[89] Hill, *From Patriots to Unionists*, p. 184.

[90] To C. Wyvill, 7 May 1785, Wyvill (ed.), *Wyvill Papers*, II, p. 456–7.

[91] 12 May 1785, *Parliamentary Register*, XVIII, pp. 298–9.

[92] McBride, *Eighteenth-Century Ireland*, p. 6.

[93] Toby Barnard, *Improving Ireland? Projectors, Prophets and Profiteers, 1641–1786* (Dublin, 2008), p. 183.

[94] Grenville to Temple, 15 December 1782, Buckingham and Chandos (ed.), *Courts and Cabinets*, I, p. 87.

should limit itself to the 'the mere lines of police'. Nevertheless, he made exceptions. The government should be active in bringing about some kind of religious rebalancing of Ireland. He had 'a grand project of exporting Catholics and importing Protestants'. He urged the recruiting of a brigade of Irish Catholics to serve in India,[95] while 'Protestant colonys, I should think, could be established in most of the Popish countys'.[96] Shelburne also attached great importance to reforming Irish education. He believed that the Irish government should sponsor 'public schools' to prevent the Catholic Church from dominating education. In his view, 'the manners of the whole country may be changed' by a programme of 'modern learning', including 'modern languages, mechanics, mathematics, and above all morality', for all pupils from seven to twenty-one.[97] As a Kerry landowner, he was well aware of the extent of the Whiteboy agitation about tithes. He thought that the tithe system was indefensible and must be replaced. He feared that a discredited Church of Ireland would in effect be replaced as the established church by the Catholics. The Church of Ireland must be made to reform. Tithes should be commuted, pluralities forbidden, and the clergy required to be resident in their parishes.[98]

The views of Lansdowne, as Shelburne had become, about what might be done for Ireland were largely the musing of a man without power after February 1783, although he is likely to have had considerable influence on Chief Secretary Orde, whose political patron he was and with whom he regularly corresponded. Pitt's much-studied Irish Propositions of 1785 were the most ambitious attempt by a British minister to change both Anglo-Irish relations and the state of Ireland.[99] The obvious purpose of the Propositions was to complete what, from the British point of view, was lacking from the constitutional settlement of 1782. The Irish had got their legislative independence, but they had jibbed at a treaty that would define their external relations with Britain—trade, defence, and relations with foreign states. They would now be offered a customs union with Britain, which would give them full access to the British market. In return they would be required to make a contribution to the common defence of the empire, that is to the cost of the Royal Navy. The possibility of commercial disputes between Britain and Ireland, and in particular of Ireland discriminating against Britain, would be removed. Pitt's ambitions, however, went further than putting relations between the two countries on a stable basis. He considered that 'the internal poverty and distress of the country is the radical cause of all the discontent that prevails'.[100] Freeing trade would bring 'lasting tranquillity and rising prosperity' to Ireland.[101] 'Real efficacy and popularity' for the government would follow and he hoped that it would then

---

[95] Orde to Lansdowne, 21 February 1786, BL Add MS 88906/1/17, f. 177.
[96] Lansdowne to Rutland, 16 January 1787, BL Add MS 88906/3/21, f. 203.
[97] To S. Oliver, 26 July 1786, BL Add MS 88906/3/18, ff. 8–9.
[98] To Rutland, 16 January 1787, BL Add MS 88906/3/21, ff. 202–3.
[99] For a recent study, see James Kelly, *Prelude to Union: Anglo-Irish Politics in the 1780s* (Cork, 1992); also the very full account in Vincent Harlow, *The Founding of the Second British Empire 1763–1793*, 2 vols. (London, 1952–64), I, pp. 558–616.
[100] To T. Orde, 19 September 1784, Ashbourne (ed.), *Pitt*, p. 87.
[101] To Rutland, 6 January 1785, *Pitt–Rutland Correspondence*, p. 75.

be possible to introduce parliamentary reform and thus to incorporate the bulk of the Protestant population into the political system.[102] Thomas Orde, the Chief Secretary, was 'convinced that G[reat] Britain would be the great gainer by a settlement which would quiet the country, and by increasing her commerce and industry pour new strength and revenue into the general stock in the custody of G [reat] Britain'.[103] The scheme failed because Pitt felt obliged to respond to pressure from British interests who feared Irish competition by strengthening the provisions for the Irish contribution and by ensuring that Ireland would be bound by British legislation on trade and navigation. Opinion in the Irish parliament saw in this an infringement of Irish legislative independence. They were not willing 'to barter constitution for commerce'.[104] The Irish government felt that it could not command a secure majority for the Propositions and therefore withdrew them.

Although the Propositions failed, the Irish parliament showed no inclination to engage in tariff wars with Britain or to conduct its own foreign and defence policies. Education and tithe reform, however, which concerned Rutland, Orde, and Pitt as well as Lansdowne, made no progress. Ambitious and comprehensive proposals made by Orde for a national system of education lapsed when he resigned his office in 1787.[105] 'By no other means', he believed 'can there be a hope of civilizing the country and making the inhabitants sensible of the advantages they derive from close connection with their neighbours in England.'[106] For the failure of their projects for Ireland's good, impatient British politicians usually blamed the Irish elite. The great benefits offered by Pitt's Propositions had been spurned by the Irish parliament, according to Orde, because of 'the unwarrantable deviation here from every ground of reason or engagement'.[107] Rutland fulminated that two seminaries 'like Eton and Westminster' might raise standards, but that in 'this barbarous country . . . every thing is a job, and abused with a *few exceptions*, from the highest to the lowest; the whole people are an interested, selfish, savage race of harpies and plunderers'.[108] Benjamin Vaughan, who tried to sell Lansdowne's ideas on education to Irish politicians, concluded that 'the Irish gentleman wants as much schooling as the Irish peasant. I could not find one modern principle brought forward in him'.[109] This was less than fair. The Irish parliament was active in promoting projects for improvement. The volume of legislation, especially on economic matters, greatly increased after 1782, even if numerous acts awarding grants and bounties to Irish manufacturing enterprises were viewed with disfavour by British free traders.[110] Nevertheless, by committing itself to the Protestant cause

[102] To Rutland, 7 October 1784, ibid. pp. 40.
[103] To Lansdowne, 21 May 1785, BL, Add MS 88906/1/17, ff. 147–8.
[104] Kelly, *Prelude to Union*, p. 196.
[105] R. B. McDowell, *Ireland in the Age of Imperialism and Revolution 1760–1801* (Oxford, 1979), pp. 93–4.
[106] To Pitt, 17 February 1787, TNA, PRO 30/8/329, ff. 295–6.
[107] Orde to Lansdowne, 14 September 1785, BL, Add MS 88906/1/17, f. 163.
[108] Rutland's notes, 14 January 1785, *Historical Manuscripts Commission: Rutland MSS*, III, p. 164.
[109] To Lansdowne, 8 November 1786, BL Add MS 88906/1/20, f. 68.
[110] See table of legislation in Joanna Innes, 'Legislating for Three Kingdoms', Julian Hoppit (ed.), *Parliaments, Nations and Identities in Britain and Ireland, 1660–1850* (Manchester, 2003), p. 31.

against the Catholic peril, the Irish government had limited its room for manoeuvre. On questions that affected the established church, above all any reform of tithes, it felt bound to defer to the wishes of the Irish parliament and the British government was not at this time inclined to exert pressure on such an issue. Pitt had accepted the policy of no further concessions to Catholics, who should, he felt, be excluded '*from any share in the representation of . . . the country*'.[111] Catholics in British North America were presumed to be hostile to the United States and therefore could be safely brought into political life. In Ireland it was politically expedient to treat them as a potential fifth column for Britain's enemies. Their condition should be improved materially, but political inclusion must be shelved for the time being. Such attitudes persisted until the outbreak of the French Revolution. Then British ministers did intervene, insisting that Irish Catholics must not be driven into the arms of French republicans and that the Irish government must sponsor reforms that among other concessions gave the franchise to some of them.

It is not easy to detect any major shift in British policy towards Ireland that might have followed from the American Revolution or even from its Irish counterpart, the winning of legislative independence. From the 1760s British governments had been pursuing increasingly interventionist policies in Ireland as in other parts of the empire. A resident Lord Lieutenant, direct management of the Irish parliament, the augmentation of the Irish army, and the large commitment of troops from the Irish establishment to America had all been signs of increasing imperial assertiveness. Whatever might happen elsewhere in the empire, Ireland was too important for such policies to be abandoned there. Even the Rockingham Whigs, with their ideals of an empire of freedom based on the cooperation of good Whigs, were not prepared to loosen ties with Ireland. They condemned armed coercion in America but were evidently prepared to contemplate it in Ireland. The 1782 'revolution' by the Irish parliament made little difference to Anglo-Irish relations. The Irish executive emerged from the events of 1782–3 'with its powers virtually intact',[112] even though it tended to use them with greater sensitivity towards the wishes of 'the gentlemen of Ireland'—as British politicians called the Irish House of Commons when they wished to be polite. In rejecting the commercial Propositions and later in supporting the British opposition over the Regency crisis caused by George III's illness in 1788–9, the gentlemen of Ireland flatly opposed the wishes of the British government. Nevertheless, in relatively peaceful times after 1784 and with no major international crisis they proved themselves generally satisfactory and compliant partners in empire. In the turbulence of the 1790s, however, their wishes could no longer be indulged nor was the British government prepared to go on indefinitely having to mediate its will through a not always reliable Irish parliament. An incorporating union between Britain and Ireland ceased to be an attractive abstract proposition and became the aim of the British government.

---

[111] See above, p. 146.
[112] Kelly, *Prelude to Union*, p. 235.

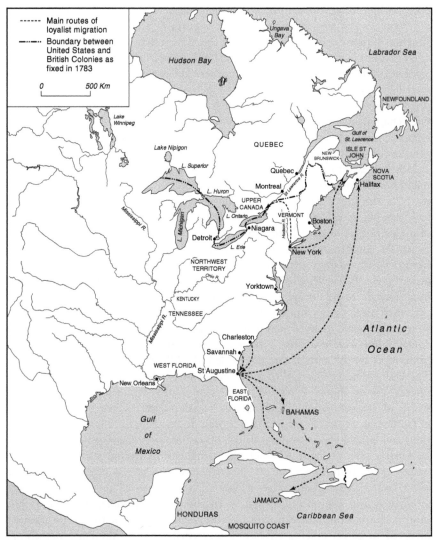

North America in the 1780s

8

The British Empire in North America after 1783

I

With the defeat of the American invasion of Quebec in 1776 and of General Burgoyne's drive southward to isolate New England in 1777, the demarcation of the areas of the continental landmass under the control of the British or of the United States remained more or less constant for the rest of the war. The British continued to occupy the posts of the Hudson's Bay Company, Newfoundland, Nova Scotia, the Isle St John (later known as Prince Edward Island), and the settled area of Quebec along the St Lawrence valley. To the west they maintained a number of garrisons at trading posts, most importantly at Niagara and Detroit. The peace recognized most of the status quo, except that by its terms, not to be fulfilled until after the signing of the Jay Treaty in 1794, the western posts were to be relinquished and the Canadian boundary was to run along the line of the Great Lakes. With the exception of the posts and East Florida, the British kept the empire in North America that they had been able to defend.

The settlements servicing the Newfoundland fisheries were a greatly valued imperial interest, above all as a 'nursery' of seamen for the Royal Navy because of the large numbers of sailors believed to be employed in the fishing fleets that came out from Britain. The fur trade through Hudson Bay was also a valued asset. The rationale for maintaining imperial rule over the other territories was less self-evident. They had been in a real sense adjuncts to the thirteen colonies. Quebec with its overwhelmingly Francophone population had been incorporated into the empire after 1763, less for any belief in its intrinsic value than because of the need to end once and for all a French threat to the colonies to the south. The furs which provided its main export had not been deemed sufficiently valuable for Britain to retain at the peace the western posts, held to be essential if large quantities of furs were to be shipped from Canada. British claims to Nova Scotia were long-standing ones, but its development within the empire had depended on the decision in 1749 to build a great naval base at Halifax primarily to protect the interests of the northern continental colonies against the French at Louisbourg. Immigration had then been encouraged and polyglot communities had been attracted there from the British Isles, Germany, and above all from New England. Its economy and that of the Isle St John, acquired in 1763, were, however, still little developed before the Revolution.

Both during and immediately after the war there were major movements of population into what remained of the British empire in North America. Opponents of the Revolution migrated overland northwards into Quebec. The majority of them, some 6,000, were settled in what was later to become Upper Canada, along the upper St Lawrence or to the north of Lakes Erie and Ontario. Native peoples in flight from American offensives clustered around the British posts in the west and some were settled in indisputably British territory north of Lake Erie. A large number of refugees left the American Atlantic ports by sea, most of them initially moving to Nova Scotia, although some also went to Quebec. By far the largest single movement was of some 30,000, including more than 3,000 free African Americans, who went mostly from New York to Nova Scotia in 1783. This loyalist exodus to British colonies made any abandonment of empire in North America scarcely conceivable, whatever doubts contemporaries might have about the value to Britain of the individual colonies.

As it became clear that the war was unlikely to end in a quick or a complete victory, the British government began to consider what might be done to provide for refugees who would need to be resettled in British colonies. A loyalist colony was envisaged at Penobscot in Maine. It seems, however, to have been assumed in London that the Americans could be induced to offer reasonable terms on which loyalists could return to their homes and that the numbers to be resettled would not be very great. Such assumptions were confounded by the bitter hostility towards Tories in all states at the end of the war. Great numbers decided not to attempt to go back to their homes when the British army left its last footholds. General Carleton in New York accepted that all who wanted to settle in British territory had the right to be shipped out and he devised mechanisms for their departure and resettlement, usually as members of associations or quasi-military companies under the authority of temporary officers.

Land was the most tangible asset that the British felt able to offer the refugees. Loyalists were settled on the land under a system of regulations which was essentially the same in each colony. All land was deemed to be disposable by the Crown outside the seigneuries in French Quebec, the very extensive grants made in the 1760s in the Isle St John, and the areas in Nova Scotia actually occupied by earlier settlers. Huge grants had been awarded in Nova Scotia in the 1760s, but as the conditions of settlement and cultivation in nearly all cases remained unfulfilled, such grants were revoked under an Order in Council of 25 July 1783 and came back to the Crown for distribution to the new immigrants.[1] Nominally consensual purchases were made in the name of the Crown from Native peoples for land required for settlement in western Quebec.[2] The terms on which the Crown disposed of its land after 1783 were roughly similar in all colonies. Above all, land was distributed free. In Quebec new land was to be held in 'seigneuries or fiefs'

---

[1] *London Gazette*, 22–6 July 1783.
[2] E.g. indenture of 22 May 1784 between 'The Sachems, War Chiefs and Principal Women of the Mississaga Indian Nation' and George III, *3rd Report of Bureau of Archives for the Province of Ontario* (Toronto, 1906), pp. 486–7.

from the Crown as seigneur,[3] a provision which was soon to cause much discontent. Elsewhere, lands were held on freehold tenure. No quit rents would be paid to the Crown for ten years. Land could only be occupied after survey and registration. Surveyors were generally instructed to lay out lands in townships of up to 100,000 acres. Each township was to include a town with small lots sited on the coast, on rivers or on the lakes of western Quebec. Larger tracts for cultivation would stretch inland. Individual allocations depended on the status of the recipient. One hundred acres was the general norm for a private in the regiments that it was government policy to disband in the colonies or to an ordinary civilian with a family. Fifty acres was added for each family member. The highest authorized grants of 1,000 acres went to field officers and to civilian notables. Junior officers and civilians of lesser importance got somewhere between 100 and 1,000 acres. It was the government's avowed intention actively to encourage settlement and cultivation, while discouraging land speculation. So grants must be limited in size and should not be made to those 'who do not mean to become immediate settlers and actually improve the lands they apply for'.[4] Grants contained provisions for a stipulated amount of land to be cultivated each year and for an oath of loyalty to be taken to the king and Parliament as 'the supreme legislature of this province'.[5]

The terms on which new lands were to be granted after 1783 were based on traditional British objectives in settling lands in America, but they also bore in places the imprint of Guy Carleton, who almost alone of those who exercised power on the British side had given serious thought to shaping the remaining British colonies. He was confident in their future, even if many of his expectations were more than a little unreal. As governor of the overwhelmingly French colony of Quebec in the 1770s he had seen the seigneurs as a 'gentrified elite' who could command the loyalty of the mass of the agrarian population.[6] Although such hopes were based on a misunderstanding of the actual position of the seigneurs in Quebec society, Carleton was still strongly committed to constructing new loyalist societies based on hierarchy and dependence, whose chief elements would be the equivalent of gentry and yeomen. This was to prove to be an unattainable objective. Beyond that Carleton fervently believed that Britain must place relations between the remaining colonies and the mother country on a new footing. The loyalists' claims for new lands from Britain were, he thought, 'their very reasonable expectation', a matter of 'justice, rather than mere favour'.[7] Possible grievances should be eliminated from the start. Quit rents should not be levied and fees must not be charged on land grants.[8] British governments apparently accepted such arguments. Huge tracts of free land were alienated, subject only to quit rents after ten years, until 1790, when William Grenville, as Secretary of State, called a halt to this largesse,

---

[3] Additional Instructions, 16 July 1783, BL, Add MS 21705, f. 142.
[4] Draft to Gov. of Nova Scotia, – June 1783, TNA, CO 217/35, f. 323.
[5] Form of grant for Nova Scotia, TNA, CO 217/59, ff. 85–6.
[6] Philip Lawson, *The Imperial Challenge: Quebec and Britain in the Age of the American Revolution* (Montreal and Kingston, 1989), p. 109.
[7] To A. Hammond, 22 September 1782, TNA, CO 5/107, ff. 214–15.
[8] To T. Townshend, 15 March 1783, Davies (ed.), *Documents*, XXI, pp. 159–60.

which he saw as squandering the resources of the Crown. Beginning with Quebec, he tried to launch a policy of reserving lands for public purposes.[9]

Actual practice in the British colonies seems rarely to have matched the high aspirations for encouraging cultivation and curbing land speculation embodied in the regulations. The acquisition of land in large blocks for future profitable disposal was certainly possible for the well connected, even if land speculation in no way matched the gigantic proportions which it was to reach in the United States. The rules for the distribution of land seem to have been applied with a strong partiality in favour of the rich and influential. A group who claimed to speak for the mass of Nova Scotia immigrants proclaimed that they had no intention of becoming tenants to 'rich gentlemen' who wanted 'to inslave our suffering brethren'.[10] Those at the bottom of the pile, the free African Americans in Nova Scotia, did worst of all. They got very meagre allocations or no land at all.[11] Poor settlers were often suspicious and militantly resentful of the rich. Nevertheless, Nova Scotia was perhaps the best poor man's country on offer in North America in 1783.

II

Beyond being places of refuge for loyalists, it was by no means clear what, apart from Newfoundland and Hudson Bay, the imperial role of the remaining colonies was to be. Assessments of their future depended to a large extent on assessments of the future of the United States. Would the United States eventually absorb the British colonies or might a continuing British presence on the North American continent be an opportunity for Britain to exercise influence over the new republic, to bring back more of its people to British allegiance through migration to Quebec or Nova Scotia or even to bring about the secession of parts of the union?

There were periodic alarms that the Americans might try to evict the British from the western posts by force, but any direct military threat by the United States to the main British colonies was recognized to be minimal. Neither the federal government nor any of the states could command forces necessary realistically to attempt any such thing. Even so, the Americans certainly hoped to see the British out of North America altogether. 'By leaps of logic peculiar to American thinking', a distinguished American scholar has put it,

> nationalism and 'natural rights' were extended to include territorial right to the North American continent; a nation conceived in liberty had a right to a homeland; in order to enjoy that liberty the people must feel secure; in order to feel secure and to enjoy the

---

[9] W. Grenville to Lord President, 20 February 1790, TNA, BT 6/20, f. 431. For the additional instruction to governors, see TNA, PC 2/134, pp. 542–3. Grenville believed that if land had been reserved for the needs of government in the thirteen colonies, it would have 'retained them to this hour in obedience and loyalty' (to Dorchester 20 October 1789, BL, Add MS 59230, f. 238).

[10] 'A Gentleman of Halifax', *A Vindication of Governor Parr and his Council* (London, 1784), pp. 28–33.

[11] See the careful examination in Ellen Gibson Wilson, *The Loyal Blacks* (New York, 1976).

freedom to develop their territory in accordance with the 'the immense designs of the Deity', they must have control of all areas strategic to their homeland.[12]

The handing over to them of Quebec and Nova Scotia had been one of the American objectives in the peace negotiations, but it had not been seriously pressed. James Monroe, who toured Quebec in 1784, explained what he thought should be America's attitude to Canada. He doubted whether it was of much commercial value to Britain and he feared that her evident unwillingness to give it up suggested that 'she either has or will have other objects'. To acquire Quebec could not, in his view, be an immediate American interest; 'we must make valuable what we have already acquired' rather than seeking extra territory. Nevertheless, by means such as restricting trade relations the United States should try to hamper the colony's development.[13]

If little was to be feared from a military attack, might not the British colonies be subverted from within by a republican fifth column infiltrating from the south? To patriotic Americans it seemed to be inevitable that the 'subjects' of empires who lived across the borders of the United States would aspire to become 'free citizens' and seek to join 'the first empire that mankind ever created on the solid foundations of truth, reason and common sense'.[14] John Jay thought that American settlers who moved into British territory would bring with them the characteristic virtues of a free and equal and, therefore, an enterprising people. 'I wish that every acre of ground that [the British] held in America was settled by natives of the United States—they would transplant their love of liberty, their spirit of enterprise, and their attachment to republicanism into countries in which it is our interest that such plants should be propagated and flourish.'[15]

The British in Canada were well aware that the American population to the south of them was an extremely mobile one, moving in huge numbers out of the older settled areas in the original thirteen colonies into new lands to the west. Some part of these mass movements would bring new settlers up to and even across the long Quebec boundary with New York and Vermont. Settlement in both states was expanding very rapidly indeed. Most of the pressure for new land in New York went westwards into the territory of Iroquoia, where the Americans had their hands full in extracting land from the Indians. In time, however, it was anticipated that the New York settlers would fill their side of the Lakes and then look northward.[16] Vermont was an immediate problem. 'The spread of settlement in that country is incredible', wrote a member of the Quebec council in 1784. He believed that there might be as many as 70,000 people in the state and that, if relations with Vermont were not managed with care, they will 'force their way into the province and take

---

[12] D. W. Meinig, *The Shaping of America: A Geographical Perspective on 500 Years of History*, I, *Atlantic America 1492–1800* (New Haven, CT, 1986), pp. 416–17.

[13] To T. Jefferson, 3 November 1784, S. M. Hamilton (ed.), *The Writings of James Monroe*, 7 vols. (New York, 1898–1903), I, pp. 42–4.

[14] J. B. Cutting to Jefferson, 16 September 1788, Julian P. Boyd et al. (eds), *The Papers of Thomas Jefferson* (Princeton, NJ, 1950–), XIII, pp. 609–10.

[15] To Lafayette, 15 July 1785, Giunta (ed.), *Emerging Nation*, II, p. 696.

[16] Dorchester to Sydney, 13 June 1787, TNA, CO 42/50, f. 398.

possession'.[17] General Frederick Haldimand, governor of Quebec, took a characteristically gloomy view of the situation after the war. 'If Great Britain hopes to retain this province, great vigilance and firmness is necessary not only to guard against the partisans of France, but against the many emissaries and well wishers, which the American states have amongst the old [Anglophone] subjects settled or who may settle in this country.' As far as possible, Quebec should be sealed off from cross-border contacts with Americans.[18]

Others opinions were more optimistic. It was not inevitable that the new empire of liberty should expand across the whole continent. It could be contained. There was an almost universal belief in Britain that the post-war United States were in dire distress and that much of the population was disaffected. A failed regime could hardly export the republican ideology on which it was based with much plausibility. In the view of Guy Carleton the population of properly governed British colonies could be rendered immune from American subversion. What had been the legitimate grievances of the thirteen colonies must be remedied and the colonial populations should have the full privileges of the British constitution, 'as far as circumstances may permit, so that we may have but one common interest, and become, as far as possible, one and the same people'.[19] Not only would colonies whose inhabitants enjoyed the ordered liberty of the British constitution have little to fear from republican subversion, but the obvious superiority of their system of government would attract migrants from the United States who could be safely absorbed into them as much needed additions to the population of the empire. Carleton had 'the most sanguine hope that the provinces which are to remain under his Majesty's dominion will suddenly become powerful, and objects of envy to those who in the present moment madly renounced the most equitable and wise system of government, for anarchy and destruction'.[20] When he returned to Quebec in 1786 as Lord Dorchester and governor he was said to welcome new migrants from America, favouring 'even the independent Whigs of America, above any *other* nation under heaven, for tho' no longer brethren, they are at least our cousins, branches from the same stock'.[21]

Lord Dorchester also hoped that good relations could be established with frontier communities of new settlers in areas adjoining Canada who had not yet been fully incorporated into the United States. Such projects were given some support by the British government.

A separatist movement in Vermont, territory claimed by New York and New Hampshire, had developed during the war. The separatists had then sought British protection and had even professed a desire to be admitted into the empire. After the war, Vermont maintained its autonomy that neither Congress nor the state of

---

[17] H. Finlay to E. Nepean, 6 November 1784, TNA, CO 42/16, f. 169.
[18] To North, 15 July 1783, TNA, CO 42/44, ff. 179–80.
[19] Memo to Lord North, 11 July and letter of 5 October 1783, Davies (ed.), *Documents*, XXI, pp. 186–7, 219–21; Memo of 20 February 1786, TNA, CO 42/49, ff. 39–40.
[20] To T. Townshend, 15 March 1783, Davies (ed.), *Documents*, XXI, p. 160.
[21] W. Smith to his wife, 10 December 1786, L. F. S. Upton (ed.), *The Diary and Selected Papers of Chief Justice William Smith 1784–1793*, 2 vols. (Toronto, 1963–5), II, p. 204.

New York had the means to crush. Contacts continued with the British in Canada. The Quebec government was ordered to avoid any political involvement but encouraged to develop commercial links. The St Lawrence ports were the main outlet for Vermont's trade, which grew with its spectacular increase in population. Carefully managed, Vermont seemed likely to become 'as advantageous to Britain as if the inhabitants were subjects of the crown' without the cost of defending or governing them.[22] When Dorchester arrived in Canada he received fresh overtures from Vermont. The outcome was that virtually all restrictions on trade between Vermont and Quebec were removed in 1787 and 1788. A group in Vermont who were opposed to integration into the United States continued, however, to press for closer relations with the British empire. One of their leaders came to London to negotiate directly in 1789. Aware that Vermont might shortly be admitted as a state within the American union, the Committee of the Privy Council reported that it was not in Britain's interest that this should happen. Areas like Vermont should be encouraged to remain 'in a state of independence, and . . . to form treaties of commerce and friendship with Great Britain'.

In 1791 Vermont did become one of the United States of America, but the committee's recommendation went further than Vermont. They hoped that 'Kentucky and all the other settlements now settling in the interior parts of the great continent of North America' would not become 'dependent on the government of the United States'.[23] At the peace settlement, Britain had seen no strong reasons for trying to maintain its title to the western lands between the Appalachians and the Mississippi. The very rapid post-war growth of settlement as Americans poured over the mountains, however, raised questions about the future of the west and of possible commercial advantages to be gained by the British in Canada. Americans feared that foreign interference would greatly exacerbate the difficult problems of establishing a stable connection between the western communities and the rest of the United States. Trade with Britain would, in Washington's view, encourage the western settlers to become 'as unconnected with us, indeed more so, than we are with South America'.[24] James Madison was concerned that they would, like those in Vermont, 'slide into . . . communication and latent connection with their British neighbours'.[25] Intelligence gathered by Dorchester indicated that new settlements were asserting their autonomy from the United States and that although they mostly saw the Mississippi, in spite of Spanish prohibitions, as the main channel for their trade, they were also interested in trading with the British via the Great Lakes and the St Lawrence.[26] John Connolly, a former loyalist officer, was reported to have come from Quebec with money from Dorchester with which to 'tamper

[22] H. Finlay to E. Nepean, 6 November 1784, TNA, CO 42/16, f. 169.
[23] Report of 17 April 1790, TNA, PRO 30/8/343, ff. 134–5.
[24] To J. Read, 3 November 1784, W. W. Abbot et al. (eds), *The Papers of George Washington: Confederation Series*, 6 vols. (Charlottesville, VA, 1992–7), II, p. 121.
[25] To Washington, 18 March 1787, ibid. V, p. 94.
[26] 'D' to Dorchester, 4 [June] 1788, TNA, CO 42/59, ff. 236–8.

with the people of Kentucky'.[27] Dorchester reported that there was support in Kentucky for refusing to become a state of the union and instead turning to Britain. A force from Kentucky might attempt to evict the Spanish from New Orleans and hand it over to the British. In Britain, John Simcoe, ex-loyalist commander and soon to be Lieutenant Governor of the new province of Upper Canada, presented the new British Foreign Secretary, William Grenville, with plans to turn Canada into 'a permanent jewel to the crown of Great Britain; a far more brilliant one than what is held by a profligate and precarious tenure in the East'. He hoped for massive immigration from the United States and for 'a permanent union of interest and of force' with Vermont and Kentucky.[28] In Grenville's opinion, it was most desirable that the new settlements in the west should not be incorporated either into the United States or into the Spanish empire and that Britain should establish 'a connection' with them without explicitly pledging overt support.[29] The Committee of the Privy Council for trade endorsed this view.[30]

William Grenville has been credited with designs for 'a commercial empire in North America' from the Mississippi to the Pacific Coast.[31] Any such plans had soon, however, to be modified to take account of the capacity that the United States was showing to draw new communities into the union. In 1792 Kentucky followed Vermont in seeking statehood. There seemed to be increasing reasons—both commercial and political, as in the need for American cooperation were war to break out in 1790 with Spain over Pacific rivalries—for Britain to establish good relations directly with the United States rather than to commit itself to transitory separatist movements in future states.[32]

Americans resented what they saw as Britain's tampering with frontier communities whose destiny seemed to them to lie in incorporation into the union. They resented even more the British failure to comply with the terms of the peace of 1783 by keeping control of a series of fur-trading posts along the frontier between Canada and the United States. By doing so the British were depriving them of access to the fur trade and were, they believed, inciting Indian hostility against them which prevented the occupation of lands by American settlers.[33] From the British point of view, as will be shown in chapter 10, continuing control of the posts was deemed essential for the security of the whole colony of Quebec. The British

---

[27] A. St Clair to J. Jay, 13 December 1788, Giunta (ed.), *Emerging Nation*, III, pp. 897–8; H. Innes to Washington, 18 December 1788, W. W. Abbot et al. (eds), *The Papers of George Washington: Presidential Series* (Charlottesville, VA, 1987–), I, pp. 188–9.

[28] Dorchester to Sydney, 11 April 1789, enclosing 'Desultory Reflexions by a Gentleman of Kentucky', TNA, CO 42/64, ff. 152–9 and to Sydney 7 June 1789, enclosing 'Observations on the Western Country', *Report on Canadian Archives for 1890* (Ottawa, 1891), pp. 108–10; Simcoe's 'Observations on the Present State of that Country', rec'd 2 March 1790, BL, Add MS 59236, ff. 17–26.

[29] To Dorchester, 20 October 1789, TNA, CO 43/10, f. 59.

[30] Report of 17 April 1790, TNA, PRO 30/8/343, ff. 134–5.

[31] Vincent T. Harlow, *The Founding of the Second British Empire 1763–1793*, 2 vols. (London, 1952–64), II, p. 609.

[32] Charles R. Ritcheson, *Aftermath of the Revolution: British Policy towards the United States 1783–1793* (Dallas, TX, 1969), pp. 156–63.

[33] For the question of the posts and of relations with Native Americans, see below, pp. 194–200.

government acquiesced in their retention, telling the United States that the British would remain in the posts so long as the Americans failed to fulfil their treaty obligations, above all their pledge to enable British merchants to recover their debts. By 1790, however, the British were beginning to look for a way out of their commitment to hold the posts. The disadvantages of antagonizing the Americans, who were developing a capacity to recover the posts by force, were coming to outweigh any advantages from holding them. A settlement by which the British withdrew was finally concluded with the Jay Treaty of 1794.

III

The boundary between American states and British colonies, agreed on paper in 1783 and given effect by the Jay Treaty, posed no great hindrance to cross-border movements of people and goods, but it did demarcate different political systems. American states, including the future state of Vermont, had their own republican constitutions. In Nova Scotia and the Isle St John a version of the system of colonial government long established throughout British America was already in existence at the end of the war. It was to be instituted in New Brunswick when it became a separate colony in 1784. A British naval officer was responsible for the government of Newfoundland. Quebec was governed under controversial arrangements devised for the special circumstances of a Francophone majority in the Quebec Act of 1774. This was to be replaced by a new constitution under an Act of 1791.

Serious consideration was first given to the post-war problems of British America by the Pitt administration once it had consolidated its hold on office in 1784. There were early indications of what seems to have been a commitment to strengthen the British presence in North America. Lord Sydney, the Secretary of State, echoed the language of the colonies' lobbies when he reportedly declared, in what was to be a much-used phrase, that Nova Scotia would become 'the envy of all the American states'.[34] The first important decision, taken at Cabinet level, was to reorganize the government of Nova Scotia, principally by the creation of a separate new colony to be called New Brunswick. No immediate decision was taken about the future government of Quebec. This would depend upon advice from Sir Guy Carleton who was to return to North America as its governor. Negotiations between Carleton and ministers were, however, to be protracted for another two years, chiefly because of Sir Guy's exacting sense of what was due to him were he to accept such an appointment. The economic role of the whole of British North America was examined by the recently established Committee of the Privy Council for trade and colonies, which had been instructed to consider the extent to which the United States should be given commercial access to the British empire, above all to the West Indies. The committee heard much unrealistically optimistic evidence about

---

[34] W. Chipman to E. Winslow, 13 March 1784, W. O. Raymond (ed.), *The Winslow Papers* (St John, NB, 1907), p. 170.

the economic potential of Nova Scotia and Quebec and concluded that in the relatively near future they should be able to meet most of the West Indies' need for the food and timber which had previously come from the thirteen colonies. Their future development, for which further immigration from the United States was highly desirable, required that they should be assured of 'proper markets'. American competition in the West Indies and in the British North American colonies must therefore be restricted.[35] Plans for creating an Anglican bishopric in Nova Scotia were known to be under considerations and parliamentary subsidies began to be paid to the Church of England in British North America for ministers' stipends and for the building of churches.

Nova Scotia initially attracted most attention because it received the main body of loyalist emigrants. On the eve of the loyalist influx in 1783, the white population of Nova Scotia was a very diverse one. Some French settlers remained after the deportation of the Acadians in 1755. New Englanders had moved into the colony in large numbers. German settlement had been encouraged and immigrants had come from the British Isles. The total population has been estimated at some 20,000 of whom 12,000 may have originated from New England. At least 30,000 loyalists were to be added to them. Nova Scotia loyalists were a very diverse set of people of British, British American, continental European, and African American origins, drawn from all over the thirteen colonies.[36] They settled on land grants made to them and created a largely new urban concentration at Port Roseway, renamed Shelburne.[37]

Nova Scotia was governed under a constitution of 1758, based on the conventional elements of governor, council, and elected assembly. The balance between these elements had been deliberately weighted to strengthen the executive power of the governor, which meant that it was regarded as 'freest from a republican mixture and most conformable to the British constitution' in all pre-revolutionary British America.[38] In spite of the large number of New England settlers, care was taken to prevent the growth of the characteristic New England system of local town administration which involved a high level of popular participation. Authority in the localities of Nova Scotia through counties was concentrated in the provincial government.[39]

Loyalist immigrants generally found the existing population and the political culture of Nova Scotia uncongenial. The loyalist elite complained of their exclusion from government offices by members of well-entrenched cliques at Halifax, who, they alleged, discharged their duties, above all the distribution of land, in corrupt and inefficient ways that were hostile to the loyalists. The loyalist communities as a whole demanded proper representation in the assembly, which in their view, in

---

[35] BL, Add MS 38388, f. 135.

[36] Loyalist society in Nova Scotia is discussed at length in ch. 12.

[37] Marion Robertson, *King's Bounty: A History of Early Shelburne* (Halifax, NS, 1983), p. 79.

[38] P. J. Marshall, *The Making and Unmaking of Empires: Britain, India and America c.1750–1783* (Oxford, 2005), p. 285.

[39] The significance of this is a major theme in Elizabeth Mancke's *The Fault Lines of Empire: Political Differentiation in Massachusetts and Nova Scotia, c.1760–1830* (New York, 2005).

spite of initial adjustments, continued to be unduly weighted in favour of the interests of the old settlers; these they denounced, unfairly recent scholarship suggests,[40] as 'republicans' who had constituted a fifth column for the Americans during the war and remained sympathetic to them after the peace. Such stories reached Guy Carleton in New York, who believed that 'the republicans have great interest and influence' in Nova Scotia and 'that some of them are in offices of trust and confidence'.[41] One of the commissioners for examining the claims of the loyalists reported that they had 'experienced every possible injury from the old inhabitants of Nova Scotia, who are even more disaffected towards the British government than any of the new states ever were'.[42]

Unable to impose their will on the existing order in Nova Scotia or on its governor, John Parr, who they saw as their enemy, some of the loyalist elite made a bid for a colony of their own to be carved out of Nova Scotia.[43] The arrival of some 14,000 people at the St John River, across the Bay of Fundy from the main peninsula of Nova Scotia, enabled a group of ex-officials and officers in the loyalist Provincial regiments, mostly from Massachusetts, to draw up a proposal for creating a separate colony in an area where the existing population was small and could be dominated. The formal case for the new colony rested on the extremely attenuated lines of communication between the St John River and the seat of government at Halifax. Much was made of the failure of the existing Nova Scotia government to bring about a quick settlement of the refugees who had gone to the St John River in such numbers. Even were the Nova Scotia government effectively able to extend its reach so far, it was central to the case for a new colony that rule from Halifax was entirely unacceptable to the new settlers there. Officials in Nova Scotia were 'vagabonds' with republican sympathies, whereas the ex-officers and the civilian refugees on the St John were 'men of the first families, of liberal education and of known probity. It is too mortifying to place them under the immediate direction of men of such different character.'[44] In short, the new colony was to be purged of the supposed political disaffection and corrupt ways of old Nova Scotia. A high-principled loyalist elite of impeccable social standing would take control of it. Such a colony would be a beacon to attract more waves of loyalist emigration from the United States.

Early in 1784 a small loyalist delegation took their case for the partition of Nova Scotia to London, where they were examined by the Privy Council. They had allies working for them in Britain, including the recently returned Sir Guy Carleton, and they got a favourable reception. The Cabinet agreed to the partition of Nova Scotia

---

[40] For the somewhat nuanced loyalty of the new England settlers, who accepted the British empire without accepting any commitment to active engagement in its cause, see ibid. pp. 66–81; J. M. Bumsted, *Understanding the Loyalists* (Sackville, NB, 1986), pp. 44–6.

[41] To Brigadier Fox, 5 September 1783, Davies (ed.), *Documents*, XXI, p. 215.

[42] T. Dundas to Cornwallis, 28 December 1786, Raymond (ed.), *Winslow Papers*, p. 337.

[43] For the creation of New Brunswick, see Ann Gorman Condon, *The Envy of the American States: The Loyalist Dream for New Brunswick* (Fredericton, NB, 1984).

[44] W. Chipman, 'Arguments for forming a Separate Province', WLCL, Sackville-Germain MSS, 16.

on 10 May 1784. The separated colony was given the name of New Brunswick and Guy Carleton's brother, Thomas, was to be its first governor. No new departure was envisaged in its constitution, which was to be 'as analogous to that of Nova Scotia as circumstances will admit'.[45] Thomas Carleton, however, thought that in Nova Scotia the assembly had made dangerous inroads into the royal prerogative in the manner of the New England colonies. He intended to restore the balance and believed that since 'a great proportion of the people have originated from New York and the provinces to the southwards', rather than from New England, it would be possible 'to take an advantage of their better habits, and by strengthening the executive power of government discountenance its leaning so much on the popular part of the constitution'.[46]

For all the promises made by the sponsors of New Brunswick that a new model colony would emerge on the banks of the River St John, the loyalists there and those in the remaining part of Nova Scotia behaved in much the same way. Rather than forming united communities, accepting the leadership of their betters who saw themselves as the embodiment of true loyalty to the empire, they were suspicious of all efforts to exercise authority over them. The claims of men who had held high office in the old colonial order or who had been senior offices in the Provincial regiments to large allocations of land were bitterly resented. As was the case with all loyalist communities, there was a general inclination to oppose executive authority. It is 'the natural disposition of people on this side of the Atlantic to kick against the King's government', the governor of Nova Scotia commented.[47] Oppositionist tendencies could become outright radicalism or, to the governor at least, republicanism. He was dismayed by the virulence with which two barristers attacked the judges in the press and in the assembly. One of them, he thought, 'aims at being the Wilkes of Nova Scotia'.[48] They have made 'a strong party chiefly among the new inhabitants who have shown a seditious factious spirit upon the occasion, many of whom have introduced republican principles, who came here on the specious pretence of loyalism'.[49]

Accusations of insubordination and republicanism were also to be made in New Brunswick.[50] The discipline of the ex-soldiers shipped to the River St John quickly broke down and they became 'an irregular and licentious body of men, irritated and disgusted to an extreme degree'.[51] There were numerous complaints about the inequitable distribution of land. Committees were formed and campaigns waged in

[45] Order in Council, 18 June 1784, Frederick Madden with David Fieldhouse (eds), *Select Documents on the Constitutional History of the British Empire and Commonwealth*, III, *Imperial Reconstruction 1763–1840: The Evolution of Alternative Systems of Colonial Government* (Westport, CT, 1987), p. 389.

[46] T. Carleton to Sydney, 25 June 1785, TNA, CO 188/3, ff. 56–7.

[47] J. Parr to Lansdowne, 15 May 1786, BL, Add MS 88906/3/18, f. 128.

[48] J. Parr to Sydney, 8 March 1788, TNA, CO 217/60, f. 173.

[49] J. Parr to E. Nepean, 18 April 1788, ibid. f. 177.

[50] D. G. Bell, *Early Loyalist St John: The Origin of New Brunswick Politics 1783–1786* (Fredericton, NB, 1983); Maya Jasanoff, *Liberty's Exiles: The Loss of America and the Remaking of the British Empire* (London, 2011), pp. 180–9.

[51] E. Winslow to B. Watson, 10 January 1784, TNA, CO 217/56, f. 386.

the press. In 1785 the governor called the first elections for the assembly. Because formal titles to land had not been issued, all male inhabitants were declared to be eligible for the franchise. The governor hoped for an assembly 'composed of worthy and respectable characters' but was dismayed by outbreaks of 'faction' and rioting and the heavy polling of opponents of the 'government men'.[52] Their election was, however, declared invalid and those who printed inflammatory material or presented 'artfull libellous petitions' were punished by the courts. By May 1786 the governor claimed that the colony had been brought to order.[53]

The 'republicanism' among loyalists which the governors of Nova Scotia and New Brunswick, and also of the Bahamas, were so quick to identify and to denounce seems generally to have been more akin to the assertion of the 'rights of Englishmen' in the years leading up to the Revolution in many North American and West Indian colonies as well as by British radicals, than to the revolutionary republicanism that took control of the new American states. The petition of 'his Majesty's dutiful and affectionate subjects' in New Brunswick against the manipulation of electoral results seems to have been characteristic. Violations of 'the rights of the people' were 'subversive of the first principles of the British constitution'. The king should use his prerogative powers to redress their grievances.[54]

Alliances between governors and loyalist elites were eventually to bring some political stability to both Nova Scotia and New Brunswick. In New Brunswick from the outset, loyalists controlled the council and held most important offices. They generally cooperated with the governor until relations broke down after 1793. In Nova Scotia what has been called a 'loyalist ascendancy' gained control after 1792 under a loyalist governor, John Wentworth, formerly of New Hampshire, with loyalists in prominent offices and dominating the council, the assembly, and most professional positions including preferment in the Anglican Church, whose first bishop, appointed in 1787, was a New York loyalist. The loyalist elites in both colonies formed connections with Federalists in the United States, but whether such regimes became 'the envy of the American states' as a whole seems unlikely. The colonies certainly did not prosper in the ways that had been planned for them. They were unable to take much advantage of the protected West Indian market. With 'primitive' infrastructures and 'a lamentable shortage of capital', their economies were largely dependent on the spending of the imperial government.[55]

IV

Post-war Quebec was still being governed under the Quebec Act of 1774, which gave it a constitution significantly different from the general model of British

---

[52] T. Carleton to Sydney, 25 October, 20 November 1785, TNA, CO 188/3, ff. 127, 153.
[53] T. Carleton to Sydney, 14 May 1786, ibid. ff. 196–7.
[54] Petition of 3 March 1786, Bell, *Early Loyalist St John*, pp. 150–2.
[55] Julian Gwyn, *Excessive Expectations: Maritime Commerce and the Economic Development of Nova Scotia 1740–1870* (Montreal and Kingston, 1998), pp. 33, 42.

colonial governments. The constitution of Quebec was peculiar to it because of what were judged to be the peculiarities of its population: they were overwhelmingly French Catholics rather than Anglophone Protestants. The right of the people of Quebec to 'the free exercise of the religion of the Church of *Rome*' was confirmed and the clergy were permitted to collect tithes. 'Matters of controversy, relative to property and civil rights' were to be settled according to 'the laws of *Canada*' rather than the common law of England. It was deemed to be inappropriate to extend elected representative government to an alien population of doubtful loyalty and anyway unused to it. So there was to be no assembly. Ordinances for 'the peace, welfare and good government' of the colony were to be made by a nominated council, subject to the governor's approval.[56]

A constitution framed to meet the special needs of a particular people was based on certain assumptions about them. What made the French Canadians different was the supposed backwardness and conservatism of the rural mass of the *habitants* of what had been New France. They were thought to be a largely apolitical people, practising subsistence agriculture, subservient to their priests and seigneurs, and potentially obedient subjects of an alien government if that government did not interfere with their beliefs and customs. As their new rulers, the British were bound both on grounds of justice and of self-interest to respect the ingrained prejudices of their subjects and to ease them only gradually into the modern commercial world. A contented people would neither rebel nor collude with foreign attacks on Canada, even if they came from France. In time, they might become a valuable source of military manpower to the empire.

The record of the French Canadians in the American War disappointed their British rulers, who often expected enthusiastic gratitude for the blessings supposedly conferred on them by the Quebec Act. Congress had called on Quebec to overthrow British rule and join the union. To speed the process American troops had invaded the colony. With 'few exceptions' the French remained 'either passive or hostile' to the British cause.[57] Nevertheless, the invading Americans did not find support on a scale and of an intensity that would have enabled them to create a new regime that might have sought to be admitted into the union. The French kept their distance from both sides and thus, the point has reasonably been made, showed themselves to be loyalists of a kind.[58]

Americans had seen the Quebec Act with its provisions for the toleration of Catholicism and for authoritarian government, let alone the expropriation of much territory claimed by individual colonies, as one of the 'intolerable acts' which justified armed resistance. People of British origin settled in Quebec generally also objected to it as subjecting them to an alien form of government which violated their rights as British subjects. In Britain the Act had been strongly opposed both in Parliament and outside it. With the ending of the war, Francophone and Anglophone committees were set up in both Montreal and Quebec to

[56] 14 Geo. III, c. 83, secs. 5, 8, 12.
[57] Hilda Neatby, *Quebec: The Revolutionary Age 1760–1791* (Toronto, 1966), p. 155.
[58] Bumsted, *Understanding the Loyalists*, pp. 46–9.

call for its replacement.[59] Petitions were sent to London asking that Quebec might like other colonies enjoy the blessings of the British constitution through the calling of an elected assembly and for English commercial law to replace provisions in the French civil law, regarded as inimical to enterprise and the economic development of the colony. Counter-petitions were launched, largely instigated by members of the Francophone elite, urging that the act be retained to safeguard the French way of life. The governor, General Haldimand, was in no doubt that pressure for more than strictly limited amendments to the Quebec Act must be resisted. 'This province can only be preserved by bringing back the Canadians to a regular subordination . . . In order to effectuate this, the authority of government must be strengthened and not diminished.'[60] British ministers' initial inclination was to temporize over the future of the Quebec Act and to postpone any decision about the introduction of representative government.

Pressures for change were, however, building up. There was increasing awareness that the French were no longer, if they had ever been, an inert people without political concerns beyond those implanted in them by their seigneurs and their clergy. They served on juries and as magistrates and sought local offices.[61] Analogies between the seigneurs and a British landowning aristocracy were recognized to be misleading. Their tenants, William Smith explained, were 'the real landholders of the province'. Britain could not rely on the mistakenly supposed ascendancy of the seigneurs or the clergy.[62] A considerable proportion of the seigneuries had actually been acquired by Anglophones.[63] The urban French bourgeois of Quebec and Montreal petitioned for the repeal of the Act and the grant of an assembly. Even if the mass of the French may not have been much concerned with representative government, many were thought to want more civil rights and legal protection from 'the caprice of men in power'.[64] There was strong agitation against the levying of labour under the *corvée* system and against the militia system. Some even thought that the *habitants* were coming to be 'tinged with Yankey politics'.[65] Yet if there seemed to be stirrings among the Francophone population, there were still presumed to be clear limits to the amount of change that they would accept. The main provisions of the French civil law on which family structures and property rights depended must be preserved.

[59] For the committees and their petitions, see F. Murray Greenwood, *Legacies of Fear: Law and Politics in Quebec in the Era of the French Revolution* (Toronto, 1993); David Milobar, 'Conservative Ideology, Metropolitan Government, and the Reform of Quebec, 1782–1791', *International History Review*, XII (1990), 45–64.

[60] To North, 24 October 1783, A. Shortt and A. G. Doughty, *Documents Relating to the Constitutional History of Canada 1759–1791*, 2nd edn, 2 vols. (Ottawa, 1918), II, pp. 736–7.

[61] Donald Fyson, 'The Canadiens and British Institutions of Local Governance in Quebec from the Conquest to the Rebellions' in Nancy Christie (ed.), *Transatlantic Subjects: Ideas, Institutions, and Social Experience in Post-Revolutionary British North America* (Montreal and Kingston, 2008), pp. 72–3.

[62] W. Smith to B. Watson, 7 November 1788, Upton (ed.), *Smith Diary*, II, p. 255.

[63] Peter Marshall, 'British North America 1760–1815' in P. J. Marshall (ed.), *The Oxford History of the British Empire*, II, *The Eighteenth Century* (Oxford, 1998), p. 389.

[64] H. Finlay to [E. Nepean], 4 September 1785, TNA, CO 42/17, f. 61.

[65] S. Holland to Roberts, 9 November 1785, ibid. f. 196.

At the time of the passing of the Quebec Act, the Anglophone population of the colony had constituted only an insignificant minority, mostly linked with the trade of Montreal or Quebec, whose claims to the rights of British subjects could be dismissed quite easily. The influx of loyalists, mainly ex-Provincial soldiers from New York, during and after the war had changed the situation. Their numbers, some 6,000 being settled immediately after the war, did not tip the balance greatly against what were assumed to be up to 100,000 French, but they took over large areas without previous European settlement, mostly to the west of the province, along the upper St Lawrence and Lakes Ontario and Erie, where they formed distinct communities.

Those who claimed to speak for the newly arrived loyalists soon began to formulate grievances against the Quebec Act from which they claimed exemption. Their main objection was that they held their grants of land under seigneurial tenure. This, they complained, subjected them 'to the rigorous rules, homages, reservations, and restrictions of the French laws and customs, which are so different from the mild tenures to which they have ever been accustomed'.[66] Some saw putting them under the same seigneurial tenure as the French as reducing them 'to the state of a conquered people who being born slaves cannot know what it is to be free'.[67] They were too far from Quebec and Montreal to be effectively administered as part of a single government. They should have their own courts, using English law, and their own Lieutenant Governor. They had not formally demanded representative government through an assembly, but there was little doubt that this was what they also hoped for. Were these things to be granted to them, they promised that many people from the United States would emigrate into what would become a new Anglophone province in order to share the great benefits of living under an English system of government.[68] Guy Carleton, who as Lord Dorchester had become governor in 1786, agreed. 'Well affected' people had already moved from the United States, he wrote. With proper encouragement, more would come to 'fill that extensive country' and bring it soon to 'a flourishing condition'.[69] They would not, however, come to live under a French system of government and land tenure, whose continuation might even drive discontented loyalists back to America.

American immigration was thought to be even more important for Quebec's development than for that of Nova Scotia. Quebec could not be permitted to stagnate indefinitely. The Committee of the Privy Council for trade and colonies had staked out its future role in a self-sufficient British Atlantic empire. It was to provide the West Indies and Newfoundland with timber and especially with great quantities of wheat and flour.[70] This required additional Anglophones, who, given official hostility to emigration from Britain, could only come from America. Some

---

[66] Petition of J. Johnson, 11 April 1785, Shortt and Doughty (eds), *Documents*, II, p. 774.

[67] P. McNiff to S. DeLancey, March 1786, Catherine S. Crary (ed.), *The Price of Loyalty: Tory Writings from the Revolutionary Era* (New York, 1973), p. 424.

[68] Johnson petition, 11 April 1785, Shortt and Doughty (eds), *Documents*, II, p. 776

[69] To W. Grenville, 27 May 1790, TNA, CO 42/67, ff. 184–5.

[70] Report of 31 May 1784, BL, Add MS 38388, f. 133.

stereotypes about French Canadians might now be questioned, but the assumption that their outlook and institutions made them a people ill-suited to the successful commercial exploitation of Quebec survived largely intact. Conventional wisdom was that 'the country is capable of great improvements', but that the 'ideas of the Canadians are very circumscribed'. Improvement therefore depended on the Anglophones, who already dominated Quebec's commercial life and were likely to produce exportable surpluses from the land on which they were settled. Their enterprise required a congenial political and legal framework. Only a government 'upon the most liberal principle of freedom will enable the country to be a commercial one'.[71] British ministers understood that 'the wealth and resources' of Canada were improving, but almost entirely due to the exertions of British and American settlers. The French were said to be 'greatly deficient in that spirit of enterprise and industry'.[72] Institutional reform and economic development were thus thought to be inseparably linked. Yet if the price of development was political reform which would alienate the mass of the French population, Canada seemed to be deadlocked.

The Pitt government was at first in no hurry to end the deadlock. In 1784 they had decided that the task of devising solutions for Quebec was to be given to Sir Guy Carleton. Carleton did not, however, get to Quebec until 1786 and then felt unable to make decisive recommendations. In the meanwhile the need for a solution was becoming increasingly urgent. The Quebec Act system of government was manifestly working badly. As the British Secretary of State observed in September 1789, Quebec was 'very far from being now in a composed or tranquil state'.[73] The nominated council was locked in rancorous disputes between reformers and conservatives. The judges were at loggerheads on how they interpreted the boundaries between the application of French and English law. Quebec's disputes were being relayed to Britain by rival petitions. The voice of the reformers calling for repeal of the Quebec Act was the loudest. They were backed by the formidable lobby of the London Canada merchants and in 1786 by the parliamentary opposition, Charles Fox proclaiming that he would have 'every government under the sanction and authority of the British dominions, founded on a principle of liberty'. He thought that the French were entitled to 'a free government', even if 'the majority of them were so blind to their own interest and ease as to refuse to accept it'.[74] The issue came up again in 1788. Governments of this period very much disliked what Shelburne called public 'clamour' leading to parliamentary interference on colonial issues; the Pitt administration wished to see clamour stilled. Finally, Quebec continued to constitute what was seen as a heavy charge on the

---

[71] 'Considerations Respecting Commerce in Canada received from Mr Mauduit' [1786], BL, Add MS 38346, f. 360.

[72] W. Grenville, 'Memorandum on Questions at Issue', copy enclosed in letter to Leeds, 15 September 1789, BL, Add MS 59230, f. 94. Shortt and Doughty (eds), *Documents*, II, pp. 970–87. The great bulk of the text is printed in Vincent Harlow and Frederick Madden (eds), *British Colonial Developments 1774–1834: Select Documents* (Oxford, 1953), pp. 197–210.

[73] Ibid. p. 202.

[74] 28 April 1786, *Parliamentary Register*, XX, p. 139.

British taxpayer. Local revenue was limited to certain duties sanctioned by a British Act of 1774. From 1778 the British Parliament had bound itself not to lay taxes on colonies and without a representative body there was no taxing authority in Quebec. It therefore received parliamentary grants to bridge the gap between its needs and what could be raised locally. In 1788 Quebec had cost the British Treasury £152,583.[75] The burden was likely to increase, a prospect that William Grenville, the new Secretary of State, viewed with as little enthusiasm as his father George Grenville had shown for colonial expenditure in the 1760s.[76] Like his father, he considered that colonies should meet their own costs.

By September 1788 the British government was apparently inclining towards a partition of Quebec, creating a separate loyalist province with British law and institutions, a proposal with which Lord Dorchester was unhappy. Definite plans for a new Canadian order were not, however, drawn up until 1789, when William Grenville took office as Secretary of State. The bill for giving Quebec a new constitution was essentially his bill. It was finally enacted in 1791.[77]

The 1791 Canada Act has attracted much attention from historians.[78] It is widely regarded as a defining statement of British imperial governance after the American Revolution, marking, for instance, 'the beginning of a new brand of imperial political engineering' that was to be applied in the future government of settlement colonies.[79] There are, however, strong elements of continuity between it and pre-Revolutionary practice as well as with the Quebec Act of 1774, which, although extensively amended, remained unrepealed. Quebec's very contentious legal system was left unreformed. The temporary deviation in 1774 from the revered maxim that British subjects of European origin could not be governed without representation was, however, abandoned. It was not possible, William Grenville believed, to go on much longer treating Quebec as an exception from other colonies. Opposition to government without representation was certain to grow in Parliament and might carry the day.[80] The example of the United States had now, in his view, to be taken into account. The debate on the Act indeed showed a marked change from previous complacency that the new America's political failure under the Confederation meant that it offered no serious competition to British regimes. The new federal Constitution was praised by both Fox and Burke. Fox thought that American governments were 'the best adapted to the situation of the people who lived under them, of any of the governments of the

---

[75] Harlow, *Second British Empire*, II, p. 754.

[76] See his Memorandum, Harlow and Madden (eds), *Colonial Developments*, p. 200. He was at this time trying to recover control over Crown lands throughout the colonial empire in order to reduce costs born by Britain.

[77] 31 Geo. III, c. 31.

[78] See, for instance, Neatby, *Quebec*, ch. 16; A. L. Burt, *The Old Province of Quebec*, 2nd edn, 2 vols. (Toronto, 1968), II, ch. 19; Harlow, *Second British Empire*, II, pp. 714–73; Peter Marshall, 'North America's Other Eighteenth-century Constitution' in T. J. Barron, O. D. Edwards and P. J. Storey (eds), *Constitutions and National Identity* (Edinburgh, 1993), pp. 101–10.

[79] Madden with Fieldhouse (eds), *Select Documents*, III, p. xxxii.

[80] Memorandum, Harlow and Madden (eds), *Colonial Development*, pp. 209–10.

ancient and modern world'.[81] Burke agreed. 'The people of America had, he believed, formed a constitution as well adapted to their circumstances as they could.'[82] Pitt was more reserved, while stating that he would not use 'republican' as 'an obnoxious term'.[83] Even if it had been politically feasible to continue to govern Quebec without an assembly, it was still undesirable to do so. Government without a local legislature was totally incompatible with enterprise and commercial development. It must inevitably 'check and depress the prosperity of the colony', Grenville wrote.[84] There was also an urgent need to raise taxes. So there must be an assembly. Because of the deep divide between Anglophones and Francophones, who mostly lived in separate territory, although the most vocal and politically active Anglophones in fact lived among the French in Montreal and Quebec, there must inevitably be two assemblies: the Anglophones could not be swamped by a French majority and the franchise could not be rigged to give the Anglophones an ascendancy over the French. Quebec must therefore be partitioned into two separate provinces, to be called Lower and Upper Canada. Under North American conditions with very wide diffusion of property, especially of land, restricting the franchise would hardly be practical. So the two assemblies would inevitably be democratic bodies. The Lower Canadian franchise was in fact 'one of the most democratic in the world' with virtually all *habitant* farmers and many artisans qualified to vote.[85]

If democracy in the assemblies could not be avoided, it must be checked. At this point breaks with the past began. Old colonial models were not to be strictly followed, but in Grenville's words, later to be much quoted, the aim was 'to assimilate the constitution of that province to that of Great Britain, as nearly as the difference arising from the manners of the people and from the present situation of the province will allow'. It was a cardinal principle in British governing circles that the failure to contain the democracy of the American colonial assemblies had been the road to revolution and ruin. The root of the trouble had been, in Grenville's view, the defective nature of the colonial councils which had failed to check the exorbitant power of the assembly. The key to balancing an over-assertive assembly was to be a prestigious and powerful Legislative Council to play the role of the House of Lords. Its members were to serve for life and it was desirable that they should constitute a colonial aristocracy with hereditary marks of honour. Grenville was thinking of a 'provincial baronetage'.[86] The governors of American colonies had also been too weak when confronted by aggressive assemblies. If they could hardly be invested with the inherited prestige and powers which continued to make the British monarchy a potent force in politics, their position could still be strengthened. They must be given adequate revenues that did not depend on the

---

[81] 8 April 1791, *Parliamentary Register*, XXIX, p. 72.
[82] 6 May 1791, ibid. p. 320.
[83] 8 April 1791, ibid. p. 76.
[84] To Thurlow, 12 September 1789, *Historical Manuscripts Commission: Fortescue MSS*, 10 vols. (London, 1892–1927), I, p. 507.
[85] Greenwood, *Legacies of Fear*, p. 47.
[86] To Dorchester, 20 October 1789. Shortt and Doughty (eds), *Documents*, II, pp. 988, 989.

assembly and have powers of patronage with which to reward their supporters. Grenville hoped that a proper Canadian equivalent to the British civil list might be provided by reserving to the Crown a proportion of all new land grants. This would also give the governor a resource with which to reward his supporters. This proposal was, in the event, dropped from the bill, although Crown Reserves were later instituted in Upper Canada, and it was replaced with a provision for land to be reserved as an endowment for the Protestant clergy, for whom support through the collection of tithes was impractical. Pitt explained in the debate that 'Protestant' was to be interpreted as the Church of England and that he hoped to see a bishop sitting in the Legislative Council.[87]

The Canada Act of 1791 fulfilled some British expectations, although ambitious hopes of assimilating colonial communities with very different social structures to a British constitutional model were doomed. Very little was raised in taxation. Governors were generally able for the next decade or so to maintain an ascendancy over the assemblies. As in New Brunswick and Nova Scotia, governors of the Canadas exercised their powers in close alliance with local elites, predominantly Anglophone in Lower as well as in Upper Canada, whose position generally depended on official patronage and office rather than on deference willingly accorded to them by the *habitants* in Lower Canada or by the increasing numbers of 'late loyalists', that is, post-1783 immigrant from the United States, settled on the land in Upper Canada. Neither group seems to have been actively committed to the ideals of an empire based on the British constitution. In 1785 Pitt had been reported as wishing to 'Anglify' Canada[88] and in the debate on the 1791 Act in response to a question he had repeated that this was his intention, although compulsion must not be used.[89] In Lower Canada there was much talk of Anglicizing by men such as William Smith but very little was attempted before the nineteenth century.[90] Immigrants from the United States to Upper Canada were likely to be attracted by cheap land and low taxes rather than by the virtues of British colonial government. The suggestion that 'most immigrants lacked ideological commitments to either empire or republic' seems realistic.[91] Protestants were, of course, a minority in Catholic Lower Canada, but the Church of England was a minority among that minority and it was a minority too in overwhelmingly Protestant Upper Canada. An Anglican missionary described the inhabitants in 1787 as 'principally Presbyterians, Anabaptists, Dutch Calvinists and New England Sectaries'.[92] Itinerant American Methodists and Baptists were later to operate effectively north of the border.

---

[87] 11 May 1791, *Parliamentary Register*, XXIX, pp. 414–15.
[88] See above, p. 88.
[89] 11 May 1791, *Parliamentary Register*, XXIX, p. 387.
[90] Greenwood, *Legacies of Fear*, pp. 52–5.
[91] Alan Taylor, 'The Late Loyalists: Northern Reflections of the Early American Republic', *Journal of the Early Republic*, XXVII (2007), 29. His arguments are elaborated in his *The Civil War of 1812: American Citizens, British Subjects, Irish Rebels and Indian Allies* (New York, 2010).
[92] J. Stuart to SPG, 20 June, 14 August 1787, Richard A. Preston (ed.), *Kingston before the War of 1812: A Collection of Documents* (Toronto, 1959), p. 120.

Pitt anticipated that 'an extension of commerce and wealth . . . would follow the introduction of the new constitution'.[93] Economic growth remained, however, sluggish. In as far as the Canadas were involved in international trade, before the boom in timber exports to Britain in the early nineteenth century, their trade was mostly cross-border with the United States rather than with other parts of the empire. They were unable to assume their allotted role of major bread provider to the British West Indies until the Americans embargoed their own shipments after 1807. Economically, as in other respects, in the early decades after American independence, British North America developed within a continental as much as within an imperial context.

Immediately after the ending of the war, there had been a mood of expansive optimism about the prospects for British North America, summed up by the much-repeated claim that the British colonies, enjoying the ordered freedom guaranteed by the British constitution and prosperity within an imperial trading system, would become the envy of the unstable American states whose union seemed to be on the point of collapse. A decade later, enthusiasts such as John Graves Simcoe, shortly to become governor of Upper Canada, or William Smith, continued to prophesy a golden future for Canada. Realistically, however, such a future must have seemed to be a long way off. Contrasts with the United States were no longer strongly in favour of the British colonies. Neither rule by governors in collaboration with official elites nor the as yet limited economic development of British North America were likely to arouse much envy south of the border. The Americans had consolidated their union and were expanding westwards. Smith could still write dismissively of the 'debility of our neighbours' and of Britain's power 'to check any councils to be meditated to her detriment by the new nation she has consented to create'.[94] But Lord Dorchester concluded by 1790 that Britain must coexist with an expanding republic on a basis of 'justice, moderation and liberality'. He thought that it would be highly desirable 'to form alliances with our neighbours, as soon as all things are well matured for that purpose'.[95]

---

[93] 11 May 1791, *Parliamentary Register*, XXIX, p. 395.
[94] To Dorchester, 5 February 1790, TNA, CO 42/67, ff. 69–70.
[95] To W. Grenville, 21 July 1790, TNA, CO 42/68, f. 277.

9

The Swing to the South

I

In his classic *Capitalism and Slavery*, first published in 1944, Eric Williams described American independence as 'the first stage in the decline of the sugar colonies'. Williams was an early exponent of what later came to be known as 'the swing to the East' in British priorities. 'The Caribbean', he wrote, 'ceased to be a British lake when the American colonies won their independence. The center of gravity in the British empire shifted from the Caribbean Sea to the Indian Ocean, from the West Indies to India.'[1] In the course of time the Caribbean did indeed become an American, not a British, lake and British imperial activities came to be focused primarily on the Indian Ocean. Yet until well into the nineteenth century there is little to suggest that the Caribbean was losing the dominant position in Britain's view of the world that it had long enjoyed. In the later phases of the American War the West Indies became the major theatre of British operations, and in the period immediately after American independence there was no diminution in British concern for the Caribbean. It is even possible to postulate that there was something like a 'swing to the South', that is a shift in focus of British preoccupations from the northern colonies with their large white populations not only to the plantation colonies of the West Indies, but also to the lands round the Gulf of Mexico and further south into Spanish America.

The French entry into the war in 1778 brought about a major shift in British strategic priorities from the North American continent to the Caribbean. Were the French to make large conquests in the West Indies, it was feared that they would strike a deadly blow at Britain's capacity to wage war. The defence of the British islands therefore became the most urgent call on Britain's resources and troops were diverted there from fighting to subdue the colonies. If anything could be saved on the mainland, there were calls that it should be the plantation colonies of the south. Georgia and South Carolina would, it was believed, be easier to subjugate and hold than the northern colonies and the wealth of their tropical staples made them a valuable prize to be kept within the empire. The new Florida colonies should be kept as well. Although West Florida had been lost to the Spanish, East Florida had been successfully defended. The southern colonies were not only desirable objects

---

[1] *Capitalism and Slavery* (London, 1944), pp. 114, 123. Williams was repeating an argument propounded by Lowell J. Ragatz in *The Fall of the Planter Class in the British Caribbean 1763–1833* (Washington, DC, 1928).

in themselves, but holding them was important to safeguard trade with the West Indies. A hostile power in possession of their ports would be able to 'inflict losses serious and immeasurable on our homeward fleets from Jamaica'.[2] British objectives in the Caribbean were, however, far from merely defensive. Not only would attacking French possessions be the best way of defending British ones, but the conquest of the French islands would cripple the French war effort. British troops from America were initially sent to attack the French in St Lucia. When Spain entered the war British operations were launched with a view to disrupting the Spanish empire in Central America. Troops were landed on the coast of what was to be Nicaragua. At the end of the war Lord Shelburne had most ambitious plans for expeditions to destabilize much of the Spanish empire.

Such designs came to very little. Instead of plundering the colonies of her enemies, Britain had to struggle hard to maintain her own. Many islands were lost, even though the greatest prize of all, Jamaica, was secured by a spectacular British naval victory. British efforts to re-establish control over South Carolina and Georgia failed. East Florida was given up as well as West Florida in the 1783 peace with Spain. The raids on Central America were largely unsuccessful and one of the two existing British toeholds there, the Mosquito Coast settlement, was renounced in 1786. Nevertheless, nearly all West Indian losses were regained at the peace and the islands quickly recovered their dominant position in Britain's post-war imperial economy. British interest in the lands around the Gulf of Mexico was kept alive. The Bahamas, hitherto a marginal British colony, were developed by loyalist migration. A considerable trade was maintained with the Floridas and Spanish Louisiana. Contact was kept up with Indian peoples on the Spanish-American frontiers and the prospects of war with Spain in 1790 led to a revival of plans for military expeditions to disrupt the empire.

The American War had inflicted very serious damage on the British West Indies. A great reduction of their trade with the continent—their main source of food, timber, and other vital supplies—created much hardship. The shipping that serviced them was vulnerable to enemy attack. Exports fell to about half their pre-war level and profits were seriously eroded. By the end of the war the French had taken all the major British islands, except for Jamaica, Barbados, and Antigua. The Spanish briefly occupied the main settlement on the Bahamas. In all cases, however, except for Tobago, British rule was restored at the peace. Within a few years there seemed to be clear indications that the plantations were recovering: shipments of produce to Britain rose above pre-war levels, slave imports forged ahead, especially into Jamaica, Grenada, and Dominica, and most of the islands appeared to be returning to profitability.[3]

---

[2] A. Campbell to W. Knox, 15 September 1782, WLCL, Knox MSS, 6: 54.

[3] See the assessment of recent research indicating recovery in Andrew Jackson O'Shaughnessy, *An Empire Divided: The American Revolution and the British Caribbean* (Philadelphia, 2000), pp. 238–9. David B. Ryden, *West Indian Slavery and British Abolition 1783–1807* (Cambridge, 2009) diagnoses 'long-term difficulties' after 1783, see p. 217.

Sections of white West Indian opinion, particularly in Jamaica, were, however, more impressed by what they saw as the post-war afflictions of the islands than by evidence of recovery.[4] Jamaica was devastated by a succession of hurricanes between 1780 and 1787 and many planters were convinced that shifts in British policies were compounding their difficulties. Jamaica's complaints reveal a strong sense of alienation from the empire whose rulers professed to value the island so highly. In 1783 a group of what the governor called 'malcontents' urged the assembly not to vote supplies for the British troops stationed on the island so long as Jamaica was 'proscribed by proclamation, and chained down by partial trade laws, while we are oppressed by improvident taxes'. The grievances of which they complained were the Order in Council of July 1783, greatly restricting American trade with the West Indies,[5] the high duties in Britain on rum as well as the increased duties imposed on sugar in the 1781 budget. They urged that Jamaica should follow the example of Ireland by forming associations to force Britain to change its policy.[6] An inflammatory pamphlet published in 1783 blamed the 'imbecility, ignorance and wickedness' of the North administration for the disasters of the American War in the Caribbean, which had only been redeemed from total catastrophe by the heroic endeavours of Rodney at the battle of the Saintes in 1782. The main theme of the pamphlet was to demand a reduction of duties on rum and the revocation of the increases in sugar duties. These were not merely 'impolitic' they were '*UNCONSTITUTIONAL because taxes have been levied on the people by those who are not their representatives*'. The British Parliament had no right to impose duties on Jamaican sugar 'since they are no more our representatives than they are the representatives of *any other part of North America*'. Jamaica should consider non-exportation and non-importation embargoes to bring Britain to her senses.[7] In more measured terms the Jamaica council and assembly sent repeated petitions to Britain asking for the reduction of duties on their exports and the lifting of restrictions on American trade. 'The existence of this country as a sugar colony' depended on redress. Jamaica had borne an 'accumulation of taxation and other hardships, until lately unheard of', but it could not be expected passively to 'await the near approach of actual famine'.[8] The Barbados agent pledged his community's love for Britain, their unwavering loyalty to the Crown and their willingness to bear any hardship for the public good, but warned that they would not accept discriminatory measures against them.[9]

For all the fury of protests and the 'threats of secession and challenges to parliamentary sovereignty', which took British West Indian opinion in the 1780s

---

[4] See Letter from Jamaica, 26 December 1786, which stressed that high output did not indicate prosperity (TNA, PRO 30/8/349, ff. 81–3).

[5] See above, p. 103.

[6] Address of 21 October 1783, enclosed in A. Campbell to North, 28 November 1783, TNA, CO 137/84, ff. 25–7.

[7] John Gardner Kemeys, *Free and Candid Reflections upon the late Additional Duties on Sugar and on Rum* (London, 1783), pp. 10, 100, 126–7.

[8] Memorial to the King, 11 December 1784, TNA, CO 137/85, ff. 240–4.

[9] Letter to the King's Ministers, 29 October 1785, TNA, BT 6/84, ff. 271–2.

into more extreme ideological positions than they had adopted during the American Revolution,[10] governors were generally able to keep control of assemblies. In Jamaica a popular Lieutenant Governor was still able to get votes of additional allowances for the royal troops. Yet the bitterness of many whites in the post-war Caribbean is unmistakable. They had a strong sense that they were getting inadequate rewards for the vital contribution that they made to the good of the empire. The West Indian interest in Britain no longer constituted a pressure group that could carry all before it as, both they and their enemies liked to believe, had been the case in the past. Representations made on their behalf by their agents, by London committees of merchants and planters, and by influential MPs appeared now to be spurned. When the West India Committee passed on a memorial to the Crown protesting about the duties and American trade restrictions from the Jamaica council and assembly, the Secretary of State complained that petitioning other than through the governor was 'disrespectful' and that ministers 'cannot support or countenance the present application without material injury to the commercial interest of this country'.[11] The West Indian whites, who were inclined to believe that the commercial interest of Britain began and ended with the prosperity of the islands, did not take kindly to finding now that the protection of British shipping took precedence to their receiving assured supplies of food and timber from the United States or that distilling rum in British North American colonies was to be encouraged to the detriment of their exports.

The truculence of West Indian complaints was not well received in Britain. During the American War official opinion in Britain had come to regard the loyalty of the British Caribbean with suspicion. Suspicions lingered on after the war. Lord Sackville, previously known as Lord George Germain, interpreted the islands' objection to 'so unexceptionable a measure' as the Order in Council of 1783 as evidence that there was 'little attachment to this country or to this government to be found among them and if America once flourishes as an independent state, our islands will seek the first opportunity of belonging to them'.[12] William Knox 'well knew how heartily disposed our West India islands were to assist the revolt of North America' and believed that through the Order in Council, for which he claimed the credit, 'he had happily defeated' the West Indians' attempt to 'transfer to the American states the profits of their commerce and to raise them a marine on the ruins of that of Great Britain'.[13] Sir Guy Carleton in his evidence in 1784 presented the Committee of the Privy Council for trade and colonies with a stark choice between the proven commitment to Britain of the loyalists in the remaining British North American colonies or the distinctly equivocal commitment of the West Indies (which was of course absorbing numerous loyalists), where 'a republican spirit' has 'in some degree spread':

---

[10] O'Shaughnessy, *Empire Divided*, pp. 245–6.
[11] Sydney to A. Clarke, 19 April 1786, TNA, CO 137/86, f. 49.
[12] To W. Knox, 20 September 1783, *Historical Manuscripts Commission, Various MSS*, VI, *Knox MSS* (London, 1909), p. 192.
[13] To W. Eden, 7 January 1786, WLCL, Knox MSS, 7: 26.

The struggle now to be decided involves a very important question, whether the United States, or the remaining British colonies in [North] America, shall engross the benefits arising from a trade between the continent and the islands; if the former succeed, their cause and their interest, political as well as commercial, must increase, and in like manner, if the loyalists prevail, they will contribute proportionately to their own and to the national strength and prosperity. The only firm hold that Great Britain has upon the remains of the American dominions, is certainly by means of the loyalists.[14]

Such pronouncements rested on unreal estimates of the capacity of the North American colonies to replace the United States in sustaining the West Indies and seriously misrepresented the political views of most of the British West Indian whites. They might be bitterly critical of British policy towards them and fiercely tenacious of what they deemed to be their constitutional rights, but this did not make them republicans.[15] Nevertheless, the tone of their opposition, added to doubts about the degree of their commitment during the war, damaged their political standing in Britain. The loyalists in the northern colonies may or may not have deserved Carleton's encomiums on their commitment to the cause of empire, but by contrast with them or even with the East India Company's servants, who were succeeding in ridding themselves of the corrupt taint of the 'nabobs', the planters seemed to be unreliable partners in empire, putting their own interests before the common good.

West Indian interests were to need all the political capital on which they could possibly draw in the years ahead as slavery and the slave trade came under attack in Britain. The next chapter will describe how these attacks were launched against an institution that had become morally disreputable and how they came to be focused in the first instance on the slave trade by which the plantations were able to replenish and expand their labour force. Mass petitions against the trade were considered by Parliament between 1789 and 1792. West Indian interests fought vigorously against abolition of the trade, while conceding the need for some regulation of it and of slavery, and were able to win what was to be a reprieve for the trade. There could, however, be little doubt that the reprieve would only be a temporary one. The conflict between the national conscience and the planters' interpretation of the needs of the West Indies was an unequal one.

Yet even if slavery had become abhorrent to British opinion and the future of the slave trade was in serious doubt, this most emphatically did not mean that empire in the West Indies had become expendable. It was confidently supposed that the greatly prized plantation agriculture would continue and indeed become more productive with a labour force that gradually ceased to be a coerced one and in course of time worked freely for wages. In the meanwhile the contribution of

---

[14] Evidence, 16 March 1784, BL, Add MSS 38388, f. 18.

[15] The case for their rejection of the republicanism and aspirations to independence of the American Revolution has been argued by O'Shaughnessy in *An Empire Divided*. For a different interpretation, stressing 'the pro-republican ideology of a large section of the inhabitants' of the British West Indies, see S. H. H. Carrington, *The British West Indies During the American Revolution* (Dordrecht, 1988), quotation on p. 130.

slave-worked agriculture to the British economy grew markedly. In the 1790s British West Indian sugar, profiting from the collapse of production in its great rival St Domingue, underwent a spectacular, if transitory expansion, especially in Jamaica.[16] In the world wars against Revolutionary and Napoleonic France, Britain was to acquire very productive new Caribbean plantation colonies worked by slaves, especially the Dutch mainland possessions that became British Guiana. These conquests greatly increased the very large contribution that the West Indies had come to make to Britain's cotton supply.

II

The American War had brought many misfortunes for the British West Indies, but one of its outcomes had been a reinforcement of both white and black refugees, displaced from the mainland by the American victories. When the British withdrew from Georgia and South Carolina in 1782 they took numerous refugees with them. In the first instance many of them moved to the British colony of East Florida, which had been successfully defended against American attacks, while others went to the Caribbean islands. In the peace settlement of 1783 Britain ceded East Florida to Spain. When the colony was evacuated in 1785 there was a wide dispersal of people. Some went north to remain under British rule in Nova Scotia. Many whites eventually went back to the United States and many slaves were sold to American planters. In spite of stories of ex-Provincial soldiers being killed when they went back,[17] it is likely that most loyalists who returned to the southern states were in no great danger. The passions which erupted in the ferocity of the back-country civil war seem to have subsided remarkably quickly. The advice from North Carolina was that 'any person that has been guilty of no cruelties may safely come back', as 'animosities bred by differences of opinion only die away so fast'.[18] The largest movements were to the Caribbean, above all to the Bahamas, where loyalist immigrants became the dominant element in the population of the islands. Others went to Jamaica and to Dominica, while a few tried to settle on the Mosquito Coast of Nicaragua, about to be handed over to Spain.

Some 10,000 whites may have left Georgia and South Carolina. The biggest element seems to have been small farmers from the Georgia and Carolina back country, who had been on the losing side in the bitter civil war set off by the British army's southern campaigns, together with artisans and craftsmen and some professional people from Savannah and Charleston. Planters on a large scale, substantial merchants, and senior royal officials or officers in the Provincial regiments tended to go to Britain. Some planters, however, tried to resume business in the Bahamas

---

[16] Ryden, *West Indian Slavery*, pp. 218–22.
[17] G. Carleton to North, 26 October 1783, TNA, CO 5/111, f. 123.
[18] N. Mason to [A. Mason], 22 February 1784, cited in Carole W. Troxler, 'The Migration of Carolina and Georgia Loyalists to Nova Scotia and New Brunswick', University of North Carolina PhD thesis, 1974, p. 167.

or in West Indian islands, taking their slaves with them. Some Provincial regiments raised in the south were disbanded at St Augustine in East Florida. A number of the soldiers chose to go to Nova Scotia, but most were dispersed throughout the Caribbean. What most distinguished the southern movements from the northern ones was the very large displacement of black people, which is described in the next chapter. Black emigrants heavily outnumbered whites. Some African Americans went to the British Caribbean colonies with guarantees of freedom; most went there as slaves, taken by owners who were seeking a new living or shipped off to be sold throughout the West Indies.

The Bahamas was the only destination where the southern loyalists were able to create what became essentially their own colony. Settling loyalists on the Bahamas was a project taken up in earnest by the Fox–North Coalition after the fall of Shelburne in 1783. William Knox, who once again enjoyed influence through Lord North, drew up a memorandum in favour of a strong settlement of loyalists in the Bahamas as a secure base to protect the Jamaican trade.[19] The obvious difficulty in settling loyalists in any numbers in the Bahamas was, however, that the land did not belong to the Crown; it belonged to a group of proprietors whose rights dated back to the seventeenth century. It had been decided in 1736 that the Crown should buy them out, but nothing had effectively been done. In September 1783 ministers determined that the project should be revived and North wrote to the Privy Council asking that the Treasury be instructed to purchase the proprietary rights. The arguments that he gave were that in equity Britain ought to find shelter for the southern as well as for the northern loyalists, who had been resettled in Nova Scotia or Quebec, and that the Bahamas were the only 'eligible' place for them to go. He threw in the consideration, widely canvassed at the time, that the Bahamas were likely to become a major producer of cotton.[20] Although it was to take another four years for the purchase to be completed, shipping was to be made immediately available to take loyalists to the Bahamas where they could be sure of receiving 'every encouragement and protection that this country can possibly afford'.[21]

Viewed realistically, whatever those who wished to promote them might assert,[22] the economic potential of the Bahamas was uncertain. The governor of East Florida described the Bahamas 'as mere rocks, fit only for fishermen'.[23] The existing population of the islands was put at 1,500 to 1,700 whites and 2,000 to 2,500 free people of colour and slaves. Agriculture was said to be little developed, the population mostly being employed at sea, running a smuggling trade, wrecking, and catching turtles. There were some valuable woods like mahogany and rich deposits of salt especially on the Turks Islands.[24] The much-vaunted potential for

[19] Undated, BL, Add MS 61864, f. 101.

[20] To Lord President, 15 September 1783, TNA, HO 43/1, pp. 183–4.

[21] North to G. Carleton, 4 December 1783, TNA, CO 5/111, f. 89.

[22] See, for instance, an account of the 'Bahama Islands', which promised 'All the natural advantages of the sugar islands' (BL, Add MS 24322, f. 102).

[23] P. Tonyn to T. Townshend, 15 May 1783, TNA, CO 5/560, f. 292.

[24] See accounts in 'Propositions Relating to the Bahamas', TNA, CO 23/26, ff. 151–3; 'Bahamas', 1 November 1785, BL, Add MS 38346, f. 56.

cotton cultivation had begun to be exploited within the last few years by planters working with small numbers of slaves. Some had become 'men of considerable property'.[25]

Loyalist migration to the Bahamas on any scale began from New York. In 1783, on the eve of the British evacuation, an association was formed with agents and a committee to act for the 400 loyalists who had engaged to settle on the island of Abaco. There they expected to harvest 'timber, log and dye wood' and to develop West Indian produce.[26] Ultimately 941 people made the journey from New York to Abaco: 217 men, 118 women, 203 children, and 403 servants, including slaves and free black people who had entered into indentures to serve for a period.[27] The governor of the Bahamas was instructed to allow heads of families 40 acres with 20 acres for additional members of households.[28] In 1783 some 600 migrants from East Florida were reported also to be settling at Abaco or moving on to Exuma. In the later stages of the exodus from East Florida, which went on until 1785, 1,033 whites and 2,214 blacks were recorded as going to the Bahamas. By 1789 the islands' population was put at 11,300, of whom 8,000 were black.[29] Some great plantation owners from East Florida shifted their operations to the Bahamas. Denys Rolle, member of a prominent Devonshire landowning family and for a time an MP, relocated some 140 slaves from Florida to Exuma to work new plantations. These eventually covered some 5,000 acres.[30] Thomas Brown from Georgia, the redoubtable colonel of the loyalist King's Rangers, took 170 slaves to the Bahamas and he too acquired great holdings ultimately amounting to 8,000 acres worked by 600 slaves.[31] He and a number of other army officers took up land in large blocks on Grand Caicos.[32] Profitable plantations on this scale were made possible by a short-lived boom in Bahamas cotton which lasted into the 1790s. Cotton also sustained a considerable number of planters with small holdings on which they employed between ten or a hundred slaves or servants on Exuma, Watling, Long Island, the Caicos Islands, and other islands to the south of the chain. An analysis of 114 surviving land grants shows an average size of holding of 382 acres.[33] The centre of government at Nassau on New Providence attracted loyalist ex-officers, merchants, and lawyers, who quickly organized a vociferous opposition to the

---

[25] O. Eve to D. Cox, 29 May 1784, TNA, CO 23/26, f. 204.

[26] Committee to G. Carleton, 25 June 1783, TNA, PRO 30/55/73, no. 8227.

[27] Sandra Riley, *Homeward Bound: A History of the Bahama Islands to 1850* (Miami, FL, 1983), pp. 140–4.

[28] Instructions to Lord Dunmore, 20 July 1787, TNA, PC 5/14, ff. 228–31.

[29] Return, 2 May 1786, TNA, CO 5/561, f. 407. Michael Craton, *A History of the Bahamas*, 2nd edn (London, 1968), p. 166.

[30] In his statement of losses, TNA, HO 42/3, ff. 124–5, Rolle described his slave labour force as 19 'tradesmen', 77 'field negroes' and 32 'rising generation', Robert Legg, *A Pioneer in Xanadu: Denys Rolle 1725–1797* (Whitchurch, Hants, 1997), pp. 125–9.

[31] Edward J. Cashin, *The King's Ranger: Thomas Brown and the American Revolution on the Southern Frontier* (Athens, GA, 1989), ch.10.

[32] Charlene J. Kozy, 'Tories Transplanted: The Caribbean Exile and Plantation Settlement of Southern Loyalists', *Georgia Historical Quarterly*, LXXV (1991), 18–42.

[33] Craton, *History of Bahamas*, p. 165.

authority of the governor.[34] Free blacks and artisans and other poor whites also established themselves there. Generalizations about the mass of ex-Florida loyalists were usually unflattering. To the governor, they were 'the scum and refuse of our unfortunate army'.[35] Another observer described them as 'the refuse of America', lawless and 'lacking respect to their superiors or even common humanity to their equals'.[36]

As in the northern colonies, the communities in the Bahamas after the inflow of loyalists were fragmented and deeply divided. Any sense of common loyalty to Crown and empire is hard to detect. There was antagonism between the new arrivals and the existing settlers. Loyalists formed parties against one another. The mass rejected the claims to authority of rich planters and former army officers. Free blacks were subjected to violence from white mobs. The scale of the inflow of new inhabitants put a severe strain on the extent of land that could be easily cultivated and on the limited possibilities for profitable employment. The Bahamas, however, had certain advantages that helped to carry it through the early stages of its population expansion. Cotton quickly grew into an important export crop, supplemented by the existing activities of wood-cutting and salt-raking. Created a free port in 1787, Nassau developed into a considerable commercial centre, trading with the French West Indies and with Spanish Louisiana, Florida, and Cuba. It was the base from which concerns like the firm of Panton and Leslie traded with Spanish territory round the Gulf of Mexico, distributing imports of British goods and shipping out furs and tropical produce to Europe.[37]

In 1782 refugees from Savannah and from Charleston had been drawn to Jamaica with its hugely productive plantation economy in considerable numbers and more were to follow after the evacuation of East Florida. Additions to the white population and to the black labour force by the slaves that white refugees brought with them seem to have been welcome in Jamaica. The Jamaica assembly exempted refugees from North America from taxation for seven years and the parochial vestry of Kingston provided relief for the impoverished, a burden against which it was to complain.[38] Some loyalists proposed to cultivate indigo if they could obtain suitable land.[39] The major grant made to them proved, however, to be a swamp which could not be drained. Few loyalist refugees seem to have had the resources to become successful planters in Jamaica.[40] Some loyalists from East Florida went on

[34] J. Maxwell to Sydney, 17 March 1784, TNA, CO 23/25, f. 104. For the turbulent politics of the loyalist Bahamas, see Maya Jasanoff, *Liberty's Exiles: The Loss of America and the Remaking of the British Empire* (London, 2011), ch. 7.

[35] J. Maxwell to A. McArthur, 9 June 1784, TNA, CO 23/25, f. 134.

[36] J. Brown to G. Elliott, 21 April 1786, TNA, CO 23/26, f. 211.

[37] William S. Coker and Thomas D. Watson, *Indian Traders of the Spanish Borderlands: Panton and Leslie and Company and John Forbes and Company, 1783–1847* (Gainesville, FL, 1986), pp. 44–5.

[38] A. Campbell to T. Townshend, 5 April 1783, TNA, CO 137/83, f. 77. Wilbur H. Siebert, 'The Legacy of the American Revolution to the British West Indies and Bahamas', *Ohio State University Bulletin*, XVII (1913), 35–9.

[39] Campbell to North, 1 August 1783 with petition, TNA, CO 137/83, ff. 142–4.

[40] Maya Jasanoff's *Liberty's Exiles*, ch. 8 contains a valuable account of the tribulations of the loyalists in Jamaica.

from Jamaica to the British settlements on the Mosquito Coast of what is now Nicaragua, largely for the extraction of logwood and mahogany. Some 330 white loyalist families with about 1,300 slaves are said to have been there at one time.[41] In 1786, under a treaty with Spain, the British settlers were ordered out of the Mosquito Coast, most going to the Honduras settlements. Mosquito Coast loyalists later petitioned for compensation for plantations and houses that they had been encouraged to set up. A return of 66 whites and 143 slaves was attached.[42]

Of the other British West Indian colonies, Dominica and St Vincent were particularly anxious to attract loyalists. Both had been conquered by the French during the war. Their small Anglophone white populations were contending with French settlers and hostile black Caribs on St Vincent, and formidable resistance from escaped slaves in Dominica. Loyalists and their slaves would be a welcome reinforcement. On both islands, however, land at the immediate disposal of the Crown was limited. Some East Florida refugees moved to Dominica. Between 460 and 470 loyalists were being given provisions there in September 1785.[43] The Dominica loyalists appear to have been mostly small planters, craftsmen, and artisans who hoped to get land grants and to carry on their trades as coopers, carpenters, tailors, or masons. They brought small numbers of slaves with them.[44] They do not, however, seem to have been able to establish a lasting presence on the island.[45] The governor of St Vincent felt that he did not have sufficient disposable land to encourage loyalist settlement, much as he would have liked to have done so.[46]

The influx of loyalists was a transforming event for many of the remaining British colonies on the North American continent where their settlement was strongly supported by the British government. In what became New Brunswick and Upper Canada the loyalists created what were essentially their own colonies and they became the dominant element in Nova Scotia. In the south the loyalists were much less successful. No southern mainland colony survived after the war. The potential of West Florida was widely recognized, but the Spanish had taken possession of it during the war and the British did not respond to American encouragement to send an expedition to recover it. East Florida had less potential and highly speculative investments after the colony's acquisition in 1763 had generally lost money. Loyalist settlement there during the war, however, stimulated development made possible by wartime conditions. East Florida replaced North and South Carolina as a source of provisions for the West Indies, of indigo and naval stores, and especially of tar and turpentine, which became the colony's staple exports. With an increasing population and with more loyalists likely to settle there,

---

[41] Sylvia R. Frey, *Water from the Rock: Black Resistance in a Revolutionary Age* (Princeton, NJ, 1991), p. 184

[42] Memorial and return 10 October 1786, TNA, CO 137/83, f. 163.

[43] Note to list of tools . . . for assisting the loyalists, [28 September 1785], TNA, CO 71/9, f. 213.

[44] See applications for relief considered by the Dominica council and assembly, ibid. ff. 258–61 and 302–3.

[45] In his 1791 book Thomas Atwood noted 'some few Americans, white people who are called American refugees' in what was still a very small British population (*History of the Island of Dominica* (London, 1791), p. 208).

[46] E. Lincoln to Sydney, 2 May, 18 August 1784, TNA, CO 260/7.

East Florida seemed to have a promising future within the British empire.[47] The Shelburne administration, however, decided to cede it to Spain as part of a settlement that involved the retention of Gibraltar. Florida proprietors offered the Spanish ambassador in London a deal whereby loyalists would remain in East Florida as 'an excellent bulwark against the United States' in return for religious, legal and commercial privileges. The Spanish would not rise to the bait and without guaranteed privileges few loyalists seem to have remained in East Florida,[48] although some went to West Florida where the Spanish were more accommodating. Most either went back to the United States or migrated to the British Caribbean. In the Bahamas, although its economic prospects were uncertain, they became the dominant element. Elsewhere, they were neither numerous enough nor do most of them seem to have had the resources to be other than marginal to existing plantation society. Outside the Bahamas the loyalist immigration did not leave much mark on the British West Indies.

III

The English had initially been drawn to the West Indies by their potential as a springboard to trade with, and to launch attacks upon, Spanish America, rather than as a source of tropical produce through plantation agriculture. That came later. Interest in the Spanish Main continued during the eighteenth-century heyday of West Indian sugar. The capacity of the Spanish empire to prevent commercial penetration and even territorial dismemberment appeared to be weakening in the face of Indian and Creole disaffection and many schemes were devised to hasten its decline by inciting revolts and establishing British enclaves on the mainland.

Spain's entry into the American War in 1779 stimulated new British designs against its empire.[49] The Spanish were to be attacked from across the Pacific via India and at New Orleans and in Central America by forces from Jamaica. At the very end of the war in 1782 Lord Shelburne had extremely ambitious plans for sending troops from New York to attack the Spanish and raise revolts from the River Plate to Peru.[50]

The Central American scheme was the only one to be put into effect. Britain had long-standing settlements in the Gulf of Honduras and on the Mosquito Coast of Nicaragua. The settlers were chiefly occupied in cutting logwood, the source of an important dye for textiles, and increasingly in shipping out mahogany to be made

---

[47] For loyalist East Florida, see Carole W. Troxler, 'Refuge, Resistance and Reward: The Southern Loyalist Claim on East Florida', *Journal of Southern History*, LV (1989), 563–96.

[48] Report of East Florida Proprietors, 19 February 1783 (*Morning Chronicle*, 22 July 1783). For Spanish accounts of the negotiations, see Del Campo to Floridablanca, 14 May 1783, and 'Articles proposed by Lord Hawke', Joseph B. Lockey (ed.), *East Florida 1783–85* (Berkeley, CA, 1949), pp. 92–3, 121–2.

[49] These are summarized in Alan Frost, *The Global Reach of Empire: Britain's Maritime Expansion in the Indian and Pacific Oceans 1764–1815* (Carlton, Victoria, 2003), pp. 95–101.

[50] See above, p. 25.

into furniture. The main plan was to recruit settlers and the bitterly anti-Spanish Miskito Indians into a force that would be strengthened by British troops from Jamaica. It would push up the San Juan River from the Mosquito Coast to Lake Nicaragua and would, it was hoped, take the towns on the Pacific Coast, thus cutting Spanish Central America in two. The plan, proposed by the governor of Jamaica, was enthusiastically received in Britain. The Secretary of State, Lord George Germain, promised four regiments from Britain, at a time of acute shortage of men for other campaigns. He hoped that it would be possible to establish a new colony of settlement in Nicaragua. The 'allurement of so fine a country and climate, the wealth of the inhabitants and the richness of the mines' would draw settlers from the West Indies and provide a haven for displaced American loyalists.[51] An initial success was won at Fort Omoa on the Honduras coast. The Nicaraguan expedition, which set out before the promised reinforcements arrived from Britain, was, however, a failure. It could not reach Lake Nicaragua and suffered great losses from disease before it was withdrawn.[52]

The immediate outcome of the American War was to strengthen rather than to weaken the Spanish empire. The British failed to break through in Central America. The Spanish conquered West Florida and took the main British settlement in the Bahamas. This was recovered at the peace, but Spain gained both West Florida and East Florida. British ministers were tempted by American offers to connive at the dispatch of troops to expel the Spanish from West Florida and thus clear them from blocking the Mississippi to American trade. The British negotiator, Richard Oswald, assured ministers that West Florida was potentially 'more productive than any part of British America'.[53] He was told that the government would be 'extremely glad' to get it back.[54] A separate article delineating boundaries if the British did recover it was included in the provisional treaty. Nothing, however, came of the project, although the treaty guaranteed that 'The navigation of the River Mississippi' should 'forever remain free and open' to British subjects. In the complex bargaining about the British retention of Gibraltar, East Florida, which had remained in British hands throughout the war, was also included in the compensations offered to Spain. Lord Shelburne argued in the debate on the treaty in the House of Lords that East Florida was of little value in terms of trade and that retaining it would not be worth future tension with Spain and the United States. It was best left in the hands of the Spanish who would not be able to develop it anyway.[55] Shelburne also sought to accommodate matters with Spain over the two British footholds in Central America, where the Spanish had succeeded in expelling

---

[51] Germain to J. Dalling, 1 March 1780, *Historical Manuscripts Commission; Stopford Sackville MSS*, 2 vols. (London, 1904–10), II, p. 284.

[52] Dr Andrew O'Shaughnessy has kindly permitted me to see an unpublished paper on the expedition, '"Let the rebellion go round": British Operations in Central America during the American Revolution'.

[53] Minutes, 29 August 1782, TNA, FO 97/157, f. 124.

[54] T. Townshend to R. Oswald, 26 October 1782, ibid. f. 166.

[55] Vincent T. Harlow, *The Founding of the Second British Empire 1763–1793*, 2 vols. (London 1952–64), I, pp. 436–7.

the Honduras settlers but had been repulsed on the Mosquito Coast. The Spanish wished to eliminate all British settlements, offering to supply the British with logwood instead. Shelburne was willing to sacrifice one of the existing settlements, that on the Mosquito Coast, for formal Spanish recognition of British rights in Honduras together with an enlargement of territory. He was aware that as Britain's supporters, 'the Mosquito Indians will find allies in parliament', but he was even more worried by the outcry that would arise 'if we do not cut log wood for ourselves, and ensure a considerable district for the purpose' in Honduras.[56]

The peace settlement of 1783 suggests that any 'swing to the South' in British strategy during the American War had been renounced. Britain's interest in the Spanish empire, which now stretched along the entire northern shore of the Gulf of Mexico, seemed henceforward to be purely commercial. Spanish trade would be encouraged through more West Indian free ports. Such a renunciation might seem to have been appropriate to Lord Shelburne with his professions of preferring trade to dominion, once he had abandoned his grandiose plans to liberate Spanish America by force. If there was such a renunciation, it was, however, by no means a complete one.

The Fox–North Coalition made a half-hearted attempt to persuade the Spanish to restore East Florida, taking up the Florida proprietors' proposal for a loyalist refuge which would act as a buffer against the United States,[57] and a much more determined one to prevent the handing back of the Mosquito Coast.[58] Such efforts suggest continuing British interest in territorial possessions on the mainland. The provisional articles of peace with Spain included clauses defining the limits of the Honduras settlements that were to be restored to Britain and stating that Britain would abandon all other claims in Central America. The Mosquito Coast was not specifically mentioned, but Lord Grantham, the British Foreign Secretary under Shelburne, had told the Spanish that in his opinion the settlement, whose only value, he thought, was as a base for smugglers, should not be retained.[59] Both the Spanish and the British negotiator, Alleyne Fitzherbert, interpreted this as a definite commitment that the Mosquito Coast was to be evacuated.[60]

Those interested in the Mosquito Coast were, however, determined that it should be retained. Their main advocate was Robert White, who called himself their agent. His voluminous writings flooded ministers' offices in his efforts to make a case for the potential of the Mosquito Coast as a valuable colony. He asserted that the Mosquito Coast was by no means to be regarded as simply a base for cutting logwood and mahogany. In the language characteristic of all colonial promoters at all times, he proclaimed that it could produce in abundance all the

[56] To Grantham, 25 December 1782, BL, Add MS 88906/3/11, ff. 48–50.
[57] See Fox's letter to Manchester, 2 July 1783 and the report of the Spanish Ambassador, del Campo, 9 August 1783, Lockey (ed.), *East Florida*, pp. 134, 138.
[58] For Anglo-Spanish diplomacy on the Mosquito Coast, see W. S. Sorsby, 'The British Superintendency of the Mosquito Shore, 1749–1787', University of London PhD thesis, 1960.
[59] Memo of 11 November 1783, BL Add MS 59238, f. 32.
[60] Fox to Manchester, 2 July 1783, Manchester to Fox, 6, 9 July 1783, TNA, FO 27/9, ff. 210–11, 259–60, 275.

important commodities of the West Indies and the southern American states. It already, he alleged, had some successful plantations and it should become a separate British colony with its own administration. The Spanish had no right to it since they had never succeeded in subduing the Miskito Indians, an independent people whom the British patronized by awarding them titles, and from whom they had received extensive grants. In the view of another propagandist, the Mosquito Coast could be 'of more importance than all the British sugar islands put together'.[61] As an additional bait, it was said to be an appropriate haven for loyalists who were known to be interested in settling there. Such assertions evidently struck a responsive cord with the Fox–North Coalition. White, whose normal expectations were that his effusions would be ignored by ministers, 'had the gratification' of being given more attention 'than ever he had received from any former administration'.[62] Charles Fox instructed the British Ambassador in Paris, who was negotiating the terms of the definitive treaty with Spain, to raise the issue of the Mosquito Coast. Fox's view was that, as it had not specifically been mentioned in the preliminary treaty, Britain was not bound to give it up. He understood it to be more important than the Honduras Bay settlements.[63] The Spanish refused to reopen the question, but no specific mention of the Mosquito Coast was made in the definitive treaty, the Cabinet feeling that they would rather leave the issue open to future dispute than put the signing of the treaty at risk by pressing the matter on Spain.[64] The Spanish subsequently threatened to take control of the Mosquito Coast by force and the British responded by dispatching forces from Jamaica. The new Pitt administration continued to insist on Britain's rights and to countenance settlement on the Mosquito Coast until November 1784, when the Cabinet decided that no further encouragement should be given.[65]

By then the government was interested in a wider diplomatic and commercial settlement with Spain. Ambitions for a colony on the Mosquito Coast were not to be allowed to get in the way of this. The governor of Jamaica was told that 'in the present situation of the affairs of this country', a war with Spain over the Mosquito Coast would be 'a very unpleasant event'.[66] Negotiations culminated in an agreement signed in London on 14 July 1786. Britain agreed formally to abandon the Mosquito Coast, the Spanish guaranteeing to avoid all acts of severity to the Miskito Indians, who joined the considerable list of Native American peoples, including the Seminole, Creeks, and Choctaw around East and West Florida, as well as the Mohawks and many others in the north, who felt themselves to have been abandoned by the British. They complained vociferously, even going to

---

[61] G. Dyer to Fox, 5 July 1783, TNA, FO 27/9, f. 255.

[62] [R. White], *The Case of the Agent to . . . the late Settlers on the Mosquito Shore* (London, 1793), p. 74.

[63] 2 July 1783, TNA, FO 27/9, ff. 210–12.

[64] The Cabinet minute of 18 July 1783 and correspondence with the king and the Duke of Manchester are in J. Fortescue (ed.), *The Correspondence of King George the Third*, 6 vols. (London, 1927–8), VI, pp. 419, 421 and Lord John Russell (ed.), *Memorials and Correspondence of Charles James Fox*, 4 vols. (London, 1853–7), II, pp. 132–4.

[65] Cabinet Minute, 15 November 1784, TNA, CO 128/3, f. 279.

[66] Sydney to A. Clarke, 2 June 1785, TNA, CO 137/85, f. 117.

Jamaica to do so. The evacuation was complete by June 1787 when 2,314 people (537 whites and free blacks and 1,677 slaves) went from the Mosquito Coast to the Honduras Bay settlement.[67] A motion in the House of Lords censuring the government for giving up 'a territory as large was Portugal' was easily defeated.[68] Not the least of Robert White's services to the settlers was his success in getting the government to inquire into claims for compensation, of course including his own arrears of salary. He threatened to petition the House of Commons and the government bought him off with a Treasury inquiry. Claims then lodged revealed that there had been ambitious but unsuccessful projects for mining gold and that some sugar had been cultivated, but that cutting mahogany was clearly the main occupation.[69]

The retreat from the Mosquito Coast and the consolidation of the Honduras settlements did not finally draw a line under projects for attacking the Spanish in Central America. When war over the Nootka Sound incident seemed likely in 1790, the American War projects were revived. Expeditions from India were to cross the Pacific. Robert White again proffered his advice. Troops were again to be sent from Jamaica to attack the mainland with the aid of the Honduras settlers.[70] British ministers established close contact with a significant Creole opponent of the Spanish imperial order, Francisco Miranda.

The handing over of the Floridas to Spain in 1783 did not mark an end to British interest in them or in the Mississippi delta and New Orleans. In re-establishing their rule the Spanish faced serious difficulties.[71] There were large Indian populations to be managed and considerable numbers of American would-be settlers were coming down the Mississippi seeking lands in West Florida or moving westwards from Georgia. To contain American inroads the Spanish needed to ally with powerful Indian peoples, above all with the Creeks but also with the Cherokee, Choctaw, and Alabama peoples. Supplies of goods, including firearms and gunpowder, were the essential underpinnings of such alliances. These had to come from British sources and to a lesser degree from the French. For supplying the Indians to the east of the Mississippi the Spanish were willing to deal with a British firm already well established in the Florida Indian trade. The firm of Panton and Leslie was permitted to retain and extend their posts in both East and West Florida.[72] Goods were shipped from the Bahamas, where the firm had its headquarters, principally to Pensacola in West Florida. In return for their extensive privileges, Panton and Leslie, hitherto committed loyalists to George III, were

---

[67] Wallace Brown, 'The Mosquito Shore and the Bay of Honduras during the Era of the American Revolution', *Belizean Studies*, XVIII (1990), 56.

[68] Lord Rawdon, 26 March 1786, *Parliamentary Register*, XXII, p. 136.

[69] J. Marsh and J. Spranger's reports to Treasury, 22 November 1790, 19 May 1791, *Journals of the House of Commons*, XLVII (1792), 431–4.

[70] Frost, *Global Reach of Empire*, pp. 228–9; Harlow, *Second British Empire*, II, p. 647.

[71] See the helpful summary of recent literature in Eliga H. Gould, 'Entangled Histories, Entangled Worlds: The English-Speaking Atlantic as a Spanish Periphery', *American Historical Review*, CXII (2007), 777–9.

[72] Coker and Watson, *Indian Traders of the Spanish Borderlands*.

willing to pledge their 'faithful adherence to the Spanish monarch' as well.[73] Nevertheless, they pointed out the advantages of their trade to the Committee of the British Privy Council, stressing that the Indians' 'passion for the English is a kind of enthusiasm' and that they 'consider the loss of the English government in that country as the greatest misfortune'.[74] Alexander McGillivray, the mixed-race Creek chief, had been in British service during the war and was a partner in Panton and Leslie. From 1788 attempts were to be made to exploit the Indians' supposed hopes of British protection against both Spain and the United States and incidentally to break the hold of Panton and Leslie over the Indian trade by a loyalist from Maryland called William Augustus Bowles with the active encouragement of Lord Dunmore, once the governor of Virginia but now the governor of the Bahamas. Dunmore had ambitions for restoring British authority over part of the Southwest. Bowles had plans to create a new independent Indian state in alliance with Britain against both Spain and the United States. He took a party of Creeks and Cherokees to Quebec. They arrived in 1790 during the Nootka Sound crisis and seemed to Lord Dorchester to be possible allies in 'any operations to dispossess the Spaniards of the Floridas and Louisiana'.[75] From Canada, Bowles went to London to lobby British ministers.[76] A number of other projects for operations against Spain, usually involving the cooperation of the United States or of groups of American settlers on the Mississippi, were being floated at the time.[77] With the settling of the disputes with Spain over access to the Pacific such projects were shelved, but they were frequently to be revived in various forms, culminating in the British disaster in 1815 when an expedition to take New Orleans was repulsed by the Americans with heavy losses.

By the middle of the nineteenth century the impulses that had so long sustained a vigorous British imperial presence in and around the Caribbean and the Gulf of Mexico had played themselves out. The British West Indian sugar plantations had been left to compete as well as they could in the British market without tariff protection against an abundance of other suppliers throughout the world. They no longer generated private or public wealth on a conspicuous scale. The tropical plantations of vital importance to the British economy were now those that grew cotton in the United States. The Spanish empire had passed away largely through the exertions of its own subjects not through the intervention of British armed force. Through the acquisition of the Floridas, Louisiana, and much more, the United States rather than Britain had become the territorial beneficiary of Spanish dismemberment. With hindsight, it is clear that the American Revolution was a dire threat the survival of European empires around the Caribbean. Yet in 1783, the United States must have seemed by far the weakest of the three competitors and Britain, even though she had just been worsted by France and Spain and by her

---

[73] Panton and Leslie's memorial, 31 July 1784, Lockey (ed.), *East Florida*, p. 259.
[74] Examination of Thomas Forbes, TNA, PRO 30/8/344, ff. 14–15.
[75] Dorchester to W. Grenville, 26 July 1790, TNA, CO 42/68, f. 280.
[76] For Bowles, see Maya Jasanoff, *Liberty's Exiles*, pp. 234–43.
[77] J. Leitch Wright, *Britain and the American Frontier 1783–1815* (Athens, GA, 1975), chs. 3 and 4.

own colonial rebellions, must have still seemed to be the strongest. The output of her existing sugar islands was recovering and in the next round of wars much new sugar territory was to be added. Her most dangerous competitor, the French colony of St Domingue, was soon to be destroyed by revolution. The Spanish empire, in spite of its effective resistance in the American War, still seemed to be ripe for liberation by British intervention. Plans were still being floated for winning unrestricted commercial access, for the seizing of trading enclaves, and even perhaps for the establishment of new colonies. Empire in and around the Caribbean continued to feature largely in British calculations for two or three decades after the loss of the thirteen colonies.

10

Empires of Righteousness
Native Americans, Enslaved Africans, and Indians

I

In a letter to a friend in March 1785, William Livingston, governor of New Jersey, reflected on the prospects for the new American empire. It was already a 'mighty structure' and certainly 'founded in righteousness', but it would 'crumble into ruin, unless by righteousness it be supported and buttressed'. In the rest of the letter Livingston discussed an issue by which the righteousness of European empires was increasingly judged, that is how they treated non-European peoples. He deplored the way in which Americans were depriving Indians of 'those lands which the Almighty had given them by prior occupancy before the ambition and avarice of Europe so abominably perverted the peaceable spirit of Christianity, under the plausible guise of converting pagans to the true faith as to carry desolation and havoc thru Asia and Africa'.[1]

Linking their treatment of the peoples of the Americas, Asia, and Africa into an indictment of the inhumanity of modern European empires was by the 1780s common practice. Its most powerful statement was the best-selling compendium of Enlightenment thought by many hands, notably that of Denis Diderot, that went under the name of the *Histoire philosophique et politique des établissements et du commerce des Européens dans les deux Indes* by the Abbé Raynal,[2] which appeared in 1772. English translations were published in London and Edinburgh in 1776. Two more followed in London in 1777 as well as a Dublin edition and an Aberdeen one in 1779. Its theme that Europeans had inflicted great damage on other peoples and were continuing to do so was accepted by most strands of opinion that could be considered as enlightened in Britain and America as well as in Europe, by many Christian activists, and also by a wider public. The British empire was certainly vulnerable with its dominant position in the slave trade, its plantation colonies worked by slaves in the Caribbean, and its new conquests in India. Some Americans saw themselves, as Alexander Hamilton put it in *The Federalist* no. 11, as fellow victims of European domination with Asians and Africans, but as now in a position

---

[1] To C. Stewart, 15 March 1785, Carl E. Prince et al. (eds), *The Papers of William Livingston*, 5 vols. (New Brunswick, NJ, 1979–88), V, pp. 176–7.
[2] Anthony Pagden, *Lords of All the World: Ideologies of Empire in Spain, Britain and France c.1500—c.1800* (New Haven, CT, 1995), pp. 163–8.

to 'vindicate the honor of the human race, and to teach that assuming brother [Europe] moderation'.[3] The new American empire had, however, a large slave population within its boundaries, had expelled or subjugated Native peoples during the early phases of settlement and, as Livingston and many others were uncomfortably aware, the great westward expansion unleashed by the war would inevitably be at the expense of other Native peoples. To some extent campaigns to bring about empires of righteousness for indigenous peoples across the world after 1783 were, as they are usually portrayed, the undertakings of self-consciously enlightened and politically radical groups together with Christian humanitarians, working in a common cause on both sides of the Atlantic. But they were also a source of Anglo-American friction and rivalry as each side tried to claim a higher degree of righteousness in a competition which in the long run and with a degree of hindsight seems to have become increasingly unreal as British and American imperial doctrines and practices converged.[4]

II

From the middle of the eighteenth century relations with the Native peoples living beyond the colonial frontiers had become the direct concern of the metropolitan British government, which entrusted dealings with them to its own officials. The experience of the Seven Years War, when so many Indians had initially fought against the British, encouraged a more interventionist policy and above all attempt, embodied in the famous proclamation of 1763, to protect them from dispossession by the land hunger of the people of the colonies. Indians had also become objects of concern to a wider public in Britain itself.[5] Money was liberally subscribed to English and Scottish missionary societies to support projects for Christianizing and civilizing 'the savages'. However limited the effect of British policies may have been, and however much Indians may have resented British attempts to order their affairs, the British generally seemed to them to be preferable to the land-hungry Americans. When fighting broke out most Indian peoples eventually sided with the British. The fate of Indian peoples, however, featured not at all in the peace negotiations. Britain was content to cede the lands of its allies to the Americans or to the Spanish without any consultation with Native opinion. A sense that they had been betrayed by their British allies was shared by outraged Native peoples from Nicaragua to the Great Lakes.

---

[3] J. R. Pole (ed.), *The Federalist* (Indianopolis, IN, 2005), p. 60.
[4] Rosemarie Zagarri, 'The Significance of the "Global Turn" for the Early American Republic: Globalization in the Age of Nation Building', *Journal of the Early American Republic*, XXXI (2011). The case for British exceptionalism is put in Van Gosse, ' "As a Nation the English are our Friends": The Emergence of African American Politics in the British Atlantic World 1772–1861', *American Historical Review*, CXIII (2008), 1003–28.
[5] Troy Bickham, *Savages within the Empire: Representations of American Indians in Eighteenth-century Britain* (Oxford, 2005).

In the south, Britain's main Native allies during the war against the Americans and the Spanish, the Cherokee, Choctaws, Chickasaws, and the Creeks and their offshoot the Seminoles, had suffered severely in the fighting. The Seminoles responded with indignant protests when they learnt that the British were evacuating East Florida. 'They do not believe it to be possible to this very hour that their ancient friends and allies will desert them.'[6] There was talk of their emigrating with the British to the Bahamas. Contacts of various kinds were to be maintained with the southern Indians by British traders and self-appointed intermediaries but, in the absence of any formal British presence, Native peoples had to come to terms with the Spanish, now again masters of the Floridas, in their efforts to check American expansion onto their lands.

In the north, the British in Canada remained in direct contact with Native peoples. In the northern sector the Indians had played a prominent role in the war. In its later stages the ruthlessness of the Americans and the much superior capacity of the British to supply and reward Indians had enabled their elaborate Indian Department to consolidate alliances with most of the frontier peoples, considerable numbers of whom had been displaced by American raids and were living near the British posts around Niagara and Detroit. As the terms of the peace leaked out, undefeated northern Indian peoples found that their lands too had been signed away without their consent by their British allies who had agreed to hand over the fur-trading posts and all territory to the south of them to the Americans 'with all convenient speed'.

Some of Britain's most committed Indian allies accepted offers of land within what was still British territory. Throughout the war British-American Provincial troops and Britain's Iroquois allies, above all the Mohawks led by the formidable warrior Joseph Brant, who held the British rank of captain, had fought together in the violent maelstrom of the Northwest borderlands. Encouraged by the British, who wished to have the Mohawks on their side of the frontier under their influence rather than under American control, Brant agreed to settle his followers in Canadian territory. Brant eventually chose a tract on the Grand River, where land was bought for him. There he was able to attract other groups of Indians to what became a flourishing township with a school, 'a handsome church with a steeple and bell, finished within, having a decent pulpit, reading desk and communion table, with convenient pews',[7] and a stately mansion for Brant himself where he entertained European visitors with tea, brandy, port, and Madeira while the Mohawks expertly danced 'Scotch reels'.[8]

The peace formally brought to an end British connections with all Indian peoples beyond the borders of Canada. Shelburne, who like other opponents of the war had regarded the alliances with Indians as indefensible because of their

---

[6] J. Douglas to North, 5 February 1784, TNA, CO 5/82, f. 430.
[7] J. Stuart to C. Inglis, 6 July 1788, Robert A. Preston (ed.), *Kingston before the War of 1812: A Collection of Documents* (Toronto, 1959), p. 137.
[8] Alan Taylor, *The Divided Ground: Indians, Settlers, and the Northern Borderlands of the American Revolution* (New York, 2006), pp. 227–8.

allegedly barbarous ways of waging war by indiscriminate murder and by scalping and torturing their victims, was happy to see them 'remitted to the care of their neighbours', who 'knew best how to tame their savage natures'.[9] In the view of men on the frontier and in Canada, an immediate severing of connections was utterly impractical and were it attempted it would have disastrous consequences for British Quebec. The British must for the moment remain in the posts and must try to continue to exercise some influence over the Indian peoples living in territory that was American by treaty but which they were far from being able to occupy effectively and where they would face bitter Indian resistance as they attempted to do so.

The fur traders, the Indian Department, and the governor of Quebec, Frederick Haldimand, all believed that immediate evacuation of the western posts would lead to catastrophe. The fur traders, whose London connections had campaigned so effectively against the peace, had great quantities of goods at the posts and demanded time to dispose of them and call in their furs. Haldimand warned the British government that continuing alliances with the Indians were essential 'for the safety of this province, which has hitherto been preserved in a great measure by their attachment'.[10] Driven by a sense of betrayal, they might well turn on Britain. Without careful British management, they would certainly be drawn into war with the Americans who were moving forward into their lands, forfeited, according to initial American policy, by their wartime alliance with Britain. The Indians would fight for land which they considered that Britain had no right to hand over to the Americans. They accepted cessions extracted by the British up to the Ohio in 1768, but contested anything beyond that. They had formed a great alliance of all the frontier peoples, including those of the south, to coordinate their resistance. Eventually no doubt the Americans would succeed in bringing about 'the destruction of the Indians', Haldimand wrote, but in the process there would be heavy losses in which the British would have a large share. 'To prevent such a disastrous event as an Indian war, is a consideration worthy the attention of both nations, and cannot be prevented so effectually as by allowing the posts in the upper country to remain as they are for some time.'[11]

Retention of the posts for the time being while urging the Americans to leave a wide swathe of territory in Indian hands as a kind of buffer became British policy for some years. Such a policy was of course dictated by the requirements of Canada's security and the needs of the fur trade. There was, however, much talk of what was due to the Indians in order to protect them from the ruthlessness of the Americans. Allegations of American cruelty to the Natives became part of the wartime rhetoric against them. 'Those very colonies who plead so high for liberty', wrote Alexander Carlyle of the Church of Scotland, were presuming that they had a right to 'drive out the heathen (a pretence in Christians no less impious than it is

[9] 17 February 1783, *Parliamentary Register*, XI, p. 68.
[10] To T. Townshend, 23 October 1782, Davies (ed.), *Documents*, XXI, p. 126.
[11] To North, 27 November 1783, TNA, CO 42/46, f. 41.

bloody,) by barbarous policy, or by force'.[12] Supporters of the war had attacked Shelburne's betrayal of Britain's Indian allies in the debates on the peace. When again briefly in office in 1783 Lord North had written of Britain's obligations to the Mohawks as a people 'justly entitled to our peculiar attention'.[13] Lord Sydney, Pitt's Secretary of State, felt it was not 'consistent with justice or good policy entirely to abandon [the Indians] to the mercy of the Americans'.[14] He made it clear, however, as did all other ministerial directives to Canada, that Indians beyond the frontier could expect no concrete measures of support and that hostilities with America on their behalf were unthinkable. When Brant arrived unbidden in London in December 1785 and asked Lord Sydney whether 'we are to be considered as his Majesty's faithful allies and to have that support and countenance, such old and true friends expect',[15] he was given no clear answer. He was, however, lavishly entertained and made much of as well as being liberally compensated for the Mohawks' wartime losses.

British members of the Indian Department and army officers on the frontier who were often closely integrated into Indian society, drew sharp contrasts between British and American Indian policy. The Mohawks who had moved to Canada, wrote one officer, will be 'much happier than those who remain with the Americans, who probably will be reduced to the same situation as the New England Indians'.[16] Major Beckwith, private emissary from the governor of Quebec, felt it appropriate to instruct Alexander Hamilton on how the United States should conduct its Indian policy through concluding 'a just and honourable peace with the savages within your limits', which would be 'greatly for the benefit of your western territory'.[17] Hamilton replied that official American policy had changed. Indians were no longer treated as conquered enemies. They were to be persuaded to sell their lands voluntarily.

Official American policy had indeed changed. Henry Knox, who as Secretary of War was directing federal Indian policy, was concerned that the new republic's reputation was at stake. Even if Congress could afford an Indian war, which it could not, 'the blood and injustice which would stain the character of the nation' would be unacceptable.[18] He believed in policies of eventual assimilation of the Indians to Christianity and settled agriculture. Projects for redeeming the Indians through missions had been joint Anglo-American ones before the Revolution and Scottish money was still being channelled to American missionaries after independence.[19] Yet circumstances were against such high-minded endeavours. British authority in Canada had a reasonable chance of being able to regulate relations between

---

[12] *The Justice and Necessity of the War with our American Colonies Examined* (Edinburgh, 1777), p. 41.

[13] To F. Haldimand, 8 August 1783, Davies (ed.), *Documents*, XXI, p. 206.

[14] To H. Hope, 6 April 1786, TNA, CO 42/49, f. 63.

[15] Brant's speech, 4 January 1786, ibid. ff. 1–2.

[16] J. Dease to Maj. Frazer, 23 February 1785, TNA, WO 28/10, f. 344.

[17] Reported conversation in Dorchester to W. Grenville, 23 November 1790, Harold C. Syrett et al. (eds), *The Papers of Alexander Hamilton*, 27 vols. (New York, 1962–1987), VII, p. 112.

[18] Paper on War Office, 15 June 1789, W. W. Abbot et al. (eds), *The Papers of George Washington: Presidential Series* (Charlottesville, VA, 1987–), II, p. 494.

[19] See below, pp. 401.

small numbers of whites and Indians in a situation where unsettled land was still relatively abundant and fur traders rather than land speculators were the strongest interest group. Loyalists who had settled in Canada professed good feelings for the Indians who had fought with them. Having been through 'the same dangers and fighting in the same cause', they felt bound 'by the strongest ties in our power to promote the wishes of these people'.[20] The American frontier, by contrast, was an extremely turbulent one. Federal attempts to impose an orderly expropriation of Indians by voluntary sales could not prevail over the interests of states like New York and Virginia, whose finances depended on quick sales of land and where land speculators were a powerful force. Even in the Northwest Territory, where Congress nominally exercised direct control, settlers were taking land and fighting off Indians regardless of what federal policy might be. The right to kill Indians became one of the rights that frontier settlers regarded as integral to the autonomy they struggled so desperately to sustain against speculators and state or federal authority.[21]

British ministers at first temporized on the issue of the evacuation of the posts. By April 1784 they had, however, decided that retention of the posts could be justified by linking it to American failures to implement other clauses of the treaty. When John Adams, as American ambassador, called for the evacuation of the posts, Pitt took the view that Britain must insist as a condition on satisfaction for America's breaches of the treaty, above all for the failure of the states to settle the debts owed to British merchants from before the war.[22] Americans were not for some years much inclined directly to challenge British intransigence, recognizing that they lacked the means to force them out.

Although they could do little about it, continued British occupation of the posts was a serious grievance to the United States and especially to the state of New York. British traders at the posts were able to maintain their operations in areas that had formally been transferred to the United States in 1783 and thus to prevent the very valuable New York fur trade from recovering from the disruptions of the war. Both Congress and the New York state government urgently needed to raise funds from land sales to enable them to meet their obligations and reduce their huge debts. Land must be obtained from Indians. Large areas were extracted from them by treaties, which the Indians later disavowed, and attempts to implement them were firmly and sometimes bloodily resisted. Americans were in no doubt, as Washington put it, that the British were 'sowing the seeds of jealousy and discontent among the various tribes of Indians on our frontier'.[23] 'So long as the British keep possession of the posts', wrote the local American military commander, 'it

[20] Petition of Provincial Regiments and Indian Department, 11 April 1785, TNA, CO 42/47, f. 58.

[21] Patrick Griffin, *American Leviathan: Empire, Nation, and Revolutionary Frontier* (New York, 2007), p. 178.

[22] To Carmarthen, 16 December 1785, BL, Egerton MS 3498, f. 155.

[23] To H. Knox, 26 December 1786, W. W. Abbot et al. (eds), *The Papers of George Washington: Confederation Series*, 6 vols. (Charlottesville, 1992–7), IV, p. 483.

is very evident that all treaties held by us with the Indians will have very little weight with them.'[24] Arthur Lee was sure that the British agents and traders incited Indians 'to murder our frontier inhabitants'.[25] Were the British to leave the posts, it was optimistically predicted that land sales in the territory across the Ohio allocated to the federal government would quickly raise enough to reduce the interest charges on the national debt to manageable proportions.[26] With the strengthening of the federal government under the Constitution, an effective United States authority, backed by limited military force, began to take root in the Northwest. Although humiliating defeats by the Indians in 1790 and 1791 eased any immediate danger to the posts, in time the Americans would inevitably become strong enough to constitute a real threat to them.

By 1794 the Americans had built up their forces for a final showdown with the Indians. For a time Anglo-American conflict was a real possibility. In spite of British weakness, Lord Dorchester, the British governor of Quebec, seemed to have abandoned his usual caution and to be encouraging Indian resistance, especially by building a new British fort well into American territory. When the Americans launched their final offensive in August 1794 the small British force in the area did nothing to aid the Indians who were defeated at the battle of Fallen Timbers and forced in the following year to cede much territory to the United States.

Well before then doubts were growing, both in Canada and in Britain, as to the need to complicate relations with the United States by holding on to posts which served no vital British interest. The British could no longer exercise a restraining influence on either Americans or Indians to prevent wars. The fur trade from the posts into territory that was American by treaty had gone through a period of great prosperity in the early 1780s. As settlement developed, however, 'the active, avaricious Americans having driven out the Indians and exhausted the hunting country' were becoming 'planters'.[27] Selling British manufactured goods to American farmers would become more profitable than the fur trade with Indians, which was shifting northwards into the relatively untapped abundance of the area beyond Lake Superior and into the Athabaska country, reached by routes which passed safely north of the posts and the 1783 boundary.[28] As part of the price for settling dangerous tensions in Anglo-American relations through the Jay Treaty negotiated in London in 1794, the British government promised to evacuate them.

By the end of the century as Americans gained full control over their side of the frontier, they were able to confine Indians into limited reservations. At the same time, the British were tightening their control over Indians in Upper Canada where

---

[24] J. Harmar to H. Knox, 6 July 1785, W. H. Smith (ed.), *The St Clair Papers: The Life and Public Services of Arthur St Clair*, 2 vols. (Cincinnati, OH, 1882), II, p. 8.

[25] To Lansdowne, 3 March 1786, Richard Henry Lee (ed.), *The Life of Arthur Lee*, 2 vols. (Boston, 1829), II, p. 167.

[26] D. Ramsay to [R. Izard], 1 December 1785, R. L. Brunhouse (ed.), *David Ramsay 1749–1815: Selections from his Writings* (Philadelphia, 1965), p. 93.

[27] H. Hamilton to Sydney, 7 April 1785, TNA, CO 42/47, f. 197.

[28] E. E. Rich, *Montreal and the Fur Trade* (Montreal, 1966).

European settlement was spreading. American and British Indian policy was converging.[29] In the period immediately after the Revolution, however, the British still valued the Indians as potential military allies and partners in the fur trade and could give them assurances of sympathy, even if they were not prepared to act effectively to protect them against American aggression.

III

Both before and after the American Revolution most British opinion almost certainly regarded the West Indian plantations as the most valuable of Britain's colonial enterprises. These plantations were worked by a huge slave population, over 200,000 in Jamaica alone, replenished by a great British slave trade. As the world's largest slave-traders, the British also supplied other colonial empires with slaves. By the time of the Revolution the slave population in the area of the new United States was larger than that of the British Caribbean, but due to the much higher rate of natural increase, imports from Africa were largely confined to the growing rice and indigo plantations of Georgia and South Carolina.

Although the use of enslaved labour was to grow throughout the British empire, by the middle of the eighteenth century the critics of slavery had won the public debate. Few were prepared to argue that the use of enslaved labour and trading in slaves were practices that could be justified except on grounds of practical necessity. By the 1760s and 1770s, to some trenchant critics in both Britain and the American colonies, such as John Wesley, Granville Sharp, and a group of American Quakers, the evil involved totally outweighed any arguments from necessity. In the 1780s such opinions not only won massive public acceptance in Britain but were translated into powerful political action which produced great petitioning campaigns for the abolition of the slave trade.[30]

Unconscionable as slavery within the British empire was to reformers, attempts to bring it to an immediate end seemed impractical. Without slaves, it was assumed that the immensely valuable plantations would cease to be viable with dire consequences for the British economy. Slavery must be reformed until it gradually withered away. Reform would come through instilling Christian beliefs and values in the slaves and by bringing them within the law and the institutions of civil society through property-holding and the development of family relationships. There would then be a gradual transformation to plantations run on a system of 'free' wage labour which, it was asserted, would be much more productive than those worked by coerced slave labour. At the best, however, such a programme could only be accomplished over a long period and would require the cooperation

---

[29] Taylor, *Divided Ground*, ch. 11.

[30] Christopher L. Brown, *Moral Capital: Foundations of British Abolitionism* (Chapel Hill, NC, 2006) is a worthy addition to David Brion Davis, *The Problem of Slavery in Western Culture* (Ithaca, NY, 1966) and Roger Anstey, *The Atlantic Slave Trade and British Abolition 1760–1810* (London, 1975) which have become classic accounts of British abolitionism.

of the white elite in the islands. To impose reform on the West Indies from Britain would be to challenge the planters' right to run their own internal affairs and was likely to be resisted. Conflicts with locally self-governing colonial communities in the aftermath of the American Revolution were not an inviting prospect. Up to a point, West Indian planters were willing to cooperate. Slave codes were being revised to limit the most gruesome of punishments, encourage Christianizing, and restrict the break-up of families. Metropolitan opinion was, however, with good reason sceptical as to how far reforms enacted in the islands would effectively change the system.

Cutting off the slave trade would be a powerful incentive to reform practices in the plantations and as a matter of commercial regulation it was indisputably a matter within the competence of the British Parliament. It was very much on sensitive British consciences that Britain was the largest slave-trader in the world. That '*rod of wickedness*', which Granville Sharp called the slave trade, was, he wrote, 'now carried on chiefly by our *Liverpool* and *Bristol* merchants'. The people of Great Britain therefore had as much complicity in the crimes of slavery as the people of the colonies.[31] The transporting of slaves across the Atlantic was known to be a horrific business in which many perished. The scandal of slaves thrown overboard from the *Zong* in 1781 was taken to epitomize the middle passage. Moreover, real reform of slave society in the West Indies was unlikely so long as waves of new slaves were being introduced. If slave mortality could no longer be made up by imports, it was presumed that masters would have no alternative but to try to prolong the lives of their slaves by better treatment and by improving the pitifully low rates of reproduction of malnourished and overworked women in the islands. Finally, the ending of the slave trade would be a victory for humanity in Africa as well as in the West Indies. By inciting Africans to kidnap other Africans or to make war on one another to create supplies of slaves, Europe was devastating West Africa. It was the duty of the British Parliament, Cambridge University insisted in a petition of 1788, to 'extend its protection to the *Africans*, the most injured and defenceless of our fellow creatures' by abolishing the slave trade.[32] Once the slave trade had ceased, other trades would take its place, spreading prosperity and all the other benefits that contemporaries associated with commerce.

The attack on the slave trade proved to be an issue on which a great coalition of supporters could be brought together. In what has been called the first 'break-through' of anti-slave-trade opinion in 1788 over a hundred petitions were sent to Parliament. Religious groups with Quakers, Protestant Dissenters, and Evangelical Anglicans in the lead provided networks for circulating vast quantities of printed material and for lobbying, coordinated by a London committee. The most extensive mobilization of popular opinion has been associated with

---

[31] *The Law of Retribution, or a Serious Warning to Great Britain and her Colonies* (London, 1776), pp. 34–5, 305.
[32] *Journals of the House of Commons*, 8 February 1788, XLIII, p. 212.

manufacturing areas in the north of England with Manchester taking the initiative in mass participation.[33] The world of parliamentary politics at which the petitions were directed contained many sympathetic to the abolitionists' cause. Evangelically inclined Anglican MPs working for national moral regeneration, for whom William Wilberforce was the great spokesman, were totally committed. So too were most activists who had been campaigning for parliamentary reform or for economy in government. Support for abolition went, however, much wider among the political elite: a good proportion of the parliamentary leadership on both sides of the House, including Pitt and Fox, were firmly engaged in the cause. William Eden, an unsentimental political careerist, was in no doubt that the slave trade was 'a damnable disgrace to the species to which I belong'.[34] Even Lord North, who seemed to be the embodiment of the vices of an earlier era and would certainly not vote for abolition, described the first Quaker petition of 1783 as having an 'object and a tendency' that 'ought to recommend it to every humane breast'.[35] In 1788 an Act was passed for regulating the conditions under which slaves could be shipped across the Atlantic and the Committee for the Privy Council for trade was commissioned to make an inquiry. The first parliamentary debate on abolition, memorably opened by Wilberforce, took place in May 1789. The slave trade was referred to a parliamentary investigation in the following year. The matter was finally put to the vote in April 1791, the motion for abolition being rejected by 163 to 88. A great new petitioning movement preceded another debate in 1792 in which immediate abolition was rejected for a gradual abolition over a period of years, but this was rejected by the House of Lords.

West Indian and slave-trading interests had at least won a reprieve. They had tried to defend themselves through petitions, the press, and the speeches of MPs well disposed to their cause.[36] Few attempts were made to refute accounts of the horrors of the slave trade. A committee of the Jamaica assembly was even prepared to concede that abuses of overcrowding and bad conditions needed to be reformed.[37] Bamber Gascoyne, MP for Liverpool, was unusual in arguing that attacks on the slave trade were based on ignorance and that it was 'neither contrary to the principles of humanity, nor disgraceful to a country'.[38] Most of those who opposed abolition argued that it must be resisted because too much was at stake. Stephen Fuller, agent for Jamaica, immediately raised a fear that was to gain great force with the massive uprisings in French St Domingue. Any attempt to change the system was to run deadly risks. He warned that rumours of abolition were

---

[33] Seymour Drescher, *Capitalism and Antislavery: British Mobilization in Comparative Perspective* (Houndmills, 1986), pp. 67–78; John Oldfield, *Popular Politics and British Anti-Slavery: The Mobilisation of Public Opinion against the Slave Trade 1787–1807* (London, 1998), pp. 45–6.

[34] To Sheffield, 28 January 1788, BL, Add MS 61980, f. 42.

[35] Brown, *Moral Capital*, p. 422.

[36] Their campaign is well analysed in David B. Ryden, *West Indian Slavery and British Abolition 1783–1807* (Cambridge, 2009), pp. 192–215.

[37] Report of [19 October 1788], TNA, CO 137/87, f. 167.

[38] 26 May 1788, *Parliamentary Register*, XXIV, pp. 9–10.

certain to set off slave revolts. Warships and marines must be immediately sent to Jamaica.[39] In a petition to the Commons he pointed out that abolition of the slave trade would endanger the £36 million that he calculated was invested in their plantations. The British Parliament must be prepared to foot a huge bill for compensation.[40] The London-based West Indian merchants and creditors put the total of capital at risk in all the islands at £70 million.[41] British African merchants made the same point about compensation. They had engaged on a trade with the full support and encouragement of the government, the Bristol merchants insisted, and were the principle conceded, that 'the property of individuals may be lessened in its value without a compensation', it would set a 'most alarming' precedent.[42] Such arguments had real force for contemporaries. African merchants and West India planters might not generally be seen in an attractive light, but they were still recognized to be the custodians of important national interests. These could not be lightly jeopardized. In his great speech in May 1789 Wilberforce argued that the plantations would not be damaged by cutting off fresh supplies of slaves and that other more valuable trades would replace the slave trade with Africa.[43] Many were not convinced. Charles Jenkinson, Lord Hawkesbury, president of the Committee of the Privy Council for trade and colonies was concerned about 'the evils that now attend the slave trade with Africa' and wished to stop it 'as soon as it can be done consistently with the real interest of the planters in the West Indies',[44] but he was well aware that:

> this trade is not only valuable in itself, but of great importance in its relation to other branches of commerce, and as it will be carried on by other countries, who will derive vast benefits from it, tho' we should even abandon it, my wish is to preserve as great a share of it as is possible to this country, and I should subject it only to such proper regulations as shall manifest a due attention to motives of humanity and justice.[45]

It is likely that such views were widely shared by those who voted against immediate abolition: they were not immune to considerations of humanity, but felt that it could be pursued at too high a price.

British opinion took great pride in the extent of the support mobilized for campaigns against the slave trade which came to be seen as expressions of Britain's distinctive commitment to liberty.[46] Rejection of slavery and of trading in human beings was equally taken by many Americans to be an essential component of the principles of universal liberty established by their Revolution. Some northern

---

[39] Petition to King, 2 July 1788, TNA, CO 137/87, f. 265. See also Fuller to Hawkesbury, 29 January 1788, cited in Ryden, *West Indian Slavery and British Abolition 1783–1807*, p. 208.

[40] Petition, 21 May 1789, *Journals of the House of Commons*, XLIV, p. 399.

[41] Resolution of 19 May 1789, Institute of Commonwealth Studies, West India Committee Minutes, reel 3.

[42] Petition, 12 May 1789, *Journals of the House of Commons*, XLIV, p. 352.

[43] *Parliamentary Register*, XXVI, pp. 137–42, 148–9.

[44] To E. Corrie, 29 February 1788, BL, Add MS 38310, f. 14.

[45] To J. Jones, 16 July 1788, ibid. f. 22.

[46] Brown, *Moral Capital*, p. 387. See also Linda Colley, *Britons: Forging the Nation 1707–1837* (New Haven, CT, 1992), pp. 355–6.

colonies had prohibited the import of slaves before the Revolution; others did so as independent states. An Act for the gradual emancipation of slaves within the state was passed by Pennsylvania in 1780. The New England states followed its example after independence. Slavery was forbidden in the new federal Northwest Territory by the Ordinance of 1787.

Most of the political elite on both sides of the Atlantic professed to regard trading in slaves and the institution of slavery as evils that should be banished from the civilized world. Even Henry Laurens, a great South Carolina planter and slave-holder, could ask whether it was 'right and virtuous to enslave hundreds of thousands of free born men and women . . . in order to enhance the value of Mr Laurens's lands'.[47] Laurens and other high-minded South Carolinans, as well as their eminent Virginian contemporaries, notoriously Jefferson and Washington,[48] but also George Mason, who thought that slavery would 'bring the judgment of heaven on a country',[49] had of course to devise compromises between their condemnations of slavery and their situation as holders of slaves. Members of the British political elite were less likely to be directly involved in Caribbean plantations, although there were one or two eminent landed families, like the Lascelles of Harewood in Yorkshire, whose fortunes were built on West Indian wealth, and stakes in West Indian property through inheritance and marriage settlements were widely diffused throughout the British upper classes.[50] A fine study of a Scottish gentry family has shown how extensively its members, both male and female, were involved in slave ownership, in Asia as well as in the Americas.[51] The politically prominent were well represented among the claimants of compensation for estates largely worked by slaves in East Florida which had been lost when the colony was handed back to Spain at the end of the war. Claimants included Alexander Wedderburn, Lord Loughborough, the future Lord Chancellor, and Henry Strachey, the peace negotiator, as well as William Grenville, who was eventually to do as much as any major politician to bring about abolition.[52] Even if they did not have direct West Indian interests, British politicians had to make compromises between their dislike of slavery and the slave trade and their sense of the great national importance of the West Indian plantation economy.

[47] To J. Bourdieu, 6 February 1783, Philip M. Hamer, et al. (eds), *The Papers of Henry Laurens*, 16 vols. (Columbia, SC, 1968–2003), XVI, p. 144. The editors of Laurens's papers, point out that he condemned slavery while still holding 300 slaves (ibid. XVI, p. xxi).

[48] A recent study has shown how well versed Washington was in the literature of anti-slavery, François Furstenberg, 'Atlantic Slavery, Atlantic Freedom, George Washington, Slavery and Transatlantic Abolitionist Networks', *William and Mary Quarterly*, 3rd ser., LXVIII (2011), 240–86.

[49] Max Ferrand (ed.), *Records of the Federal Convention of 1787*, 4 vols. (New York, 1937), II, p. 370.

[50] For a later period, see Nicholas Draper, *The Price of Emancipation: Slave-ownership, Compensation and British Society at the End of Slavery* (Cambridge, 2010).

[51] Emma Rothschild, *The Inner Life of Empires: An Eighteenth-Century History* (Princeton, NJ, 2011), pp. 154–70

[52] The claims may be found in TNA, T 77, TS 11/985–90 and AO 12/3. Grenville and his brother Thomas had inherited a claim for land mostly worked by servants imported from around the Mediterranean rather than by slaves (TNA, T 77/7, f. 152).

Such similarities would suggest that there was abundant room for Anglo-American cooperation for common ends and against easily identifiable enemies, such as the British slave-merchants, West Indian planters, and the planters of Georgia and South Carolina, who were importing slaves and would resolutely and successfully oppose any writing of anti-slavery provisions into the new Constitution of the United States. There certainly was cordial transatlantic cooperation between individuals, such as Benjamin Rush and Granville Sharp. Publications were exchanged and British luminaries of anti-slavery, such as Sharp or Thomas Clarkson, were honoured by the American anti-slavery societies. The College of William and Mary, Alma Mater of the Virginia slave-holding gentry, honoured Sharp in 1791. There was also, however, antagonism, competitive point-scoring, and even accusations of hypocrisy between Britons and Americans.[53]

During the war the identification of the Americans with slavery had been a major theme in British condemnations of the Revolution. Dr Johnson's famous quip about 'the loudest yelps for liberty' coming from 'the drivers of negroes' was one of many. A government pamphleteer replied to American outrage that the governor of Virginia had incited slave resistance by asking how those who proclaimed that 'all men are equal' could 'complain of *the offer of freedom* held out to those wretched beings'.[54] An exchange between Richard Price and Henry Laurens, two men who wished one another well and were united in their professions of hostility to slavery, illustrates the scope for continuing Anglo-American controversy about slavery after the war. In his *Observations on the Importance of the American Revolution* of 1784 Price had pointed out that Americans would not 'deserve the liberty for which they have been contending' until they had rid themselves of slavery. He commended to them the example of Britain, where a slave became 'a *freeman*, the moment he set foot on *British* ground'.[55] As well as retailing a somewhat distorted version of the famous judgment on Somerset's case of 1772, Price was showing a very characteristic British assumption about slavery: it was an un-British institution, solely devised and practised in the colonies. He and others who strongly sympathized with the American cause had no inhibitions in lecturing the new republics on their absolute duty to get rid of slavery as soon as possible and later in condemning the settlement in the constitutional Convention that allowed slave-trading to continue for a further twenty-one years and made some provision for the return of fugitive slaves. Granville Sharp expressed the disappointment of British anti-slavery campaigners that the Convention had not lived up to the 'declarations of Congress, so frequently repeated during the contest with Britain'.[56] For George Dillwyn, an American Quaker in London, the Convention was 'setting at naught *the Power* of God' to which Americans had appealed in their struggle with Britain.[57] Laurens

[53] The Anglo-American anti-slavery alliances, but not the conflicts, are brought out in Betty Fladeland, *Men and Brothers: Anglo-American Antislavery Cooperation* (Urbana, IL, 1972).

[54] [John Lind], *An Answer to the Declaration of the American Congress* (London, 1776), p. 107.

[55] pp. 83–4.

[56] To Pennsylvania Society for Abolition of Slavery, 28 February 1788, *The American Museum*, IV (1788), 414.

[57] W. H. [Hodgson] (ed.), *The Life and Travels of John Pemberton* (London, 1844), p. 273.

delivered a stinging retort in return to Price. He could not be serious in commending Britain's example. 'Britain is the fountain head from whence we have been supplied with slaves.' The British Parliament would 'enslave Asia, Africa, America and Europe too if they durst for increasing their own navigation and commerce'.[58] John Jay was willing to accept a rebuke delivered to him by Granville Sharp. It was, he agreed, 'very inconsistent' with American 'declarations on the subject of human rights to permit a single slave to be found within their jurisdiction', but he still questioned Britain's right to take the high moral ground, pointing out that 'India and Africa experience unmerited oppression from nations that have been long distinguished by their attachment to their civil and religious liberties, but who have expended not much less blood and treasure in violating the rights of others than in defending their own.'[59] Underlying American retorts was the assumption that slavery had been forced on them by the British determination to dump slaves on them. This assumption was as misleading, but also as comforting, to Americans as the assumption that slavery was an exclusively colonial phenomenon, was misleading but comforting to British opinion. Americans were in their own view the victims in Jefferson's memorable words intended for the Declaration of Independence of the 'piratical warfare... of the CHRISTIAN King of Great Britain' who had forced slaves on them and had then vetoed all their efforts 'to prohibit or to restrain this execrable commerce'.[60]

The fate of slaves who fled to the British army during the course of the war provoked bitter accusations of hypocrisy and bad faith. Many ex-slaves left American territory when the British withdrew, either going to the British West Indian colonies or to the Bahamas, often via East Florida, or going northwards to Nova Scotia. The British version of this exodus was usually that these were people who had fled from slavery and been given various pledges of freedom by British officers by which the British government was bound. The most explicit pledge was that by the British commander-in-chief, Sir Henry Clinton, in 1779. Clinton's proclamation had been intended primarily to deter blacks from serving in the rebel army. Any African person in the American forces who was captured by the British would be sold as a slave, but those who escaped to the British lines from American masters should be given protection and 'be allowed to pursue any occupation they chose without molestation or being reclaimable by their former owners'.[61] To return people to slavery, and no doubt to the vengeance of their former owners, who had fled to the British expecting these terms would be a violation of the national honour. The American version was that many slaves had been stolen from their owners and commandeered as booty by the British. They were being shipped away for sale. Thus the British were conducting a kind of slave trade for their own

[58] To Price, 1 February 1785, Hamer et al. (eds), *Laurens Papers*, XVI, pp. 533–4.

[59] Jay on behalf of Society for Promoting the Manumission of Slaves to London Committee, [post May 1788], Henry P. Johnston (ed.), *The Correspondence and Public Papers of John Jay*, 4 vols. (New York, 1890–3), III, p. 341.

[60] 'Original Rough Draft', Julian P. Boyd et al. (eds), *The Papers of Thomas Jefferson* (Princeton, NJ, 1950–), I, p. 426.

[61] 'Précis Relative to Negroes', TNA, CO 5/8, f. 112.

profit. Furthermore, the seventh clause of the preliminary terms of peace, signed on 30 November 1782, forbade the further 'carrying away any negroes or other property' by the British when they withdrew. Most ex-slaves left New York for Nova Scotia after the signing of the treaty and thus in the American view in clear violation of it.

On the shipments out of the southern ports of Charleston, Savannah, or St Augustine in Florida, the Americans may have had a better case than historians often seem to be willing to allow them. Great numbers of slaves fled to the British army during its southern campaigns. When the British withdrew from their last enclaves in the south many people of African origin went with them. Some left as free people, having been able to establish their claims under the British promises. They went to places of their own choosing. Most left as slaves. Some were carried away by British or loyalist masters who were transferring their activities to other British colonies. Most were sold to new owners in the Caribbean or the United States.

Estimates for the number of black people who went from Savannah with the British in 1782 vary from 2,500 to 3,500 and possibly higher.[62] Most who went did so as slaves. Loyalist planters shipped them off in large numbers. The governor of Georgia, Sir James Wright, asked for shipping to take 2,000 slaves belonging to fifteen associates to Jamaica.[63] Slaves belonging to William Knox, under-secretary to Lord George Germain, were consigned to Jamaica, the governor promising to do all he could 'towards employing them in a way useful to their owners and agreeable to themselves'.[64] What he gained from disposing of them helped Knox to buy an estate in Pembrokeshire 'of upwards of one thousand pounds a year', an income on which he hoped to support his claim to become a baronet.[65] The number of black people shipped out of Charleston, estimated at 8,000 or 10,000,[66] was much larger than those going from Savannah. Some left Charleston with guarantees of freedom. Most blacks, however, left Charleston as slaves. Many of them were taken with their fleeing loyalist owners, whose claims to property prevailed over any British pledges of freedom. Others, in spite of British proclamations against illegal shipments were said to have been 'fraudulently removed by persons of flagitious character' who had no right to them and were being sold throughout the West Indies.[67] It was widely believed by Americans that a huge slave trade was being conducted by the British involving the removal of 12,000 slaves from Charleston as

---

[62] Cf. Cassandra Pybus, 'Jefferson's Faulty Math: The Question of Slave Defections in the American Revolution', *William and Mary Quarterly*, 3rd ser., LXII (2005), 262 and Sylvia R. Frey, *Water from the Rock: Black Resistance in a Revolutionary Age* (Princeton, NJ, 1991), p. 174.

[63] Wilbur H. Siebert, *Loyalists in East Florida 1774–1785*, 2 vols. (Deland, FL, 1929), II, p. 347; Wright stated that he had 526 slaves in his employment in 1776. The patriots confiscated them, but he recovered many of them after the British re-occupation and insured 220 to go to Jamaica in 1782 (Schedule of Losses, 15 September 1783, TNA, AO 13/84, ff. 644–6).

[64] A. Campbell to W. Knox, 15 September 1782, WLCL, Knox MSS, 6: 54.

[65] To North, 8 November 1783, BL, Add MS 61867 f. 154.

[66] Pybus, 'Jefferson's Faulty Math', pp. 262–3; Frey, *Water from the Rock*, p. 174.

[67] J. Cruden to P. Tonyn, 27 April 1783, TNA, CO 5/109, f. 375; to Sydney, 2 January 1784, TNA, FO 4/3, ff. 22–3.

the 'booty' of the British army,[68] often with great cruelty, including the concealing 'up to 200 negroes like beef or pork' in barrels, in which a number of them died.[69]

A considerable proportion of the people of African origin who had been shipped out of Savannah or Charleston were initially taken to East Florida. When East Florida was about to be handed over to the Spanish, they, together with slaves already working on the Florida plantations, were dispersed through the Caribbean and the southern United States. Some 6,500 people of African origin were listed as having left Florida.[70] Many of those who could maintain their free status chose to go to the Bahamas where numerous white loyalists were also going, but some were said to prefer Jamaica or the Windward Islands.[71] The majority of Africans who left East Florida did so as slaves at their owners' bidding. They were shipped in large numbers to the Bahamas. Loyalists going to the Bahamas were said to have 'very little money, but many have from ten to a hundred negroes'.[72] Some slaves were sent to Jamaica, although slaves from the continent were regarded by Jamaica planters as too 'soft' for the rigours of sugar cultivations and many of them were later sold back into the United States.[73] Some large slave-holders sent their slaves for sale in Dominica in the Windward Islands.[74] It is likely that many sent there were subsequently shipped on to the French islands. There was much selling of Florida slaves to the United States as Georgia and South Carolina planters sought to recruit a new labour force.

The forced dispersal of slaves around the Caribbean and the southern United States not only disrupted their lives but exposed them to new disease environments and work regimes and in many cases to early death. Judith Shivers took her slaves to Jamaica, where, like others, she found the market overstocked, so she sent them to Dominica. There the climate 'greatly effected the health of her negroes' so that two died and 'no benefit could be got' from the rest, whom she would have to sell at a low price.[75] Lord Hawke, heir to the Florida estates of his father, the great admiral, claimed compensation for slaves, especially children, who had died when sent for sale to Dominica.[76] Having failed to sell his slaves at a high price in ready money to the Spanish in Florida, Patrick Tonyn, last British governor of East Florida, sent sixty-nine slaves to Dominica but fifteen died before they could be sold there and he got a low price for the rest.[77] A 'sickness' caused 'by their removal from the province of East Florida' to the Bahamas killed 42 of the 143 slaves shipped by

---

[68] B. Vaughan to R. Oswald, 14 November 1782, WLCL, Shelburne MSS, 70, p. 389

[69] E. Pendleton to J. Madison, 23 December 1782, David J. Mays (ed.), *The Letters and Papers of Edmund Pendleton*, 2 vols. (Charlottesville, VA, 1967), II, p. 436.

[70] Return of 2 May 1786, TNA, CO 5/561, f. 407.

[71] P. Tonyn to G. Carleton, 11 September 1783, TNA, CO 5/111, f. 26.

[72] W. Walker to E. Lincoln, 28 January 1784, TNA, CO 260/7, unpaginated.

[73] Maya Jasanoff, *Liberty's Exiles: The Loss of America and the Remaking of the British Empire* (London, 2011), pp. 258–9.

[74] J. Orde to Sydney, 24 August 1785, TNA, CO 71/9, f. 193.

[75] TNA, AO 12/3, f. 159.

[76] Letter to Claims Commission, 7 March 1788, TNA, T 77/8, ff. 51–2.

[77] 'List of Negroes', 21 August 1785, TNA, T 77/17, f. 235 and note on slave prices, TNA, TS 11/996, pp. 13–14.

Denys Rolle, an East Florida planter.[78] For those African Americans whose pledges of freedom were protected, the British 'evacuation of America' at the end of the war may indeed have been 'the most significant act of emancipation in early American history'.[79] African Americans who were able to maintain their free status included the Baptist ministers Moses Baker and George Liele, who went from Georgia to Jamaica.[80] Such people seem, however, to have been only a small minority of those who left the southern states. For the large number of those who remained slaves at the mercy of their owners' to dispose of them as they saw fit, the war's consequences could be dire. The diaspora of 'loyalist' African Americans meant for most of them little more than being traded around the Caribbean or back to the United States.

Black people who had made their way to New York also left with the British when they withdrew in 1783. Over 3,000 of them went to Nova Scotia. The number was considerably smaller than those who left from the southern ports, but the proportion who went with guaranteed freedom and not as slaves was very much higher. The migration of ex-slaves from New York to Nova Scotia provoked British-American recrimination at the very highest level and has attracted some fine historical writing.[81]

General Guy Carleton, the British commander-in-chief, laid down the principle that any black person who had come to New York before the end of hostilities and claimed protection under the British proclamations was free to go wherever he or she wished. The great majority chose to go to Nova Scotia and were settled there with the white refugees. Carleton saw this as an issue of high principle. The New York blacks could not be deprived of 'that liberty I found them possessed of'. He did not consider that any British government would consent to so 'notorious breach of the public faith towards people of any complection' by handing them back.[82] A document compiled some time after the war, probably by his secretary, Maurice Morgann, attributed to Carleton the view that ex-slaves were 'British subjects'. Those officers supervising the evacuation of New York were said to have acted on the principle that 'the *British constitution*' did not allow slavery but held out '*freedom* and *protection* to all who come within and claimed its protection'.[83] At a meeting with Washington in May 1783 Carleton refused to hand over the ex-slaves who had joined the British before the signing of the treaty, although compensation would be paid for them. Carleton's stand was endorsed by British

---

[78] TNA, TS 11/989, pp. 240–1, 269.

[79] C. Pybus, 'Jefferson's Faulty Math', p. 264.

[80] John W. Pulis, 'Bridging Troubled Waters: Moses Baker, George Liele and the African American Diaspora to Jamaica' in Pulis (ed.), *Moving On: Black Loyalists in the Afro-Atlantic World* (New York, 1999), pp. 186–92.

[81] James W. St G. Walker, *The Black Loyalists: The Search for a Promised Land in Nova Scotia and Sierra Leone 1783–1870* (London, 1976); Ellen Gibson Wilson, *The Loyal Blacks* (New York, 1976); Graham Russell Hodges (ed.), *The Black Loyalist Directory: African Americans in Exile after the American Revolution* (New York, 1996); Simon Schama, *Rough Crossings: Britain, the Slaves and the American Revolution* (London, 2005).

[82] To Washington, 12 May 1783, TNA, CO 5/109, f. 314.

[83] 'Precis Relative to Negroes' and 'Negroes', TNA, CO 5/8, ff. 112 and 86–7.

political opinion. Lord North regarded it as 'an act of justice'[84] and Charles Fox considered that 'no man of honour' could have returned the ex-slaves.[85] Alexander Hamilton, who held strong anti-slavery views, thought that the British were entirely justified.[86] Some other Americans, however, saw the British insistence on their national honour as a transparent device to hide their designs to appropriate slaves for their own purposes and were deeply cynical about British claims to superior humanity. Many Virginia planters were outraged at what they saw as the abduction of their slaves. Washington, who suspected that missing slaves of his own were in New York but saw little hope of recovering any unless they were willing to return voluntarily,[87] felt that he had to take the matter up with Carleton. He was described, probably by Maurice Morgann who was present at their meeting, as having demanded the return of the slaves 'with all the grossness and ferocity of a captain of banditti'.[88] This no doubt distorted account of how Washington conducted himself illustrates the extent to which British opinion believed that they had gained the moral ascendancy on the question of fugitive slaves, as on the treatment of Native Americans.

Although most blacks who went to Nova Scotia kept their freedom, they did not prosper there and suffered much discrimination. They were in theory entitled to allocations of land on the same scale as other refugees. Their grants were, however, generally much smaller and many got no land at all. Most had to work for wages, usually under terms of indenture for a specified period. The black loyalist community remained an impoverished one, living, it has been said, in ways 'not altogether different from the life of slavery they had left behind'.[89] Whereas whites who could not make a living in Nova Scotia tended to remove themselves to the United States, few blacks seem to have been willing to take the risk of being re-enslaved. In 1792, however, over 1,000 of them took a risk of a different sort. They enlisted to go to Africa, to what they hoped would be a more spacious freedom offered them in Sierra Leone.

Harsh as the treatment of many blacks in Nova Scotia had been, the British could perhaps claim that promises of freedom had been honoured in the face of the American determination to return runaways to servitude. In the much larger exodus to the south the British record was much more equivocal.

The story of how General Nathanael Greene found slaves for the plantations expropriated from loyalists, which had been awarded to him by Georgia and South Carolina in recognition for his great services in driving the British out of their states, shows how far both sides remained entangled with slavery after the war. Greene had been brought up a Quaker in Rhode Island. One of his Quaker correspondents

---

[84] To Carleton, 8 August 1783, TNA, CO 5/110, f. 65.
[85] To D. Hartley, 9 August 1783, TNA, FO 4/2, f. 202.
[86] Conversation with G. Beckwith, October 1789, Syrett et al. (eds), *Hamilton Papers*, V, p. 487.
[87] To B. Harrison, 30 April 1783, John C. Fitzpatrick (ed.), *The Writings of George Washington*, 39 vols. (Washington, DC, 1931–44), XXVI, p. 370.
[88] '7th Article', WLCL, Shelburne MSS, 87: 389.
[89] Walker, *Black Loyalists*, p. 58.

urged him to take a public stand against using 'the labour of slaves' on his estates.[90] Greene, who urgently needed the profits from his plantations to put his tangled finances to rights, gave him a sadly evasive answer. 'On the subject of slavery, nothing can be said in its defence. But you are much mistaken respecting my influence in this business.' He hoped that the condition of the slaves on the estates 'will not be worse but better'.[91] His agents obtained slaves for him from his former enemies the British, buying them from British slave-traders who brought them to Charleston or making purchases at St Augustine in East Florida from the British owners of plantations who wished to dispose of their slaves before the Spanish took over.

IV

Empire in India was an issue that set Britain and America apart from one another. For Americans of the revolutionary generation, Britain's imperial ambitions in India were one of the most alarming signs of the decline in Britain of that libertarian virtue that, they thought, had once joined British and Americans in an empire of freedom. The British were establishing a despotic regime in Asia, the home of despotism. The poison of Asiatic despotism and luxury would inevitably corrupt the mother country as it had corrupted Rome. Americans refused to allow tea to be landed in 1773, not only because it was taxed by the British Parliament, but because it was shipped by the East India Company, who in India had 'by the most unparalleled barbarities, extortions, and monopolies, stripped the miserable inhabitants of their property, and reduced whole provinces to indigence and ruin' and who now 'cast their eyes on America, as a new theatre whereon to exercise their talents of rapine, oppression and cruelty'.[92] During the war Americans saw the peoples of India as fellow victims of British tyranny who were so 'enervated by effeminacy' that, unlike the manly Americans, they could not effectively resist.[93] They had, however, produced a formidable warrior in Haidar Ali of Mysore, whose feats against the British were celebrated in America, Philadelphia merchants calling a fighting ship the *Hyder Ally*. In the second edition of 1785 of his sermon on *The United States Elevated to Glory and Honour*, Ezra Stiles prophesied that '*Bengal* and the *East Indies*' would soon 'be delivered from the cruelty and injustice of the British government there'.[94] Much about British India continued to appear in print in independent America.[95]

---

[90] Letter of W. Mifflin, 4 October 1783, Richard K. Showman et al. (eds), *The Papers of General Nathanael Greene*, 13 vols. (Chapel Hill, NC, 1976–2003), XIII, p. 158.

[91] To W. Mifflin, [November 1783], ibid. XIII, p. 192.

[92] John Dickinson cited in James R. Fichter, *So Great a Proffit: How the East Indies Trade Transformed Anglo-American Capitalism* (Cambridge, MA, 2010), pp. 19–20.

[93] Congress to Jamaica Assembly, 25 July 1775 cited in David Armitage, *The Declaration of Independence: A Global History* (Cambridge, MA, 2007), p. 51.

[94] (Worcester, MA, 1785), p. 83 fn.

[95] Zagarri, 'The Significance of the "Global Turn"', p. 11.

Much British opinion would in the past generally have agreed with the American view of empire in India as an aberration, vulnerable to being overthrown; after 1783 fewer and fewer British people did so. Instead, they began to see themselves as becoming righteous rulers of what would be an enduring empire. Chapter 6 tried to show how reforms in the immediate aftermath of the American War seemed to have created a stable system of government for British India, while the East India Company's operations appeared to be prospering to Britain's advantage in what proved to be a relatively brief interval of peace between world wars. Anxieties about empire in India went, however, much further than concerns about the mismanagement of what should be a major national asset. The East India Company had not only proved to be a wasteful steward of great potential resources; it had tarnished Britain's honour by oppressive rule. Its misdeeds had been publicized throughout Europe, most obviously by the Abbé Raynal. The misfortunes of the war in America were sometimes attributed to divine displeasure at British crimes in India. Alexander Carlyle, who had castigated the Americans for the way they treated their Native peoples, turned his fire on his own countrymen in India in the same pamphlet. 'Can we believe', he asked, 'that deeds have been committed...by natives of these islands, that will make the odious names of Cortes and Pizarro be forgotten and stain the British annals to the latest posterity?'[96] The Unitarian divine, Theophilus Lindsey, thought that 'Our territorial possessions in the East Indies, are and have been the cause of misery to millions of the natives, and a sink of corruption that has contributed to undo us.'[97] George III, always a reliable guide to conventional opinion, deplored in 1784 'those shocking enormities in India that disgrace human nature and if not put a stop to threaten the expulsion of the Company out of that wealthy region'.[98] At the highest level of national politics this sense of outrage about British rule in India was finding expression in the attacks that Edmund Burke was launching against the Governor General, Warren Hastings, which were to lead to the House of Commons voting in 1787 that he should be impeached in the House of Lords.

Those who were trying to reform British India insisted that Britain's profit must not be pursued at the expense of British honour. Rather, it was commonly supposed that reform to make India profitable to Britain and reform to do justice to Britain's Indian subjects were complementary, not conflicting, aims. Britain's national reputation and her wealth would grow together in a well-regulated empire. The benefits that Britain expected to derive from India depended on Indian prosperity. Britain was not embarked on a raid to plunder Indian resources; she was laying the foundations for an enduring empire. Those who were shocked by what they understood to be Britain's record in India rarely advocated the abandonment of empire. Nor did they reject the notion that Britain was entitled to profit from well governed Indian provinces. Burke believed that were Britain to rule its

[96] *The Justice and Necessity of the War*, p. 42.
[97] To W. Russell, 30 January 1784, G. M. Ditchfield (ed.), *The Letters of Theophilus Lindsey (1723–1808)*, I, *1747–1786* (London, 2007), p. 414.
[98] To Pitt, 17 July 1784, TNA, PRO 30/8/103, f. 115.

Indian possessions with justice, it could reasonably expect to receive 'a revenue ample enough beyond all the most extravagant expectations and to justify to the world the mysterious ways of that astonishing dispensation of Providence by which we had acquired dominion where nature had almost forbid intercourse'.[99] In particular, British political power must not be used to impose an unequal commercial relationship that would impoverish India. Belief that a free commerce between peoples all over the globe was beneficial to both sides of the exchange was an axiom not just of British reformers but of enlightened opinion in general. Commerce without force was a great civilizing agent, but trade based on coercion was ultimately destructive to both parties. A merchant armed with political power, as was the East India Company, had the potential for great abuses. American trade in India in practice depended on operating within the British imperial framework, but Americans envisaged the trade that the new United States was beginning to conduct with Asia as quite unlike that of the British. It was a peaceful exchange that would be welcomed by Asian peoples, not a monopoly imposed on them by force. John Jay urged that the British should abandon empire and 'tribute', that is the taxation of their provinces; 'cease to treat these unhappy natives as slaves'; and be content to trade with Indians 'as with other independent kingdoms'.[100] The British were not prepared to give up either empire or tribute, but it was official policy that the Company's monopoly should be regulated to ensure just prices for Indian producers and artisans.

The abuses of the Company's rule were to be curbed by prohibitions in the 1784 India Act on malpractices such as unjust wars, bribery, or loans at extortionate rates of interest, by punishing offenders (in practice only Warren Hastings was brought to trial) and by reforms enacted in India. These were to be the work of Lord Cornwallis who took office in 1786 as the Governor General chosen by the Pitt administration. In stark contrast to his reputation among American patriots in South Carolina as a war criminal, Cornwallis quickly established himself as a Governor General who would embody a new age of righteous government in British India, enforcing strict economy on the Company's establishments and prosecuting corruption and oppression while rewarding conscientious service among the Company's European servants. William Jones, thought to be the most eminent contemporary European scholar of Asian languages, who became a royal judge in India, described Cornwallis and his deputy as 'perhaps, the most virtuous governors in the world'.[101] That the British regime in India had enlisted the services of so universally admired a scholar as Jones seemed to add lustre to it. The British were assuming the role of interpreters to a worldwide audience of the Indian culture that they professed to be cherishing. The willingness of Jones, virtually a republican in British politics and a committed supporter of the American

---

[99] Cited in Paul Langford (ed.), *The Writings and Speeches of Edmund Burke* (Oxford, 1991–), vol. VI, ed. P. J. Marshall, *India: The Launching of the Hastings Impeachment 1786–1788*, Introduction, p. 35.
[100] To B. Vaughan, 30 November 1784, Johnston (ed.), *Correspondence of Jay*, III, p. 134.
[101] To J. E. Wilmot, 3 October 1787, Garland Cannon (ed.), *The Letters of Sir William Jones*, 2 vols. (Oxford, 1970), II, p. 781.

cause in the war, to endorse empire in India shows how far India had become a dividing point between otherwise like-minded people in Britain and America.

The government of Bengal under Cornwallis was increasingly presented to the British public as not only upright but as an agent of Indian improvement. In the 1770s under Hastings the British had been committed to recreating indigenous institutions so as to enable the Company's subjects to be ruled according to what were regarded as their own traditions. Under Cornwallis, while still professing their commitment to preserving Indian law and custom and extending full toleration to Indian religion, the Company's officials felt free to innovate in order to give Indians the great benefits of secure personal and property rights which were considered to be new to them. British India was becoming 'an empire of improvement and enlightenment rather than constitutional restoration'.[102] The Hindu masses of eastern India were reputedly the special beneficiaries of the new order. They were conventionally depicted as mild, inoffensive, and highly industrious people who had been exploited by despotic Islamic regimes and by rapacious Company servants in the past. Guaranteed rights were now to replace capricious despotism. Hindus would be 'more happy, better protected, and more secure' than ever before.[103] Cornwallis became something of a cult figure as the embodiment of a benevolent governor. Poetic effusions prophesied that 'Thy mild protection of an injur'd land, / Shall form the epoch whence whole realms shall date, / With hearts exultant their amended fate.'[104]

The trial of Warren Hastings was launched in the House of Lords in 1788 with high spectacle. Although it was to fizzle out after seven years in public indifference or hostility, there are indications of widespread approval for what seemed an act of atonement and cleansing of Britain's reputation. An MP contrasted the satisfaction at the way in which Parliament was 'stretching out the strong arm of justice to punish the degradation of British honour and humanity in the east' with its failure so far 'to dispense the blessings of their protection and liberty to the poor Africans, who were serving in the west'.[105] Alexander Haliday, a Belfast Presbyterian, commended Burke and his allies for doing something 'to redeem the Hindoos essentially from a most rapacious tyranny and to reserve the British name from infamy and detestation ... I wish', he added, 'the wretches to the south of this unfriended isle, who are equally miserable though not quite so innocent as the others, could meet with as able and persevering advocates.'[106] To Abigail Adams, observing the proceedings from London, what was being revealed about British rule in India was what a victorious Britain would have done in America: 'The same

---

[102] Robert Travers, *Ideology and Empire in Eighteenth-Century India: The British in Bengal* (Cambridge, 2007), p. 244.

[103] *A Short Review of the British Government in India* (London, 1790), p. 106.

[104] *The Hero. A Poetic Epistle Respectfully Addressed to Marquis Cornwallis* (Cambridge, 1794), p. 15.

[105] Lord Belgrave, 16 June 1788, *Parliamentary Register*, XXIV, p. 110. See also Henry Beaufoy's speech on same day, ibid. p. 110.

[106] To Charlemont, 22 June 1787, *Historical Manuscripts Commission: Charlemont MSS*, 2 vols. (London, 1891–4), II, p. 55.

scenes would probably have taken place as have been acted in India...England could have produced more than one Hastings.'[107]

Whatever Americans might believe to the contrary, many British people were now sure that they had created a righteous empire in India. The sensational success of Raynal's *Histoire des deux Indes* was one indication of how morally vulnerable contemporary empires had become, not only at home but in the opinion of enlightened Europe. In their own eyes at least, the way in which they had protected Native Americans and the slaves who had taken refuge with them, the vigour of their campaigns against the slave trade and the benevolence of their rule in India constituted a powerful answer to critics. They certainly felt that they had nothing to fear by comparison with the Americans.

---

[107] To I. Smith, 12 March 1787, L. H. Butterfield et al. (eds), *Adams Family Correspondence* (Cambridge, MA, 1963–), VIII, pp. 8–9.

PART II
TRANSATLANTIC COMMUNITIES

11

Crossing the Ocean

I

On the eve of the Revolution people moved freely around the British Atlantic empire in large numbers. Migration to America from the British Isles, especially from Scotland and Ireland, was running at a very high level: nearly 44,000 people left for the thirteen colonies from 1770 to 1775.[1] There were smaller movements to Nova Scotia and of predominantly Irish servants to Newfoundland. Although the volume of their migration had passed its peak, numerous Germans were still crossing the Atlantic to the thirteen colonies. So too were people from Africa. The old slave colonies around the Chesapeake no longer depended on importing fresh labour, but some 25,000 enslaved Africans were brought in to supply the booming plantation economies of Georgia and South Carolina in the early 1770s.[2]

There were few legal impediments to free movement within the British Atlantic empire. British subjects, that is both those born in the British Isles or in British dependencies, formed what has been called a single 'community of allegiance' and generally had a right to go to any part of the king's dominions. British ministers were, for instance, alarmed at the volume of emigration from Scotland to America in the 1770s but accepted that they had no powers to restrict it. Foreign Europeans who migrated to the colonies generally found naturalization processes in force which enabled them also to become British subjects without much difficulty.[3] Enslaved Africans were not deemed eligible to be British subjects and their movements were rigorously controlled.

Right up to the Revolution, many Americans seem to have accepted their membership of a single community of allegiance to the king of Great Britain with enthusiasm. Their sense of themselves as being generic 'Americans' rather than British subjects appears to have been weak. Their strongest loyalties are likely to have been to their particular colony and then to the British 'nation'. British opinion was more likely than they were themselves to classify them as

---

[1] James M. Horn, 'British Diaspora: Emigration from Britain, 1680–1815' in P. J. Marshall (ed.), *The Oxford History of the British Empire*, II, *The Eighteenth Century* (Oxford, 1998), p. 32. Bernard Bailyn, *Voyagers to the West: Emigration from Britain to America on the Eve of the Revolution* (London, 1987) is the canonical account of these great movements.

[2] 'The Trans-Atlantic Slave Trade Data Base', <http://www.slavevoyages.org>.

[3] James H. Kettner, *The Development of American Citizenship 1608–1870* (Chapel Hill, NC, 1978), chs. 4, 5.

undifferentiated Americans. To the British they were, of course, fellow subjects, but whether they were seen by many as full members of the nation seems doubtful.[4]

When the Americans declared their independence, in their own eyes they ceased to be British subjects. Subjecthood implied protection in return for allegiance and George III had openly withdrawn his protection from his subjects in the thirteen colonies and was indeed making war on them. They were therefore free to give their allegiance elsewhere. Congress proclaimed that 'all persons residing within any of the united colonies, and deriving protection from the laws of the same, owe allegiance to the said laws'. Those who continued to adhere to the king were 'guilty of treason'.[5] Individual states enforced their own oaths of allegiance. The formal British position was that subjects could not renounce their allegiance. Americans who refused to obey the Crown were therefore committing treason. Both sides, however, found these doctrines impossible to enforce to their logical conclusion. The British generally treated those captured in America, but not those taken on the high seas and brought to Britain, as prisoners of war rather than as rebels guilty of treason. The Americans too generally treated captured loyalist soldiers as prisoners rather than traitors.

In 1783 Britain acknowledged that the former thirteen colonies were now 'free, sovereign and independent states'. Ideas of some kind of surviving common citizenship were floated by Lord Shelburne and by John Jay, but nothing came of them. A separate American nationality had clearly come into being. From the outset, Americans stressed that they were citizens of a new republic, no longer subjects of a monarchy. A citizen was a '*unit* of a mass of free people who collectively possess sovereignty', David Ramsay explained, whereas a subject is '*under* the power of another'.[6] There were still, however, considerable difficulties in defining who was British and who was American. These uncertainties involved, for the Americans, people who had been born before the Declaration of Independence or, for the British, those born before the peace had been signed in 1783.

Long-established British doctrine was that 'if the King lost any of his dominions, those born in them while he was King still retained their status as subjects, even though they might acquire a new status as the subjects of a ruler to whom these dominions had passed'.[7] Logically this meant that all those born in America before 1783 could be both British subjects and American citizens. Some argued that since this was the case, it was possible for an American loyalist to remain a British subject while still living in America.[8] In December 1784, however, the British law officers promulgated what seems to have been a modified version of this doctrine: 'a person born a subject of his Majesty in America, previous to the separation of the American states from Great Britain, has not by virtue of such separation lost his capacity of

---

[4] Stephen Conway, 'From Fellow Nationals to Foreigners: British Perceptions of the Americans, circa 1739–1783', *William and Mary Quarterly*, 3rd ser., LXIX (2002), 65–100.

[5] Kettner, *Development*, p. 179.

[6] [David Ramsay], *A Dissertation on the Manner of Acquiring the Character and Privileges of a Citizen of the United States* (Charleston, SC, 1789), p. 3.

[7] W. S. Holdsworth, *History of the English Law*, 14 vols. (London, 1903–52), IX, p. 84.

[8] George Chalmers, *Opinions on Interesting Subjects of Public Law and Commercial Policy arising from American Independence*, 2nd edn (London, 1785), p. 7.

continuing in the allegiance of his Majesty within any part of his dominions'.[9] This presumably ended all doubts that American loyalists, who vehemently asserted that they were 'as perfectly subjects of the British state as any man in London or Middlesex',[10] remained British subjects provided that they lived outside the United States. Henry Cruger was an interesting example of a person born in America who remained a British subject in Britain. He had been an MP for Bristol from 1774 to 1780 and was elected again in 1784. His opponents then tried to unseat him on the grounds that he was 'a native of one of the United States of America', that he had sided with the patriots in America in the closing stages of the war and that he had taken an oath of loyalty to one of the states, renouncing his allegiance and becoming an alien 'actually or virtually'.[11] Cruger's supporters denied that he had taken any such oath.[12] The House of Commons committee that heard the petition against him found Cruger duly elected, presumably because, even if he had taken an oath in America, he still remained a British subject. While a wide interpretation of British subjecthood was no doubt much to the advantage of merchants, like Cruger, who wished to carry on business and hold property on both sides of the Atlantic, it could be highly disadvantageous to a large category of people, that is to seafarers. The Royal Navy was inclined to deem that any sailor on a nominally American ship who could not prove that he had been born in America was a British subject and thus fair game for impressment. Claims by British-born sailors that they had become naturalized Americans were often dismissed.

In establishing their own category of citizenship Americans inevitably disrupted the old community of allegiance of the British empire. American citizens could not retain their allegiance to the Crown. British-born people who did not choose to be citizens of an American state therefore became aliens. To the outraged horror of the loyalists, the British seemed to be prepared to accept a distinction that was made in the 5th article of the peace treaty between American-born loyalists and 'real British subjects'. These were British-born people whose 'only particular interest in America consisted in holding lands and property there'.[13] To Americans, they were aliens to whom, under British pressure, they were prepared to offer special terms for recovering their pre-war debts, whereas they regarded American-born loyalists as their own disloyal citizens to whom nothing was due. There was an obvious disparity between Britain's generous treatment of Americans in Britain, who had the rights of British subjects, and the way in which British subjects were treated in America as aliens. John Jay was told by the British consul in Philadelphia that Americans had suffered 'no deprivation of any right of holding or acquiring property in England' and that British subjects in America should enjoy the same

---

[9] Opinion of 13 December 1784, TNA, HO 48/1, f. 113.

[10] *The Case and Claim of the American Loyalists Impartially Stated and Considered* (London, [1783]), p. 34.

[11] *Journals of the House of Commons*, 9 February 1785, XL, p. 506. The case for and against Cruger was argued in *Felix Farley's Bristol Journal* throughout April 1784.

[12] M. Dawes, *Observations on the Mode of Electing Representatives in Parliament for the City of Bristol* (Bristol and London, 1784), p. 37.

[13] US Commissioners to R. Livingston, 18 July 1783, Giunta (ed.), *Emerging Nation*, I, p. 885.

benefits. John Adams, American minister in London, agreed.[14] But by 1789 only Pennsylvania was allowing foreigners to own land.[15] Were British subjects permitted to acquire land, it was said that they 'would try to hold us again in a species of slavery by getting mortgages and other holds on our lands'.[16] Those aliens who held land in America, even if they acquired it in settlement of debts, were theoretically liable to be required to forfeit it to the state. There were fears, apparently based on a decision in Maryland, that some American courts might indeed order the forfeiting of British-owned estates.

Before the Revolution, the thirteen colonies had to a large extent controlled the naturalization processes by which immigrants became British subjects. After 1783 the states had complete freedom to determine who were or were not to become citizens. It was anticipated that there would be a massive influx of new citizens and that prospect was generally welcomed. That the new America should become an 'asylum', a term famously used by Thomas Paine in *Common Sense* but with a long ancestry and widely taken up by others, for the poor and oppressed of Europe became part of the ideology of Revolutionary America. America's future role in the world would be, in Washington's words, to succour 'the poor, the needy and oppressed of the earth' on 'the fertile plains of the Ohio'.[17] John Adams thought that Britain's distressed state after the war would 'drive great numbers to our country'. America must, he felt, become 'an asylum, worthy to receive all who may wish to fly to it'.[18] Although there was little questioning of the principle that population growth through immigration was highly desirable or that America should envisage itself as a welcoming asylum for the world, there was much discussion as to whether certain categories of immigrant might not be appropriate for the new republic and whether measures should be taken to exclude such people or at least to prevent them from becoming citizens.[19] In some ways the immigration policies of independent America became more restrictive, at least in theory, than those of the old colonies. The irredeemably idle and dissolute or the politically unregenerate were to be guarded against. It was hoped that new immigrants would have 'a clear and conscious attachment to and familiarity with republican principles'.[20] In some states there was for a short time at least a prejudice against admitting British people in general. Scots were specifically to be excluded from Georgia. South Carolina was urged to stop the British 'flocking here and, by their riches and address, overrun the country, and turn out those who fought and

---

[14] P. Bond to Leeds, 15 August 1789, TNA, FO 4/7, ff. 160–1; Adams to Jefferson, 19 January 1786, Julian P. Boyd et al. (eds), *The Papers of Thomas Jefferson* (Princeton, NJ, 1950–), IX, p. 182; see also Kettner, *Development of Citizenship*, pp. 204–5.

[15] P. Bond to Carmarthen, 19 February 1789, TNA, FO 4/7, f. 45.

[16] H. Williamson to T. Ruston, 12 February 1784, Paul H. Smith (ed.), *Letters of Delegates to Congress 1774 to 1789*, 26 vols. (Washington, DC, 1976–2000), XXI, pp. 352–3.

[17] To D. Humphreys, 25 July 1785, W. W. Abbot, et al. (eds), *The Papers of George Washington: Confederation Series*, 6 vols. (Charlottesville, VA, 1992–7), III, p. 152.

[18] To J. Warren, 21 March 1783, *Warren-Adams Letters*, 2 vols. (Boston, 1917–25). II, p. 199.

[19] Marilyn. C. Baseler, *'An Asylum for Mankind': America, 1607–1800* (Ithaca, NY, 1998), ch. 6; Kettner, *Development of Citizenship*, ch. 8.

[20] Ibid. p. 231.

conquered and gained the independence of America'.[21] Americans were acutely sensitive to any supposed attempts by Europe to jettison its human waste on their shores. Before the Revolution poor whites had been shipped over in great numbers as indentured servants bound to labour for fixed periods. With the ending of the war questions were asked as to whether the resumption of such a system was compatible with 'the idea of liberty this country has so happily established'.[22] Although the importing of indentured labour was set to diminish in the future,[23] war had 'greatly exhausted this country of servants' and the practice was revived in 1783.[24] Washington approved of purchasers of land who brought in 'able bodied men indented for a certain time' to cultivate it.[25]

Two other well-established sources for importing labour did, however, come under sustained attack. Importing Africans as slaves virtually ceased except in the far south. After the war, most American states were not prepared to sanction the importing of enslaved Africans. Georgia and South Carolina were, however, determined to try to rebuild their slave labour forces that had been dispersed during the war. David Ramsay, a South Carolina opponent of the slave trade, wrote that opposition would incur 'calumny and public odium . . . without the least prospect of . . . being able to put a stop to the inhuman traffic'.[26] British merchants were virtually the only suppliers. Some 8,735 slaves were disembarked, most at Charleston with some at Savannah, in three years from 1783–5. In 1786 the South Carolina assembly debated a prohibition on further imports as economically and socially undesirable. A temporary prohibition was enacted in 1787. Further imports virtually ceased for a time, reviving in the 1790s and expanding greatly before the formal ending of the trade in 1808.[27] There were strong objections to the importation of British convicts, which was effectively terminated within a few years. Shipments from England stopped almost at once. The Irish parliament passed an Act for transporting convicts to 'plantations in America' in 1786 and a limited flow continued from Ireland until 1788,[28] but shortly afterwards, when a cargo of Irish convicts was turned away from Newfoundland, British ministers concluded that they could not compel even their own remaining American colonies to accept convicts.[29]

---

[21] John C. Meleney, *The Public Life of Aedanus Burke* (Columbia, SC, 1989), pp. 126–7.

[22] Baseler, p. 231.

[23] Robert Steinfeld, *The Invention of Free Labor* (Chapel Hill, NC, 1991).

[24] 'Genuine copies of authentic letters' in 'A Concise Account of the Provinces of North America', William E. Van Vugt (ed.), *British Immigration to the United States 1776–1914*, 4 vols. (London, 2009), I, p. 254.

[25] To R. Henderson, 19 June 1788, Abbot et al. (eds), *Washington Papers: Confederation Series*, VI, p. 340.

[26] To B. Rush, 22 August 1784, Robert L. Brunhouse (ed.), *David Ramsay 1749–1815: Selections from his Writings* (Philadelphia, 1963), p. 76.

[27] 'Trans-Atlantic Slave Trade Database', <http//www.slavevoyages.org>.

[28] Maurice J. Bric, *Ireland, Philadelphia and the Re-invention of America 1760–1800* (Dublin, 2008), p. 126.

[29] W. Grenville to Fitzgibbon, 2 December 1789, *Historical Manuscripts Commission: Fortescue MSS*, 10 vols. (London, 1892–1927), I, pp. 548–9.

The fracturing of a single Atlantic community of allegiance into two political units, the British empire and the United States, potentially created some obstacles to the free movement of people. The British, as this chapter will show, tried to prevent the emigration of skilled artisans, but otherwise did not impose restrictions. The Americans tried to define concepts of republican citizenship from which undesirable immigrants might be excluded. In practice, however, such changes seem to have had little if any effect in restricting the flow of people across the Atlantic. Citizenship was easily acquired in most American states. If need be, migrants seem to have had no great difficulty in assuming American or British identities and in affirming the republican principles of an American state or in pledging their assent to the sovereignty of the king-in-Parliament in British colonies, if so required. Once peace had been restored, patterns of transoceanic migration in the 1780s generally returned to what they had been before the war, except that convicts ceased to be shipped. It seems likely that the overall total of emigrants from the British Isles to the United States in the 1780s was at least comparable to what it had been in the hectic years immediately before the Revolution.

II

The war stopped normal migration from 1775 to 1783, but it brought large numbers of British and German soldiers to fight in America. Enlisting in a regiment bound for America was a well recognized way for a person without means to start a new life there. It had obvious affinities with indentured civilian service: a man committed himself to serve for a period of years in America in return for a free passage and his keep. The turning of soldiers into settlers was given some official encouragement. In 1763 the governors of American colonies had been authorized to make grants of land to officers and men of the king's forces who chose to take their discharge in America after the Seven Years War. The same offer was made in 1783, although it was of course confined to those who were willing to take up land in the remaining British colonies. Upwards of 1,600 regular British and German soldiers after they were disbanded chose to go to Nova Scotia and a small number took land in the colony of Quebec.[30]

Although the numbers cannot be quantified with any precision at all, there can be no doubt that a considerable body of ex-soldiers remained in the United States rather than returning home with their regiments at the end of the war or going to the British colonies. Henry Laurens reflected that 'many thousands have become useful inhabitants of the country they were sent to devastate'.[31] Some of those that remained had deserted during the course of the war. An incomplete return compiled by the War Office calculated that between 1774 and 1780 a total of

---

[30] List of Corps Disbanded, TNA, CO 217/57, f. 157.
[31] To W. McCulloch, 9 March 1782, Philip M. Hamer et al. (eds), *The Papers of Henry Laurens*, 16 vols. (Columbia, SC, 1968–2003), XV, p. 472.

2,195 men deserted from British regiments.[32] British officers believed that there were numerous deserters still in America at the end of the war. An officer who went to Lancaster in Pennsylvania reported that that there are 'a very great number' of them 'in or about this town and indeed dispersed throughout the country'.[33] To encourage them to accept passages home, an order was issued in May 1783 remitting capital punishment for the offence of desertion.[34]

Other British soldiers who stayed in America after the war had been captured by the Americans. The most economical way of dealing with them was to hire them out as labourers to employers on whom the cost of their keep would fall and who executed a bond guaranteeing that they would not abscond. Congress officially recognized such practices in the closing stages of the war, when prisoners were permitted to buy their discharge by a period of labour and then to take the oath of allegiance and become citizens of one of the states.[35] Many British prisoners wished for nothing more than to be repatriated. Exchanged prisoners coming back to Britain in 1778 'burst into tears of joy at landing, others prostrate on the ground thanked God for being restored to their country'.[36] But the prospect of remaining in America, to which they had become accustomed and where wages were high and there was the promise of cheap and accessible land, seems to have been sufficiently alluring for a considerable number to pass up the chance of going home at the end of the war. Men with craft skills were greatly valued in America and must have been particularly tempted. The British commander-in-chief at the end of the war, Sir Guy Carleton, embarked those prisoners who had been released and brought to New York in 1783 after nearly six years of captivity as quickly as possible. He believed that otherwise, once they had received fresh clothing and the large arrears of pay due to them, 'the connections' that they had 'formed, during their long residence in this country' would induce them to remain in America.[37]

The British were uncertain about the precise number of prisoners held by the Americans in the closing stages of the war. The War Office confessed that it had 'not the means of ascertaining the number lost by captivity, having no account of what the whole number of prisoners taken in any one year may be, or of the prisoners that may be have been exchanged in the course of it'.[38] Carleton put the total at nearly 12,000 in May 1782, which seems to have been high, even allowing for the 6,000 or so British troops who had surrendered at Yorktown.[39] Washington assessed the number to be handed over at 5,000 to 6,000.[40] By the end of May

---

[32] 'An Account of the Men Lost and Disabled in His Majesty's Land Service', January 1781, BL, Add MS 38375, ff. 74–5.

[33] A. Clarke to G. Carleton, 13 May 1783, TNA, CO 5/109, f. 296.

[34] Order of 14 May 1783, TNA, WO 1/13, f. 58.

[35] 21 June 1782, Worthington C. Ford (ed.), *Journals of the Continental Congress, 1774–1789*, 34 vols. (Washington, DC, 1904–37), XXII, pp. 343–4.

[36] G. Yonge to J. Almon, 3 January 1778, BL, Add MS 20733, f. 148.

[37] To Sir G. Yonge, 26 May 1783, TNA, WO 1/13, f. 40.

[38] Account, January 1781, BL, Add MS 38375, ff. 74–5.

[39] To W. Ellis, 8 May 1782, TNA, CO 5/105, f. 88.

[40] To A. Hamilton, 22 April 1783, Harold C. Syrett et al. (eds), *The Papers of Alexander Hamilton*, 27 vols. (New York, 1962–87), III, p. 334.

1783 4,900 had been brought to New York and a few more were to follow.[41] The officer who had been sent to collect the prisoners from Pennsylvania reported that this was 'very far short' of what he had been led to expect, but did not anticipate significant additions.[42] It seems clear that a significant if unknown number of British prisoners chose to become immigrants into the United States of America.

That German troops would become immigrants in large numbers was commonly assumed. From the early stages of the war the Americans had actively sought to lure German soldiers into joining the German community already established in America. German prisoners were extensively put out to work, often for fellow Germans. Deserters were promised 50 acres of land. By the end of the war the Americans were actively recruiting them into the Continental Army in return for promises of land and cash bounties. Later recruits sent to make up the German regiments in America were said by the Hessian General Knyphausen to have enlisted with a specific view 'to get over here in some manner, and never to see Europe again'.[43] Desertion became particularly frequent in the last years of the war. The Hessians at New York in 1783 waiting to go back to Europe were reported to be deserting in great numbers, saying that 'they are so much prejudiced in favour of the soil, government and inhabitants of America that they mean to become inhabitants of it'.[44] Nearly 3,000 Hessians were stated as having deserted in the course of the war and when the Hessians were finally withdrawn 3,014 were listed as remaining in America, a total which did not include the contingents of other princes.[45] 'Almost a quarter of the German troops', it has been suggested, 'made a conscious decision not to return to Europe.'[46]

Captured Americans were often enlisted willy-nilly into British forces. As the story of the men of a British regiment made up of prisoners captured in South Carolina suggests, most of those incorporated into the British army during the war probably eventually returned to the United States, although some settled in Nova Scotia.[47] Many captured American seamen were compelled to serve in the Royal Navy. This could take them to distant parts of the world. Richard Low was serving 'with a number of other Americans' in HMS *Defence* in India at the end of the war.[48] The Admiralty agreed to release him and other prisoners,[49] but some elected to remain with the British. Jacob Nagle of Reading, Pennsylvania, was a

---

[41] G. Carleton to T. Townshend, 28 May 1783, TNA, PRO 30/55/70, no. 7800. See returns in TNA, CO 5/109, ff. 308, 388.

[42] A. Clarke to G. Carleton, 27 May 1783, TNA, PRO 30/55/70, no. 7785.

[43] Cited in Rodney Atwood, *The Hessians: Mercenaries from Hesse-Kassel in the American Revolution* (Cambridge, 1980), p. 205.

[44] John Shy (ed.), *Winding Down: The Revolutionary War Letters of Lieutenant Benjamin Gilbert of Massachusetts 1780–3* (Ann Arbor, MI, 1989), p. 108.

[45] Atwood, *The Hessians*, pp. 194, 256.

[46] Charles P. Neimeyer, *America Goes to War: A Social History of the Continental Army* (New York, 1996), p. 63.

[47] See below, pp. 249–51.

[48] J. Carter to J. Adams, 19 April 1785, TNA, FO 4/3, f. 341.

[49] Admiralty to Carmarthen, 7 December 1785, ibid. f. 376.

conspicuous example. He was taken off an American privateer, forced to serve on a British warship, and eventually brought back to Britain. He continued to serve in the Royal Navy with credit for many years before finally returning to America.[50]

III

It was widely expected that there would be a massive resumption of free emigration from Britain immediately after the ending of the war. Well before the formal ratification of the peace, paragraphs in the British press were announcing that '*Emigration*, that alarming evil, which threatens all our devoted country through all its coasts, is already beginning its frightful devastations in different parts of Ireland ... [G]reat part of Scotland and Ireland, nay the north and western parts of England itself, will soon be depopulated.'[51] What was called 'a spirit of emigration' was said to be abroad throughout the British Isles. It was expected that post-war hardship, accentuated by poor harvests and high food prices in 1782 and 1783 would greatly augment the flow. Americans were also confident that the new America would exert a magnetic pull on those who saw the chance not just of escaping poverty but of living in a just society, purged of the vices of old Europe.

Concern that hardship would drive people to America focused most strongly on Scotland and above all on the Highlands. John Knox, a London bookseller, in his passionately polemical *View of the British Empire, more especially Scotland* of 1784 took it on himself to publicize the distresses of the Highlands. 'Neglected by government; forsaken or oppressed by the gentry,... the Highlands of Scotland ... are the seats of oppression, poverty, famine, anguish, and wild despair.' In what he called the famine of 1782, 'many hundred persons languished and died'. Highlanders had emigrated to America in large numbers before the war closed the ports, and they would do so again if urgent measures were not taken.[52] Other parts of Scotland were also distressed after the war. In 1784 it was said that the 'load of taxes,... the decay of trade and manufactures and particularly, the scarcity for a long time, and high prices of grain' were driving 'the poorer sort' towards emigration.[53] 'Can there be any occasion to remind you', an Aberdeen preacher told his audience, 'that the spirit of emigration very strongly prevails through a great part of North Britain?' Without immediate action, 'the northern parts of this island, already considerably depopulated, may in time, become almost a desert'.[54] In 1786 there was still talk of 'starving Highlanders' and it was asserted without any

[50] John C. Dann (ed.), *The Nagle Journal: A Diary of the Life of Jacob Nagle, Sailor, from the Year 1775 to 1841* (New York, 1988).

[51] *Public Advertiser*, 27 February 1783.

[52] pp. 8, 78.

[53] M. Ross to J. Witherspoon, 12 July 1784, Ashbel Green, *The Life of the Revd John Witherspoon*, ed. Henry Lyttleton Savage (Princeton, NJ, 1973), p. 210.

[54] William Duff, *National Prosperity the Consequence of National Virtue; and National Ruin the Effect of National Wickedness: A Sermon* (Aberdeen, 1785), pp. 92–3.

evidence that 30,000 had gone to America since the war and still more were about to leave.[55]

Much of Ireland suffered from what has been called a 'subsistence crisis' in the years 1782 to 1784.[56] Reports of hardship stimulating emigration came principally from Dublin and from the north. In June 1783 the Dublin magistrates reported a 'great scarcity of grain' in the city, while a threefold increase in the price of oatmeal was provoking disorder in Ulster.[57] Shortages and high prices continued over the winter of 1783–4.[58] By June 1783 emigrants were said to be going to America from the north of Ireland 'with an eagerness never known before'.[59] The turbulent weavers from the Earl of Meath's Liberty in Dublin, who complained bitterly that British imports were destroying their livelihood, reportedly 'declared their readiness for a general emigration'.[60]

Prominent Americans were frequently told about groups in the British Isles who wished to enjoy the freedom that America had so recently won for itself. Franklin, in particular, was bombarded with requests for his support for such people. A party of artisans in the Lancashire textile trades at Stockport told him that they wished to improve their lives in America and ardently desired to escape from 'the hand of oppression that our rulers lay upon all the governed' and to live in 'a free state governed by HONEST MEN'.[61] Contrary to British beliefs that he was actively soliciting emigrants, Franklin warned them to think carefully before embarking. They could expect no government support in America.[62] Undeterred, they were about to take ship from Londonderry in August 1782 when they were rudely interrupted. The administration had got wind of the scheme through an informer in Stockport and the Lord Lieutenant of Ireland was asked to arrest them. Five men were apprehended but the case against them could not be sustained. It was an offence for artificers to be encouraged to leave the king's dominions, but until the peace was formally ratified America was part of the king's dominions. The arrested emigrants were discharged and induced to give their services to the new textile works being established in Ireland.[63]

Friends of the new America who were men of substance told their American contacts that they hoped to go there themselves and to bring numerous followers with them. The Earl of Buchan, a Scottish nobleman of liberal views, wrote that 'Many of my acquaintance . . . seem disposed to seek an asylum on the other side of

---

[55] H. Beaufoy, 20 June 1786, *Parliamentary Register*, XX, p. 392.

[56] James Kelly, 'Scarcity and Poor Relief in Eighteenth-century Ireland: The Subsistence Crisis of 1782–4', *Irish Historical Studies*, XXVIII (1992–3), 38–62.

[57] Northington to North, 26 June 1783, TNA, HO 100/9, f. 181.

[58] Northington to Sydney, 26 January 1784, TNA, HO 100/12, ff. 68–71.

[59] *Morning Herald*, 13 June 1783.

[60] Ibid. 22 July 1783.

[61] H. Royle et al. to Franklin, [23 November 1781], Leonard W. Labaree et al. (eds), *The Papers of Benjamin Franklin* (New Haven, CT, 1959–), XXXVI, p. 107.

[62] To E. Clegg, 26 April 1782, ibid. XXXVII, pp. 226–7.

[63] Their story can be traced in numerous letters in the Home Office Domestic papers (TNA, HO 42/1) and in the Lord Lieutenant's correspondence (TNA, HO 100/3). See also the account of the episode in Robert Glen, 'Industrial Wayfarers: Benjamin Franklin and a Case of Machine Smuggling in the 1780s', *Business History*, XXIII (1981), 309–26.

the Attlantic.' He hoped to promote the settlement of Scots in America who were 'friends to the principles which gave independence to that country'.[64] Franklin was also told in a letter from Anglesey of plans for a mass emigration of at least 1,000 discontented Welsh people, led by 'men of property and opulence'.[65] John Jay too heard about the discontents of the Welsh from an Anglican clergyman who, 'with many more of the Principality of Wales, intend, if God willing, to cross the Atlantic to a land of freedom and liberty' won for humanity by 'the immortal Washington'.[66] Washington himself was told that in Scotland 'oppression is reduced to a system' and that 'four young gentlemen' were willing to lead the thousands of poor Scots who wished to flee from this oppression by emigrating.[67] Thomas Pownall, former governor of Massachusetts, envisaged the United States as, 'that branch of the English nation' that was now '*my country*' and hoped to buy land there and to bring over with him 'a number of experienced farmers and usefull labourers'.[68] There is, however, no evidence that these professions of admiration for American principles produced any significant movement of migrants to America. Ideologically moti-vated emigration was the product of a harsher climate against political and religious dissent in Britain in the 1790s and of oppression in Ireland before and after the rebellion of 1798.[69]

Post-war British governments were immediately deluged with calls both in the press and in Parliament for action to stem a supposed epidemic of emigration. There seems to have been a general consensus among ministers that emigration was an evil that must be resisted. This was a view shared by all shades of British opinion. Irish patriots as well as the Irish administration deplored it. Fears of the economic collapse likely to follow depopulation, especially in Ireland and Scotland, were as lively as they had been before the Revolution.[70] That an independent America should prosper at Britain's expense now made emigration even more unpalatable. This was a case made with particular force by Phineas Bond, the energetic and strongly opinionated American loyalist who served as British consul at Philadelphia. While Britain haemorrhaged its population, he wrote, American employers gained the labour that they urgently needed and American merchants and ship-owners profited from the passenger trade.[71] No distinction was usually made between emigration to British North American colonies, which might reasonably have been regarded as being in the national interest, and emigration to the alien United States. All emigration, except for the transportation of convicts, was deemed undesirable. The governor of the Isle St John, later the colony of Prince Edward Island, was

---

[64] Letter of 18 February 1783, Labaree et al. (eds), *Franklin Papers*, XXXIX, pp. 186–7.

[65] Summary of letter, of H. Jones 9 April 1783, ibid. XXXIX, p. 55.

[66] Letter of J. Price, 29 October 1783, Henry P. Johnston (ed.), *The Correspondence and Public Papers of John Jay*, 4 vols. (New York, 1890–3), III, p. 92.

[67] Letter of C. MacIver, [November 1784], Abbot, et al. (eds), *Washington Papers: Confederation Series*, II, pp. 158–9.

[68] To J. Bowdoin, 28 February 1783, 'The Bowdoin and Temple Papers, II', *Collections of the Massachusetts Historical Society*, 7th Ser., VI (1907), 4.

[69] Michael Durey, *Transatlantic Radicals and the Early American Republic* (Lawrence, KS, 1997).

[70] Bailyn, *Voyagers to the West*, pp. 36–42.

[71] E.g. Bond to Leeds, 15 August 1789, TNA, FO 4/7, f. 166.

warned by Lord George Germain, even before the ending of the war, not to expect migrants from Britain: 'This country and Ireland being too much exhausted to admit any of their inhabitants to people distant territories.'[72]

In trying to curb emigration after 1783, ministers were very much in the same situation as their predecessors had been before the Revolution. Although estimates of the outflow of people of varying degrees of credibility were freely bandied about, they had no reliable statistics for migration until the establishment of British consuls in major American ports later in the 1780s. Nor, whatever the actual scale of the problem might be, did governments believe that they had effective powers to prohibit people leaving the country. As the author of 'Hints to restrain Emigration' put it, 'policy ought to exert every nerve ... to restrain the alarming emigration from this country to America', but measures 'to confine the inhabitants of a free country' were unacceptable.[73] Laws did, however, exist which made it an offence for skilled workers to go abroad or for industrial machinery to be exported. Apparently believing the stories about numerous American agents trying to recruit artisans,[74] the government published a notice in the *London Gazette* in February 1784 warning of the penalties and those who encouraged them to go would incur.[75] This seems to have had a deterrent effect on recruiting even unskilled indentured servants for America. The Irish parliament passed its own Act prohibiting the seducing of artisans and manufacturers into going abroad in 1785. Prominent Americans in Britain were thought to be actively promoting emigration; Henry Laurens—without, it would seem, any foundation—was publicly accused of doing so.[76] Suspicions about John Witherspoon, president of the College of New Jersey, whose supposed designs the Scottish administration were urged by the Secretary of State to counter,[77] had a little more substance. Witherspoon had been a most active promoter of emigration from Scotland before the Revolution and, when he returned to Britain in 1784, he had a commission from Washington to recruit tenants for his western lands. He was, however, much too circumspect to attempt anything of the kind, believing that the government would pounce on him if even a weaver or a blacksmith took ship to America under his auspices.[78]

It was commonly held that emigration was not only damaging to Britain but that would-be emigrants needed to be dissuaded for their own good. Admonitory pamphlets were brought out and the British and Irish papers were full of warnings about conditions in America: government there was unstable and property insecure, taxes were exorbitant, stories of high wages and cheap land were illusory, new migrants would meet with ill-treatment and hostility. Josiah Wedgwood published

---

[72] Cited in J. M. Bumsted, *The People's Clearance: Highland Emigration to British North America 1770–1815* (Edinburgh, 1982), p. 71.

[73] 'Memorandum for Col. North', n.d., TNA, HO 42/3, f. 342.

[74] E.g. *Public Advertiser*, 30 March 1784.

[75] See above, pp. 111–12.

[76] John King, *Thoughts on the Difficulties and Distresses in which the Peace of 1783 has involved the People of England*, 5th edn (London, 1783), p. 33.

[77] Sydney to T. Miller, 16 July 1784, TNA, HO 102/2, p. 48.

[78] Washington to Witherspoon, 10 March 1784, Witherspoon to Washington, 14 April 1785, Abbot et al. (eds), *Washington Papers: Confederation Series*, I, pp. 198–9; II, p. 497.

a pamphlet trying to dissuade any workman in the potteries from emigrating. America was the destination that would be 'the most hurtful to our particular business'. He gave examples of migrants who had come to a bad end in America.[79]

If not much could be done—beyond threats and cajolery—physically to prevent people from emigrating, panic about emigration was an important stimulus for measures for improvements in Britain that might keep people at home. Most concern was focused on conditions in Scotland. Fear that an important source of military manpower would be drained away reinforced the attention directed to the Highlands.[80] Highland Societies were formed in Edinburgh and London to consider means of alleviating poverty. In August 1784 Henry Dundas, the second most powerful minister in the Pitt administration, moved for the repeal of the Forfeited Estates Act of 1746, which had been intended to emancipate the Highlands from the hold of disaffected chiefs. Repeal was a measure he had advocated before the outbreak of the Revolution.[81] He believed that with their lands restored to them the Highland chieftains would cherish their followers and dissuade them from becoming 'adventurers to seek a better fortune in America'.[82] Lord Sydney, the Secretary of State, strongly supported the proposal. 'It would rivet great numbers of Highlanders, who would not think of going from home when they knew that those for whom they had an affection from their earliest youth were to be put in possession of their family estates.'[83] Much attention was given to revitalizing the fisheries in Scottish waters, which would, it was hoped, provide plentiful employment for the Highlands as an alternative to emigration.

Popular anxieties were generally aroused by greatly exaggerated fears of the actual scale of emigration. In the case of Ireland, however, rumours had real substance. Emigration from Ireland resumed soon after the war and it constituted by far the largest element in British migration to America throughout the 1780s.[84] A ship took emigrants from Londonderry as early as August 1782.[85] The formal conclusion of the peace unleashed a wave of Irish emigrants. Estimates put the total for 1783 as high as 5,000 with even larger numbers in 1784, the peak year of the decade. Around 10,000 seems to be a generally acceptable total for that year but some scholars suggest that it was very much higher.[86] Thereafter the rate levelled off at, it is supposed, an average of 5,000 a year for the rest of the decade.

---

[79] *An Address to the Workmen in the Pottery on the Subject of Entering into the Service of Foreign Manufacturers* (Newcastle, Staffs., 1783), pp. 4–5, 8.

[80] Andrew MacKillop, *'More Fruitful than the Soil'; Army, Empire and the Scottish Highlands 1715–1815* (East Linton, 2000), p. 180.

[81] Bailyn, *Voyagers to the West*, pp. 46–8.

[82] 2 August 1784, *Parliamentary Register*, XVI, p. 323.

[83] 16 August 1784, ibid. XVI, p. 89.

[84] On Irish emigration, see Kerby A. Miller, *Emigrants and Exiles: Ireland and the Irish Exodus to North America* (New York, 1985); James Kelly, 'The Resumption of Emigration from Ireland after the American War of Independence, 1783–1787', *Studia Hibernica*, XXIV (1984–8), 61–88; M. A. Jones, 'Ulster Emigration 1783–1815' in E. E. R. Green (ed.), *Essays in Scotch-Irish History*, 2nd edn (Belfast, 1992); Kerby A. Miller et al. (eds), *Irish Immigrants in the Land of Canaan: Letters and Memoirs from Colonial and Revolutionary America* (New York, 2003); Bric, *Ireland, Philadelphia*.

[85] See information of W. Clarke, 6 August 1782, TNA, HO 42/1, f. 295.

[86] Notably Kelly, 'The Resumption of Emigration', p. 79.

There were at first clear continuities between post-war Irish immigration and the pattern established before the war.[87] Most of the emigrants again left from ports in the north—Londonderry, Belfast, Newry, and Larne—taking passengers largely drawn from Ulster, although people from other parts of Ireland and even from Britain made their way to northern ports to get a passage. Thirty-six families were said to have gone from the Clyde to take ship for America from Belfast in June 1783.[88] The dominance of the northern ports reflected the extent to which the trade in people was closely integrated with other forms of Irish-American trade. Ships bringing back American flax seed for the Ulster linen industry found passengers a valuable outward cargo. Immigrants went to Charleston, Baltimore, and New York, but most were landed at the ports on the Delaware, above all at Philadelphia. There a number of well-established Irish merchant houses took a prominent role in organizing the passenger trade. As had been the case before the war, a considerable proportion of the first post-war Irish emigrants seem to have been indentured servants. Immediately after the war, Irish indentured servants from Waterford were said to be being advertised for sale 'like negroes' at Charleston.[89] Other servants embarked as 'redemptioners', who paid for the cost of their passage on arrival, usually by an advance of wages from an employer or by contributions from friends or relatives already in America. A British consul reported that the treatment of servants on overcrowded ships was 'oppressive and cruel' and that on their arrival they were likely to be carried into 'the back country' under the guard of 'severe and brutal drovers'.[90] Harsh post-war conditions in Ireland no doubt swelled the number of people willing to mortgage their services in order to get to America. The war had created a serious shortage of labour and there was said to be an 'excellent market' for servants at Philadelphia in 1783.[91] At Baltimore, where Washington's agents and presumably those of other Virginia and Maryland planters looked for likely craftsmen, the demand for masons and bricklayers was such that servants were able to negotiate reductions in their period of service from the usual four years to only a year and a half.[92] With the recession brought about by the supply of British goods beyond the capacity of Americans to pay for them, the demand dried up. The Lord Lieutenant of Ireland reported in August 1784 that the captain of an immigrant ship had found no sale for his servants and had therefore 'to give them away to prevent them starving'. He thought that fewer servants were likely to be shipped in future.[93]

Passengers who paid their way largely replaced servants. Fare-paying migrants were likely to be people of some substance, whose motives in crossing the Atlantic

[87] For the pre-war trade, see Thomas M. Truxes, *Irish-American Trade, 1660–1783* (Cambridge, 1983).

[88] *Caledonian Mercury*, 21 June 1783.

[89] *Public Advertiser*, 16 March 1784.

[90] P. Bond to Carmarthen, 16 November 1788, TNA, FO 4/6, f. 313.

[91] Letter of 16 September 1783 in 'A Concise Account of North America', Van Vugt (ed.), *British Immigration*, I, p. 249.

[92] T. Tilghman to Washington, 15 July 1784, W. W. Abbot et al. (eds), *Washington Papers: Confederation Series*, I, p. 529

[93] Rutland to Sydney, 19 August 1784, TNA, HO 100/14, ff. 58–9.

were not necessarily to escape deprivation but to take the opportunities for leading a better life that America seemed to offer. They have been described as 'the first visibly "modern" Irish emigrants', not fleeing from hardship or persecution, but responding to 'economic development in the transatlantic world'.[94] From the mid 1780s they were leaving when Ulster in particular was undergoing a phase of economic expansion after the immediate post-war depression. Most of the Irish arriving on the Delaware in 1789 were said to be 'people in tolerably good plight with some property beforehand, and who have come out to settle as farmers or to engage as artificers'.[95] Few servants were noted among those who came in through Charleston towards the end of the decade. Most of them were in search of land in the interior of North and South Carolina.[96] By the end of the 1780s a number of emigrants from the North of Ireland were reported to be settling in Kentucky.[97] More family parties and fewer single males went. Protestants, especially Presbyterians, were still dominant, but increasing numbers of Catholics were also emigrating.

Scottish migration to America, even though so much was being written about the depopulation of the Highlands, got under way after the war much more slowly than did Irish emigration. Many people might wish to emigrate but the means by which they could do so had yet to be re-established. One of John Witherspoon's correspondents from Montrose in eastern Scotland told him in a most informative letter of the difficulties faced by the poor who wished to cross the Atlantic. The lack of ships going to America from the east-coast ports forced would-be emigrants to take themselves to Glasgow first. There the government's threats about the laws against seducing skilled artisans to go overseas were making merchants wary of offering indentures to servants. Such terms as were available were harsh. The alternative was for a would-be emigrant to pay for his own passage, but anyone who could afford to do that 'may be reckoned a rich man at present'. Steerage passages cost six guineas.[98] A clergyman at Tong in the Isle of Lewis reported 'a murmur about emigration running thro' the common people', stimulated, he thought, by the talk of 'a few old soldiers', but it would not turn into 'the phrenzy of 1773' without a leader or the arrival of a ship from the Clyde looking for human cargo.[99]

For the poor especially, unless they were prepared to go as servants, moving to America required the aid of 'networks', that is of local leaders, commercial firms, religious groups, entrepreneurs and promoters and, above all, 'the countless informal kinship and friendship networks that spanned the Atlantic', to arrange passages and settle them in work or on the land. Such connections were responsible for 'the majority of free British migration to America' in the years before the Revolution.[100]

---

[94] Miller, *Emigrants and Exiles*, p. 191. See also Bric, *Ireland, Philadelphia*, pp. 94–8.
[95] Bond to Leeds, 10 November 1789, TNA, FO 4/8, f. 162.
[96] Miller's Report, 21 January 1791, ibid. f. 58.
[97] 'Observations on the Colony of Kentucky', BL, Add MS 59083, f. 79.
[98] Letter of C. Nesbit, 16 March 1784, Green, *Life of Witherspoon*, pp. 221–3.
[99] J. Downie to G. Gillanders, 10 May 1784, National Archives of Scotland, GD 427/220/7.
[100] Barbara De Wolfe, *Discoveries of America: Personal Accounts of British Emigrants to North America during the Revolutionary Era* (Cambridge, 1997), pp. 23–4.

Scots would travel within networks of other Scots from the same areas or the same congregations. Many Scottish-American communities had, however, been damaged and displaced during the war. Strong measures had been taken in Maryland and Virginia against the powerful Glasgow merchant houses which had controlled much of the Chesapeake's trade and had brought in many young Scots to serve them. After the war, the houses were mainly concerned with recovering their debts, not with recruiting to extend their activities. The frontier counties of the Mohawk or upper Hudson valleys of New York, the territory of Sir William Johnson, the great patron and provider of tenancies for waves of newly-arrived Scots, had been ravaged by ferocious fighting. Johnson's family with many of their Scottish followers had been forced to take refuge in Canada. Before the war Highland Scots had also flooded into North Carolina. There too they had experienced military defeat. Scots were well represented among the loyalist refugees who fled from North Carolina. By 1790, however, some Highland immigrants were reported to be coming back to North Carolina through Charleston.[101]

In due time after the war, Scottish groups which had been dispersed into British territory, began to reach back across the Atlantic to encourage other Scots to come out and join them. Those who had been uprooted from up-state New York included a group of Roman Catholics from around Glen Garry in Inverness-shire who had emigrated in 1773.[102] Many of them supported the royal cause during the war and subsequently established themselves in the western parts of Quebec in what was to become the new colony of Upper Canada, where a block of land was initially allocated specifically for Catholics. Other Highlanders, including many Catholics, later left Scotland to join them. Two ship-loads came in 1786. A ship from Greenock was reported to have brought 520 Highlanders to Quebec in September 1786. They had signed bills to repay the merchant who had financed the voyage. From Quebec they moved up the St Lawrence to join their clansmen and co-religionists in Upper Canada. Another ship in the same year brought 320 via Philadelphia and New York and then overland to Canada.[103] Many more from Inverness-shire and the western islands followed in 1790 and 1791, most of them going to another already established settlement of Highlanders at Pictou in Nova Scotia where John Witherspoon had been instrumental in bringing Scots in the 1770s.[104] With the ending of the war, land around Pictou was allocated to predominantly Scottish soldiers who had fought for the Crown in American Provincial regiments. Other Scots moved there from the United States. In 1784 the Pictou Presbyterians petitioned to Scotland for a minister and in 1786 they got what they had asked for, a minister from the Secession Church who could preach both in Gaelic and English. He found an impoverished community. Many of the

---

[101] G. Miller to Leeds, 28 January 1790, TNA, FO 4/8, f. 58.

[102] Bailyn, *Voyagers to the West*, pp. 582–3.

[103] R. McDonnell to A. Macdonnell, 1 April 1786, Allan I. Macinnes et al. (eds), *Scotland and the Americas, c.1650–c.1939: A Documentary Source Book* (Edinburgh, 2002), p. 176; L. H. Copsey, *The Scottish Pioneers of Upper Canada 1784–1855* (Toronto, 2005), pp. 21–3; Royce MacGillivray and Ewan Ross, *A History of Glengarry* (Belleville, Ont., 1979), pp. 6–11.

[104] Bailyn, *Voyagers to the West*, pp. 390–7.

Highlanders were illiterate and there was as yet no town, no church, nor school.[105] In 1791 they were reinforced by 1,300 people, mostly Catholics who left the Highlands for Pictou.[106]

To contemporaries the last few years before the outbreak of fighting in America in 1775 had been a time of a hectic and alarming spate of emigration. Current estimates suggest that of the 45,000 or so who went, there had been slightly more leaving from Ireland than from Scotland with England not very far behind.[107] In the 1780s the overall volume of emigration from the British Isles may not have been very different from what it had been in the 1770s, but the great change was the decline of the movements of English and Scots and the very marked increase in Irish emigration. The temporary disruption of pre-war links is a plausible explanation for the decline of Scottish emigration in the 1780s, which was later to recover. The decline of the English is, however, puzzling. Brisk emigration from London is said to have resumed in 1783; a total of 372 emigrants were reported to have left on American ships between March and August.[108] Thereafter there are few references in consular or other reports to specifically English migrants arriving in America. The English were no doubt subsumed into the general figures. In the five years from 1770 to 1775 English and Welsh immigration into the thirteen colonies has been put at 11,700.[109] It seems most unlikely that the total from 1783 to 1789 was anything approaching that. A lower volume of English emigration may in part be attributable to a less severe increase in post-war food prices by comparison with Scotland and Ireland and to opportunities for employment in England benefiting more immediately from the spurt in manufacturing and the quick recovery of overseas trade that followed the ending of the war. By contrast with the decline of English and Scots, there clearly was a great increase in the number of Irish crossing the Atlantic after the war. A careful calculation of Irish coming through Philadelphia alone puts them at 32,000 for 1783–9.[110] Additions have to be made for other significant ports: Charleston, Baltimore, and New York. An overall figure of about 40,000 for the 1780s might be appropriate.

Post-war Irish migration was resumed on a large scale and was directed primarily to the United States. Scottish emigration was slower to take off and a considerable proportion went to British North American colonies. In what sense was the difference between Ireland and Scotland a consequence of the disruption of empire

---

[105] George Patterson (ed.), *Memoirs of the Rev. James MacGregor* (Edinburgh, 1859); George Patterson, *A History of the County of Pictou, Nova Scotia* (Montreal, 1877).

[106] Bumsted, *People's Clearance*, p. 74; A. McDonald to Bishop Hay, 11 July 1791, Macinnes et al. (eds), *Scotland and the Americas*, pp. 45–6.

[107] Figures for 1770–5 are drawn from Horn, 'British Diaspora', Marshall (ed.), *Oxford History of the British Empire*, II, table 2.2, p. 32.

[108] E.g. E. Watson to J. Adams, 30 April 1783, Robert J. Taylor et al. (eds), *The Papers of John Adams* (Cambridge, MA, 1977–), XIV, p. 462; *Morning Herald*, 15 August 1783.

[109] Horn, 'British Diaspora', p. 32.

[110] Bric, *Ireland, Philadelphia*, p. 306. The British consul at Philadelphia put the total of immigrants into the port from 1783 to 1789 at 27,716, some 2,000 of whom were Germans; 'the rest consisted of Irish and a very few Scotch' (P. Bond to Leeds, 16 November 1789, TNA, FO 4/8, f. 162).

and the attainment of American independence? It is tempting to suggest that the tendency of Scots to settle in British colonies rather than in the United States was a deliberate political choice, the consequence of strong Scottish support for the policies of the British government during the war. Scots were indeed warned that, as they were 'peculiarly obnoxious to the United States on account of the active part they have taken against them', emigrants there 'will probably meet with very little encouragement'.[111] In 1782 a Georgia law laid down that, as 'the people of Scotland have in general enacted a decided inimicallity to the civil liberties of America', Scots immigrants would be deported unless they had taken an active part in the American cause.[112] Conversely, it might be supposed that, given Ireland's recent conflicts with British authority, when Irish migrants had a chance of escaping from British domination by going to now independent American states, they would take it. There was indeed a strong sense of fellow feeling for the new America in Ulster. An Ulster land agent warned his employer that 'the same spirit that made our farmers take up arms and desert the plough' to join the Volunteers 'will infallibly drive them to America if oppressed at home...Our People adore the manly firmness and courage of their relatives in America, and when a peace is established, will flock there in thousands, if not tied by the indulgence and humanity of their landlords to their native soil.'[113] Some Scots thought the same. Nova Scotia was said to be unpopular with some would-be emigrants, 'who have a sort of notion of freedom, and are not ambitious of any more of the blessings of his Majesty's government'.[114] It seems unlikely, however, that the bulk of those who crossed the Atlantic chose their destination primarily on political considerations. Those leaving Scotland were naturally drawn to joining Scottish communities in America wherever they might be settled. Since the vicissitudes of war meant that major communities were now settled in surviving British colonies, many Scottish emigrants therefore chose to go there. Most Irish did not go to British colonies. Political sympathies were probably an added inducement to go to the United States for those from Ulster, but the routes along which the Irish went to an independent America after 1783 were those long fixed by the pattern of Irish trade and settlement. They merged into Irish communities that had survived the upheavals of the war in the port cities, especially in Philadelphia, and in the western back country. In choosing their destinations prospective emigrants no doubt endeavoured to inform themselves of the advantages of different parts of America. Considerations like the availability of land, the terms on which it could be had, levels of taxation, or commercial opportunities might appear to be in favour of either an American state or a British colony. In the last resort, however, choice was relatively limited: as they had done before the war, most migrants went where the facilities in terms of shipping and the organization

[111] *Caledonian Mercury*, 23 April 1783.
[112] Kettner, *Development of Citizenship*, p. 216.
[113] J. Moore to A. Annersley, 22 June 1782, W. H. Crawford (ed.), *Letters from an Ulster Land Agent 1774–85* (Belfast, 1976), p. 39.
[114] C. Nesbit to J. Witherspoon, 16 March 1784, Green, *Life of Witherspoon*, p. 221.

provided by networks to which they belonged made it practical for them to go. In the 1790s America began to attract refugees from British or Irish political and religious persecution, but it seems doubtful whether the political reconfiguration brought about by the Revolution had any major effect on the changes in the pattern of transatlantic migration that were taking place immediately after 1783.

IV

As soon as the war ended Americans flocked to Britain, as they had done before the war, on relatively short visits of business or pleasure or to take up studies, particularly of medicine in Edinburgh or of the law in London. Aspiring American merchants poured into Britain 'from every quarter of their late dispersions (much as we are told the Jews will one day assemble at Jerusalem)' to 'go as far as their money or credit will carry them in purchase of goods' to ship home.[115] Budding American painters again came to London. These included John Trumbull, Mather Brown, and William Dunlap, who arrived in 1785 aged nineteen and lived a convivial life, consorting with young British officers who had served in America.[116] In August 1783 American officers were to be seen in London 'sporting their black and white cockades' and being 'treated with the utmost civility by many people'.[117] A new cohort of young 'transatlantics' began to frequent the New England Coffee House.[118]

There was nothing new about the appearance of American seamen, merchants, tourists, or students in the streets of British towns. What was new was a stream of people who had fled from persecution not to the British colonies in North America or around the Caribbean but to Britain itself. Anglican clergy driven out of their parishes in New England or the middle colonies were prominent among the early exiles. A wide range of people followed with the evacuation of Boston in 1776, of Philadelphia in 1778, later of the southern ports, and finally in 1783 of New York. What are for the most part the sad stories of their experiences in Britain have often been told. Their expectations of an early return in the wake of a victorious British army were dashed as the years passed. They found Britain an excessively costly place for people who had lost nearly everything they possessed. British people often seemed to be uncaring and unfriendly. Their advice was generally ignored by those in power and they found the protracted business of soliciting employment or compensation from a cumbersome bureaucracy or from

---

[115] Silas Deane to Simeon Deane, 1 April 1783, 'The Deane Papers', *Collections of the Connecticut Historical Society*, XXIII (1930), 172–3.

[116] William Dunlap, *History of the Rise and Progress of the Arts of Design in the United States*, 2 vols. in 3 (New York, 1834; repr. 1969), I, p. 260.

[117] *Morning Herald*, 19 August 1783. Joseph Reed's experiences were less happy. In London in 1784 he found that 'the character of an American officer . . . is far from drawing respect', William B. Reed (ed.), *Life and Correspondence of Joseph Reed*, 2 vols. (Philadelphia, 1847), II, p. 404.

[118] F. Curwen to W. Pynchon, 9 May 1784, Andrew Oliver (ed.), *The Journal of Samuel Curwen Loyalist*, 2 vols. (New Haven, CT, 1972), II, p. 990 fn.

neglectful would-be patrons mortifying in the extreme. They were frankly home-sick, consorting with one another, and—judging by the company that came to the house of Abigail Adams, wife of the United States minister—with other Americans who had been their patriot enemies.[119] Much as they might have reverenced Britain from afar as their home, 'the loyalists realised how American they were only after they had abandoned America'.[120] In the course of time a good many of them drifted back to the United States or sought a more congenial refuge in Britain's remaining colonies.

About 7,000 in all are estimated to have come to Britain at least for a time. They were for the most part people who had been of some substance or ambition, officials, landowners, merchants who had traded by sea, clergy, or other profes-sional people who were willing and able to get themselves across the Atlantic. They were not representative of the great bulk of those displaced by war and Revolution, who were small farmers, often from the back country stretching from New York to Georgia, or urban artisans and petty traders. Many of these belonged to ethnic or religious minorities who probably had little if any sense of Britain as 'home'. Such people generally moved to other parts of North America or to the Caribbean.

People of African origin also moved to Britain during and immediately after the war. They are likely to have come on warships into whose crews they had been recruited in America, with British regiments returning home or as servants and dependants of white loyalists or returning British officers. Their numbers are very hard to estimate. They only became an object of public attention in Britain when they came to be seen as part of the problem of the conspicuous deprivation among the London 'Black Poor' in 1785 and 1786. Many of those whose sufferings required urgent charitable relief were then said to 'have served Britain, [to] have fought under her colours, and after having quitted the service of their American masters, depending on the promise of protection held out to them by British Governors and Commanders, are now left to perish by famine and cold'.[121] Recent research confirms that a considerable proportion of the African population of London in the 1780s were indeed recent arrivals from North America or the West Indies.[122] A small number left no doubt of their loyalist credentials when they applied, usually with very meagre success, for compensation for their losses from the commission considering loyalist claims.[123] A return to Africa through the

---

[119] E.g. her letters to E. Shaw, 28, [29] July 1784, L. H. Butterfield et al. (eds), *Adams Family Correspondence* (Cambridge, MA, 1963–), V, pp. 403, 406.

[120] Mary Beth Norton, *The British-Americans: The Loyalist Exiles in England 1774–1789* (London, 1974), p. 41. See also Maya Jasanoff, *Liberty's Exiles: The Loss of America and the Remaking of the British Empire* (London, 2011), ch. 4.

[121] *Public Advertiser*, 19 January 1786, cited Anthony J. Barker, *The African Link: British Attitudes to the Negro in the Era of the Atlantic Slave Trade 1550–1807* (London, 1978), p. 32.

[122] Stephen J. Braidwood, *Black Poor and White Philanthropists: London's Blacks and the Foundation of the Sierra Leone Settlement* (Liverpool, 1994), pp. 23–7.

[123] Some of their claims are analysed in Simon Schama, *Rough Crossings: Britain, the Slaves and the American Revolution* (London, 2005), pp. 175–80.

project of the new settlement of Sierra Leone was, however, envisaged in part as recompense to African loyalists who had come to Britain. At least half of the 347 blacks going in the first venture are thought to have been ex-slaves recently arrived from America.[124]

---

[124] Mary Beth Norton, 'The Fate of Some Black Loyalists of the American Revolution', *Journal of Negro History*, LVIII (1973), 417.

12

British Communities in North America after 1783

I

The greater part of the territory on the North American continent that remained British after American independence, that is Nova Scotia, the Isle St John, New-foundland, and Quebec, had been recently acquired by Britain and was thinly settled. The biggest element of the colonial population was the French who had stayed in Quebec after its conquest. The loss of the thirteen colonies however, brought important gains to these possessions that had previously been on the fringes of empire. Above all, they gained a sudden accession of new inhabitants who left the United States during and immediately after the war. These new immigrants became a strong presence in what remained of Nova Scotia and dominated the new colonies of New Brunswick and Upper Canada which were carved out for them in the west of Nova Scotia and of Quebec. The importance of this wave of migration in ensuring that there would ultimately be a British as well as an American continental empire can hardly be doubted. They held the fort, so to speak, until the arrival of large waves of immigration direct from the British Isles began in the 1830s.

Although they were to ensure the survival of a British North American empire, the people who left the United States were not obviously very different from those who remained there. Quite a lot of them were recent emigrants from Britain, but those with prominent British connections under the old colonial order—royal officials, international merchants, or Anglican clergy—were only a relatively small element in a mass of farmers, back-country settlers, urban artisans and traders, or servants. A considerable portion of them hardly counted as British at all. Ethnic and religious minorities not fully assimilated into the mainstream of American society were well represented among them. Over 3,000 African Americans went to Nova Scotia as free people and an uncertain number were carried there and to Quebec as slaves. Native American settlements were formed in Quebec by refugees from territory handed over to the United States. The first language of a good number of migrants of European origin was likely to be German, some form of Dutch, or the Gaelic spoken in the Scottish Highlands.

What is assumed to have distinguished this diverse range of people and to have made them British as opposed to American is not their origins, their social status, or their connections with the mother country, but their political commitments. Those who left the United States were collectively called 'loyalists' by their British contemporaries and so they have been called ever since. Their migrations are now often described as the loyalist diaspora. This implies a dispersal of people who had aligned themselves with the losing side in the war and after the collapse of the British regimes in the old thirteen colonies were driven to flee by persecution or by their aversion to the new order. Forced out of the United States, the great bulk of them resorted to territory still under British rule. There they presumably wished to continue to live as subjects of the British empire whose institutions and values they would uphold.

Very large numbers of those who left the new United States for British colonies undoubtedly did so because they feared for life and limb or felt themselves to be alienated from the new republican order and were determined to live under a British one. There is a huge body of testimony describing persecution and suffering, often very grievous. Recorded professions of aversion to the new order and enthusiasm for the British constitution and British concepts of liberty naturally came mostly from the propertied and the literate, especially in their claims for compensation for their losses, but such sentiments were by no means confined to them. An ex-slave who went to Nova Scotia proclaimed his political commitment when he called himself 'British Freedom'.[1]

Nevertheless, the concept of a loyalist diaspora needs to be interpreted with some discrimination. There was no close correlation between being a loyalist and being an emigrant. It is likely that only a small proportion of those who had loyalist sympathies actually emigrated; perhaps 80,000 out of a very rough estimate of half a million potentially disaffected did so.[2] On the other hand, fear and hatred of the Revolution may not have been the dominant motives for some those who did leave. Of the 'wide range of inhabitants' of the old thirteen colonies who moved to British North America it has been suggested that 'loyalists in the strict sense composed but one element'.[3]

American patriots did not systematically expel their enemies. They generally wished to force them into conformity rather than drive them out. Few people were put to death by order of any state. Actions by local activists were another matter. They certainly killed those they saw as their opponents in some numbers, notably in what amounted to civil wars in the Carolinas, New Jersey, and the northern counties of New York. Local committees which took on themselves the task of enforcing conformity of opinion in support of the Revolution did their utmost to cow dissenters into submission. Yet, even if it can rarely have looked like that to those that they terrorized, they usually purported to act by due legal process and their aim was to 'reincorporate' their enemies into revolutionary society rather than

---

[1] Simon Schama, *Rough Crossings: Britain, the Slaves and the American Revolution* (London, 2005), pp. 12–13.
[2] Paul H. Smith, 'The American Loyalists: Notes on their Organization and Numerical Strength', *William and Mary Quarterly*, 3rd ser., XXV (1968), 269.
[3] Peter Marshall, 'British North America 1760–1815' in P. J. Marshall (ed.), *Oxford History of the British Empire*, II, *The Eighteenth Century* (Oxford, 1998), p. 381.

to expel or destroy them.[4] Reincorporation could, however, be an extremely brutal process: imprisonment, deportation, confiscations, beatings, and other forms of violence and acts of public humiliation were commonly inflicted. Grievous as the sufferings of many individuals could be, the rigour with which penal sanctions were enforced or popular revenge was exacted varied greatly according to place and time. In the early years of the war those who would not join in the popular mobilization by taking oaths of loyalty to the principles of the Revolution could suffer severely. At the end of the war there was a frenzy of popular hatred against those dubbed Tories. For long periods, however, in many of the states if loyalists kept their heads down they could expect to coexist, no doubt uneasily, with patriots. A recent study has stressed that loyalists and patriots in New York state did not necessarily live in relations of unremitting hostility to one another. People 'often put family concerns over the demands of congresses, committees and generals'.[5] An examination of a single community in New York shows how the desire to maintain some sort of consensus could be 'stronger than political causes'.[6] Even quite conspicuous people could manage to keep out of trouble. His friends were in no doubt that James Brooks, an English-born office-holder under the old regime in Maryland, was 'a very good loyalist', but he was a self-confessed 'quiet man'. He thought it 'possible that a real loyalist might continue in that country during the whole war and preserve his loyalty'. He himself was deprived of his offices but stayed on in Annapolis until October 1779. The worst that happened to him was that he had to pay £10 for refusing to take the new Association oath of loyalty to the republic, was 'once insulted and hurt' and had to practise subterfuge when 'success to General Washington' was proposed; he drained his glass but did not repeat the words.[7]

Whether people left their homes probably often depended on whether they had a reasonable chance of getting away with safety: when the British army left an area, for instance, many loyalists went with them. Some who left had little choice as to whether they left or not. Male heads of households no doubt took women and children with them as a matter of course. Servants probably had no alternative but to follow their masters and mistresses. Slaves were shipped out of the United States to destinations chosen for them by their loyalist masters. Of those who could exercise some freedom of choice, fear of persecution or strength of ideological conviction may well have been mixed with calculations about the prospects awaiting those who moved to British colonies.

In any attempt to explain its full scale, the loyalist diaspora cannot be entirely separated from a greater American diaspora that was also taking place after the

---

[4] T. H. Breen, *American Insurgents, American Patriots: The Revolution of the People* (New York, 2010), pp. 213, 216.

[5] Judith L. Van Buskirk, *Generous Enemies: Patriots and Loyalists in Revolutionary New York* (Philadelphia, 2002), p. 47.

[6] Jonathan Clarke, 'The Problem of Allegiance in Revolutionary Poughkeepsie' in David Hall et al. (eds), *Saints and Revolutionaries: Essays in Early American History* (New York, 1984), p. 309.

[7] H. E. Egerton (ed.), *The Royal Commission on the Losses and Services of American Loyalists 1783–1785* (New York, 1915), pp. 292–4.

ending of the war. It was a part of it. The American Revolution unleashed a great movement of people from east to west within the United States, whose territory by the terms of the peace of 1783 now extended to the Mississippi and the Great Lakes. Western settlement spread into what were to become the new states of Ohio, Kentucky and Tennessee. In the Southwest, American settlement moved relentlessly towards the Mississippi and infiltrated into western Florida, which had been restored by Britain to Spain at the peace. New Englanders were moving north into Maine and Vermont.

'The typical loyalist' going to the British American colonies, J. M. Bumsted has written, 'was probably little different in most respects from the American settler the region might under other circumstances have hoped to attract.'[8] Many who went to the British colonies, like the multitude of Americans who were migrating to the west, were looking for land to enable them to maintain themselves as independent farmers. The British offered land on exceptionally generous terms. Land available in Nova Scotia might not be comparable to the fabled lands of the west, but it was probably not much inferior to the land drawing many migrants to Maine and Vermont, it was free, and new settlers would not have to fight Indians for it. Merchants and artisans had a chance of remaking their lives in British settlements. 'Several considerable builders and merchants' were said to have gone from New York to Nova Scotia to build ships there.[9] Carleton commended the application of New York 'merchants' for lots in the new town of Shelburne, Nova Scotia. They had 'a view to the same commercial undertaking' as others who had already moved.[10] Whereas the American states paid for labour and services in depreciated paper, if they paid at all, the British paid in hard cash. Migrants to British colonies would be transported free by sea and fed for some time after their arrival. This was a significant consideration in times of extreme economic dislocation and desperate hardship in the closing years of the war, when 'not one man to twenty' discharged from a Massachusetts regiment of the Continental Army had 'a single farthing' to get home and many were reduced to begging or to going to New York to look for work on the ships that were to take the British troops away.[11] The governor of Nova Scotia certainly thought that there was a considerable number 'who came here with a view only of receiving his Majesty's bounty of land, provisions &c.' and had then sold their land grant for whatever it would raise and had gone back to the United States.[12] In bad times they can hardly be blamed for doing so.

---

[8] '1763–83: Resettlement and Rebellion' in Phillip A. Buckner and John G. Reid (eds), *The Atlantic Region to Confederation: A History* (Toronto, 1994), p. 181.

[9] Brook Watson's evidence, 20 March 1784 to Privy Council Committee, BL, Add MS 38388, f. 32.

[10] To Parr, 19 November 1783, TNA, PRO 30/55/86, no. 9652. For a cogent discussion of those who might have seen Nova Scotia as 'a source of opportunity', see Neil MacKinnon, *This Unfriendly Soil: The Loyalist Experience in Nova Scotia, 1783–1791* (Kingston and Montreal, 1986), pp. 55–7.

[11] John Shy (ed.), *Winding Down: The Revolutionary War Letters of Lieutenant Benjamin Gilbert of Massachusetts 1780–3* (Ann Arbor, MI, 1989), pp. 107, 108.

[12] To Lansdowne 3 September 1787, BL, Add MS 88906/3/18, f. 130. See also his letter to E. Nepean, 13 July 1787, TNA, CO 217/60, f. 28.

To try to distinguish, as contemporaries such as the commissioners for settling loyalist claims felt that they must do, between 'real' loyalists, committed to Crown and empire, and opportunistic loyalists, seeking a better life in material terms, is probably to oversimplify in many cases. Motives are likely to have been mixed for very many people. They might have fallen foul of the new order, but their decision to leave may also have been influenced by their hopes of bettering themselves or at least getting through hard times under the British. Many of them were soon to be disappointed with what they found in the British colonies and went back quickly to the United States, particularly from Nova Scotia. Thus the migration of people to the British continental colonies can perhaps be interpreted as something not entirely distinct from other migratory movements across the continent at the same time. Recognizing that those who went to the British colonies could in varying degrees be both loyalist refugees, stigmatized for their actions and their beliefs, and Americans on the move, either at the behest of others or seeking their own advantage, may give us a clearer understanding of their aspirations and of the nature of the societies that they were to establish within the framework of the British empire. British policy-makers and the loyalist elites intended that these societies should be distinctively British and shaped by British values, but the mass of those who went ensured that they also developed strong similarities to those societies that other migratory Americans were trying to create in other parts of the continent.

Flight to the British colonies to the northward began during the war and reached its peak when New York was evacuated in 1783. Some 30,000 went by sea to Nova Scotia; of those 14,000 settled in the valley of the River St John to form the nucleus of what became the separate colony of New Brunswick in 1784. Some 500 moved on to what was already an established colony, the Isle St John, later to be Prince Edward Island.[13] Throughout the war people had been fleeing overland into the colony of Quebec. Some had clustered around British military posts on the frontier, notably at Detroit and Niagara. Most others had moved up the route from New York past Lake Champlain to the largely French settlements on the lower St Lawrence. Some 1,300 came from New York by sea. Once the fighting stopped, the governor of Quebec directed refugees from the United States to new settlements on the north side of Lakes Erie and Ontario and along the upper course of the St Lawrence. A few went to the Atlantic coast. It is estimated that about 6,000 people were initially resettled in Quebec.

II

Men who had been under arms formed an important element of those who were migrating to British territory. Some of these troops were British and German regular soldiers who had accepted the Crown's offer of colonial land; the great

---

[13] Evidence about the numbers of emigrants is helpfully examined in the Appendix: 'Measuring the Exodus', to Maya Jasanoff, *Liberty's Exiles: The Loss of America and the Remaking of the British Empire* (London, 2011), pp. 351 ff.

majority were drawn from the 22,000 or so who had joined what were called Provincial regiments, recruited in North America to fight for the British Crown.[14] At the end of the war, the regiments were disbanded and the soldiers were encouraged to settle in the remaining colonies. Provincials and their dependants constituted the great majority in the new townships settled in what became Upper Canada.[15] The 4,000 ex-soldiers going to what became New Brunswick were about half of those initially settled there.[16] In Nova Scotia, where men from eleven battalions, including some who had come from the southern colonies, were disbanded, former soldiers were an important element.[17] It was British policy that Provincials should be kept together once they had been demobilized. Their settlements 'should resemble in some degree the cantonments of an army, with such distinctions of favour to the officers as will enable them to preserve their authority'. The rank and file would be allocated land on a scale appropriate to yeomen farmers and the officers with larger grants would become a landed elite, serving as magistrates. The ex-military settlers could quickly be re-embodied as a militia to check any American threat to British territory. It was to reinforce the boundary with Massachusetts that Guy Carleton directed that the bulk of the men of Provincial corps should be settled on the Rivers St John or St Croix in what became New Brunswick, rather than in peninsular Nova Scotia.[18]

British designs for turning the Provincial regiments into military settlers, in which the hierarchical relationship of officers and men would be preserved, reflected a somewhat idealized view of what the Provincial regiments had actually been. Lord George Germain urged the British commander-in-chief in 1779 to give a strong preference in selecting Provincial officers to men who were 'natives of America and are of weight and influence and have property in that country'.[19] They would then be able to recruit soldiers attached to them. Officers and men would be bound by ties of deference and obligation as well as by loyalty to the Crown. Some of the colonels of Provincial regiments certainly were American grandees of high standing who could presumably attract recruits from the localities over which they exerted influence. Great New York landowners like Beverley Robinson[20] or Oliver DeLancey raised regiments. So did Sir John Johnson, who had inherited Sir William Johnson's estates on the New York frontier and was able, when he fled to Canada, to take with him many of the Johnson tenants, mostly Highland Scots who had very recently moved to

---

[14] This figure is derived from the research of Paul H. Smith in 'The American Loyalists', 259–77.

[15] J. Johnson's Return, July 1784, *Report on Canadian Archives for 1888* (Ottawa, 1889), p. 753.

[16] Return of 24 November 1783, TNA, CO 5/111. Ann Gorman Condon estimates disbanded soldiers to have constituted about a half of New Brunswick's early population, *The Envy of the American States: The Loyalist Dream for New Brunswick* (Fredericton, NB, 1984), p. 2; see also Wallace Brown, 'Loyalist Military Settlement in New Brunswick' in Robert S. Allen et al. (eds), *Loyal Americans* (Ottawa, 1983), pp. 82–3.

[17] List of corps disbanded in Nova Scotia, 1784–5, TNA, CO 217/57; see also return of 1,661 Provincial officers and men and an overall total including dependants of 3,225 in TNA, WO 36/3.

[18] Carleton to J. Parr, 26 April 1783, Davies (ed.), *Documents*, XXI, p. 164; Memorandum Respecting the Provincial Officers, TNA, PRO 30/55/72, no 7999.

[19] To H. Clinton, 23 January 1779, Davies (ed.), *Documents*, XVII, p. 46.

[20] On him see Jasanoff, *Liberty's Exiles*, pp. 34–6.

America, and to recruit them into the King's Royal Regiment of New York. Cortlandt Skinner, former Speaker of the New Jersey assembly and in British eyes 'one of the most respectable men from the continent of America', probably had 1,500 men under arms in four battalions of New Jersey Volunteers.[21] Many of those who commanded Provincial regiments can, however, be more accurately described as military entrepreneurs than as American gentlemen 'of weight and influence'. The most highly esteemed regiments were commanded by British regulars, John Graves Simcoe, Banastre Tarleton, and Lord Rawdon, or by men of no particular social eminence but with a talent for hard and ruthless warfare, such as Edmund Fanning, whose King's American Regiment burnt towns in raids on the Connecticut coast, or Thomas Brown, a recent immigrant from Yorkshire, who claimed to have raised 1,200 men mostly from South Carolina for his Rangers who fought ferociously on the borders of East Florida and Georgia.[22]

The right to raise a regiment was extremely attractive because of the material benefits which it offered. The commandant of a corps could appoint his officers, a much-prized source of patronage. He had profitable perquisites from equipping, clothing, and supplying his men. When a regiment had reached its stipulated size the colonel and his officers would be confirmed in their local ranks in America and paid their full salaries. Regiments that won special renown, and no doubt had particularly well-connected colonels, might win the great prize of being put on the British establishment. Provincial officers at the end of the war mounted a successful campaign for British half-pay when their regiments were disbanded. All Provincial officers expected to receive very substantial land grants in addition to their emoluments.

Although the rewards of the Provincial service depended on raising men, very few regiments were ever up to full strength. Soldiers were in very short supply and neither local influence nor military reputation of themselves were likely to be sufficient to bring them in. Sir John Johnson had won the right to raise two battalions but, the governor of Quebec observed, 'notwithstanding his great interests in the country and his indefatigable efforts to raise men, he has not been able in the course of four years to compleat the first'. Major John Butler, whose Rangers operating out of Niagara terrorized the New York frontier, was unable to raise the eight companies for which he had stipulated, even though 'his obtaining the rank of Lieutenant Colonel and his son that of Major depends upon his success'.[23] Edward Winslow, who was responsible for mustering Provincial regiments, pointed out that men in the early phases of the war generally expected to serve in their own provinces under officers known to them. As the British reduced the force of their own regulars in America after 1778, however, Provincial regiments ceased to be treated as local militia serving under their own leaders in their own neighbourhoods, but became

---

[21] Edward Alfred Jones (ed.), *The Loyalists of New Jersey* (Newark, NJ, 1927), pp. 191–3.

[22] Edward J. Cashin, *The King's Ranger: Thomas Brown and the American Revolution on the Southern Frontier* (Athens, GA, 1989).

[23] F. Haldimand to G. Johnson, 10 February 1780, cited in Philip Ranlet, *The New York Loyalists* (Knoxville, TN, 1986), p. 136.

substitutes for regular battalions, to be posted wherever they might be needed. Provincials drawn from around New York, for instance, made up a major part of the British army dispatched to the south. Sent all over the continent, placed not under local gentry but under what Winslow called the 'coxcombs—fools—and blackguards', who, he thought, increasingly got Provincial commissions and subjected to rigorous military discipline, 'the soldiers, unaccustomed to severity, have been made miserable and unhappy'.[24] A letter to a friend living on the Mohawk River found on the body of a deserter from the 2nd battalion of the King's Royal Regiment of New York, who had fled from one of the Canadian posts but had been tracked and killed by the Indians sent after him, which was the usual fate of deserters on the Canadian frontier, is chilling testimony both of unhappiness and severity. The soldier who wrote the letter was serving 'sore against my will and several young fellows of the neighbourhood who would wish to be at home again out of this cursed bondage and hard usage'.[25] Instead of quick victories, many Provincial recruits had experienced defeat or after they had declared their loyalty had seen their homelands abandoned to their patriot enemies by the withdrawal of the British army from New Jersey and Pennsylvania. Many men from the farming communities of the upper Hudson Valley or the Green Mountains of Vermont made the tragic miscalculation of joining General Burgoyne's invading force. After the surrender at Saratoga, they had little alternative to fleeing to Canada, where they were enlisted into Provincial corps.

In the later stages of the war, those recruiting for the Provincial regiments could not rely on the local influence of notables. Recruiting parties were sent out from British bases into American territory. Single men without land or family, often recent immigrants who had come to America as indentured servants, seem to have been the staple material. When British recruiters worked over the numerous prisoners captured around New York in 1776 for the Queen's Regiment or for Rogers' Rangers, what they got were mostly 'Irish or English, and were generally servants whose masters had sent them with the militia to show their Whigism and their patriotism'.[26] The Royal Highland Emigrants, who were conspicuous in the defence of Canada in 1775 and 1776 and were later settled in Nova Scotia as the 84th foot, gathered in Scots from the last ships bringing immigrants and recruited heavily from among the predominantly Irish servants shipped out from Cork and Waterford to work in the fisheries of Newfoundland.[27] With many unemployed by the disruption of the fisheries during the war and with uncertain food supplies producing near famine conditions in Newfoundland, such men can have needed

---

[24] To Maj. Barry, 13 November 1778, W. O. Raymond (ed.), *The Winslow Papers* (St John, NB, 1901), pp. 40–1. These grievances were raised in an undated loyalist petition to the Crown and both House of Parliament and 'the people of Britain' written just after Yorktown (TNA, CO 5/82, f. 232).
[25] Enclosed in J. Ross to Maj. Lernoult, 26 November 1782, TNA, WO 28/8, f. 266.
[26] Howard H. Peckham (ed.), *Memoirs of the Life of John Adlum in the Revolutionary War* (Chicago, 1968), p. 86.
[27] R. Duff to Dartmouth, 14 November 1775, TNA, CO 94/32, f. 104; J. Parr to Sydney, 2 June 1786, TNA, CO 217/58, f. 51. There were more Irish than Scots in a return of 84th Foot on 1 January 1783, TNA, WO 28/10, f. 205.

little inducement to enlist. The 'scum of the jails' were said frequently to be recruited into Provincial regiments.[28] Great numbers of escaped slaves served the British in various irregular formations or as Pioneers, and some were formally enlisted in the Provincial regiments. In 1777 'all negroes and molattoes and other improper persons' were ordered to be discharged but black people undoubtedly continued to be recruited. The King's American Dragoons, for instance, fighting in South Carolina had what was called 'a seapoy troop (gens de couleur)' riding with them.[29] Deserters from the Continental Army were especially prized. One of the most highly esteemed of all the Provincial regiments, the Volunteers of Ireland, was composed of Irish deserters, under the command of British regulars rather than American officers.[30] According to General Nathanael Greene, 'soldiers long in the service become more indifferent which side they serve'. He hazarded the guess that a third of the British force that he was fighting in in the south are 'deserters from our army, and prisoners enlisted from our captives'.[31]

Whoever they were, recruits had to be bought. They were promised land after the war and in its later stages received bounties. Since so much depended on raising men, officers were prepared to put their own money into funds to pay extra bounties. The officers of the King's American Dragoons paid an extra seven guineas per recruit out of their own pockets.[32] Colonel John Hamilton claimed to have paid £5,580 to raise 1,150 men for the North Carolina Volunteers.[33] Scarcity of potential recruits led rival commanders to 'lay claim to the same men', leading to 'ridiculous' disputes.[34] The British Provincial regiments were ultimately in competition, not only with one another, but with the states which were seeking recruits for the Continental Army also by offering ever higher bounties; it is possible, especially in the south, that they may have been actually competing for the same men.[35]

In the early stages of the war, Edward Winslow surmised that 'The pleasure of gratifying revenge for recent persecutions and injuries, or a flush of romantic military ardor were the inducement to engage' into the Provincial regiments.[36] What the foot-loose recent immigrants who joined up in the later years of the war for a substantial bounty—perhaps as an alternative to indentured servitude to a civilian employer—and had a tendency to change sides, felt about the cause of king and empire for which they fought is hard to fathom. Some nominal Provincial formations, such as the 'cowboys' who operated around New York or the elements

---

[28] A. Middleton, 'Sketch of the Present Mode of Recruiting', BL, Add MS 38343, f. 282.

[29] T. W. Braxted, 'The Black Pioneers and Others' in John W. Pulis (ed.), *Moving On: Black Loyalists in the Afro-Atlantic World* (New York, 1999), pp. 4–7; B. Thompson to Germain, 11 January 1782, *Historical Manuscripts Commission: Stopford Sackville MSS*, 2 vols. (London, 1904–10), II, p. 250.

[30] H. Clinton to Germain, 23 October 1778, Davies (ed.), *Documents*, XV, pp. 227–8.

[31] To S. Huntington, 10 May 1781, Richard K. Showman et al. (eds), *The Papers of General Nathanael Greene*, 13 vols. (Chapel Hill, NC, 1976–2003), VIII, p. 234.

[32] 'A Short Account of the King's American Dragoons', TNA, HO 42/2, f. 323.

[33] See his petition, TNA, FO 4/5, f. 198.

[34] Maj. Nairne to Maj. Lernoult, 1 December 1780, TNA, WO 28/4, f. 113.

[35] For Virginia's problems in raising its quotas, see Michael A. McDonnell, *The Politics of War: Race, Class and Conflict in Revolutionary Virginia* (Chapel Hill, NC, 2007), pp. 389–93.

[36] To Maj. Barry, 13 November 1778, Raymond (ed.), *Winslow Papers*, p. 41.

of the King's Rangers in East Florida and Georgia, degenerated into bandits, plundering indiscriminately.[37]

The ambiguities of motive and allegiance are brought out in an extreme form by the men of a particular unit whose vicissitudes took them from serving in the Continental Army in South Carolina, to being captured by the British, enrolled in a Provincial regiment in Jamaica, and ultimately being settled in Nova Scotia after the war. These were the men of what came to be called the Duke of Cumberland's Regiment. Their colonel, Lord Charles Montagu, was also a deeply ambiguous figure in his own right. He was the brother of the Duke of Manchester, one of the inner circle of the Rockingham Whig political connection, who was an opponent of the war. Montagu had been governor of South Carolina in the 1760s and was on good terms with those who were to become leading patriots, including Henry Laurens. Montagu told General William Moultrie, who had been captured at Charleston in 1780, that he regretted the 'unfortunate war' and 'thought the Americans injured'.[38] It was even reported that he had offered his services as a commander of troops to Franklin in Paris.[39] Montagu tried to use the initial British victories in South Carolina to recoup his losses, including the confiscation of 18,000 acres in South Carolina that he had accumulated as governor, which he valued at £36,830,[40] by relaunching his career as a military entrepreneur. The capture of Charleston gave the British 5,618 Continentals and militia as prisoners.[41] Most of these prisoners were kept on ships off Charleston where they died in large numbers, especially in a smallpox epidemic. Montagu saw the potential for raising a Provincial regiment and tried to recruit them. With extraordinary fortitude, considering the horror of the conditions under which they were being held on the prison ships, those whom he approached told him that 'as they had fought in a cause that appeared to them a just one, no hardship should compel them to desert that, nor no advantage should compel them to engage in any other'.[42] When he put a different proposition to them, that they would not be used against Americans, but should join a regiment that would go to Jamaica to fight the French and the Spanish, with the prospect of a raid on the Spanish Main, 500 of them assented. Basic information has survived for 187 of these. Some two-thirds gave their place of birth as in America, most in Virginia or North Carolina, whose Continental regiments had provided the bulk of the prisoners. Men born in England and Ireland were the largest element of the rest. The great majority of the prisoners were in their twenties.[43] Embodied as the Duke of Cumberland's regiment in February 1781, the men set off for Jamaica. Quixotically, Montagu offered their

[37] Harry M. Ward, *Between the Lines: Banditti of the American Revolution* (Westport, CT, 2002).
[38] Letters of 11, 12 March 1781, William Moultrie, *Memoirs of the American Revolution so far as it related to the States of North and South Carolina and Georgia*, 2 vols. (New York, 1802), II, pp. 166–71.
[39] David Ramsay, *The History of the Revolution of South-Carolina from a British Province to an Independent State*, 2 vols. (Trenton, NJ, 1785), II, p. 289.
[40] Memorial of Lord Charles Montagu, TNA, AO 13/133, f. 113.
[41] H. Clinton to Germain, 4 June 1780, Davies (ed.), *Documents*, XVI, p. 344.
[42] Montagu to J. Dalling, 1 October 1781, TNA, CO 137/82, f. 12.
[43] Murtie J. Clark, *Loyalists in the Southern Campaign of the Revolutionary War*, 3 vols. (Baltimore, MD, 1981), I, pp. 471–4.

command to the captive General William Moultrie as a step 'to the reconciliation we all wish for'. Moultrie rejected this proposition as an insult to his honour.[44]

In Jamaica, Montagu won praise for turning out a body of men 'conspicuous for good discipline, military appearance and the most regular conduct'.[45] If Montagu did well by his men, they certainly did well by him. He obtained the rank of lieutenant colonel and made his son a captain. He was given permission to raise a second battalion stipulating that he be promoted to the rank of colonel for doing so.[46] The second battalion, which included men taken out of jail,[47] was raised in New York. At the end of the war, Montagu's regiment was disbanded in Jamaica. The officers were put on half-pay and Montagu set his sights on Nova Scotia. Although he was told that he might have the governorship of Jamaica, he wished to exchange that, while still drawing an income from it, for the governorship of Nova Scotia, where he asked for 12,000 acres of land to compensate for what he had lost in South Carolina.[48] Three hundred of his men were prepared to go to Nova Scotia with him. They arrived in the winter of 1783 in a state of destitution and later moved onto land allocated to them at Chedabucto Bay, where they founded a township which they called Manchester, in honour of their colonel's brother. Montagu was reported to be 'indefatigable' in his efforts to get his men settled,[49] but he died on 3 February 1784 'at a little hut in the woods of Nova Scotia and was committed to the earth with much military foppery and ridiculous parade'.[50] He died in debt.[51]

It would be difficult to apply the term loyalist to the soldiers of the Duke of Cumberland's regiment who ended up in Nova Scotia. Whatever they may have thought about serving the Crown, the only positive evidence of their commitments that they gave was their remarkable tenacity in refusing to fight against the Americans whose cause they regarded as just, a view which their colonel professed to share. Nor did many of them appear to have the desirable attributes of settlers on new lands. Successful pioneering required the labour of a family unit as well as tenacity and experience of the wilderness. The first settlers at Manchester included only nine women to 144 men.[52] The rank and file of the first battalion of the regiment later petitioned for potential wives to be sent to them from England to enable them 'to succeed and prosper'.[53] Most of them showed no inclination to attempt to clear the holdings allotted to them, but disposed of them 'for a dollar, or a pair of shoes—or a few pounds of tobacco—but most for a gallon of New England rum and quit the country without taking any residence'. Quitting the

---

[44] Moultrie, *Memoirs*, II, pp. 166–71.
[45] A. Campbell to Col. Fitzherbert, 12 July 1783, TNA, WO 1/52, f. 319.
[46] G. Yonge to T. Townshend, 7 September 1782, TNA, HO 42/1, f. 117.
[47] Return of Prisoners in the Provost, 24 May 1783, TNA, PRO 30/55/70, no. 7762.
[48] Montagu to Manchester, 20 December 1783, WLCL, Manchester MSS.
[49] J. Parr to Shelburne, 24 January 1784, BL, Add MS 88906/3/18, f. 104.
[50] MacKinnon, *This Unfriendly Soil*, p. 85.
[51] Manchester to J. Parr, 20 December 1785, TNA, CO 217/57, f. 220.
[52] Carole W. Troxler, 'The Migration of Carolina and Georgia Loyalists to Nova Scotia and New Brunswick', University of North Carolina, PhD thesis, 1974, p. 118.
[53] Petition of J. Mills, TNA, CO 217/57, f. 221.

country meant going back to the United States where the prospects of employment for a single man were likely to be much more promising. By 1788 only thirty privates of the regiment were thought to be anywhere near the Chedabucto grant. After Lord Charles Montagu's death, many of the officers of his regiment left Nova Scotia, although they did their best to secure their land grants, presumably as an investment for the future.[54] In 1786 the settlers at Manchester described themselves as 'loyalists and emigrants from the southern parts of North America, principally reduced officers and disbanded soldiers . . . in general in low circumstances'.[55]

The inability or unwillingness of disbanded Provincial soldiers to cultivate their lands and the tendency for their former officers to leave the colony seems to have been repeated in other parts of Nova Scotia. The process of allocating land on the St John River, the future New Brunswick, was a protracted one; during the delay, the disbanded soldiers revealed themselves to be 'an irregular licentious body of men, irritated and disgusted to an extreme degree', prone to crime and disobedient to their former officers.[56] When the settlement was made, only one-tenth of the lots were taken up and many of those were quickly abandoned. Dissatisfied men trickled back to the United States.[57] Some of the disbanded German soldiers in Nova Scotia were said not to have the 'industry to cultivate a wilderness' and to get 'so frequently drunk, that they neglected all manner of cultivation'.[58] A British officer thought that the policy of what he called 'bribing soldiers of the line', that is British regulars, with land to settle in Nova Scotia was entirely misconceived. They were mostly 'tradesmen' not farmers, and would be much better off in Britain rather than 'starving here or gone to the states'.[59] Provincial NCOs were said to have been more enthusiastic settlers. Edward Winslow related how he was entreated by 'Those respectable sergeants' of regiments that he listed, 'once hospitable yeomen of the country. . . . "Sir, we have served all the war. Your honor is witness how faithfully. We were promised land, we expected you had obtained it for us,—we like the country—only let us have a spit of our own".'[60]

Provincial officers were well treated. Senior officers were entitled to grants of 1,000 acres. For some these became estates on which they resided while they built new lives for themselves in exile in Nova Scotia. Most, however, seem to have taken little interest in developing their holdings, treating them as an asset for subsequent resale. The governor of Nova Scotia noted that a considerable number of officers had gone to Britain.[61] All benefited greatly from the award of half-pay for life for Provincial officers as for officers in disbanded British regiments. They obtained this concession in 1783 after intensive lobbying in London. Their cause was particularly

---

[54] J. Wentworth to J. Parr, 5 March 1788, TNA, CO 217/61, ff. 55–6.
[55] Rhodes House MSS, SPG Journals, 17 November 1786, vol. 24, p. 353.
[56] E. Winslow to B. Watson, 10 January 1784, TNA, CO 217/56, ff. 394–5.
[57] Brown, 'Loyalist Military Settlement in New Brunswick' in Allen et al. (eds), *Loyal Americans*, p. 84.
[58] J. Parr to Sydney, 8 November 1788, TNA, CO 217/61, ff. 1–2.
[59] T. Dundas to Cornwallis, 28 December 1785, Raymond (ed.), *Winslow Papers*, p. 338.
[60] To W. Chipman, 26 November 1784, ibid. p. 188.
[61] J. Parr to Sydney, 10 August 1784, TNA, CO 217/56, f. 214.

taken up by Lord North, in office in coalition with Charles Fox in the summer of 1783. He was briefed by the politically adept Benjamin Thompson of the King's American Dragoons and presented the case of these 'faithful subjects and gallant soldiers' to the House of Commons on 27 June 1783. It was carried in the face of some opposition, Pitt denouncing it as a hang-over from 'the profusion and wasteful system' of the late war.[62] One of the arguments deployed for giving the officers half-pay was that it would enable them to support the role of colonial gentry that Carleton envisaged for them.[63] The expectation that the disbanded Provincial regiments should remain essentially in being in their new settlements, both as a defensive shield for the colony and, through their sense of hierarchy and subordination, as an antidote to the contagion of republican levelling, was entirely unrealistic.

With the winding down of the war, most Provincial soldiers in Quebec or along the Canadian land frontier seem to have hoped that it would be possible for them to go home. It became clear, however, that too much blood had been shed and too much resentment had been aroused for them to resume their lives in the new New York state from whence most of them had come.[64] They would have to accept what was on offer for them in Quebec. Most of them went to land allocated by the governor of Quebec on the western course of the St Lawrence river or on the northern shore of Lake Ontario or Lake Erie, away from the main areas of French settlement.

The soldiers who were disbanded in Quebec seem to have been much better adapted to settle in the wilderness than those who went to Nova Scotia. Those who had served in the two battalions of Sir John Johnson's Royal Regiment of New York or in the Rangers were mostly people of Scottish or German origin who had been 'bred to the cultivation of new lands' in the northern counties of New York before the war.[65] With 'a few exceptions', they were said not to have been 'persons of great property and consequence' when they fled.[66] Many of their officers came from the same background, being described as 'farmers of property' or 'wealthy farmers', again overwhelmingly from New York.[67] Even so, the rank and file were no more willing to accept the continuing authority of their officers than were the soldiers in Nova Scotia. In 1787 it was reported that 'a very dangerous jealousy and want of confidence mutually subsisted in that settlement, between the majority of the settlers, and their late officers'.[68] There was a much higher proportion of families to single men than seems to have been the case with the regiments that went to

---

[62] *Parliamentary Register*, X, pp. 237, 243. Thompson's correspondence with North is in TNA, HO 42/4, ff. 242, 244, 286–7, 309.

[63] Memorandum respecting the Provincial Officers, TNA, PRO 30/55/72, no. 7999.

[64] E.g. see letter about Butler's Rangers from Capt. Potts to F. Haldimand, 14 August 1783, Catherine S. Crary (ed.), *The Price of Loyalty: Tory Writings from the Revolutionary Era* (New York, 1973), p. 388.

[65] W. Marsh to R. Mathews, 19 August 1782, BL, Add MS 21821, f. 398.

[66] H. Hope to T. Dundas and J. Pemberton, 29 January 1786, TNA, CO 42/49, f. 105.

[67] Returns for the Royal Regiment of New York and for Edward Jesssup's Loyal Rangers, TNA, CO 42/46.

[68] Report of J. Collins and W. Powell, 18 August 1787, Richard A. Preston (ed.), *Kingston before the War of 1812: A Collection of Documents* (Toronto, 1959), p. 122.

Nova Scotia. Some men had been able to take women and children with them when they fled to Canada and the Americans generally made no difficulties about permitting the families of others subsequently to make their way there later.[69] A return of 1784 listed 947 women and 2,235 children to 1,866 men.[70]

The new settlers in Quebec were not easily governable. Those who tried to organize them found them 'both needy and unruly'.[71] A magistrate recalled his early encounters with 'a turbulent crew' who 'at the first forming of the settlement were perfect strangers both to the laws of God and man'.[72] The Anglican clergyman who had the care of them described his parish as consisting 'chiefly of the New York loyal refugees, a description of men not remarkable for either religion, or industry or honesty'.[73] But their British officers seem to have thought well of those who had served through the war. For 'the chearfullness and spirit, to which they have submitted to all dutys for these three years under my command', one officer warmly supported their claim to land.[74] They seem generally to have taken up the grants made to them and to have stayed on them.

III

In addition to the disbanded soldiers, a flood of civilian refugees came to Nova Scotia after 1783. Those who went were not solely seeking land. Good quality agricultural soils were confined to limited areas. Elsewhere the existing settlers were heavily engaged in fishing and timber extraction as well as farming. Ports, notably Halifax which was also a major British military and naval base, attracted merchants and artisans. Guy Carleton took an optimistic view of the civilian refugees. They were, he wrote, 'merchants, farmers and mechanics, and many persons of large property'.[75] He anticipated that they would prove to be 'real efficient settlers, already acquainted with all the necessary arts of culture and habituated to situations of the like kind'.[76] Edward Winslow wrote of the arrivals on the St John River, 'There are assembled here an immense multitude (not of dissolute vagrants such as commonly make the first efforts to settle new colonies) but gentlemen of education—farmers, formerly independent—and reputable mechanics'.[77] The Governor

[69] Linda Kerber, *Women of the Republic* (Chapel Hill, NC, 1980), p. 123.

[70] TNA, PRO 30/8/346, f. 46. See also Janice Potter MacKinnon, *While the Women only Wept: Loyalist Refugee Women in Eastern Ontario* (Montreal and Kingston, 1993). On the St John River in what became New Brunswick, a muster of 1784 gave 585 women to 1,877 men (W. O. Raymond, 'Loyalists in Arms', *Collections of the New Brunswick Historical Society*, II (1899), 222–3).

[71] N. McLean to A. Evans, 28 February 1785, TNA, WO 28/10, f. 329.

[72] Memorial of A. Paterson, 6 September 1792, Ontario Archives, C Series, RG 8, vol. 15.

[73] J. Stuart to C. Inglis, 6 July 1788, Preston (ed.), *Kingston before the War of 1812*, p. 135.

[74] J. Ross to Maj. Lernoult, 22 June 1783, TNA, WO 28/8, f. 335.

[75] To Parr, 22 August 1783, *Historical Manuscripts Commission: American MSS*, 4 vols. (London, 1904–9), IV, p. 295.

[76] To A. Hammond, 22 September 1782, TNA, CO 5/107, f. 215.

[77] To W. Chipman, 26 April 1784, Raymond (ed.), *Winslow Papers*, p. 192.

of Nova Scotia was less impressed by those who had just come under his jurisdiction. He wrote of them that

> they made a most heterogenious mixture of loyalty and *pretended* loyalty, different sects
> of religions (almost all sorts), disbanded soldiers and sailors of all nations, several ships
> with emigrants from Scotland and Ireland, convicts and sweepings of the streets of
> London by the Lord Mayor, near 3000 negroes from the different parts of the
> continent, some of them desperate villains, the tout ensemble a choice sett . . . The
> Germans and the Highlanders make by far the best and quietest settlers.[78]

From the largest new settlement at Port Roseway, soon to be named Shelburne, Benjamin Marston, one of those engaged in surveying, wrote of

> a collection of characters very unfit for the business they have undertaken. Barbers,
> shoemakers and all kinds of mechanics bred and used to live in great towns, they are
> inured to habits very unfit for undertakings which require hardiness, resolution,
> industry and patience.[79]

Recent scholarship tends towards the verdicts of Governor Parr and Benjamin Marston. Those who migrated to Nova Scotia were certainly very diverse in origin. They came to what was already a fragmented society, whose main elements, in addition to its Native American inhabitants, were the remnants of the French-speaking Acadians; 'foreign Protestants', mostly German-speakers, shipped in after 1748; New England 'planters' encouraged to take up land in the Seven Years War; and immigrants from the British Isles from the 1760s, mostly Scottish or from northern England. There was little integration among the existing settlers and still less between them and those who came after 1783, who were given to complaining of the 'republicanism' of those already there. The largest contingent of the loyalist immigrants, at least 40 per cent and probably more, came from New York. The 'mechanics', whom Marston noted at Shelburne, had largely come from New York city. Among others, nearly all the artificers employed in the British Engineer Department there chose to go to Nova Scotia, mostly to Halifax.[80] Of the middle colonies, considerable numbers came from New Jersey and rather fewer from Pennsylvania. The New England states were 'represented more by quality than quantity'; there was a high proportion of office-holders, lawyers, and clergy. Perhaps as many as 15 per cent came from the south, including the larger part of the ex-slaves and some of the rank and file of the North and South Carolina Provincial regiments who had ended up in Florida and from there moved up to Nova Scotia.[81] Migrants from the different states tended to keep apart. Parr wrote of conflict between the New Englanders and the rest.[82] Ethnically too, the new settlers were very divided and tended to live apart from one another. Scots,

---

[78] J. Parr to Lansdowne, 1 May 1785, BL, Add MS 88906/3/18, f. 119.
[79] Diary, 24 May 1783, W. O. Raymond, 'The Founding of Shelburne', *New Brunswick Historical Society Collections*, VIII (1909), 214.
[80] List of 13 November 1783, TNA, PRO 30/55/86, no. 9606.
[81] MacKinnon, *This Unfriendly Soil*, pp. 59–61.
[82] Ibid. p. 95.

Irish, German, and African Americans generally settled with those with those of their own community. Forty-seven families of the German Reformed Calvinist Church of New York asked to be able to live together 'in one place' in the Nova Scotia 'wilderness . . . under the mild influence of British rule'.[83] Disbanded German soldiers who gave up their lots were said to have become 'servants to their countrymen, the old German inhabitants'.[84] Parr did not underestimate the extent of religious diversity. The established Church of England was very much a sect among many other sects. Professed loyalty to the Crown and the experience of exile did not provide any over-arching sense of unity to the very miscellaneous range of people subsumed under the name of loyalists.

Socially there seems to have been a convergence towards a mass of people of limited means who had enjoyed a degree of independence, if a precarious one, as small farmers or artisans before the upheavals of war and exile. Farmers from New York and parts of Connecticut and New Jersey with artisans and craftsmen from New York city, constituted the majority of occupations designated on the lists of those going to what became New Brunswick.[85] The typical refugee to Nova Scotia from the Carolinas and Georgia has been described as a small farmer from the back country who had owned some 100 to 400 acres of which he might have cultivated 15 to 40 acres.[86] Below them, the numerous servants who are likely to have been serving in the disbanded Provincial regiments or those who came with the family of their employers had not previously enjoyed any semblance of independence. Nor had the mass of the over 3,000 free blacks who had been slaves, still less those who remained enslaved. At the other end of the scale, the number of men of property and high social standing in the old thirteen colonies who chose to settle in Nova Scotia was limited, rather more choosing New Brunswick. Loyalists with the highest ambitions and best connections seem generally to have decided to go to Britain.[87]

It seems likely that the preference of many who were crowded into New York at the end of the British occupation would have been to return to their homes once fighting had stopped. An upsurge of militant popular hostility against any compromise with enemies of the Revolution, which took place in all states at the end of the war and was particularly fervent in New York, made this impossible. When British forces pulled back from outlying areas that they had dominated in Westchester County, indiscriminate violence with beatings and robbery immediately followed.[88] The crisis which had produced the great exodus was, however, over quite soon. State authorities generally curbed local committees who had taken the law into their own hands and penal policies were moderated. Although further

---

[83] Memorial of J. M. Kern, 10 June 1783, TNA, PRO 30/55/71, no. 7962.

[84] Parr to Sydney, 8 November 1788, TNA, CO 217/61, f. 1.

[85] Esther Clark Wright, *The Loyalists of New Brunswick* (Fredericton, NB, 1955), p. 161; see lists in D. G. Bell, *Early Loyalist Saint John* (Fredericton, NB, 1983), pp. 255–345.

[86] Troxler, 'The Migration of Carolina and Georgia Loyalists', pp. 4, 181.

[87] MacKinnon, *Unfriendly Soil*, pp. 62–4.

[88] Ranlet, *New York Loyalists*, pp. 165–6; 'Humble Address of the Freeholders of the County of West Chester' to Carleton, TNA, PRO 30/55/70, no. 7843.

measures were enacted against loyalists in 1783 and 1784, New York followed the path of other states in ceasing to enforce and then in repealing measures that had been taken against them. Those who had fled in 1783 could in a year or two contemplate returning to the United States without fearing that they would suffer any very dire consequences. Many evidently did so. Estimates of the numbers who left New Brunswick, usually to the United States but also to Upper Canada, vary widely, but they seem to have been considerably lower than those who left Nova Scotia.[89] There what has been described as an 'epidemic return' to the United States took place.[90] The decline of population was most spectacular in Shelburne. The town had grown very quickly indeed, being the destination of most of the artisans and other urban dwellers from New York. Within a year there may have been 8,000 people living in and around Shelburne.[91] It failed, however, to capture a sufficient share of Nova Scotia's seaborne trade and to develop other commercial activities to enable it to support such a population. Many soldiers disbanded in Nova Scotia, like those of the Duke of Cumberland's Regiment, fled from land that they could not cultivate with any prospect of success. They too tended to go back to the United States.

To some extent at least, losses to the United States were counterbalanced by new immigrants from them into the British colonies. It was part of the rhetoric of the loyalist leadership that the exodus of 1783 had only taken off a section of the mass of Americans who pined to live once again under royal government and were becoming increasingly disaffected with the abject failures of the republican regimes in the states. British ministers were assured that 'The number of loyalists who still remain in the different states and who are passionately desirous of removing themselves to the province of Nova Scotia' was 'incredible'.[92] So long as a check was kept on the movement of 'disaffected persons', this was a prospect that was welcomed in London. The Committee of the Privy Council with responsibility for trade and colonies was assured in 1784 that 'great additional numbers are likely to emigrate from the countries under the dominion of the United States and to settle in Nova Scotia and that proposals have been made from all over the continent for permission to come there'.[93] An application to settle came in October 1783 from a group said to represent 150 families who styled themselves Connecticut loyalists. The governor gave them 'every encouragement'. He had been told that 'at least a fourth part of that colony would follow them'.[94] Quakers from New York, New Jersey, and Pennsylvania also applied to settle. Several hundred of them created a new settlement at Beaver Harbour in New Brunswick, which did not prosper and

---

[89] Bell, *Early Loyalist Saint John*, pp. 35, 133; Condon, *Envy of the American States*, p. 187; Wright, *Loyalists of New Brunswick*, pp. 212–15; Brown, 'Loyalist Military Settlement in New Brunswick', p. 84.

[90] MacKinnon, *Unfriendly Soil*, p. 178.

[91] Marion Robertson, *King's Bounty: A History of Early Shelburne* (Halifax, NS, 1983), p. 79.

[92] J. Haliburton's 'Remarks' to E. Nepean, TNA, CO 217/35, f. 336.

[93] Report of 31 May 1784, BL, Add MS 38388, f. 135. The committee were repeating Carleton's evidence of 16 March 1784, ibid. f. 18.

[94] 'Subscribers' to J. Parr, [October 1783], TNA, CO, 217/56, f. 103; Parr to Shelburne, 25 October 1783, BL, Add MS 88906/3/18, f. 101.

was nearly wiped out by fires.[95] Parr expected other movements. Presumably referring to Shays's rebellion, he thought that recent 'dissentions' will give us 'as many inhabittants from Massachusetts, Connecticut &c. as we may want'.[96]

Many movements of families or of individuals between the United States or the British colonies presumably also took place without governments having cognizance of them. Before the war there had been very close connections between New England and Nova Scotia. Many New Englanders migrated there while retaining links with the communities from which they had departed. Esteemed New England preachers were welcomed in Nova Scotia. The war no doubt disrupted these links, but they seem to have been resumed with the peace. People evidently travelled freely across the international boundary between the British empire and the United States which formally separated Maine from New Brunswick and goods were exchanged even more freely, even if authorities on both sides of the line condemned such exchanges as 'smuggling'.

Whereas those travelling from the United States to Nova Scotia generally came by sea, Quebec had a long land frontier with Vermont and New York. Crossings of the frontier were hard to control in any case and official policy came to accept that Quebec should not try to exclude immigrants from the United States but should welcome them. 'Our true interest is to keep this country, and with that view this province ought to be an offered asylum to all discontented Americans' was an aspiration being expressed as early as 1784.[97] The actual volume of migration from America in these early years is hard to quantify. The Surveyor General of Quebec settled 3,000 people from the United States in 1786 and 1787.[98] The population of what became Upper Canada grew from 6,000 in 1784 to 14,000 in 1791. In 1788 it was estimated that 20,000 to 30,000 Americans could be added to Canada's population in the next twelve months if given the right inducements.[99] An Act of Parliament was passed in 1790 to give 'encouragement . . . to persons that are disposed to come to settle in certain of his Majesty's colonies and plantations', including Quebec and the Bahamas. They would be required to take an oath of allegiance and were permitted to bring their belongings, including slaves, without paying duties.[100]

In trying to explain why people might choose to move from the United States into British colonies there is no need to accept the explanations current in British circles of a huge reserve of closet loyalists waiting their chance to leave or of massive disillusionment with the early republic. Certain ethnic and religious minorities who had earned the hostility of patriots by their attempts to maintain neutrality during the war were, however, still ill at ease in the new United States and were easily

---

[95] A. J. Mekeel, 'The Quaker-Loyalist Migration to New Brunswick and Nova Scotia', *Bulletin of the Friends Historical Association*, XXXIII (1943), 65–75; 'Quaker-Loyalist Settlement in New Brunswick and Nova Scotia', ibid. XXXVI (1947), 26–38.

[96] To E. Nepean, 5 February 1787, TNA, CO 217/60, f. 12.

[97] H. Finlay to A. Todd, 5 May 1784, TNA, CO 42/16, f. 117.

[98] P. A[llaire] to G. Yonge, 5 October 1787, TNA, FO 4/5, f. 323.

[99] H. Finlay to E. Nepean, 14 April 1788, TNA, CO 42/61, f. 170.

[100] 30 Geo. III, c. 27.

persuadable to move. Whereas the American states found neutrality hard to tolerate during the crisis of the war, neutrality, as with the Quebec French or the Nova Scotia New Englanders, could pass for loyalty for the British. Communities, like the Quakers, who wished to follow their own way of life with a minimum of involvement with the outside world found that the British generally left them alone, whereas the Americans might not. Groups of American Quakers, who were still facing problems over issues such as whether they should pay taxes to discharge war debts, might expect to find that British rule would be less exigent in its demands.

Most 'late loyalists' who travelled in the years after 1783 probably did not take much ideological baggage with them into exile. Their concerns are likely to have been more material. There could be a persuasive economic case for moving from the United States. The debts incurred during the war and the measures being adopted by the states to pay them off caused hardship to many in a period of falling prices in the 1780s. Taxation levels were high and some states insisted that taxes be collected in specie. Failure to pay was leading to court orders that land be forfeited. There were vigorous protests against such apparently draconian measures. Overt resistance was strongest in New England, but 'pockets of defiance' were 'flaring up from New Jersey to South Carolina'.[101] It would not be surprising if some sufferers were inclined to try their luck with the British. Low taxes in the British colonies were reported to be 'a great inducement to poor people, whose property is daily taken by execution to pay taxes which are now four times more than was ever known'.[102] As well as lower taxes, those moving to the British colonies would expect to get their land free; anywhere in America they would be required to pay for it. There might also be commercial advantages in choosing to go to a British colony. Some merchants from the United States were attracted by the advantages of settling in Nova Scotia. There their ships would be registered as British and they would have access to imperial trades, notably to the British West Indies, from which Americans were nominally excluded. Those members of the Nantucket whaling community, generally Quakers, who relocated to Dartmouth in Nova Scotia to avoid paying the prohibitive British duties on imported American oil, were a conspicuous example of people who migrated to put themselves inside the British commercial system.

Nova Scotia, New Brunswick, and those parts of Quebec that became Upper Canada were British colonies. British rule shaped their institutions, the tenure by which they held their lands and the commercial system within which they conducted much of their trade. The British Treasury was far more lavish in what it spent in the colonies than any American government could be. The state-supported Church of England was a presence in all the British colonies. The societies in these British colonies cannot, however, be described as British in any very positive sense in this period. They were made up of a mosaic of communities, divided ethnically, religiously, and by the parts of the old thirteen colonies from which most of them

---

[101] Richard B. Morris, *The Forging of the Union 1781 to 1789* (New York, 1967), p. 264.
[102] P. A[llaire], to G. Yonge, 5 October 1787, TNA, FO 4/5, f. 324.

had emigrated. If they were anything beyond their community identities, in a general sense they were Americans, even if they did not feel any commitment to the United States. A trickle of migrants was beginning to come directly from Britain, but the greater part of them had come recently from the American states, even if they had been first-generation immigrants. Once the turmoil of the war and its immediate aftermath had subsided, links with the states were restored. People moved easily between colonies and states. Loyalist and patriot allegiances no doubt remained enduring legacies of the war, but with the passing of time other considerations played an increasingly important part in shaping decisions as to which side of the frontier a person might choose to live.

Those colonies that remained under British rule after the war became part of an empire with aspirations to asserting its differences from the United States and to self-sufficiency. But they also remained part of a wider British Atlantic world which still included the United States. People, goods and ideas continued to move to and from the American states and the British colonies. Those who were called loyalists constituted important elements of the Anglophone population of the colonies. Attempts to construct distinctive societies on British principles came, however, to very little. On the northern frontier of the United States, the Anglo-American war that broke out in 1812 has been described as a 'civil war between kindred peoples, recently and incompletely separated by the American Revolution'.[103] Nevertheless, British North America survived as part of the British empire. In 1812 and perhaps on other occasions, most of those who had chosen to live there may not have been much enthused with the values that its rulers believed it to embody, but they still had no strong incentive to wish for an end to its separation from the United States. Their expectations from politics may not have been very high and the British order served them well enough: it gave them land and left them alone.

---

[103] Alan Taylor, *The Civil War of 1812: American Citizens, British Subjects, Irish Rebels and Indian Allies* (New York, 2010), p. 6.

13

The Course of Trade

I

On the eve of the Revolution the trade of the thirteen North American colonies was very closely integrated into the British empire. Fifty-eight per cent of what the colonies exported in the years 1768 to 1772 went to Britain itself and 27 per cent went to the British West Indies.[1] The North American colonies imported sugar, rum, and molasses from the West Indies and fruit and wine from southern Europe, but the great bulk of their imports consisted of manufactured goods supplied by Britain. America had become the most important overseas market for what Britain manufactured. In 1772–3 North America and the West Indies took 37 per cent of British domestic exports.[2]

The close integration of the colonies with Britain and its other colonial possessions was underpinned by Acts passed by the British Parliament, whose main provisions were outlined at the beginning of chapter 5. The enforcement of this system of regulation was often fallible, but the economic integration of Britain and the colonies depended on much more than enactments on paper. The dynamism of the eighteenth-century British economy would have pulled British America into its orbit regardless of legal provisions, and the development of the colonial economies on any scale without a close association with Britain would scarcely have been possible. For some American commodities, Britain was the largest market and therefore their natural destination; others were processed in Britain and re-exported by British merchants throughout Europe. Because of their quality and cheapness and because American tastes were usually close to British ones, British manufactured goods had a strong competitive advantage in American markets. British credit was the vital lubricant of the Anglo-American trading system. American planters and entrepreneurs were often financed by British merchants in setting up their plantations and businesses and in recruiting their labour force of slaves shipped from Africa or servants from Europe. British goods could normally be obtained by American merchants for re-selling in the colonies on up to a year's credit.

Merchants and shipping were the essential elements of an integrated Atlantic economy. British and American merchants operated on both sides of the ocean and

---

[1] James F. Shepherd and Gary M. Walton, 'Economic Change after the American Revolution: Pre- and Post-War Comparisons of Maritime Shipping and Trade', *Explorations in Economic History*, XIII (1976), 406.

[2] Phyllis Deane and W. A. Cole, *British Economic Growth 1688–1959* (Cambridge, 1969), p. 34.

under the Navigation Acts no distinction was made between ships built in the colonies or in Britain. In the southern colonies the great staple exports, tobacco and rice, were for the most part dispatched to Britain by the agents resident in America of British merchant houses on British-owned ships for sale in British ports. In the main ports of the middle and New England colonies there were long-established American merchant communities with their own ships. They transacted most of the inter-American trade between North America and the West Indies and a considerable part of the transatlantic trade as well, ordering goods through their British correspondents and consigning cargoes to them. American merchants often spent periods in Britain, as did British merchants in America. Great numbers of ships were built in the colonies and either operated by American owners or sold in Britain.

The war that broke out in 1775 severely disrupted Anglo-American trade. Both sides resorted to economic warfare. The Americans banned trade with Britain and its colonies, while the British Prohibitory Act declared 'all manner of trade and commerce' by the colonies to be illegal. The navy was encouraged to make prizes of all American ships and privateers were later commissioned to operate against them. American privateers retaliated in full measure. Many ships were lost on both sides and others were diverted from trade into privateering. The customary arrangements for supplying goods on long credit made British concerns very vulnerable to a sudden rupture of commercial relations. Debts from before the war owed to British merchants amounted to some £3 million.[3] Some individual claims were very high indeed. The London house of Champion and Dickason stated that out of £300,000 owing to them for woollens and other manufactured good shipped to New England on the eve of the war, £100,000 had been lost.[4]

The breakdown of trade was, however, by no means complete. The French complained bitterly about 'an immense commerce with England' during the war.[5] British goods came into America in ever increasing quantities through New York, which was occupied by the British army from 1776 until the end of the war. From New York they passed freely into many other states.[6] After the British army seized Charleston in South Carolina in 1780, numerous British merchants followed in its wake. They sold goods 'to a very great amount', hoping for repayment in rice and indigo.[7] Bermuda was a base for much smuggling into America. British goods were even said to be shipped directly from Britain without undue difficulty to ports under the full authority of the independent states, especially in New England. British manufactures also reached America from European ports and via the neutral West Indian islands, notably through Dutch St Eustatius. By the last years of the war estimates were putting British exports to the ex-colonies at some two-thirds of

[3] Jacob M. Price, 'Capital and Credit in the British-Chesapeake Trade, 1750–1775' in V. B. Platt and D. C. Skaggs (eds), *Of Mother Country and Plantations* (Bowling Green, OH, 1971), p. 8.

[4] Memorial of August 1784, TNA, BT 6/85, f. 46.

[5] Luzerne to Vegennes, 21 March 1781, translation in Giunta, *Emerging Nation*, I, p. 159.

[6] Richard Buel, *In Irons: Britain's Naval Supremacy and the American Revolutionary Economy* (New Haven, CT, 1998), pp. 226–7.

[7] See petition of 18 January 1783, TNA, CO 5/108, f. 78.

their pre-war total.[8] The official values for American exports are less spectacular, but still show a sharp increase in the later years of the war.[9] Belief in the buoyancy of wartime exports encouraged British polemicists to argue that American dependence on British goods was so complete that no concessions needed to be made after the war to retain their market.[10] The immediate shipping out of huge quantities of British goods as soon as the peace had been concluded suggests, however, that a large unsatisfied demand for them had built up during a long war.

Although they now could be exported without restriction, beyond those that the Royal Navy sought to impose, to other European countries, the production of American export staples declined during the war. Wartime tobacco output has been estimated at only about one-third of its pre-war level.[11] There were strong trends towards greater self-sufficiency. There was not much incentive to cultivate crops for export in a partially blockaded America or, as a British consul later pointed out, for a farmer to 'look further than the nurture of his own family'. He probably could not obtain imported goods for any surplus he produced, which anyway might be requisitioned or plundered for the needs of whichever army controlled the area.[12] Labour became scarce. The white labouring poor were the chief source of recruits for the Continental Army and the British loyalist regiments, while the slaves fled from plantations in large numbers when the British invaded the south. Basic manufacturing, on the other hand, increased, above all for military needs and to fill the gap left by the decline of imports.

The effects of wartime dislocation were to be felt for some years after independence. If the American economy grew at all, its progress was likely to have been slow until about 1790 and there was a pronounced check in the mid 1780s. The recovery of overseas trade and the development of an independent American merchant marine were hampered by British restrictions imposed after the war on access to what had been important markets, especially in the West Indies, but some caution about their adverse effect would probably be justified. Certain trades, such as whaling, were devastated, when the British put prohibitive duties on imports of American whale oil. The British retention of trading posts along the Canadian frontier effectively prevented any revival of the American fur trade. A great Massachusetts merchant pointed out the ways in which the post-war British restrictions disrupted the intricate networks of trade through which New England

---

[8] *Morning Herald*, 28 February 1783. The source of these figures is not identified.

[9] Stephen Conway, *The British Isles and the War of American Independence* (Oxford, 2000), pp. 67–8.

[10] E.g. [Lord Sheffield], *Observations on the Commerce of the American States*, 2nd edn (London 1784), p. 276.

[11] Jacob M. Price, 'Reflections on the Economy of Revolutionary America' in Ronald Hoffman et al. (eds), *The Economy of Early America: The Revolutionary Period 1763–1790* (Charlottesville, VA, 1988), p. 318.

[12] P. Bond to Leeds, 10 November 1789, TNA, FO 4/8, f. 153. The effect of the shortage of imported goods on grain production is a major theme of Buel's *In Irons*. For the wartime problems, especially labour shortages, crippling American agriculture, see Allan Kulikoff, *From British Peasants to American Colonial Farmers* (Chapel Hill, NC, 2000), pp. 256–75.

was able to obtain the means of paying for its British imports.[13] On the other hand, although British prohibitions produced a marked fall in the officially recorded value of exports to the British West Indies, growing trade with Spanish, French, and Dutch colonies meant that Caribbean trade as a whole exceeded its pre-war level by 1790. American shipbuilding revived in spite of British exclusions. By 1790–2, the total tonnage of American shipping was probably some 50 to 80 per cent above what it had been before the Revolution.[14]

II

As soon as hostilities ceased, there was a spectacular boom in Anglo-American trade, focused primarily on the import into America of huge quantities of British manufactured goods.[15] British and American merchants crossed the Atlantic in great numbers to buy and sell British goods. On 1 April 1783 Silas Deane, now living in exile in Britain, reported that Americans were buying goods 'as far as their money or credit will carry them'.[16] There were to be many complaints of Americans without means who abused the credit so readily extended to them,[17] but the press reported 'that several American merchants of the first consequence' had also arrived.[18] These included major operators, such as William Bingham, a partner of Robert Morris, who had made a great fortune as Congress's agent in the French West Indies and was resuming a connection in London with the Barings, into whose family two of his daughters were to marry, and Jeremiah Wadsworth, a Connecticut merchant and former military commissary.[19]

Once hostilities ceased, American ports were quickly, to some it seemed in retrospect too quickly and with far too little regulation, reopened to British ships. British merchants flocked back, notably to Philadelphia, seeking orders and they were joined by individual adventurers who brought over goods with them as a speculation for sale in rented premises.[20] The return of the British to the Chesapeake was slower. The predominantly Scottish merchant community had been

[13] S. Higginson to J. Adams, 8 August 1785, 'Letters of Stephen Higginson, 1783–1804', *Annual Report of the American Historical Association for 1896*, 2 vols. (Washington, DC, 1897), I, pp. 719–23.
[14] Shepherd and Walton, 'Economic Change', p. 419. For a summary of current debates about the post-war American economy as a whole, see Cathy Matson, 'A House of Many Mansions: Some Thoughts on the Field of Economic History' in Matson (ed.), *The Economy of Early America: Historical Perspectives and New Directions* (University Park, PA, 2006), pp. 40–8.
[15] For an account of this boom in Philadelphia, the principal port involved, see Thomas M. Doerflinger, *A Vigorous Spirit of Enterprise: Merchants and Economic Development in Revolutionary Philadelphia* (Chapel Hill, NC, 1986), pp. 243 ff.
[16] To Simeon Deane, 1 April 1783, 'The Deane Papers', *Collections of the Connecticut Historical Society*, XXIII (1930), 172.
[17] E.g. H. Martin to T. Jefferson, 15 November 1784, Julian P. Boyd et al. (eds), *The Papers of Thomas Jefferson* (Princeton, NJ, 1950–), VII, p. 522.
[18] *Morning Herald*, 2 July 1783.
[19] See Richard A. East, *Business Enterprise in the American Revolutionary Era* (New York, 1938), pp. 141–4 for Bingham and pp. 82–100 for Wadsworth.
[20] Doerflinger, *Spirit of Enterprise*, p. 245.

unpopular before the war and Lord Dunmore's attempts to arm the slaves, naval raids, and the ravages of Lord Cornwallis on his last campaign left deep resentments in Virginia. A bill that would have permitted British subjects to return to Virginia immediately after the war was rejected with popular acclamation. By 1784, however, many Scottish stores were again selling imported British goods in Virginia.[21] British merchants had followed the British army first into Georgia in 1779 and then into South Carolina after 1780. Some stayed behind in Savannah and in Charleston after they were evacuated. British merchants at Charleston even contracted to clothe the southern Continental Army.[22] The British quickly resumed the supply of slaves to South Carolina and to Georgia. In three years from 1783 some 8,750 slaves were landed from British ships in North American ports, the great bulk— 7,391—at Charleston and a little over 800 at Savannah.[23] A report on South Carolina's trade at the end of 1784 noted that the extent of the credit that the British offered gave them 'a very large proportion of the import trade' of the state.[24]

Initially British imports faced competition in the northern ports from the French and the Dutch, but they were soon regaining their old dominant position. In September 1783 Robert Morris reported that 'Our commerce is flowing very fast towards Great Britain.' British goods, he wrote, were cheap, their merchants gave long credit and were 'attentive and punctual'.[25] The Irish joined in the bonanza. An 'immense quantity of goods' were reported to have been sent out, 'by all accounts, so hastily and ill manufactured that they should not seem likely to promote the success of this commerce'.[26] Large shipments from Britain in 1783, added to stocks built up in New York in the last stages of the war, quickly glutted the market. By 1784 British dry goods were being sold in Boston and New York at auction at much less than their sterling cost.[27] A New York merchant wondered how the Americans could possibly pay for the goods that were pouring in: 'Our warehouses from one end of the continent to the other seem a pile of riches, which the resources of this country cannot answer for in many years to come.'[28] Henry Laurens believed that more goods were crossing the Atlantic than 'can be sold in three years and more perhaps than will be paid for in ten'.[29] In 1783 at official values £1

---

[21] T. M. Devine, *The Tobacco Lords: A Study of the Tobacco Merchants of Glasgow and their Trading Activities, c.1740–90* (Edinburgh, 1975), p. 164.

[22] J. Banks's Statement, [15 February 1783], Richard K. Showman et al. (eds), *The Papers of General Nathanael Greene*, 13 vols. (Chapel Hill, NC, 1976–2003), XII, p. 445

[23] 'The Trans-Atlantic Slave Trade Data Base', <http://www.slavevoyages.org>.

[24] G. A. Hall's Report, 31 December 1784, Boyd et al. (eds), *Jefferson Papers*, VIII, p. 201.

[25] To B. Franklin, 30 September 1783, E. James Ferguson et al. (eds), *The Papers of Robert Morris* (Pittsburgh, PA, 1973–), VIII, p. 557.

[26] T. Orde to W. Pitt, 31 August 1784, TNA, PRO 30/8/329. f. 126.

[27] J. Sebor to S. Deane, 10 November 1784, 'Deane Papers', p. 201.

[28] Cited in Kenneth Morgan, 'Business Networks in the British Export Trade to North America, 1750–1800' in John J. McCusker and Morgan (eds), *The Early Modern Atlantic Economy* (Cambridge, 2000), pp. 53–4.

[29] To J. Woodrop, 28 June 1783, Philip M. Hamer et al. (eds), *The Papers of Henry Laurens*, 16 vols. (Columbia, SC, 1968–2003), XVI, p. 221.

million worth of British goods were imported into the United States. Some £3.6 million followed in 1784, a figure only exceeded before the war in 1771.[30]

As Laurens anticipated, payment for these vast quantities of goods obligingly supplied on credit was to be a most serious problem. In the later years of the war specie had been dispensed for supplies and services by the British and French armies and had been earned by those American ships that could evade the British blockade and deliver supplies at Havana, especially for the Franco-Spanish fleets in the West Indies. In April 1783 specie was said to be plentiful in Pennsylvania, New York, and New England.[31] It quickly became scarce. At the end of the year Francis Baring noted that silver was flowing into Britain from America so that 'we shall soon get back from thence the greater part of the guineas and dollars which we sent thither' during the war.[32] By 1785 John Adams was reporting that America was bring drained of its circulating specie to pay off debts to Britain.[33] William Bingham made the same point two years later: 'The merchants and factors of the British, soon accumulated the greatest portion of specie in the country, in return for their merchandize, and shipped it to Europe.'[34] A total of £2.1 million was calculated to have gone to Britain in specie from Philadelphia and New York in the first three years since the peace. This was thought to be more than all the specie remaining in the whole United States.[35]

As specie became scarce, the export of American commodities became increasingly important to British merchants as the means by which they could secure payment for their shipments of manufactured goods. In spite of much hostility to them, British merchants eventually won back a considerable part of the stake that they had held in the major southern staples. On 24 July 1783 the first tobacco ship from Virginia since the war came into Bristol to be greeted by 'a considerable number of very respectable tradesmen' and a 'band of music'.[36] By 1785 Madison was despairing of his hopes of breaking 'the Scotch tyranny' over Virginia. 'Our trade was never more compleatly monopolised by G. B. when it was under the direction of the British parliament than it is at the moment.' Virginia's merchants 'are almost all connected with that country' and Virginia was entirely dependent on British shipping.[37] Direct shipments of tobacco to British ports were, however, declining by the end of the decade. Those ports that had transhipped tobacco for France, above all Glasgow, were worst affected as tobacco went directly to French ports, but from 1789 to 1791 64 per cent of American shipments were still going to Britain.[38] Even when tobacco went directly to Europe, British merchants and

---

[30] B. R. Mitchell, *British Historical Statistics* (Cambridge, 1988), p. 494.

[31] S. Inglis to F. and J. Baring, 25 April 1783, Ferguson et al. (eds), *Morris Papers*, VII, p. 753.

[32] To Shelburne, 11 November 1783, BL, Add MS 88906/1/1, f. 97.

[33] To J. Jay, 17 June 1785, Charles F. Adams (ed.), *The Works of John Adams*, 10 vols. (Boston, 1850–56), VIII, p. 270.

[34] To Lansdowne, 4 March 1787, Giunta (ed.), *Emerging Nation*, III, p. 440.

[35] P. A[llaire] to [G. Yonge], 5 July 1786, TNA, FO 4/4, f. 223.

[36] *London Recorder*, 27 July 1783.

[37] To J. Monroe, 21 June 1785, William T. Hutchinson et al. (eds), *The Papers of James Madison* (Chicago and Charlottesville, VA, 1962–), VIII, p. 307.

[38] Jacob M. Price, *France and the Chesapeake*, 2 vols. (Ann Arbor, MI, 1973), II, pp. 732–3.

British ships were heavily involved. In 1789 Glasgow merchants thought that three-quarters of the 200 or 250 ships employed in the American tobacco trade were British.[39] A large part of the rice exported from South Carolina was also handled by British merchants and exported in British ships. Edward Rutledge described it 'as a shameful, and an unnatural relic of our former dependance'.[40] The partners of a Charleston merchant house were grieved 'to see nine tenth of our produce carried out of our ports by British vessels, and in walking our streets, whether convinced by the dialect, or the names of those who supply our wants, that we should rather conceive ourselves in the Highlands of Scotland than in an American state'.[41] After the war, South Carolina rice, like the tobacco of Maryland, Virginia, or North Carolina, increasingly began to be exported directly to Europe, albeit still often in British ships.

Although British merchants enjoyed considerable success in directing American exports to Britain, the gap between the official values of these exports and what America imported from Britain was huge. Even in 1786, a year in which there was a dip in imports after the great post-war boom in imported manufactures, the value of exports was still around half of the value of what Americans were importing.[42] Official values of cargoes were at best an imperfect indicator and omitted much. As was the case before the war, Americans could settle their obligations to Britain by what they earned exporting to continental Europe or to the West Indies. In the early 1780s, however, such earnings were probably considerably lower than they had been before the Revolution. American trade with southern Europe, important in the colonial period but now threatened by North African corsairs, was reported to be at a low ebb, while exports to northern Europe, which were increasing significantly at the end of the decade, at first grew slowly. Earnings from shipping, of great importance in the late colonial period, were also at a low level as the American mercantile marine took time to recover from the ravages of the war and the immediate post-war dominance of British ships, reinforced by British prohibitions on the use of American ships to supply British colonies. Silas Deane's foreboding as early as April 1783 that 'America will probably be as deeply indebted to this country, as at any former period, and I fear without the same ability to pay',[43] was fully justified. Large new debts were being added to the great body of undischarged debts accumulated before the war.

Robert Morris took a relaxed view about mounting debts, believing in the eventual capacity of 'this growing country' to generate a surplus of exports over imports. Until then, 'the capitalists of Europe will by one means or other be drawn in to make the needful advances and we can afford to pay for them'.[44] He was, however, very much an exception. For most of his contemporaries, American indebtedness to Britain was, like other aspects of Anglo-American commerce, a

[39] Glasgow Merchants' Answer, 26 November 1789, TNA, BT 6/20, f. 298.
[40] To T. Jefferson, 23 October 1787, Boyd et al. (eds), *Jefferson Papers*, XII, p. 263.
[41] Brailsford and Mavis to T. Jefferson, 31 October 1787, ibid. XII, pp. 298–9.
[42] Mitchell, *Historical Statistics*, p. 494.
[43] To Simeon Deane, 1 April 1786, 'Deane Papers', p. 173.
[44] To B. Vaughan, 27 November 1783, Ferguson et al. (eds), *Morris Papers*, VIII, p. 787.

morally charged issue; they were a tie of continuing dependence that must be broken. Debt had political consequences too. The British government was using Americans' failure to honour their obligation to pay their pre-war debts as a pretext for not evacuating the fur-trade posts, as they were bound by the treaty to do. The British negotiators in Paris had been instructed to press hard for a clause giving creditors full freedom to recover their debts 'in sterling money', rather than in devalued paper. The Americans had conceded this easily. To most of the American elite the payment of just debts was a binding obligation that could not be evaded. It was necessary to ensure the respect of other nations which they ardently desired for the new republic. The matter looked rather different for many in the Chesapeake states of Virginia and Maryland, by far the largest source of the pre-war debts, often owed by small farmers and or by people opening up land on the frontier, rather than by great planters.[45] How could the British have the gall to claim the repayment of debts after the way in which their troops and ships had ravaged Virginia? They too were not observing the treaty, failing to return the slaves that had fled to them or to pay the stipulated compensation. In any case, immediate repayment was totally impractical. Virginia's debts were put at £2 million or more, which Jefferson, who believed that non-payment would leave 'our character stained with infamy among all nations and to all times',[46] considered to be ten times the available circulating cash in the state. Did the creditors want an immediate sale of their debtors' property? If so, it would only sell for rock-bottom prices. Payment would take a long time and would depend on the recovery of Virginia's economy.[47] On his brief visit to Britain in 1786, Jefferson saw the spokesman for the Scottish creditors, and they came close to an agreement for repayment by instalments over five years.[48] Such sweet reasonableness was not reproduced in public exchanges. 'The British merchant is in some states positively, in others virtually, prohibited by the legislature from recovering his property', it was alleged.[49] States made laws hostile to the recovery of debts. Courts were said to be biased against British creditors and even if they were not, to be intimidated from doing them justice by popular pressure. The creditors protested loudly and frequently. They had set up a committee in 1783 to lobby the government either to take action against America or to pay them compensation from the British Treasury. Retaining the northern posts and refusing to settle disputes about the ex-slaves who had been shipped to British colonies became the British countermeasures. The American leadership certainly wished to settle the debt question, above all to get the British out of the fur-trade posts, but, as in other matters, they were deeply embarrassed by their inability to impose their will on the states. John Jay, as Secretary of State, eventually

---

[45] Charles R, Ritcheson, *Aftermath of Revolution: British Policy Towards the United States 1783–1795* (Dallas, TX, 1969), p. 66.

[46] To J. Monroe, 10 May 1786, Boyd et al. (eds), *Jefferson Papers*, IX, p. 501. An authoritative estimate is that the Chesapeake States owed £1.95 million without including interest which the British creditors claimed (Price, 'Capital and Credit in the British-Chesapeake Trade', p. 8).

[47] To A. McCaul, 19 April 1786, Boyd et al. (eds), *Jefferson Papers*, IX, pp. 388–90.

[48] Jefferson to J. Jay, 23 April 1786, ibid. IX, p. 404.

[49] 'State of the Grievances' of British Merchants, 28 February 1786, TNA, FO 4/4, f. 47.

took charge of the matter and Congress ruled that state acts contrary to the treaty must be repealed.[50] The British creditors were not at first appeased, but settlements were gradually made over a long period. Under the terms of the Jay Treaty of 1794 the United States government made a cash payment towards settling debts. By the early nineteenth century Glasgow creditors had recovered a considerable proportion of what they were owed.[51]

The debts clocked up since the peace by those who had taken great quantities of goods on generous credit received much less attention, although very large sums were at stake. One London house was said to be owed £778,000 for themselves and other creditors for whom they were trustees.[52] Abigail Adams greatly disapproved of her countrymen who 'have most materially injured themselves by running here in shoals after the peace and obtaining a credit that they cannot support' and she spared a thought for the plight of their creditors.[53] Her husband was sure that Americans felt 'their moral characters, and their reputation as men, as well as their credit as merchants' to be involved in paying off their debts.[54] The new wave of British creditors were not always so sure. They too found the American courts unsympathetic and the state laws 'extremely defective, and involved in great doubt and perplexity'.[55] The 'relaxed state of legal proceedings' in America were said to enable the American partners in an Anglo-American partnership to default on obligations of £53,000 for which the London partner was put in confinement by the firm's creditors.[56] A Scottish merchant with long experience of Virginia planters reflected that in the old days he did not believe 'there was in general an honester sett of people on the face of the earth, but wonderfully have they changed of late years'.[57] Whether they were victims of American sharp practice or, probably more often, of their own imprudence, British exporters had little alternative but to write off part of their debts and try to be more careful in future. The drying up of credit was widely reported. There were complaints of a stagnation of trade, particularly in 1786. The volume of British exports did not reach the dizzy heights of 1784 until 1790 and 1791.

By the end of the decade the imbalance in Anglo-American trade was becoming less acute. American exports were growing. More tobacco and rice were being shipped to Europe but exports of cereals were overtaking them and becoming the major item in direct trade with Britain. Protective duties under the British Corn Laws were reduced when prices in Britain exceeded a certain level, last set in an Act of 1773. In the late 1780s grain prices were beginning a sustained rise.[58] At the

---

[50] Report of 13 October 1786, Giunta (ed.), *Emerging Nation*, III, pp. 333 ff.

[51] Devine, *Tobacco Lords*, p. 159.

[52] Enclosure in W. Harvard to Carmarthen, 20 December 1785, BL, Add MS 38375, f. 132; see also TNA, PRO 30/8/344, f. 114.

[53] To J. Q. Adams, 6 September 1785, L. H. Butterfield et al. (eds) *Adams Family Correspondence* (Cambridge MA, 1963–), VI, p. 344.

[54] To J. Jay, 17 June 1785, C. Adams (ed.), *Adams Works*, VIII, p. 270.

[55] Submission to Carmarthen, n.d., TNA, PRO, 30/8/344, f. 99.

[56] Mr Harvard's 'State of Facts', ibid. f. 114.

[57] A. McCaul to T. Jefferson, 14 August 1788, Boyd et al. (eds), *Jefferson Papers*, XIII, p. 513.

[58] See graph in M. J. Daunton, *Progress and Poverty; An Economic and Social History of Britain 1700–1850* (Oxford, 1998), p. 34.

same time, American grain harvests were producing surpluses on a scale to take advantage of export opportunities. British consuls reported that the output of cereals was increasing greatly in New York and in Pennsylvania, where there was 'a vast improvement of the land', and was spreading to Maryland and Virginia, where cereals were replacing tobacco.[59] The Committee of the Privy Council believed that in normal years European grain production and consumption were more or less in balance; in time of scarcity 'the deficiency can only be supported from the harvest of America'.[60] By 1789 grain had become 'one of the chief remittances America can make', according to a Liverpool merchant.[61] Britain was developing a role as entrepôt for the re-export of American grain to southern Europe.[62] Suspension of American grain imports in 1788 to prevent the spread of a scourge called the Hessian fly from America to Britain brought petitions from British west-coast ports for the trade to be resumed to relieve local shortages.

The United States was also beginning to attract funds from Britain on a large scale. After the signing of the peace, there had been numerous press reports of a possible revival of interest in purchasing American land, which had attracted so many British speculators in the 1760s and 1770s. 'Gentlemen of unencumbered and independent fortunes' were said to be considering taking up land that, it was predicted, would increase in value by fifteen years' purchase in three years.[63] One William Green felt himself 'a little disposed to speculate in American property' and was willing to lay out £5,000 for an estate in New York of 10,000 acres.[64] Some American speculators were keen to encourage European investors to buy land from them. Such people hoped that the enacting of the Constitution would encourage Europeans to believe that their funds were now more secure in America and would thus stimulate the land market.[65] In uncertain conditions, however, not least about the rights of aliens to hold land, which had only been definitely legalized in Pennsylvania,[66] it is unlikely that many such transactions were concluded. A characteristically grandiose scheme by Robert Morris to finance huge purchases of American land by loans in Europe of up to $400,000 came to nothing in the Netherlands as well as in Britain.[67] If sales of land remained sluggish until the 1790s, from 1788 Europeans with funds to spare began to show a keen interest in investing them in American securities, especially when it was known that the new federal government under Alexander Hamilton's direction would assume the states' debts.

---

[59] J. Temple to Leeds, 23 September 1789, P. Bond to Leeds, 10 November 1789, TNA, FO 4/7, f. 203, FO 4/8, ff. 153–4.

[60] Report, 3 March 1790, BL, Add MS 38392, f. 46.

[61] H. Wilckens to Hawkesbury, 29 March 1789, BL Add MS 38224, f. 63.

[62] Report of Committee of the Privy Council, 27 November 1789, BL, Add MS 38349, f. 305.

[63] *Public Advertiser*, 29 January 1783.

[64] To C. Champlin, 5 September 1783, 'The Commerce of Rhode Island 1726–1800, II', *Collections of the Massachusetts Historical Society*, 7th ser., X (1915), 185.

[65] M. Fisher to R. Barclay, 20 October 1787, cited in Terry Bouton, '*The People*', *the Founders and the Troubled Ending of the American Revolution* (New York, 2007), p. 179.

[66] P. Bond to Leeds, 3 January 1791, TNA, FO 4/9, f. 21.

[67] Memorandum of Agreement, [20 March 1783] and J. Vaughan to Morris, 2 June 1783, Ferguson et al. (eds), *Morris Papers*, VII, p. 616; VIII, pp. 145–7.

In 1789 Gouverneur Morris in London persuaded a syndicate, including Francis Baring, to invest in $600,000 of American securities.[68] British merchants trading to America were said to be speculating on a large scale in American 'floating paper'. Many small British investors in American funds have been identified.[69] As a consequence of big shipments of wheat to Britain and a great inflow of British funds for American securities, in 1790 the rate of exchange between the two countries became favourable to the United States, 'almost for the first time in living memory'.[70]

The inflow of foreign funds, either to purchase land or American securities, was another ideologically loaded issue. Like Robert Morris, Alexander Hamilton had no inhibitions about drawing on the resources of Europe to fund the development of America. By 1790 Hamilton believed that the United States was in the happy position of being able to borrow as much as might be wanted in Europe and that the interest which they paid was likely to fall.[71] Tench Coxe, an enthusiast for the development of American manufactures, hoped that 'informed and judicious foreigners' would help to provide the capital for them.[72] For Jefferson and Madison, on the other hand, British funds invested in America were as toxic to republican virtue as British goods. 'Money in all its shapes is influence', Madison wrote. 'Our monied institutions consequently form another great engine of British influence. Our bank is a powerful one. Their capital belongs in a great part to Britons, or to proprietors interested in the British connection.'[73]

III

Shipping was the most contentious of all Anglo-American commercial issues. The Proclamation of 2 July 1783 and the measures sponsored by the Committee of the Privy Council were aimed at excluding the Americans from the carrying trade of the British empire, above all to and from the West Indies, with the desirable consequence, at least for some of those most closely involved, of stunting the development of an American maritime marine as well stimulating the expansion of Britain's own shipping. Americans deeply resented the attempted exclusion of their ships from the British West Indies and they were determined that they should develop merchant shipping on a scale that befitted their sense of themselves as an

---

[68] E James Ferguson, *The Power of the Purse: A History of American Public Finance, 1776–1790* (Chapel Hill, NC, 1961), p. 265.

[69] Ritcheson, *Aftermath of Revolution*, p. 208.

[70] Ferguson, *Power of the Purse*, pp. 261–9; conversation of William Johnson with George Beckwith in Dorchester to W. Grenville, 27 May 1790, *Report on Canadian Archives for 1890* (Ottawa, 1891), pp. 140–1.

[71] Report on the Public Credit, [9 January 1790], Harold C. Syrett et al. (eds), *The Papers of Alexander Hamilton*, 27 vols. (New York, 1962–87), VI, pp. 89–90.

[72] 'Thoughts on the Present Situation of the United States', *The American Museum*, IV (1788), 403.

[73] Essay on 'Foreign Influence', 23 January 1799, Hutchinson et al. (eds), *Madison Papers*, XVII, p. 219.

independent nation. British opinion quickly came to believe that restrictive measures were successfully achieving most of Britain's objectives. The American pre-
war contribution of about one-third of the empire's shipping had been replaced by
a great expansion of British-built ships. Some 100,000 tons were thought to have
been added by 1786, when the number of ships 'now upon the stocks in England,
exceeded that of any former year'.[74] In 1788 584 new ships totalling 42,586 tons
were built.[75] The exclusion of American ships from the West Indies was claimed to
be effective and, moreover, was said to have been achieved without any detriment
to the interests of the planters who had received timber and provisions from North
America in British ships 'fully sufficient to their supply'.[76] Bold assertions were
made about the supremacy of British shipping, not only between North America
and the West Indies but in all other Atlantic trades. It was said that British ships
'almost wholly engross the carrying trade' of America, a claim supported by a return
of 215 British ships of over 27,000 tons at the port of Philadelphia in 1788.[77]
British sources estimated that seven-eighths of the trade of the states south of the
Chesapeake was being carried in British ships.[78]

Claims made for the dominance of British shipping in the trade of the United
States in the years immediately after the war had substance but were more than a
little exaggerated. West Indian planters totally rejected assertions that they were
being adequately supplied from North America by timber and provisions brought
in British ships. They continued to petition and agitate against the Proclamation of
July 1783. A letter from Jamaica complained that the price of imports was twice
what it should be and that the market for Jamaican molasses in the United States
had collapsed.[79] The chairman of the West India Committee told the Committee
of the Privy Council that the choice was whether American ships would be allowed
into the British islands legally or 'clandestinely'. He believed that 'a great part of the
present supply' was being brought in by American ships fraudulently registered as
British.[80] According to an American, 'our merchants find no difficulty in getting
their vessels registered in the English islands, save a little expence; all the
custom house officers have their price'.[81] 'A Briton and a Loyalist' was outraged
by the number 'of vessels American built, owned by American citizens, and
navigated by American seamen or by Irish or British renegadoes', that hoisted
British colours when it suited them.[82] American supplies were also extensively
shipped into the British islands via foreign European ones. To counter this, trade
with foreign islands was forbidden by an Act of 1787. Were this Act strictly
enforced, it would, the West India Committee alleged, have reduced the British

---

[74] Grey Cooper, 16 June 1786, *Parliamentary Register*, XX, p. 384.
[75] T. Irving, memorandum for Committee of Merchants, [1789], TNA, BT 6/20, f. 273.
[76] William Grenville, 11 February 1788, *Parliamentary Register*, XXIII, pp. 178–9.
[77] P. Bond to Carmarthen, 4 January 1789, TNA, FO 4/7, f. 1.
[78] Report of Committee of the Privy Council, 28 January 1791, TNA, FO 4/9, f. 105.
[79] Jamaica Letter, 26 December 1786, TNA, PRO 30/8/349, ff. 81–2.
[80] Evidence on 17 May 1784, BL, Add MS 38388, ff. 109–10.
[81] J. Sebor to S. Deane, 10 November 1784, 'Deane Papers', pp. 203–4.
[82] To North, 22 April 1785, BL, Add MS 61864, f. 40.

islands to starvation.[83] There were legal loopholes in the Proclamation of 1783 and the 1787 Act. The governors of the West Indian islands could proclaim an emergency and temporarily allow in American ships or permit trade with the foreign islands. This, under the pressure, it was alleged, of the planters on their councils, they did on many occasions.[84]

Keeping American ships with American goods out of Nova Scotia and the other British North American maritime colonies was even more of an intractable problem than excluding them from the West Indies. Nova Scotia was said to have become 'a nursery for American seamen and a market for American produce', rather than being part of the British imperial commercial system.[85] The British colonies continued to need large supplies which could only be provided by the United States. These could come easily into Nova Scotia through the fleets of American boats that were permitted under the terms of the peace to fish off its coasts and to dry their catch on shore. At the new settlement of Manchester in Nova Scotia it was said that 'you can scarce enter a house but see an American package'.[86] The customs officials at Halifax were accused of issuing the necessary documents, no doubt for a suitable return, to enable American ships to pass as British.[87] The economies of northern New England and Nova Scotia and New Brunswick were closely integrated in ways that did not show much regard for imperial regulations.[88] The governor of Nova Scotia believed that it was impossible to stop American rum from being smuggled into those parts of Nova Scotia around the Bay of Fundy from 'the vicinity of the Massachusetts country to this province'.[89]

In February 1789 the Committee of the Privy Council repeated with satisfaction the claim by the British consul based at Philadelphia that with 215 ships of 27,000 tons British shipping 'almost wholly engrosses the carrying trade' of America. This was proof, according to them, of the 'beneficial effects of the new regulations of trade'.[90] Yet a return for Philadelphia in 1788 had put the total of American ships entering the port at 596 with a tonnage of 43,136.[91] The evidence that the American shipbuilding industry was recovering fast from the damage inflicted on it by the war and by post-war uncertainties was clear. Within a few years American ships were becoming very competitive. In 1789 Alexander Hamilton was advised by William Bingham that while a British ship of 200 tons would cost £13 per ton, an American one would cost £8 10s a ton. The American ship could be sailed

---

[83] R. Neave and S. Long to Sydney, 30 September 1787, TNA, BT 6/20, f. 63.

[84] Selwyn H. H. Carrington, 'The United States and the British West Indian Trade, 1783–1807' in Roderick A. McDonald (ed.), *West Indian Accounts: Essays on the History of the British West Indies and the Atlantic Economy in Honour of Richard Sheridan* (Kingston, 1996), pp. 149–68.

[85] G. Leonard to E. Nepean, 2 November 1787, TNA, CO 217/60, f. 245.

[86] Lodge and Armstrong to G. Leonard, 9 September 1787, TNA, BT 6/59, no. 28.

[87] Report of Surveyors of Customs, 24 March 1788, TNA, CO 217/60, f. 191.

[88] Joshua M. Smith, *Borderland Smuggling: Patriots, Loyalists, and Illicit Trade in the Northeast, 1783–1820* (Gainesville, FL, 2006).

[89] J. Parr to Sydney, 2 September 1787, TNA, CO 217/60, f. 49.

[90] Minutes, 5 February 1789, BL, Add MS 38391, f. 96.

[91] TNA, BT 6/20, f. 226.

15 per cent cheaper than an English one and 'the quickness of their voyages far exceeds that of the European ships'.[92]

The opening up of trade with Asia was taken as the most obvious demonstration of American maritime prowess. Most American ships in the early years went no further than to the Dutch Cape of Good Hope or to the islands of Mauritius and Réunion, opened to American trade by the French government. They took lumber and provisions and came back with coffee, cotton, and Indian piece goods. Dutch records show that five American ships went at least as far as the Cape in 1785–6. In 1788–9 and 1789–90 sixteen and nineteen did so.[93] A few, including the much celebrated *Empress of China* which made the first American voyage to China in 1784, went as far as Canton for tea.[94] The European wars from 1793 were to enable Americans as neutral carriers to expand their Asian trade very greatly.

In the Atlantic, Americans believed that they could now 'afford to carry as cheap as almost any Europeans'.[95] Competition in the early months of 1790 between British and American ships was causing a 'ferment' at Liverpool, which after 1783 was taking over much of the American trade previously handled by London.[96] Exporters through Liverpool of 'valuable manufactured goods of Manchester and Yorkshire' were reported to be giving American ships the preference.[97] The tables had to begun to turn: the successes which British ships had achieved in winning freights in American ports immediately after the war were now beginning to be matched by American success in winning freights to and from British ports. In the years 1790 to 1792, 45 per cent of the ships coming into American ports from Britain were American ones. By 1802 the proportion was to be 77 per cent.[98] By then the tables had turned completely. American ships were to dominate transatlantic Anglo-American trade in war, and later in peace.

IV

The ratification of the new American Constitution and the formation of the first federal administration was for both British and Americans the occasion for systematic examinations of Anglo-American trade, particularly focusing on shipping. On the British side the examination was conducted by the Committee of the Privy Council. Questions were sent to the Committee of Merchants Trading to America and to bodies able to speak for mercantile opinion in London, Bristol, Liverpool, Glasgow, and Edinburgh. In the United States, largely on the initiative of James

---

[92] 25 November 1789, Syrett et al. (eds), *Hamilton Papers*, V, pp. 555–6.

[93] James R. Fichter, *So Great a Proffit: How the East Indies Trade Transformed Anglo-American Capitalism* (Cambridge, MA, 2010), p. 38.

[94] B. Lincoln to A. Hamilton, 22 December 1789, Syrett et al. (eds), *Hamilton Papers*, VI, p. 29.

[95] S. Higginson to A. Hamilton, 20 May 1790, ibid. VI, p. 425.

[96] Peter Maw, 'Yorkshire and Lancashire Ascendant: England's Textile Exports to New York and Philadelphia, 1750–1805', *Economic History Review*, LXIII (2010), 734–65.

[97] H. Wilckens to Hawkesbury, 29 September 1789, TNA, BT 6/20, f. 243.

[98] François Crouzet, 'America and the Crisis of the British Imperial Economy, 1803–1807' in McCusker and Morgan (eds), *Early Modern Atlantic Economy*, pp. 305–6.

Madison, Congress debated whether federal duties should be laid on foreign ships and, if so, whether there should be discrimination against countries who had not signed treaties of commerce with America, above all against Britain.

The main questions asked by the Committee of the Privy Council were what had been the effects of duties levied on British trade by the individual states, what would be the likely outcome of duties to be levied on all American ports by the authority of Congress, and whether Britain should retaliate.[99] Lord Hawkesbury—the title now assumed by Charles Jenkinson—had received complaints from a Liverpool merchant called Henry Wilckens, who told him that 'nothing but the firm hope of government here giving them assistance and shackling the Americans in return could cause them to continue the trade another voyage'.[100] The Liverpool merchants called for action. They wanted Britain to retaliate to the point where the duties were equal on both sides. This, they believed, would force the Americans into negotiations for a commercial treaty.[101] Other ports had different views. They accepted that the American states had discriminated against them, but they regarded the burdens as having done relatively little damage to a very valuable trade. Any new federal duties were not likely to be unduly penal. They looked forward to more stable relations under the new Constitution. So they strongly advised against retaliation that, in the words of the Glasgow response, would only prolong 'that animosity that has unhappily so long prevailed' and prevent 'that return of harmony which would be so comfortable and beneficial to both'. 'The trade to and from the United States is of very great importance to the navigation, to the shipowners as well as to the mercantile interest of this country.'[102] One Bristol group went even further and argued that what was damaging American trade were duties laid in Britain on American exports, not those imposed on the other side of the Atlantic.[103] This view was put even more strongly in another paper in the Committee's archive. 'The fact is that their port charges of every kind are far more moderate than our own.'[104] The general advice was that the role of government should be to promote reconciliation not to incite confrontation. Rather late in the day, Hawkesbury seems to have come to the same view. 'I could wish that all the differences between them and us were settled, if possible in an amicable manner and think it right therefore to discourage every thing that may tend to create fresh animosity between the subjects of the two countries.'[105] The Committee of the Privy Council's report, submitted on 28 January 1791, accepted the majority view among the merchants. It recommended that since attempts to introduce discrimination against Britain had failed for the time being in Congress, retaliatory duties would for the moment be inappropriate. Negotiations should be opened to improve commercial relations. It was to be hoped that past resentments would

[99] Minutes of 13 October 1789, BL, Add MS 38391, f. 186.
[100] 21 January 1790, TNA, BT 6/20, f. 402.
[101] Liverpool's answers, 25 November 1789, ibid. ff. 281–2.
[102] Glasgow answers, 26 November 1789, ibid. f. 295.
[103] Bristol Merchants' answer, 11 December 1789, ibid. f. 286.
[104] 'Paper from Mr Milligan', 20 October 1789, ibid. f. 258.
[105] To H. Wilckens, 25 January 1790, BL, Add MS 38310, f. 47.

subside and that 'ancient habits and the recollections of former connections might bring back the people of these states to a more favourable disposition to Great Britain'.[106]

The Committee then turned its attention, as it had been required to do by the Secretary of State, to giving advice on the position that Britain should adopt in any future negotiations with the new United States government, were such negotiations to take place. The underlying assumption of the report was that Britain's record towards the United States since 1783 had been beyond reproach. In the face of breaches of treaty provision about debts and irrational commercial restrictions by individual states, Britain had shown forbearance. In some respects Lord Hawkesbury's view of America seems to have mellowed. The report welcomed the Constitution and the new federal order. It assumed that Congress would 'act upon a larger scale and in support of a more extensive and general interest' than the states had done. The injustices that the states had committed on British merchants and British creditors would, it was assumed, be redressed.[107] The report, however, had few suggestions about significant concessions that might be offered by Britain in any negotiations. On the point that most interested Americans—access to the West Indies by American ships—the Committee recommended no concession whatsoever. Britain could 'never submit even to treat' on this.[108] In places Hawkesbury allowed a cloven hoof to show. The supposed success of British ships in capturing most of the trade between North America and the West Indies was a matter for satisfaction, not just because it stimulated British shipping but because 'it took from the navigation of the United States as much as it added to that of Great Britain'.[109] The report concluded that, although it hoped for better things from the Americans, if they proved recalcitrant, it was of no great concern for Britain. With very few viable exports, America had no alternative to trading with Britain.[110] The tone of the report, which with some justice has been dismissed as 'mean-minded and backward-looking, a particularly reactionary form of mercantilism',[111] alarmed those who were acting for Britain in the United States.[112] They felt with good reason that it would play into the hands of those like Jefferson and Madison who saw Britain as an unreconcilable enemy. It also included some highly indiscreet references to the formation of an 'English party' in American politics. It was indeed to be exploited by Jefferson.

With the enacting of the Constitution, the possibility now existed for a unified American commercial policy. James Madison sought to direct such a policy, just as Lord Hawkesbury had for some years sought to direct Britain's commercial policy. It is not very likely that James Madison and Lord Hawkesbury thought well of one

---

[106] Report of 28 January 1791, TNA, FO 4/9, f. 149.
[107] Ibid. f. 122.
[108] Ibid. f. 150.
[109] Ibid. f. 111.
[110] Ibid. ff. 151–2.
[111] Stanley Elkins and Eric McKiterick, *The Age of Federalism: The Early American Republic, 1788–1800* (New York, 1993), p. 380.
[112] Ritcheson, *Aftermath of Revolution*, pp. 136–7.

another. The British view of Madison was that he was 'a gentleman of the first abilities' but with very unsound views about trade;[113] American views of Hawkesbury were much less flattering; he was seen as an incorrigible foe of America, doing all he could to cramp its trade. To Americans who cherished old myths, he seemed to be the reincarnation of Lord Bute, exercising 'secret influence with his sovereign'.[114] There were, however, very marked similarities between the objectives that Hawkesbury and Madison had set themselves and in the obstacles that they faced in trying to attain them. Both were economic nationalists seeking to make their respective countries self-sufficient, above all in shipping and ultimately in naval power. Once the United States had attained independence, Hawkesbury was determined that American shipping should not have a stake in the trade of the British empire. Madison was equally determined to break what he regarded as the neo-colonial dominance of British shipping over America. A strong merchant marine was for Madison, as for Hawkesbury, the basis of naval power. 'Was it not', Madison said, 'for the necessity we are under of having some naval strength', he would be for free trade with the whole world, but Americans must have 'a navy and seamen of our own'.[115] In trying to achieve his objectives, Hawkesbury certainly enjoyed more advantages than Madison had. Madison's huge resources of knowledge and his iron sense of purpose assured him of a leading role in the House of Representatives, but he had no official position in the new federal executive, where he had a most formidable opponent with views diametrically opposed to his in Alexander Hamilton, who openly told a British contact of his disapproval of the discriminatory duties against British shipping to which Madison was committed.[116] Hawkesbury, by contrast, was firmly entrenched in the Pitt administration and seems to have encountered very little opposition from his colleagues until William Grenville, the new Secretary of State responsible for foreign affairs, began to assert his ideas on American policy from 1791. Grenville's increasing concern for more flexible relations with the United States would not then necessarily coincide with Hawkesbury's views.

Yet both Hawkesbury and Madison faced serious difficulties in implementing policies of which the underlying aim was to prise apart and subordinate to national objectives a mass of Anglo-American connections that had survived even during the war, when the French complained that far too many English commercial agents were being 'tolerated in the midst of the continent',[117] and may even have grown stronger in some respects since 1783. When consulted by Hawkesbury in 1789, British merchants, with the partial exception of those from Liverpool, told him that

---

[113] P. Bond to Carmarthen, 29 April 1789, TNA, FO 4/7, f. 84. See also the exchange between George Beckwith, who supposed that Madison's 'character for good sense and other qualifications' would dispose him to more enlightened views about Britain, and Hamilton, who lamented that 'although this gentleman is a clever man, he is little acquainted with the world' (Record of conversation, [October 1789], Syrett et al. (eds), *Hamilton Papers*, V, p. 488).

[114] J. B. Cutting to T. Jefferson, 26 June 1788, Boyd et al. (eds), *Jefferson Papers*, XIII, p. 291.

[115] House of Representatives, 4 May 1789, Hutchinson et al. (eds), *Madison Papers*, XII, p. 125.

[116] Conversation with G. Beckwith [October 1789], Syrett et al. (eds), *Hamilton Papers*, V, pp. 488–9.

[117] Luzerne to Vergennes, 21 March 1781, translation in Giunta (ed.), *Emerging Nation*, I, p. 159.

while they welcomed government action in certain areas like the recovery of debts, they wished to be free to cultivate a 'comfortable' and 'beneficial' harmony with the Americans, whose market was so important to them. Madison got something of the same message in the debates on his duties in the House of Representatives, also in 1789. Few were prepared to say that they were willing to accept British dominance or that, in theory, measures to cut the British down to size were not fully justified. Nevertheless, John Laurance from New York told the House that it was not for the federal government to tell American merchants with whom they should trade. 'If they find it their interest or convenience to form connexions with the subjects of one nation in preference to another, why should the government interfere to dissolve it?'[118] William Smith of South Carolina gave a firm exposition of a characteristic southern perspective. The development of an American merchant marine, which would inevitably be a predominantly New England one, was no doubt a most desirable objective, but could it replace the British in fulfilling southern needs? 'British merchants send out their goods upon credit; they establish agents and houses to deal them out to planters as they are wanted, and take their crops in return.' Could the New Englanders do this? For the moment, like them or not, the British were indispensable.[119] Madison's discriminatory duties passed the House by a large majority to be defeated in the Senate ostensibly in the name of stronger action. Madison was to renew the struggle, but he feared, rightly, that 'It will probably come to nothing, many of the members of both Houses having shown by the nature of their arguments that they do not think the U.S. ought to risk the scanty privileges G.B. now vouchsafes by an effort to extend them.'[120] Hamilton may well have been right when he told his British friend that most American merchants 'with few exceptions were against every species of distinction' against Britain.[121]

The interconnectedness of Britain and America largely frustrated the self-sufficiency which Lord Hawkesbury and James Madison and those on both sides of the Atlantic who thought like them tried to cultivate. Hawkesbury's principal aim was that Britain should have a merchant marine solely built and crewed in Britain itself from which American participation would have been purged. He also hoped that the remaining components of the British empire in America could form a closely integrated whole from which the United States would be excluded. Newfoundland would draw its food and timber supplies from the British mainland colonies and would provide fish for the West Indies, while Nova Scotia, New Brunswick, and Quebec would supply the islands with timber and such provisions as they did not get from the British Isles. These trades were solely to be conducted in British ships. Madison wanted to foster an American merchant marine and thus greatly to reduce the British role in carrying American trade. He hoped in general that America would be able to break out of its colonial framework in which most of its trade had

---

[118] 21 April 1789, *Annals of the First Congress of the United States* (Washington, 1834), I, p. 184.
[119] 7 May 1789, ibid. I, pp. 286–7.
[120] To W. Nicholas, 18 July 1789, Hutchinson et al. (eds), *Madison Papers*, XII, p. 294.
[121] Syrett et al. (eds), *Hamilton Papers*, V, p. 488.

centred on Britain, exporting its commodities to a wide variety of markets and diversifying the sources of its imports. Americans should emancipate themselves equally from the grip of British credit and a craving for British fashion.

As far as shipping was concerned, both Hawkesbury and Madison could draw comfort from the available statistics—based, on the British side, on more comprehensive registration after the 1786 Navigation Act. Both at first sight showed sizeable increases in the number of 'British' and 'American' ships. Closer examination might suggest more nuanced conclusions. Attempts to define ships as either exclusively British or exclusively American were fraught with difficulties. Joint Anglo-American ownership was extremely common, as the British consul in Philadelphia pointed out in 1787.[122] This enabled the owners to evade American duties or British prohibitions as it suited them. As early as 1786 Hawkesbury had been warned that 'British' ships were being built in the United States.[123] In 1790 he was told that 'a Manchester house, who has an establishment at Philadelphia, and is very rich . . . has several vessels now in the stocks' in America.[124] The first American consul in London found it equally difficult to determine whether a ship was British or American. American registers were often given to 'a person in America on his swearing that he is the sole owner when it is notorious, that the principal resides here and that the person in whose name the register is granted, is no more or less than an agent, or junior partner'.[125] Both the complex patterns of Anglo-American connections and the way in which ships could assume diverse identities at will is illustrated by the case of the *Hydra*. This was a 300-ton ship owned by a British merchant called William Green. In 1784 he intended to defy the East India Company's monopoly by taking the *Hydra* from London to Asia under American colours. To obtain these and the American Letters of Navigation given to ships going to Asia, he asked his uncle, Christopher Champlin of Newport, Rhode Island, to declare himself to be the ship's owner with Green as his supercargo. Champlin's connection in the ship was in reality no more than a commission on the cargo. As further security, Green applied to Rhode Island for naturalization for himself. In Bengal, Green intended to sell his cargo and obtain goods for the return voyage to America through British private traders. When he got to Asia, presumably because he also called at the French settlement of Chandernagore, he found French colours of more use to him than American ones. The ship came back to Newport via the Dutch West Indian island of St Eustatius.[126] For all the ingenuity with which the *Hydra* changed its national allegiance in order to outwit commercial regulations, the voyage appears to have been unsuccessful. With 'money growing scarcer every day', the cargo,

[122] P. Bond to Carmarthen, 14 May 1787, Giunta (ed.), *Emerging Nation*, III, p. 504.
[123] Letter of M. Gregory, 8 June 1786, BL, Add MS 38219, f. 170.
[124] Letter of H. Wilckens, 21 January 1790, TNA, BT 6/20, f. 402.
[125] J. Johnson to T. Jefferson, 26 February 1791, Boyd et al. (eds), *Jefferson Papers*, XIX, p. 340.
[126] The voyage of the *Hydra* is abundantly documented in 'The Commerce of Rhode Island 1726–1800, II', *Collections of the Massachusetts Historical Society*, 7th ser., X (1915). See also, Holden Furber, *John Company at Work* (Cambridge, MA, 1951), p. 144.

seven-eighths of which were said to be owned by English investors, did not find a ready sale at Newport in 1786.[127]

Seamen were the crucial consideration behind all policies of national maritime self-sufficiency. Official policy in both countries was that British or American ships should be crewed by British or American seamen, available to be mobilized for national navies. Under the famous British Navigation Act, three-quarters of the crew of a British ship were required to be British, while Madison aspired to ensure that America had seamen of its own for its own naval needs. Seamen were, however, as prone to shifting between being British or American as easily as the ships in which they sailed. British sailors were said to be easily induced to serve on American ships by the higher wages paid on them. William Bingham believed that the crews of ships sailing from Philadelphia in 1789 were 'mostly foreigners'.[128] The British consul at Philadelphia agreed that 'A vast proportion of mariners, employed in navigating American ships are foreigners—too many of whom, I am sorry to say, are his Majesty's natural born subjects.'[129] By January 1790 Hawkesbury was hearing stories about 'the methods the Americans pursue in enticing our sailors from the service of British merchants'.[130] In the immediate post-war years, however, many 'Americans' were believed to be serving on British ships. The impressment of American sailors for the Royal Navy, which was to cause so much bitterness in the Revolutionary and Napoleonic Wars, first surfaced in 1790 when a press was ordered to man the navy for the crisis with Spain over Nootka Sound. There were bitter complaints about the impressment of Americans. A contemporary American account estimated that 4,000 or 5,000 Americans were regularly employed on the British ships that came into the port of London in the 1780s and that 2,000 of the 13,000 seamen impressed in 1790 were Americans. British officials usually ordered the release of individuals about whom representations were made, but argued that 'the similarities of manners, language &c.' made discrimination almost impossible.[131] To their respective publics, British and American seamen seemed to be the embodiment of national qualities—republican liberty or British freedom.[132] In reality it was by no means easy to distinguish British from American seamen who assumed whichever identity suited them best at the time.

If separate British and American merchant marines became established, subject to much fuzziness as to what constituted a 'British' or an 'American' ship or a British or American sailor, Hawkesbury's hopes that the United States could be excluded from the trade of British colonies and Madison's aspirations for a much reduced British stake in the American economy remained a long way from

---

[127] P. A[llaire] to [G. Yonge], 5 July 1786, TNA, FO 4/4, f. 223.

[128] To A. Hamilton, 25 November 1789, Syrett et al. (eds), *Hamilton Papers*, V, p. 557.

[129] P. Bond to Leeds, 18 September 1790, TNA, FO 4/8, f. 348.

[130] To H. Wilckens, 25 January 1790, BL, Add MS. 38310, f. 47.

[131] Julian P. Boyd, 'The Impressment of Hugh Purdie and Others' in Boyd et al. (eds), *Jefferson Papers*, XVIII, pp. 310–24; see also J. Johnson to Jefferson, 2 November 1790, ibid. XVII, p. 670; and G. Morris to Leeds, 24 September 1790, W.W. Abbot et al. (eds), *The Papers of George Washington: Presidential Series* (Charlottesville, VA, 1987–), VI, p. 505.

[132] For the association of American seamen with the cause of liberty, see Paul A. Gilje, *Liberty on the Waterfront: American Maritime Culture in the Age of Revolution* (Philadelphia, 2004).

fulfilment. Both the British West Indies and the British North American colonies depended, as in the past, on supplies from the old thirteen colonies. The indications that a large part of these cargoes came illegally in American ships are clear. While the British could not keep American ships and commodities out of their empire, Americans could not free themselves from British commercial dominance. By 1790, with the exception of the new Asian commerce, the main outlines of America's intercontinental trade were not yet essentially different from what they had been in the colonial period. Although they went to a wider range of European countries than before the Revolution, American exports to Europe still consisted of the same basic commodities of the colonial era, such as tobacco, rice, timber, or naval stores, with grain and flour assuming greater importance. Many of them continued to go via Britain. American manufacturing was yet to develop on a scale that would reduce the flow of manufactured imports, which still came largely from Britain. Above all, at every level, from the dealings of Robert Morris and William Bingham with the Barings downwards, American merchants traded in close collaboration with British merchants and on British credit. Even the Indian and Chinese trade, vaunted as the symbol of America's new commercial independence, depended in their early stages to a large extent on British finance and on the goods and services provided in Asia by British subjects, if they were not, like the *Hydra*, essentially British ventures under American colours. The British consul in Philadelphia described American Asian trade as a channel for the agents of the European East India companies to send home their fortunes.[133] By this he meant that the Americans funded their trade with money borrowed from European company employees in Asia, to be repaid in Europe when the cargoes were sold. As the Committee of the Privy Council noted in its 1791 report, American trade as a whole depended on British capital to a 'much greater degree than the commerce carried on with any other foreign country. In all commercial matters the merchants of Great Britain continue still to have a close connection with the subjects of the United States.'[134] A study of Liverpool and Philadelphia has concluded that for the merchants of both ports 'political factors often came second to financial expediency' so that, regardless of political developments, 'traders around the Atlantic continued doing what they were good at—distributing goods! Their shared sense of common interests made them a coherent community.'[135] Economic nationalists in both Britain and the United States might regard such a situation as undesirable, but the strength of the economic interconnectedness of Britain and American commerce frustrated most of their efforts to prise them apart.

---

[133] P. Bond to Carmarthen, 2 July 1787, TNA, FO 4/5, ff. 191–2.
[134] Report, 28 January 1791, TNA, FO 4/9, f. 133.
[135] Sheryllynne Haggerty, *The British Atlantic Trading Community, 1760–1810: Men, Women and the Distribution of Goods* (Leiden, 2006), p. 250.

14

Customs in Common

I

Before the great disruption of the American Revolution, Great Britain and Ireland together with the British colonies in the Caribbean and along the North American mainland were more than an empire held together by the exercise of authority from Britain; they can be described as a British Atlantic world defined by movements of people, flows of trade and by common values as well as by common allegiance. Native Americans, enslaved Africans, French Canadians, and many Catholic Irish generally felt themselves to be excluded from this community of values, but the dominant elements in all British territories together with the great mass of those who could trace their roots back to the British Isles were likely to be fully committed to them. There is indeed much to suggest that in the American colonies a common commitment to values emanating from Britain was growing stronger rather than weaker in the years immediately before the Revolution. Some historians have described this as a process of spreading Anglicization.

After independence, many members of the new American elite hoped that the people of the United States would free themselves from the cultural dominance of Europe in general and of Britain in particular and would come to live by values appropriate to the great experiment in republican government on which the United States was embarked. As Benjamin Rush put it, the American Revolution involved far more than changing 'forms of government'; it required a 'revolution in our principles, opinions, and manners'.[1] Independence brought some immediate diminution of British influences. American lawmaking and American courts, for instance, were no longer subject to any British supervision and formal links between American Protestant denominations and their British brethren weakened—Anglicans and Methodists, in particular, becoming effectively autonomous. In general, however, as is hardly surprising considering the strength of links before 1776, anything approaching a revolution 'in principles, opinions, and manners' had yet to be accomplished in the time-span covered by this book. Communications across the Atlantic, movements of people, and flows of trade quickly revived and the former thirteen colonies remained strongly Anglicized, as they had been before the Revolution.

---

[1] To R. Price, 25 May 1786, L. H. Butterfield (ed.), *The Letters of Benjamin Rush*, 2 vols. (Princeton, NJ, 1951), I, p. 388.

At the outbreak of the Revolution British communities throughout the world had in general come to conceive of themselves, in the striking formulation of David Armitage, as parts of an empire that was 'Protestant, commercial, maritime and free'.[2] These remained distinctive features of the post-war British Atlantic world, including those parts now outside the empire. With the exception of Ireland and Quebec, it was still a predominantly Protestant world, even if denominational patterns were changing. A very large volume of trade continued to flow between the territories of what had been the old Atlantic empire, now carried not by a single imperial merchant marine but by the competing shipping of Britain and of the United States, which was becoming an aspiring maritime power in its own right. Both the white population of the United States and white Anglophones within the post-1783 British Atlantic empire envisaged themselves as free peoples, although they differed profoundly in their interpretations about the constitutional arrangements that would best ensure freedom. Americans had rejected any subordination to the British Parliament and ultimately to the authority of the British Crown as incompatible with their freedom, while the extent to which their professedly republican institutions appeared to be under popular domination was regarded by most British opinion as subversive of the balanced government under law that was essential to true liberty.

II

If British mixed monarchy or American republics appeared to offer different and conflicting ways of ensuring the liberty of free peoples, both British and Americans still essentially agreed after 1776 as to what constituted liberty. For both American citizens and British subjects liberty consisted of rights defined by English law, that is by the common law and certain statutes concerned with civil rights. The common law remained a common Anglo-American inheritance cherished on both sides of the Atlantic. Society existed, according to Sir William Blackstone, the great expounder of the laws of England, 'to protect individuals in the enjoyment of their absolute rights, which were vested in them by the immutable laws of nature'. These rights took concrete form as 'political and civil liberty'. Liberty was an 'inestimable blessing' which the 'laws of England' were 'peculiarly adapted' to preserve even for 'the meanest subject'.[3] Americans might believe that current practice in Britain had departed far from such ideals, but they were still ideals to which even the most radical American subscribed. They too revered the common law, which, embodying natural law, reason and the ancient customs of the English people, was believed to have taken its first definitive form under the Anglo-Saxons. It had suffered many adulterations and corruptions from the Norman conquest onwards, but its essential principles had been reasserted by the Glorious Revolution, although they still needed to be carefully guarded and Americans believed that

---

[2] *The Ideological Origins of the British Empire* (Cambridge, 2000), p. 195.
[3] *Commentaries on the Laws of England*, 9th edn, 4 vols (London, 1783), I, pp. 124, 126–7.

there had been much further backsliding in recent times in Britain. Between 1776 and 1784 eleven out of the thirteen new American states made 'directly or indirectly, some provisions for the reception of the common law'.[4]

Americans believed that they had taken English law with them across the ocean, adjusting it to local conditions and supplementing it by enacting their own laws to meet local needs, as they were empowered to do so long as their laws were not repugnant to the laws of England. How much of the law of England applied in the colonies was uncertain. Much of it, Blackstone pointed out, was 'neither necessary nor convenient' for colonial societies. The crucial issue was, however, who had the final authority to determine what the colonies could or could not adopt. Blackstone insisted that such matters must ultimately be determined by the king through his Privy Council.[5] From the later seventeenth century, however, colonial populations increasingly maintained that, like Englishmen in England, they were entitled, as a matter of inherent right not of royal grant, to live under the protection of those provisions of the common law confirmed by certain English statutes that established the essential rights of all freeborn Englishmen. These guaranteed trial by jury and secured them 'against imprisonment, loss of life, or dispossession of property without due process of law' and from 'taxation without consent'. In their own eyes and in those of at least some British lawyers, they had in the course of time succeeded in establishing their right to 'traditional English legal guarantees of life, liberty and property'.[6] Defence of common law rights was to feature prominently in controversies leading up to the Revolution. Congress resolved in its Declaration of Rights and Grievances of 1774 that the colonies were 'entitled to the common law of England'. In the Declaration of Independence the king was accused of having deprived 'us in many cases of the benefits of trial by jury' and of having 'abolished the free system of English laws' in favour of French Canadian civil law in the neighbouring province of Quebec.

Blackstone thought that 'the artificial refinements and distinctions' that had evolved in the legal arrangements of 'a great and commercial people' in Britain would not be needed in 'infant' colonies.[7] By the eighteenth century, however, common law 'refinements and distinctions' were being adopted to settle disputes over debts and contracts in what were becoming increasingly commercialized colonial societies.[8] Such litigation required specialized lawyers learned in the law in the English manner. Historians have seen the widening diffusion of the common law throughout the eighteenth century as a process of Anglicization.[9] By the

---

[4] Morton J. Horwitz, *The Transformation of American Law 1780–1860* (Cambridge, MA, 1977), p. 4.

[5] Blackstone, *Commentaries*, I, p. 108.

[6] Jack P. Greene, *Peripheries and Center: Constitutional Development in the Extended Polities of the British Empire and the United States 1607–1788* (Athens, GA, 1986), pp. 25–7.

[7] *Commentaries*, I, p. 108.

[8] James A. Henretta, 'Magistrates, Common Law Lawyers, Legislators: The Three Legal Systems of British America' in Michael Grossberg and Christopher Tomlins (eds), *The Cambridge History of Law in America*, I, *Early America (1580–1815)* (Cambridge, 2008), p. 570.

[9] John M. Murrin, 'The Legal Transformation: the Bench and the Bar in Eighteenth-century Massachusetts' in Stanley N. Katz (ed.), *Colonial America: Essays in Politics and Social Development* (New York, 1983), pp. 415–49.

outbreak of the Revolution, Massachusetts lawyers had developed 'a graded profession based on their perception of an English model'.[10] English professional divisions between attorneys and barristers were established and appropriate wigs and robes were adopted. Learning in the refinements of the common law had to be derived from England. For a favoured few it was obtained by study at the Inns of Court in London. Over one hundred American students, mostly from the southern colonies, enrolled at the Inns from 1755 to 1775.[11] Most aspiring practitioners learnt from reports of cases decided in England or from English books. Although he was extremely hostile to the constitutional claims of the colonies and his doctrine of parliamentary sovereignty was repugnant to them, Blackstone was extensively studied and greatly admired in America. The *Commentaries* were reprinted in Philadelphia in 1771–2 and again in 1774. 'I hear', Edmund Burke said in 1775, 'that they have sold nearly as many of Blackstone's Commentaries in America as in England.'[12]

The association of a professionalized common law with English influence— the proportion of loyalists among prominent lawyers turned out to be quite high in the northern states—made it potentially vulnerable in post-Revolution America. James Madison called the common law 'this *monarchical* code'. Had it been fully applied in the new states, it 'would have brought over from G[reat] B[ritain] a thousand heterogeneous and anti-republican doctrines, and even the *ecclesiastical hierarchy itself*'.[13] It was vulnerable for other reasons as well. In a new order in which the people were sovereign, their will expressed in legislation must surely prevail over a law based on custom and on what were now foreign statutes enacted in the sometimes remote past. The common law seemed intricate, cumbersome, and uncertain in its operations, giving judges—such as the sinister, to some Americans, Lord Mansfield—far too much leeway to improvise. American reformers, like those in Britain and Europe, urged that the law should be reformed on scientific principles. For all his reverence for the ancient common law, Jefferson was one of these. He called for a thorough revision of the law 'with a single eye to reason, and the good of those for whose government it was framed'.[14] There were complaints of 'the tedious delay: intricacies—labyrinths—perplexities etc. which continually involve the most simple actions in our courts'.[15] Resort to an opaque law to enforce debts in a time of economic dislocation was denounced as a source of oppression in disorders in western Massachusetts in 1786. Some important changes were made, as with the abolition of entail and primogeniture in Virginia's inheritance law, and complex

[10] Gerard W. Gawalt, *The Promise of Power: The Emergence of a Legal Profession in Massachusetts 1760–1840* (Westport, CT, 1979), p. 29.
[11] Julie Flavell, *When London Was Capital of America* (New Haven, CT, 2010), p. 85.
[12] 'Speech on Conciliation with America', Paul Langford (ed.), *The Writings and Speeches of Edmund Burke* (Cambridge, 1981–), III, ed. Warren M. Elofson and John A. Woods, *Party, Parliament and the American War 1774–1780* (1996), p. 123.
[13] To Washington, 18 October 1787, W. W. Abbot et al. *The Papers of George Washington: Confederation Series*, 6 vols. (Charlottesville, VA, 1992–7), V, pp. 382–3.
[14] Cited in Kevin J. Hayes, *The Road to Monticello: The Life and Mind of Thomas Jefferson* (New York, 2008), p. 207.
[15] *Massachusetts Centinel*, 24 September 1785, cited in Gawalt, *Promise of Power*, p. 50.

forms of pleading were increasingly simplified. Systematic codifications of the law, however, came to little where they were attempted. Much of the common law survived.

Whatever defects might be alleged against it, the English common law was indelibly identified with liberty and with the security of the individual and of his property. This ensured its survival and indeed its expansion. The common law was established both in new British colonies that were predominantly Anglophone and in new American states. Insistence on their right to the common law was prominent in the demands of loyalists for their own province of Upper Canada to be carved out of Quebec with its French civil law. American settlers establishing what were to become new states expected the same. The common law was adopted without question in Kentucky. The Northwest Ordinance of 1787 laid down that its inhabitants were entitled to 'judicial proceedings according to the course of the common law'.[16] Three or four American students a year, mostly from South Carolina, still went to the Middle Temple in the 1780s.[17] The 'judicious' Blackstone, as Alexander Hamilton called him, maintained his supremacy until well into the nineteenth century, when American law reports and the first widely received American legal treatises began to appear.

Even before the Revolution, Americans had been adapting the common law to the circumstances of their particular colonies. Each colony developed its own version. The process of adaptation continued after independence as the law was purged of what were seen as elements incompatible with republican societies together with what were regarded as later English corruptions and distortions. Americans came to pride themselves that they had produced 'a system of laws that . . . combined the purest forms of English legal heritage with their own innovations to create a superior common law system that became an integral part of their American identities'. The persistence of a common law that had been Americanized and republicanized could not be seen as evidence of 'cultural dependence'.[18]

III

America's leaders hoped to reshape not only their law but many other aspects of their European and most especially their British cultural inheritance. They too should be Americanized and take on a republican tone. '[O]ur people, altho' enlightened and virtuous', John Adams wrote at the end of the war, 'have had their minds and hearts habitually filled with all the passions of a dependent, subordinate people, that is to say with fear, with diffidence and distrust of themselves, with

---

[16] Northwest Ordinance, Art. 2. For the spread of the common law beyond the old thirteen colonies, see Jack P. Greene, 'The Cultural Dimensions of Political Transfers: An Aspect of the European Occupation of the Americas', *Early American Studies*, VI (2008), 1–26.

[17] C. E. A. Bedwell, 'American Middle Templars', *American Historical Review*, XXV (1920), 688–9.

[18] Ellen Holmes Pearson, 'Revising Custom, Embracing Choice: Early American Legal Scholars and the Republicanization of the Common Law' in Eliga H. Gould and Peter S. Onuf (eds), *Empire and Nation: The American Revolution in the Atlantic World* (Baltimore, MD, 2005), p. 111.

admiration of foreigners'. They must rid themselves of their 'fear and self diffidence on the one hand, and of this excessive admiration of foreigners on the other'.[19] Abigail Adams explained why English influences were particularly insidious and why they must be resisted. Their luxuries, their venality, and profligacy' were 'worse than Egyptian bondage'.

> Our intercourse with any other country cannot for a long time have so great a tendency to injure our morals and manners as this, for speaking the same language, descended from the same ancestors, professing the same religion, with all our habits and prejudices in favour of it, its very vices, like those of our near kindred, we wish to cover and extenuate.[20]

Benjamin Rush feared that the end of the fighting would 'unnerve the resentments of America and introduce among us all the consequences of English habits and manners with English manufactures'.[21]

A variety of proposals were floated for encouraging the cultural autonomy of the new republic and enabling it to take its proper place in the international republic of learning. This should be a dominant one, since leadership in the arts and sciences was inevitably passing from east to west and the United States was the beneficiary of this inexorable process. 'The present is an age of philosophy, and America, the empire of reason', Joel Barlow, poet and diplomat proclaimed. 'Here neither the pageantry of courts nor the gloom of superstition have dazzled or beclouded the mind.'[22] Not only should the new republic be marked by the distinction of its savants and its artists, but it must also have a highly educated population. The mass of Americans should be proficient not in the refined learning of old Europe, but in the practical knowledge of everyday life. The artificialities of conventional politeness needed be replaced by the direct communication of solid information and virtuous conduct in the letters of the new republic.[23] The lexicographer Noah Webster felt that America must shake off the linguistic shackles of Britain and develop its own language. The usage of England itself 'should no longer be *our* standard'. The 'taste of her writers is already corrupted and her language on the decline'.[24]

America's leadership hoped that the new republic would no longer be part of what has been called Britain's 'empire of goods' with its tastes shaped by British tastes through the consumption of vast quantities of imported British items.[25]

---

[19] To President of Congress, 5 September 1783, Robert J. Taylor et al. (eds), *The Papers of John Adams* (Cambridge, MA, 1977–), XV, p. 255.

[20] To C. Tufts, 21 February 1786, L. H. Butterfield et al. (eds), *The Adams Family Correspondence* (Cambridge, MA, 1963–), VII, p. 71.

[21] To N. Greene, 15 April 1782, Butterfield (ed.), *Letters of Benjamin Rush*, I, p. 286.

[22] Cited in Brooke Hindle, *The Pursuit of Science in Revolutionary America, 1735–1789* (Chapel Hill, NC, 1956), p. 253.

[23] Michael Warner, *The Letters of the Republic: Publication and the Public Sphere in Eighteenth-century America* (Cambridge, MA, 1990), pp. 123–51.

[24] Cited in Joseph J. Ellis, *After the Revolution: Profiles of Early American Culture* (New York, 1979), p. 184.

[25] The concept is that of T. H. Breen; see his *The Marketplace of Revolution: How Consumer Politics Shaped American Independence* (New York, 2004).

Resumption of British imports on a large scale would constitute a serious challenge to the virtue of the new republic. They were the embodiment of the values of a corrupt, hierarchical society, encouraging extravagance and display instead of republican simplicity. Everything possible, David Ramsay, historian of the Revolution, urged, should be done to 'counter-act that ruinous propensity we have for foreign superfluities and to excite us with the long neglected virtues of industry and frugality'.[26] Americans, Jefferson wrote, should repent of the sins of consuming imported goods and ask themselves: 'Can you become rigorously frugal? Can you despise European modes, European follies and vices?'[27] Such exhortations had little effect. Immediately after the war, British goods began to be imported on a scale that far exceeded America's capacity to pay for them. The success of British exports depended on their relative cheapness and the long credit extended by British merchants; but, to the vexation of patriotic Americans, it also reflected the prestige of British goods in the eyes of American consumers. 'The English having formed our taste', Robert Morris wrote, were after the war 'in a position to gratify that taste by the nature and fashion of their manufactures'.[28] At the highest levels of American society some now chose French objects as an alternative to the prevailing British designs and furnishings,[29] but in mass consumption the British had little competition.

Many heard exhortations to frugality but, if they obeyed them they did so by a process of republicanizing and Americanizing luxury and refinement in ways which strict republicans were most unlikely to approve. After independence Americans with social ambitions still 'modeled their lives after the aristocrats of a society that was supposedly repudiated at the founding of the nation'. They succeeded, however, in devising compromises which at least satisfied such scruples as they may have felt. 'By simply avoiding excess, a term impossible of precise definition, the provincial gentry cleared the way to construct costlier houses according to standards of ever more refined taste, thinking of themselves not as effete aristocrats but merely as republican gentlemen.'[30] In matters of dress, men aspiring to republican gentility felt that they should avoid imported excesses, such as Spitalfields silk waistcoats and other fopperies, but they did not reject fashion altogether. Rather they replaced 'one fashion orthodoxy with another'.[31] The recreations of the refined continued to be modelled on British aristocratic mores. 'The Revolution, for all the talk of

---

[26] D. Ramsay to J. Eliot, 6 August 1785, Robert L. Brunhouse (ed.), *David Ramsay, 1749–1815: Selections from his Writings* (Philadelphia, 1965), p. 91.

[27] To N. Tracy, 17 August 1785, Julian P. Boyd et al. (eds), *The Papers of Thomas Jefferson* (Princeton, NJ, 1950–), VIII, p. 399.

[28] To B. Franklin, 30 September 1783, E. James Ferguson et al. (eds), *The Papers of Robert Morris* (Pittsburgh, PA, 1973–), VIII, p. 557.

[29] D. L. Berquist, ' "The Honours of a Court" or "the Severity of Virtue": Household Furniture and Cultural Aspirations in Philadelphia' in Catherine E. Hutchins (ed.), *Shaping a National Culture: The Philadelphia Experience, 1750–1800* (Winterthur, DL, 1994), pp. 323–4.

[30] Richard L. Bushman, *The Refinement of America: Persons, Houses, Cities* (New York, 1992), pp. xix, 197.

[31] Linzy Brekke, ' "To Make a Figure": Clothing and the Politics of Male Identity in Eighteenth-Century America' in John Styles and Amanda Vickery (eds), *Gender, Taste, and Material Culture in Britain and North America, 1700–1830* (New Haven, CT, 2006), pp. 240–1.

republicans about simplicity, equality and virtue, did not alter the play of private society.' Assemblies, clubs, salons, coffee house, and tea tables all reappeared. Public entertainments held around the serving of tea, the most flagrant imported corruption, were a particular affront to strict republican sensibilities. Yet such entertainments took place even in Boston. Dancing manuals, such as *A Collection of Figures of the Newest and Most Fashionable Country-Dances*, were published.[32] Commercial theatre, outlawed by Congress during the war, revived with imported British actors often taking prominent parts.

Ambitions for the American reading public to be supplied with books published in the United States which would propagate a republican view of life remained largely unfulfilled. Webster was immediately successful with his 'spellers', his grammar and his dictionary, but most other projects came to very little. 'Visions of the "rising glory" of American literature burst like bubbles on the financial markets of the early national economy.'[33] What was financially viable was not publishing new American books, beyond a range of cheaper items such as almanacs and devotional works well established long before the Revolution, but importing great quantities of British ones and producing American editions of some of them. An American printer recalled in 1810 that 'For many years after the peace of 1783 books could be imported into the United States and sold cheaper than they could be printed here.'[34] Jedidiah Morse's *Geography Made Easy* with its emphasis on the geography of America sold well, but those who wished to see American children educated in American ways still had to use English books, even though 'a very great proportion' of those 'which are in general use', apart from Greek and Latin texts, came to be reprinted in America by the 1790s.[35] 'One surprising consequence of American independence from the British empire was to reinforce the anglicization of print that culturally was a strong feature of the pre-war decades.'[36]

American painters continued to go to Britain to learn their calling, albeit often under the eminent Americans resident in London, notably Benjamin West or John Singleton Copley. Americans still saw British approbation as recognition of their country's artistic and literary accomplishments. Washington took pleasure that 'critics in England . . . speak highly of the American poetical geniuses (and their praises may be more relied upon as they seem to be reluctantly exhorted)'.[37] Philip Freneau, one of the poetical geniuses that he had in mind, put the matter more

---

[32] David S. Shields, *Civil Tongues and Polite Letters in British America* (Chapel Hill, NC, 1997), pp. 309, 311.

[33] Robert A. Gross, 'An Extensive Republic' in Gross and Mary Kelley (eds), *A History of the Book in America*, II, *An Extensive Republic: Print Culture and Society in the New Nation, 1790–1840* (Chapel Hill, NC, 2010), p. 17.

[34] James Raven, 'The Importation of Books in the Eighteenth Century' in Hugh Amory and David. D. Hall (eds), *A History of the Book in America*, I, *The Colonial Book in the Atlantic World* (Cambridge, 2000), p. 195.

[35] Tench Coxe, *A View of the United States of America in a Series of Papers* (London, 1794), p. 160.

[36] Hugh Amory and David D. Hall, 'Afterword' in Amory and Hall (eds), *The Colonial Book*, p. 482.

[37] To Lafayette, 28 May 1788, Abbot et al. (eds), *Washington Papers: Confederation Series*, VI, p. 298.

robustly. 'Can we never be thought to have learning or grace / unless it be brought from that horrible place / Where tyranny reigns with her impudent face[?]'[38]

American aspirations to scientific achievement had taken root in the colonial period. The first learned societies and medical schools had been established and fifty-three Americans had been admitted to the Royal Society of London. One American, Benjamin Franklin, had achieved a worldwide reputation for his work on electricity and was ultimately to become 'one of the most recognised people in the Western Hemisphere'.[39] As was only to be expected, colonial American science was very much an offshoot of British science. American societies followed British models, corresponded with their British exemplars, and sought their recognition. Metropolitan patronage was readily extended to them and there was something like an Atlantic community of learning. Individual fellows of the Royal Society, notably the Quaker botanist Peter Collinson, acted as intermediaries between a not unresponsive Society and aspiring colonials. Even Franklin can be described as 'a colonial client' who had to resort to 'the meticulous cultivation of friends and patrons'.[40] A measured verdict is that, although 'as tutor, exemplar, and encourager to American science', the Society inevitably had 'serious weaknesses', it still 'shaped to a considerable degree . . . English science and its provincial reflection in America'.[41] The London Society of Arts was particularly assiduous in cultivating American contacts. Its overtly utilitarian aims of encouraging the development of useful products throughout the empire, especially by paying premiums, coincided with the bias towards the utilitarian of much early American science. Americans joined the Society in considerable numbers and competed eagerly for its premiums.[42]

Would scientific endeavour in an independent America remain a 'provincial reflection' of British science? Ambitious Americans hoped that it would not. They wished to be a fully autonomous part of an international scientific community. American societies, however, continued to follow the pattern of the British Royal Society or the London Society of Arts. They were voluntary clubs, covering all areas of 'philosophy' with a strong bias towards practical improvement, whose membership included a high proportion of the well connected. The Pennsylvania Act reincorporating the American Philosophical Society in 1780 stated that 'the experience of ages shows that improvements of a public nature, are best carried on by societies of learned and ingenious men, uniting their labours without regard to nation, sect, or party, in one grand pursuit'.[43] The aims of the American Academy

---

[38] Amory and Hall, 'Afterword' in Amory and Hall (eds), *The Colonial Book*, p. 483.

[39] Joyce E. Chaplin, *The First Scientific American: Benjamin Franklin and the Pursuit of Genius* (New York, 2006), p. 1.

[40] Ibid. p. 133.

[41] George F. Frick, 'The Royal Society in America' in Alexandra Oleson and Sanborn C. Brown (eds), *The Pursuit of Knowledge in the Early American Republic: American Scientific and Learned Societies from Colonial Times to the Civil War* (Baltimore, MD, 1976), p. 81.

[42] D. G. C. Allan, ' "The Present Unhappy Disputes:" The Society and the Loss of the American Colonies' in Allan and John L. Abbott (eds), *The Virtuoso Tribe of Arts and Sciences: Studies in the Eighteenth-Century Work and Membership of the London Society of Arts* (Athens, GA, 1992), pp. 214–36.

[43] *Transactions of the American Philosophical Society*, II (1786), xi.

of Arts and Sciences founded at Boston in 1780 stressed the practical applications of science. 'The principal figure' on its corporate seal was Minerva:

> At her right-hand is a field of Indian corn, the native grain of *America* . . . About the feet of Minerva are scattered several instruments of husbandry. On her left-hand are a quadrant and a telescope, a prospect of the sea, with a ship steering towards the town . . . The device represents the situation of a new country, depending principally on agriculture but attending at the same time to arms, commerce, and the sciences.[44]

The New York Society for Promoting Useful Knowledge of 1784 was even more explicitly utilitarian in its aims.

If the forms of the early post-war societies were generally British, the aspirations that they embodied were undoubtedly American. American science would enable the American people to exploit the vast potential wealth of 'this country of North-America, which the goodness of Providence hath given us to inherit'.[45] Scientific knowledge would, the new American Academy proclaimed, 'advance the interest, honor, dignity, and happiness of a free, independent, and virtuous people'.[46] The progress of American science would refute slighting European opinions about America, of which the two most resented were, surprisingly, propagated by its French allies rather than by its British enemies. In his *Notes on the State of Virginia* Jefferson entered the lists against Buffon, who had argued that the fauna of America were smaller and inferior to those of the old world and, against Raynal, who had asserted that 'America has not yet produced one good poet, one able mathematician, one man of genius in a single art or a single science'. On the contrary, Jefferson insisted that, 'of the geniuses which adorn the present age, America contributes its full share'. He cited Washington (a genius at warfare) and Franklin and Rittenhouse as scientific geniuses.[47]

Some of the formal links of a British Atlantic community of science were dismantled after the war. After 1774 the overseas premiums of the Society of Arts were only awarded to inhabitants of what remained British colonies. American membership of British societies became generally confined to those who were honoured with foreign membership, like James Bowdoin, elected in 1788 to the Royal Society as president of the American Academy of Arts and Sciences, or David Rittenhouse, elected in 1796 as president of the Philosophical Society. Alexander Hamilton became a corresponding member of the Society of Arts in 1788. Americans tended increasingly to publish their findings in the journals of their own societies. Four contributions from Franklin appeared in the first post-war volume of the American Philosophical Society's *Transactions*. From the opening of Charles Willson Peale's Philadelphia Museum in 1786, American specimens and curiosities came to be displayed in America rather than being sent to Europe.

---

[44] Walter Muir Whitehill, 'Early Learned Societies in Boston and Vicinity' in Oleson and Brown (eds), *Pursuit of Knowledge*, pp. 153–4.

[45] *Transactions of American Philosophical Society*, II (1786), xi.

[46] Charter of American Academy, cited in Whitehill, 'Early Learned Societies', p. 153.

[47] *Notes on the State of Virginia*, ed. William Peden (Chapel Hill, NC, 1955), pp. 64–5.

Long residence in France gave Franklin and Jefferson, who had been able to argue his case face to face with Buffon, a close involvement with French science. The overseas contacts of most Americans tended, however, to revert to Britain after the war. Joseph Banks, president of the Royal Society since 1778, assiduously cultivated Franklin, suppressing in their correspondence his strong aversion to the American Revolution.[48] Although Banks was increasingly involved in projects to enlist science in the service of the British state, he and Franklin exchanged uplifting sentiments about how science transcended national concerns. Franklin looked forward to a return to those 'peaceful times when I could sit down in sweet society with my English philosophic friends'.[49] The Royal Society evidently regarded Franklin as one of their own. In 1790 Caleb Whitefoord, who had been at the peace negotiations, presented the Society with a portrait that he had commissioned, showing 'the great philosopher such as he was', to be hung in the Great Room with portraits of other 'illustrious persons'.[50] After the war British scientists in general seem to have slipped easily back into the role of patrons of up-and-coming American science. The zoologist Thomas Pennant commended the volume of the *Transactions* of the American Philosophical Society that appeared in 1786. In America 'science of every kind begins to flourish', he wrote.[51] Whatever strict republicans might have hoped, some American scientists still saw themselves as clients. Benjamin Waterhouse, Professor of Physic at Harvard, sent Banks his published medical lectures 'that you may form some opinion of our feeble endeavours to diffuse useful knowledge . . . We look up to the English as our elder bretheren in science.'[52] With the peace, American medical students returned to Edinburgh or the London hospitals.[53] Agricultural improvement, which was the major preoccupation of American applied science, drew heavily on British writings and practices. The Philadelphia Society for the promotion of Agriculture admitted from the beginning that 'it looked to England for guidance'. Arthur Young was revered on both sides of the Atlantic.[54]

Britain clearly continued to exercise a powerful cultural dominance over the new America in its early years of independence. Lip service might be paid to cultivating republican life styles of simplicity and frugality and to the merit of buying native rather than foreign goods, but imports from Britain were still highly valued and Americans who could afford to do so still pursued refinement of living on models that were derived from Europe and, above all, from Britain. The American public continued to read British books, to build and furnish their houses in British ways, and to follow British sartorial fashion. Everything that Jefferson was hearing in Paris

[48] John Gascoigne, *Science in the Service of Empire: Joseph Banks, the British State and the Uses of Science in the Age of Revolution* (Cambridge, 1998), p. 43.

[49] To Banks, 9 September 1782, Leonard W. Labaree et al. (eds), *The Papers of Benjamin Franklin* (New Haven, CT, 1959–), XXXVIII, pp. 84–5.

[50] Whitefoord to J. Banks, 3 December 1790, Neil Chambers (ed.), *The Scientific Correspondence of Joseph Banks*, 6 vols. (London, 2007), IV, pp. 22–3.

[51] *The Literary Life of the Late Thomas Pennant Esquire by Himself* (London, 1793), pp. 29–30.

[52] Letter of 10 August 1787, Chambers (ed.), *Banks Scientific Correspondence*, III, pp. 306–7.

[53] Hindle, *Pursuit of Science*, pp. 281–3.

[54] Ibid. pp. 358–62.

about his fellow Americans 'fills me', he wrote in 1786, 'with despair as to their recovery from their vassalage to Great Britain. Fashion and folly is plunging them deeper and deeper into distress.'[55]

Nevertheless, it seems likely that the war and independence probably speeded the Americanization and even perhaps the republicanization of things that had originated in Britain. Over a long period, but with increasing speed after 1783, Americans incorporated the English common law and adapted it to produce what seemed to them to be a distinctive American common law. As the following chapter will try to show, after independence Protestant denominations across the Atlantic, the Episcopal Church, the Methodists, the Presbyterians, and the Baptists, all became more distinctively American, as the Congregationalists had long been. American Protestant Christianity began to develop its own characteristics, marked by the fervour of evangelical revivals, even though this was far from the kind of rational, undogmatic beliefs, tending to unitarianism and even to deism, that the leaders of the Revolution had envisaged as appropriate to a republic. Even gentility and refinement were becoming Americanized. The point has been made that the standards of American polite society might be derived from Europe but that post-war American society, without a court, an aristocracy, a dominant theatre, or indeed a recognized national capital to set its tone, was 'profoundly different' from any society in Europe. In America 'Old World fashions, discourses, and behaviors combined with local improvisations' in different ways in different American cities.[56] What came to be seen as distinctively American in many other respects probably evolved out of gradual processes of adapting old world, and especially British, originals to new world conditions.

---

[55] To T. Pleasants, 8 May 1786, Boyd et al. (eds), *Jefferson Papers*, IX, p. 472.
[56] Shields, *Civil Tongues and Polite Letters*, p. 309.

15

Transatlantic Protestants

I

Protestant denominations that had been transplanted from the British Isles to North America maintained close ties throughout the colonial period with their fellow Protestants in Britain. Like those of other informal networks, such links were generally becoming more close-knit in the years before the Revolution. Some denominations recognized the spiritual authority of parent churches in Britain; others saw themselves as autonomous. All, however, looked for support from Britain in various ways. The colonial clergy was for the most part American, but ministers, evangelists, and college teachers still came out from Britain. Devotional and scholarly books were sent across the Atlantic in great quantities. Virtually all denominations in America sought money from their connections in Britain, above all for founding and sustaining the new colleges launched in the mid eighteenth century. Denominational rivalry was often intense, so British supporters were lobbied to use their influence with the government or with Parliament in order to win advantages for their American colleagues over their rivals and to protect their interests in dealing with colonial authorities.

The Church of England was formally, if not necessarily in practice, the least autonomous of the denominations and the most dependent on Britain.[1] Without its own bishops, it was subject to the Bishop of London. Its clergy had to go to England for ordination. It received powerful aid from the Society for the Propagation of the Gospel, the SPG. On the eve of the Revolution the Society was maintaining seventy-seven missionary clergy in North America at the cost of more than £5,000 a year.[2] Nearly all the Society's missionaries ministered to the white colonial population, but it was also committed to missions to the Native Americans, above all to the Six Nations. Although it was established in five colonies and in part of a sixth and its support was growing markedly, the Church of England in America was in essence no more than a denomination in competition with other denominations.

The Congregationalists were the oldest of the Dissenting denominations in America. They had the status of an established church in Massachusetts, Connecticut, and New Hampshire. Relatively secure in their privileges and with long-established colleges, they had less need of British support. New England Congregationalists,

---

[1] For a valuable recent assessment of the position of the Church in America, see Jeremy Gregory, 'Refashioning Puritan New England: The Church of England in British North America, c.1680–c.1770', *Transactions of the Royal Historical Society*, 6th ser., XX (2010), 85–112.
[2] C. F. Pascoe, *Two Hundred Years of the S.P.G.*, 2 vols. (London, 1901), I, pp. 79; II, pp. 830–1.

however, kept in close touch with sympathetic English radicals, such as Thomas Hollis, a great benefactor of Harvard, about supposed threats to them from across the ocean. By contrast, Presbyterians, fuelled by large-scale immigration from Ulster as well as from Scotland, were a relatively new and rapidly expanding denomination in eighteenth-century America, especially in the middle colonies where they spread into frontier areas. They sent appeals to Britain for money, ministers, and support. In 1760 the General Synod of Ulster sponsored a collection for Presbyterian ministers who had suffered in the war that had ravaged the frontier of Pennsylvania.[3] The Presbyterian Synods of New York and Philadelphia told the General Assembly in 1772 that they looked on their 'connection with the Church of Scotland' as 'the means of securing our constitutional privileges especially our religious liberties'.[4] American Baptists were slower to organize, but from mid century the New England Baptists formed their Warren Association, opened Rhode Island College (the future Brown University), and began to lobby for aid from home, principally in support of their resistance to paying Congregational church rates.

The boundaries between Dissenting denominations were not rigid. A group in Britain, including notable luminaries such as Joseph Priestley and Richard Price, have come to be known as Rational Dissenters.[5] They tended to heterodox theological views, especially about the Trinity, and to political radicalism. They drew support principally from English Presbyterians but included men who had left the Anglican Church. They enjoyed the esteem of like-minded Americans, usually free-thinking, politically radical laymen rather than clerics. The Church of Scotland's Society for the Propagation of Christian Knowledge was another example of cooperation across denominations. It channelled money raised in Britain for Indian missions through inter-denominational boards of correspondents in America.[6] In England the Dissenting denominations worked together easily through the organization called the Dissenting Deputies.[7] On the eve of the Revolution, John Witherspoon, Presbyterian president of the College of New Jersey, saw the Dissenting Deputies as important allies in 'the grand struggle' for 'religious liberty', which 'we or posterity may be called upon to make in the glorious cause in which the happiness of thousands yet unborn may be deeply interested'.[8]

The revivals of the Great Awakening in America of the 1730s and 1740s profoundly affected Congregationalists, Presbyterians, Baptists, and some Anglicans,

---

[3] *Records of the General Synod of Ulster from 1691 to 1820*, 3 vols. (Belfast, 1890–8), II, pp. 436–7, 467–8.

[4] Andrew Hook, *Scotland and America; A Study of Cultural Relations 1750–1835* (Glasgow, 1975), p. 32.

[5] See the essays on them in Knut Haakonssen (ed.), *Enlightenment and Religion: Rational Dissent in Eighteenth-century Britain* (Cambridge, 1996).

[6] Minutes of General Meetings of SSPCK, vol. 5, National Archives of Scotland, GD 95/1/5; *State of the Society in Scotland for Propagating Christian Knowledge* (London, 1771), pp. 16–19.

[7] Alison Gilbert Olson, *Making the Empire Work: London and the American Interest Groups 1690–1790* (Cambridge, MA, 1992), p. 100. Professor Olson's work is an invaluable guide to transatlantic religious connections.

[8] Minutes of meeting of 19 October 1774, Guildhall Library, Dissenting Deputies Minute Book, II, p. 180.

causing deep divisions within rather than between denominations. Revivals created new and vibrant links across the Atlantic. There were similar phenomena in the British Isles, most notably at Cambuslang in Scotland. The great Anglican orator George Whitefield exercised his charismatic powers on both sides of the Atlantic. News of providential happenings was eagerly passed to and fro across the ocean. Ministers and congregations were linked in Concerts of Prayer.[9] On the eve of the Revolution, the Methodist revival within the Anglican Church was beginning to gain a foothold in the middle colonies and John Wesley was dispatching itinerant preachers to America.[10]

Quakers stood entirely outside the Dissenting denominations. They were highly organized on both sides of the Atlantic. Yearly Meetings in the colonies and in Britain exchanged detailed 'Epistles'. British Quakers made extended tours of the colonies, attending meetings and living with American Quaker families. American Quakers did the same in Britain. In London there was a structure of committees to keep a close watch on matters of concern to Quakers in America as well as Britain.[11] The British Quaker elite of merchants and professional men was rich and respectful of authority and the Quakers were said to be 'a body of people of great weight and much esteemed here'.[12]

Behind the willingness of British Christians to lay out their money on a very large scale, £24,000 on colonial colleges alone between 1749 and 1775,[13] and to deploy such influence as they could wield in American causes, lay a strong sense of transatlantic Protestant communities. The sense of commitment that bound America to Britain seems to have ranged from the exalted fellow feeling of those who found themselves caught up in revivals, which they knew were also sweeping through the colonies, to the preoccupations of leading figures such as the Archbishop of Canterbury, Thomas Secker, for whom in the words of his contemporary biographer:

> The advancement of true piety and learning, the conversion of the *Indians* and the *Negroes*, as far as it was practicable, the establishment of proper schools, the distribution of useful books, the good conduct of the missionaries, the preservation of peace and harmony amongst the different religious communities in those parts of the *British* empire; ... had a very large share in his thoughts.[14]

---

[9] Susan O'Brien, 'A Transatlantic Community of Saints: The Great Awakening and the First Evangelical Network.1735–55', *American Historical Review*, XCI (1986), 811–32; Michael J. Crawford, *Seasons of Grace: Colonial New England's Revivalist Tradition in its British Context* (Oxford, 1991).

[10] Dee E. Andrews, *Methodists and Revolutionary America 1760–1800: The Shaping of an Evangelical Culture* (Princeton, NJ, 2000).

[11] Olson, *Making the Empire Work*, p. 99.

[12] T. Penn to W. Peters, 7 July 1756, Historical Society of Pennsylvania, Thomas Penn Letter Books, VI, f. 316.

[13] Beverly McAnear, 'The Raising of Funds by Colonial Colleges', *Mississippi Historical Review*, XXXVIII (1952).

[14] Beilby Porteus, *A Review of the Life and Character of the Right Rev. Dr Thomas Secker*, 5th edn (London, 1797), pp. 67–8. For Secker's American interests, see Robert G. Ingram, *Religion, Reform and Modernity in the Eighteenth Century: Thomas Secker and the Church of England* (Woodbridge, 2007), ch. 7.

The biographer of John Erskine, prominent in the Popular Party of the Church of Scotland and therefore a man of an entirely different outlook from Secker, wrote of Erskine's wide network of American correspondents and that 'his connections with America had a strong hold on his mind... His solicitude for her prosperity, and especially for her progress in literature and religion was always expressed with eagerness and affection.' At the beginning of the American War, he urged conciliation 'for the cause of religion,... as much as he pleaded the cause of political expediency'.[15] Few British secular notables could match the commitment to America of eminent divines like Secker and Erskine.

Many Americans had come to believe that their country had a unique destiny in God's providential designs for the world.[16] So too did some people in Britain. Thomas Randall, a radical within the Church of Scotland, wrote in 1767 that he had 'long thought that the intentions of Providence (after the abuse of our great mercies and our dreadful degeneracy)' was 'to fix the great seat of truth and righteousness in America'.[17] The Anglican polemicist George Horne hoped to see 'the clouds of infidelity disperse before the sun of righteousness, rising to the American, perhaps as he sets in the European world'.[18] For the many British people who saw themselves as in varying degrees part of a network of transatlantic Protestant communities, revolution and war were catastrophic events which sundered cherished links and shattered expectations. Many saw these happenings as divine chastisement for national dereliction. Sermon after sermon from all denominations called for national repentance and reform of manners. Beyond that they blamed human agency. Some attributed the disaster to the rebellious ambitions of the Americans, others to the high-handed and oppressive intransigence of government and Parliament.

II

All Protestant denominations on both sides of the Atlantic, even the Quakers who had great difficulty in defining the neutrality to which they wished to adhere,[19] were divided by the Revolution. This was certainly the case with Anglicans, although many saw the Revolution as aimed against them. From the outset it was denounced in Britain as a plot to overthrow both Church and State. This view was summed up in a newspaper paragraph in 1776, which identified New England as

---

[15] Henry Moncrieff Wellwood, *An Account of the Life and Writings of John Erskine* (Edinburgh, 1818), pp. 163, 400.

[16] Nathan O. Hatch, *The Sacred Cause of Liberty: Republican Thought and the Millennium in Revolutionary New England* (New Haven, CT, 1977); Ruth Bloch, *Visionary Republic: Millennial Themes in American Thought* (New York, 1988); Nicholas Guyatt, *Providence and the Invention of the United States, 1607–1876* (Cambridge, 2007).

[17] Letter to J. Witherspoon, [4 March 1767], in L. H. Butterfield (ed.), *John Witherspoon Comes to America: A Documentary Account* (Princeton, NJ, 1953), p. 29.

[18] George Horne, *An Apology for Certain Gentlemen in the University of Oxford* (Oxford, 1756), pp. 26–7.

[19] Olson, *Making the Empire Work*, pp. 168–9, 180–1.

the cradle of revolt. 'They are republicans in politics—puritans in religion—and of consequence disaffected to the established government in Britain in church and state.'[20] The 1770s in America were thus a replay of the 1640s in England. Presbyterians soon came to be joined with Congregationalists as fomenters of rebellion. That Anglican clergy were the most conspicuous early victims of the Revolution heightened the impression that it was a war against the Church. A group consisting largely of SPG missionaries, who had been trying to sustain Anglicanism in New England or in the middle colonies, soon had to flee to Britain. Their sufferings were publicized by the SPG. 'Numerous indeed and truly pitiable are the accounts received by the Society.'[21] Preaching at Oxford, the exiled Myles Cooper, president of King's College in New York, assured his audience that he 'could unfold such scenes of persecution and cruelty as would excite the indignation and horror of every soul in this assembly'.[22] The view that religious Dissent was at the heart of the rebellion was shared in some degree in official circles. Lord George Germain believed that the other colonies had been 'gradually seduced into rebellion' by the Massachusetts 'Independants' (Congregationalists).[23] British Dissenters were accused of aiding and abetting their American allies in their rebellious projects. A newspaper paragraph of 1776 accused the British Dissenters of wishing to overthrow Church and State 'with the assistance of their friends in America'.[24] The role that British Dissenters were assumed to have had in inciting revolt in America later became a stock weapon in Anglican polemics against them, as in controversies over the Test and Corporation Acts.

Any simple view of Anglicans as the victims of revolution and of Dissenters as its propagators would, however, be highly misleading. A large segment of the revolutionary leadership was Anglican. Throughout the colonies as a whole only about a quarter of the clergy emigrated. Anglicans became most embattled with the Revolution in New England, New York, and New Jersey, where they were in a minority and where there was a previous history of conflict. In Virginia and Maryland and further south, where the Church was established, a large majority of the Anglican laity and many of the clergy seem to have sided with the Revolution or at least to have accepted it.[25] The ardent patriot William Lee explained to an Anglican parson in his native Virginia that he saw 'most clearly the work of providence in this American business' and then asked, 'Do I not talk like a true

---

[20] 'Pacificus', *Morning Chronicle*, 8 August 1776.

[21] *An Abstract of the Proceedings of the Society for the Propagation of the Gospel in Foreign Parts for 1776* (London, 1776), p. 37.

[22] Myles Cooper, *National Humiliation and Repentance Recommended and the Causes of the Present Rebellion in America Assigned* (Oxford, 1777), p. 19.

[23] Letter to W. Howe, 18 October 1776, *Historical Manuscripts Commission: Stopford Sackville MSS*, 2 vols. (London, 1904–10), II, p. 43.

[24] 'No Dissenter', *General Evening Post*, 27–30 April 1776.

[25] For an analysis of the allegiance of the Anglican clergy, see James B. Bell, *A War of Religion: Dissenters, Anglicans and the American Revolution* (Houndmills, 2008), pp. 195–210; see also D. J. Holmes, 'The Episcopal Church and the American Revolution', *Historical Magazine of the Protestant Episcopal Church*, XLVII (1978), 261–91.

Church of England man, not a High Church man?'[26] By High Church men, he meant in particular the New England or New York Anglicans. In England the bishops and Church hierarchy almost without exception opposed the Revolution, as did most of the lower clergy. It has, however, been suggested that members of the Anglican laity constituted the majority of those who petitioned against the war in 1775.[27]

Propositions equating Dissenters with supporters of the Revolution must be severely qualified.[28] Such propositions would certainly apply to the majority of Congregationalists in America and to most exponents of Rational Dissent in England. The same would probably be the case for most Presbyterians of Irish origin in America and for many Presbyterians in Ireland itself.[29] Scottish Presbyterians in America, however, were by no means united behind the Revolution. Many, especially in New York and the Carolinas, fought for the Crown and then emigrated to Quebec or Nova Scotia. The official institutions of the Church of Scotland were firmly pro-government and this probably reflected the views of a majority of the political nation in Scotland. The SSPCK stopped sending money to the College of New Jersey when they judged that the colony was 'in a state of rebellion against the crown of Great Britain'.[30] There was, however, a considerable Popular Party within the Kirk who opposed the war and may have had wide support.[31] After the war, John Witherspoon came to believe that there was much sympathy for America among 'the common sort' in Scotland.[32]

The allegiance of English Dissenters, that is of Congregationalists, Presbyterians, and Baptists, who were not members of the Rational Dissenting congregations, is a contentious issue.[33] James Bradley's conclusion based, on very impressive research, is that in the petitioning movement against the war of 1775 'the great majority of Dissenters gave strong support to conciliatory measures'.[34] Dismay and revulsion at the prospect of civil war and at the policies of the government that seemed to be provoking it was not, however, necessarily the same as being 'pro-American', often as that elision is made. As the war ground on year after year and it became clear that

---

[26] Letter to Rev. Mr Hurt, 15 March 1775, Virginia Historical Society, MS L 51, f. 415.

[27] James E. Bradley, *Popular Politics and the American Revolution in England: Petitions, the Crown and Public Opinion* (Macon, GA, 1986), p. 192.

[28] J. C. D. Clark's *The Language of Liberty 1660–1832: Political Discourse and Social Dynamics in the Anglo-American World* (Cambridge, 1994) identifies those Dissenters most prone to revolutionary involvement: in England those with heterodox views on the Trinity and a much wider range in America caught up with evangelical and revivalist enthusiasm, who provided the mass support for the Revolution.

[29] Ian McBride, *Scripture Politics: Ulster Presbyterianism and Irish Radicalism in the Late Eighteenth Century* (Oxford, 1998).

[30] National Archives of Scotland, GD/95/1/5, p. 217.

[31] R. K. Donovan, 'The Popular Party of the Church of Scotland and the American Revolution' in Richard B. Sher and J. L. Smitten (eds), *Scotland and America in the Age of Enlightenment* (Edinburgh, 1990), pp. 81–99.

[32] See above, p. 83.

[33] See discussion in Clark, *Language of Liberty*, pp. 329–35; Olson, *Making the Empire Work*, p. 152.

[34] James E. Bradley, *Religion, Revolution and English Radicalism: Nonconformity in Eighteenth-century Politics and Society* (Cambridge, 1990), p. 398.

Americans would accept nothing short of independence (an eventuality which even most Rational Dissenters deplored)[35] and would go so far as to ally with Britain's hereditary Catholic enemies to get it, their cause seemed less attractive to many. The views of John Rogers, Congregationalist minister of Long Lane Chapel, Southwark, and perhaps significantly a 'strict Calvinist', may be characteristic. He was 'a Whig as to the American quarrel but against the Americans on the point of separation'. He 'much faulted the Americans for their severities to the friends of Great Britain and most of all for joining the interests of the chief Popish powers' and he regretted that so much money had been sent to them in the past.[36] When William Gordon, an Independent, returned to England, having served as chaplain to the Massachusetts Congress, he commented on 'the coolness with which I have been treated by several, even of my brethren in the ministry' and he knew of London Dissenting ministers 'who would have rejoiced to have had the promoters or encouragers of revolution, whether in civil or sacred orders, hanged as rebels'.[37] He was 'abused and insulted by one of his brethren in a coffe[e] house where the Dissenting ministers meet every Tuesday'.[38]

III

American independence and the accelerating pace of new developments in the religious life of the post-revolutionary United States brought about changes in the pattern of relations between the transatlantic denominations. Independence meant that links were now between equals and no longer based on deference or on the rendering of services by the British, while in America 'a profound religious upsurge' was beginning to produce 'a vastly altered religious landscape'.[39] The relative strength of the denominations changed markedly. Anglicans, Congregationalists, and Presbyterians all lost ground, while Methodists and Baptists flourished mightily. Fervent evangelical revivals that marked the first stages of what became a Second Great Awakening fragmented the denominations. Eventually there were to be 'not just Baptists but General Baptists, Regular Baptists, Free Will Baptists, Separate Baptists, Dutch River Baptists, Permanent Baptists, and Two-Seed-in-the-Spirit Baptists'.[40] New cults completely outside the older denominations sprang up in profusion. Everywhere the existing structures of religious authority and the ministry of a regularly ordained clergy were coming to be called

[35] A point well made by Colin Bonwick, 'English Dissenters and the American Revolution' in H. C. Allen and Roger Thompson (eds), *Contrast and Connections: Bicentennial Essays in American History* (London, 1976), p. 104.

[36] L. F. S. Upton (ed.), *The Diary and Selected Papers of Chief Justice William Smith 1784–1793*, 2 vols. (Toronto, 1963–5), I, p. 41.

[37] Letter to J. Manning, 13 September 1786, Reuben A. Guild, *Early History of Brown University*, repr. (New York, 1980), p. 441.

[38] Abigail Adams to J. Q. Adams, 22 July 1786, L. H. Butterfield et al. (eds), *Adams Family Correspondence* (Cambridge, 1963–), VII, p. 284.

[39] Nathan O. Hatch, *The Democratization of American Christianity* (New Haven, CT, 1989), p. 4.

[40] Gordon S. Wood, *Empire of Liberty, A History of the Early Republic* (New York, 2009), p. 610.

in question. Religious revivals spread throughout British colonies, especially in Nova Scotia, where they caused dismay to secular authority, as well as through the United States. In Britain religious denominations were also to come under pressure from popular revivals, but the challenges developed later and had less cataclysmic results.

Most American Protestants not surprisingly saw the hand of divine Providence in their victory. 'Nothing', for John Witherspoon, was 'more manifest than that the separation of this country from Britain has been of God'. The British had been vainly resisting 'the course of Providence'.[41] It was widely believed that the new republic had a God-given destiny to redeem the world. God had willed the success of America in the war because of the future that He intended for it.[42] The Warren Baptist Association of New England regarded the Revolution as 'one important step towards bringing in the glory of the latter day ... Nor is it at all improbable that America is reserved in the mind of Jehovah to be the grand theatre on which the divine redeemer will accomplish glorious things.'[43] Some British divines were also prepared to see God's hand in the emergence of an independent America. The Unitarian Newcome Cappe, in a sermon at York in 1781, suggested that 'It may be the purpose of providence, beyond that friendly ocean to prepare an asylum for the calamities which are coming on a land that will not be reformed.'[44] Most British Protestants were, however, rather more reserved. War had strained relations with their American brethren and initial reports from the newly independent republics were often far from encouraging.

American Anglicans experienced the most complete withdrawal of British authority and drying up of British support. The Church of England in America had come out of the war badly damaged. The 311 clergymen on the eve of the Revolution had shrunk to 141 by the peace.[45] Many churches had been closed and their congregations dispersed. The financial support accorded to the Church in the ex-colonies where it had been established was taken away as disestablishment was enforced in the new states. In spite of the entreaties by the Connecticut clergy that 'to their former calamities this insupportable one may not be added,—the being discarded by the Society',[46] discarded they were. The SPG interpreted its charter, which directed its attention to the spiritual needs of 'our plantations, colonies and factories beyond the seas' as precluding activities outside the dominions of the Crown. In April 1785 it decided that it would no longer pay stipends to missionaries in the United States, but that it would do its best to provide for those who were willing to go to the surviving British colonies.[47] In spite of the

[41] 'Sermon Delivered at a Public Thanksgiving after Peace', *Works of the Rev. John Witherspoon*, 2nd edn, 4 vols. (Philadelphia, 1802), III, p. 79.

[42] Bloch, *Visionary Republic*.

[43] William G. McLoughlin, *New England Dissent 1660–1833 The Baptists and the Separation of Church and State*, 2 vols. (Cambridge, MA, 1971), II, pp. 741–2.

[44] *A Sermon Preached on Wednesday 21st of February 1781, the Late Day of National Humiliation* (London, 1781), p. 17. For other examples, see Guyatt, *Providence and the United States*, pp. 126–7.

[45] Bell, *A War of Religion*, p. 198.

[46] Letter of 6 May 1783, Rhodes House Library, SPG Journals, 23, p. 142.

[47] Rhodes House Library, SPG Journals, 24, pp. 81–2.

dismay of the Connecticut clergy at the loss of the SPG's support, Anglicanism in Connecticut was said to have survived the war with seventy congregations, 'many of them large and making a majority of the inhabitants of large towns', and with 40,000 adherents in all.[48]

The war also disrupted the SPG's missions to Native Americans. The territory of the Six Nations was bitterly fought over and in 1783 was ceded to the United States. The Society, however, accepted responsibility for the Mohawk communities, believed to be under the authority of the Anglican military hero, Joseph Brant, who had relocated north of Lake Erie in Canada. There the Mohawks had a new church built for them, which Brant wished to have 'decently ornamented' including the royal arms, as 'vastly pleasing to the congregation, as well as striking their visiting Indian neighbours with awe and respect'.[49] The Scottish Society continued after the war to pay the salaries of missionaries to the Indians operating in what was now the territory of the United States. It renewed its payments to Samuel Kirkland, who as Congress's emissary to the Oneida had tried to rally them against the British during the war, and was gratified to hear that 'his success among the Indians had greatly exceeded anything formerly known to the Society'.[50] Kirkland continued to receive his salary from Scotland until 1796.[51] By then, however, public zeal in Britain for Native American conversion had largely evaporated. Missionary enthusiasm was increasingly directed towards enslaved Africans and the new Indian subjects of the East India Company.

Without the privileges that they had enjoyed under the colonial order or the support that had been channelled to them from Britain through the SPG, American Anglicans had to rebuild a Church seriously damaged by war. Once Anglicans could no longer be seen as an agent of imperial authority, America's secular leadership, committed to the principles of religious freedom, was not unsympathetic to their designs. In Jeffersonian circles the Episcopal Church was commended as 'liberal' by comparison with revivalist sects that were 'bigoted and illiberal' and it was expected that it would become 'truly respectable' when it reformed itself.[52] To stand on their own feet, American Anglicans, however, initially needed acts of English authority. Candidates for ordination still had to go to Britain and to swear allegiance to the Crown. In 1784 a bill was passed in the British Parliament, put forward by the Bishop of London, enabling foreign subjects to be ordained by English bishops without swearing the oath of allegiance.[53] The question of an American bishop, which had proved so contentious in the past,

---

[48] S. Seabury to M. Cooper, 31 August 1782, National Archives of Scotland, CH 12/12/2007. See also C. Inglis to SPG, 6 May 1782, J. W. Lydekker, *The Life and Letters of Charles Inglis* (London, 1936), p. 208.

[49] D. Claus to E. Nepean, 24 April 1787, TNA, CO 42/19, f. 127.

[50] Minutes of 11 November 1784 and 3 January 1788, National Archives of Scotland, GD/95/1/5, pp. 298, 327.

[51] Alan Taylor, *The Divided Ground: Indians, Settlers and the Northern Borderlands of the American Revolution* (New York, 2006), pp. 209, 370–1, 374.

[52] J. Page to T. Jefferson, 23 August 1785, Julian P. Boyd et al. (eds), *The Papers of Thomas Jefferson* (Princeton, NJ, 1950–), VIII, p. 428.

[53] 24 Geo. III, c. 35.

remained to be resolved. In the view of the republican elite, it now presented no real problems. A bishop without any claim to temporal authority would be acceptable.[54]

The English bishops and the British government moved slowly and cautiously. The bishops were lobbied by two conflicting elements among the American Anglicans. First in the field were the High Church clergy of New England. They were alarmed by the plans of other American Anglicans for what seemed to be a Church under lay authority. 'A bishop, it seems, is to have no more power than a lay member. Doctrine, discipline, liturgies &c. are all to be under lay control.'[55] They thought it 'their duty to reject such a spurious substitute for episcopacy'.[56] In 1783 they dispatched Samuel Seabury of Connecticut to go to London to seek consecration from the English bishops. He made little progress, being told that the bishops would not act without the approval of the British government and that the government was wary of giving offence in the United States. After a year he decided to by-pass the English bishops and ask for consecration from bishops who felt no obligation to obey British secular authority. These were the bishops of the Episcopal Church of Scotland, often regarded in England as 'downright Jacobites'.[57] Seabury was consecrated by them as Bishop of Connecticut at Aberdeen in November 1784. This was an outcome that had been foreseen even before Seabury left America and it was one that appealed strongly to the High Church clergy in Connecticut. In Seabury's view, the connection between the Church of England and the British state was far too 'intimate', whereas from the Scots 'a free, valid and purely ecclesiastical episcopacy may . . . pass into the western world'.[58]

The majority of American Anglicans, including those who had sided with the Revolution, proceeded very differently. They hoped to rebuild the Anglican Church from the parish level upwards. State associations of clergy and laity came together and elected delegates to represent them at national conventions.[59] The similarities with republican secular constitution-making were obvious. Benjamin Rush reported that the new episcopal Church would be 'the most popular church in America. They have adopted a form of ecclesiastical government purely republican.'[60] To those who sought to defend the Anglican tradition, this was 'a motley mixture of episcopacy, presbytery and ecclesiastical republicanism'; the English

---

[54] There were exceptions. Rufus King was 'very much dissatisfied' with the appointment of bishops. He thought that 'an equality in the teachers of religion and a dependence on the people, is an republican sentiment' (letter to E. Gerry, 6 May 1785, Paul H. Smith (ed.), *Letters of Delegates to Congress 1774–1789*, 26 vols. (Washington DC, 1976–2000), XXII, p. 385).

[55] S. Seabury to J. Skinner, 27 December 1784, National Archives of Scotland, CH 12/12/2017.

[56] A Jarvis to Archbishop of York, 21 April 1784, National Archives of Scotland, CH 12/12/1995.

[57] G. Sharp to B. Rush 10 October 1785, John A. Woods (ed.), 'The Correspondence of Benjamin Rush and Granville Sharp', *Journal of American Studies*, I, (1967), 27.

[58] Letter to Connecticut Clergy, 26 July 1784, E. Edwards Beardsley, *The Life and Correspondence of the Right Reverend Samuel Seabury* (Boston, 1881) p. 137.

[59] Frederick V. Mills, *Bishops by Ballot: An Eighteenth-century Ecclesiastical Revolution* (New York, 1978) p. 156; Nancy L. Rhoden, *Revolutionary Anglicanism; The Colonial Church of England Clergy during the American Revolution* (New York, 1999).

[60] To R. Price, 15 October 1785, D. O. Thomas and W. Bernard Peach (eds), *The Correspondence of Richard Price*, 3 vols. (Cardiff and Durham, NC, 1983–94), II, p. 307.

bishops must be expected to reject 'a scheme formed with such a design to degrade the episcopal order' when the Philadelphia Convention submitted it to them in 1785 together with their revised liturgy and the names of candidates to be consecrated as their first bishops.[61] The English bishops were certainly concerned at trends in the liturgy, particularly about alterations to the Creeds which seemed to them to show Socinian tendencies.[62] They were wary about sanctioning something that 'will be called a branch of the Church of England, but afterwards may appear to have departed from it essentially, either in doctrine or discipline',[63] but they had little scope for effective intervention. They agreed to consecrate the three candidates to be sent over, even though two of them had played active roles in the Revolution and the third, Dr Provoost of New York, certainly had highly suspect views about the Trinity.[64] Nevertheless, they swallowed their misgivings. The Archbishop of Canterbury was reported to have told an American episcopal clergyman that the bishops 'from the bottom of their hearts wished our prosperity, and would do all in their power to promote it', that the government had no objections, and that the king had 'expressed great satisfaction' in it.[65] An Act of Parliament was duly passed authorizing the consecration of American bishops 'without taking the oaths of allegiance and supremacy and the oath of due obedience to the archbishop of the time'.[66]

The English bishops cannot have had much enthusiasm for what they had done and were to show very little interest in the new Episcopal Church of the United States with its quasi-republican institutions. They had got out of a difficult situation as well as they could. The alternatives were even worse. If they did not consecrate bishops for the Philadelphia Convention, future conventions might assume the power of licensing clergy for themselves, others might resort to the Scottish 'Jacobites', and the bishops were warned that Wesley had sanctioned superintendents in America who were calling themselves bishops and ordaining their own Methodist clergy.[67] They chose to cut their losses in the United States and to focus their attention elsewhere, above all on the principal remaining British North American colonies, Nova Scotia and Quebec.

Here the SPG acted in close cooperation with the British government which helped them to construct what were essentially state-supported Anglican churches directly financed by parliamentary grants. This strategy was based on debatable assumptions: that Dissenters had inspired the Revolution, that the great bulk of Anglicans had been loyal and, most debatable of all, that a large majority of those

---

[61] T. Chandler to W. Johnson, 28 December 1785, E. Edwards Beardsley, *The Life and Correspondence of Samuel Johnson, DD*, 3rd edn (Boston, 1887), p. 370.

[62] G. Sharp to B. Franklin 19 August 1786, Lambeth Palace Library, SPG Papers, 8, f. 195.

[63] Letter of English Bishops, 24 February 1786, William White, *Memoirs of the Protestant Episcopal Church in the United States of America*, 2nd edn (New York, 1836), p. 298.

[64] He 'inclined to opinions little less than of a Socinian character' (Samuel Wilberforce, *A History of the Protestant Episcopal Church in America* (London, 1844), p. 264).

[65] R. Peters to W. White etc., 4 March 1786, White, *Memoirs*, pp. 330–1.

[66] 26 Geo. III, c. 84.

[67] A. Beach to SPG, 8 February 1785, Rhodes House Library, SPG Journals, 24, p. 102; G. Sharp to Archbishop, 15 September 1785, Lambeth Palace Library, SPG Papers, 8, f. 190.

who were emigrating from the United States to Quebec and Nova Scotia were Anglicans.[68] The Church of England was therefore to be built up as a bulwark against sedition and a check on American expansion. Guy Carleton and William Knox were fervent advocates of such policies. 'The prevalence of the Church of England in those colonies', Knox wrote, 'is the best security that Great Britain can have for their fidelity and attachment to her interests.'[69] Ministers were persuaded. Government grants supplemented the Society's salaries of missionaries in Nova Scotia, New Brunswick, Cape Breton Island, and Quebec and paid for church and parsonage house-building in New Brunswick and Cape Breton Island.[70] In 1787 the New York loyalist Charles Inglis was appointed the first bishop of Nova Scotia. An Anglican college and schools were to be opened in Nova Scotia.

The Church of England sought to entrench itself with the aid of the secular power in the face of a majority in Nova Scotia drawn from very diverse Protestant sects together with a considerable Catholic element. In 1772 a Yorkshire Methodist arriving in Nova Scotia had noted that 'the people here are of different perswasion in religion[.] They are mostly Presbyterian and Baptists[.] The Church of England are fewer than either.'[71] He correctly anticipated that Methodist missionaries would reap a rich harvest. Henry Alline, with his doctrines of universal salvation cutting across denominational allegiances, reaped an even richer harvest on his missionary peregrinations throughout Nova Scotia until his death in 1784. There was official concern about the political dangers of religious diversity among the existing Nova Scotia population. The Presbyterian community at Halifax set a cat among the pigeons by inviting a protégé of John Witherspoon to come from New Jersey to minister to them. This was taken to be part of a 'concerted plan' of subversion.[72] The loyalists, far from being solidly Anglican, introduced further elements of religious diversity. The governor described them as being drawn from 'almost all sorts' of 'different sects of religion'.[73] 'What disturbed and perplexed' Governor Parr most on a tour of his province was:

> the cursed enthusiastic spirit of religion, which has crept in throughout the interiour parts, new light springs out of other new lights, making fanaticism even ashamed of itself. I could not have believed it, had I not been an eye witness, to these deluded mortals seeking the Lord in the high roads and bye ways, young girls under twenty crying and lamenting in a piteous manner, tears running fast down their cheeks, looking at the house where an illiterate, ignorant rascal was tormenting scripture and religion, at another place a shoemaker equally ignorant was holding forth, also to a numerous congregation, one side of the country chiefly Anabaptists, mixed with

---

[68] For a strong exposition of these views see Guy Carleton to North, 26 August 1783, TNA, CO 5/110, f. 257.

[69] Letter to C. Jenkinson, 3 April 1786, BL, Add MS 38219, f. 59.

[70] Rhodes House Library, SPG Journals, 20 October 1786, 24, pp. 345, 392.

[71] J. Metcalf to A. Gill, August 1772, Barbara De Wolfe (ed.), *Discoveries of America: Personal Accounts of British Emigrants to North America during the Revolutionary Era* (Cambridge, 1997), p. 46.

[72] G. Carleton to North, 8 November 1783, TNA, CO 5/111, f. 133; also J. Parr to G. Carleton, 23 October 1783, 15 February 1784, TNA, CO 5/111, f. 131, CO 217/56, f. 363.

[73] J. Parr to Lansdowne, 1 May 1785, BL, Add MS 88906/3/18, f. 119.

various sects, Sandiemonians, Swedenbergers, &c. and all these exclusive of Methodists the greatest number are Dissenters who are divided among themselves such as Presbiterians, Seceders and Independants, from these various opinions, the Established Church is almost totally deserted in the interior parts.[74]

The diary of the Congregationalist Simeon Perkins at Liverpool illustrates the remarkable range of religious experiences available in Nova Scotia. He listened to Henry Alline, to a variety of Methodists, to Anglicans, including the bishop when he went to Halifax, to Quakers, to New Lights, to various black preachers, and he attended a 'love feast', which he found 'very solemn and decent'.[75] The Anglican clergy felt themselves to be fighting a losing battle. At Cornwallis, 'Almost all the inhabitants . . . are wild enthusiasts, of every denomination,—Independents, Presbyterians, Allanists &c. &c.', while families from England 'have lost all relish for the pure worship of the Church of England; and calling themselves Methodists, run about the country exhorting'.[76]

In Quebec, Anglicans were swamped by a huge French Catholic majority. Among Anglophone communities, the Church of England was again a minority. The commercial groups who had moved into the towns after the conquest were likely to be either Scottish Presbyterians or New England Congregationalists. In Montreal, Dissenters were said to be 'far the majority'.[77] The loyalists who settled in Quebec along the upper St Lawrence were described as being 'principally Presbyterians, Anabaptists, Dutch Calvinists and New England sectaries'. The 'real members of the Episcopal Church bore a very small proportion to the numerous sects of Dissenters'.[78] A sizeable proportion of the loyalist ex-soldiers in Quebec, 'whether Highlanders, [French] Canadians or Germans', were Catholics.[79]

In Nova Scotia, New Brunswick, and what was to be Upper Canada, the Church of England after 1783 became what it had been in the thirteen colonies, a Protestant denomination competing with other Protestant denominations. In spite of strong government backing, nowhere was it dominant.[80] Yet although Anglicans in writing home to enlist support usually spoke of competition and threats, there is much evidence of coexistence and even of cooperation across denominations. Where clergy were very few and far between, as was nearly always the case, the religiously minded would resort to wherever they could find one and they seem rarely to have been turned away whatever their denominational allegiance. Simeon Perkins's eclecticism

---

[74] J. Parr to Lansdowne, 3 September 1787, ibid. f. 131.

[75] D. C. Harvey (ed.), *The Diary of Simeon Perkins 1780–1789* (Toronto, 1958).

[76] J. Wiswall to SPG, 12 December 1783, Rhodes House Library, SPG Journals, 23, p. 303.

[77] J. Stuart to SPG, n.d., ibid. 24, p. 3.

[78] J. Stuart to C Inglis, 20 June and 14 August 1787, 6 July 1788, Richard A. Preston (ed.), *Kingston before the War of 1812: A Collection of Documents* (Toronto, 1959), pp. 120, 135.

[79] J. MacKenna to F. Haldimand, 27 August 1783, BL, Add MS, 21874, f. 48.

[80] There is an illuminating account of the problems subsequently faced by the Church of England in British North America in Michael Gauvreau, 'The Dividends of Empire: Church Establishment and Contested British Identities in the Canadas and the Maritimes, 1780–1850' in Nancy Christie (ed.), *Transatlantic Subjects: Ideas, Institutions, and Social Experience in British North America* (Montreal and Kingston, 2008), pp. 199–250.

which drew him to a gamut of clergy, ranging from itinerant black preachers to an Anglican bishop, was not unusual.

By the end of the Revolutionary War, Methodists in America had moved far out of the fold of the Church of England and were effectively placing themselves beyond any control that Wesley might hope to exert over them. Identified with collaboration with Britain, Methodists had suffered severely during the Revolution, but they made a most remarkable recovery. By 1788 they were claiming 1,000 preachers and over 30,000 adherents, and numbers were growing with astonishing speed. Methodism was also spreading very rapidly in Nova Scotia. Francis Asbury, who had emerged as the leading American superintendent, later styling himself bishop, was prepared to accept 'union but no subordination, connexion but no subjection' with Methodism in Britain.[81] The charter that enabled him to assert his independent leadership was the instructions sent by Wesley in 1784, recognizing that the Americans were now 'totally disentangled both from the state and from the English hierarchy' and that, while he would not ordain ministers in England, he saw no alternative to empowering his superintendents to ordain them in America.[82] This they proceeded to do to good effect, setting up their own church structure, the Methodist Episcopal Church, at Baltimore in 1784. Wesley clearly regretted the ensuing separation. When later asked why he had conceded so much in 1784, he was reported to have said that:

> As soon as we had made peace with America, and allowed them their independence, all religious connexion, between this country and the independent colonies was at an end; in consequence of which the sectaries fell to work to increase their several parties, and the Anabaptists in particular were carrying all before them. Something had to be done, without loss of time, for his poor people as he called them in America; he had therefore taken the steps in question, with the hope of preventing further disorders.[83]

Whatever Wesley's motives may have been, the American Methodists were able to seize the chance of going their own way, leaving Wesley with only a nominal authority over them.[84]

The Revolution may have been a defeat for the Church of England in America, albeit one to which many American Anglicans and Methodists responded in creative ways. For British Dissenters, a category often stretched to include Scottish Presbyterians, however inappropriately in view of the established status of the Church of Scotland, it is generally assumed to have been a victory. Religious freedom, at least in principle, was inscribed in all the new state constitutions. Many are presumed to have found the new order in Church and State across the Atlantic much preferable to that

---

[81] Letter to J. Winscon, 15 August 1788, Elmer T. J. Clark et al. (eds), *Journal and Letters of Francis Asbury*, 3 vols. (London and Nashville, TN, 1958), II, p. 63. For Asbury, see John H. Wigger, *American Saint: Francis Asbury and the Methodists* (Oxford, 2009).

[82] Letter of 10 September 1784 in John Telford (ed.), *The Letters of the Rev. John Wesley*, 8 vols. (London, 1931), VII, pp. 238–9.

[83] William Jones, *Memoirs of the Life and Writings of George Horne, Late Bishop of Norwich* (London, 1795), pp. 155–6.

[84] See the account in Andrews, *Methodists and Revolutionary America*.

in Britain. Robert Southey wrote of British Nonconformists after 1783 that 'New England was more the country of their hearts than the England wherein they had been born and bred.'[85] This might have been true when Southey wrote it in the early nineteenth century, but in the immediate aftermath of the war, which a number of them had ultimately come to support, many British Dissenters seem to have been doubtful about the new America.

Rational Dissenters were an obvious exception. They had generally opposed the war and they enthusiastically welcomed the new state constitutions. In his *Observations on the Importance of the American Revolution and of the Means of Making it a Benefit to the World* of 1784 Richard Price particularly commended what he rather over-optimistically interpreted as the total separation of Church and State throughout the new states.[86] The United States were now happily free of 'tyrannical laws against heresy and schism, and...slavish hierarchies and religious establishments'.[87] For Thomas Brand Hollis, 'The Virginia declaration of toleration or rather against intolerance, surpasses for spirit and good sense anything of its kind in Europe.'[88] John Jebb anticipated that American independence would be 'a great event...in the civil and religious history of mankind...The Gospel will flourish in consequence of the true spirit of toleration being established in the transatlantic world.'[89] Rational Dissenting ministers happily consorted with John Adams, the first American ambassador in London. The Adams family regularly attended Price's meeting house. The rise at the expense of strict Calvinism of liberal Unitarian and Universalist doctrines among the New England clergy, particularly in Boston, enabled the Rational Dissenters to establish new links across the Atlantic and to extend their influence. The London Unitarian Theophilus Lindsey was delighted to record that a 'loyalist high churchman' had been driven out of the Anglican King's Chapel in Boston and that the service there had been 'altered from Trinitarian to Unitarian'.[90] In 1791 an outraged Philadelphia Presbyterian wrote of the Boston ministers that 'Some are Calvinists, some Universalist, some Arminians, some Arians and at least one a Socinian'. Yet 'they will meet and shake hands, and talk of politics and science, and laugh and eat raisins and almonds, and apples and cakes, and drink wine and tea, and then go about their business when they please'.[91] Such people were natural soul-mates for British Rational Dissenters, even if their influence in the United States was in sharp decline in face of revivalist movements.

---

[85] Cited in Anthony Lincoln, *Some Political and Social Ideas of English Dissent 1763–1800* (Cambridge, 1938), p. 26.

[86] James H. Hutson, *Church and State in America; The First Two Centuries* (New York, 2008), pp. 104–5.

[87] (London, 1784), pp. 3, 19.

[88] To J. Willard, n.d., 'Joseph Willard Letters', *Proceedings of the Massachusetts Historical Society*, XLIII (1909–10), 622.

[89] To C. Wyvill, 27 September 1781, C. Wyvill (ed.), *Political Papers*, 6 vols. (York, 1794–1804), IV, p. 511.

[90] Letter to W. Tayleur, 7 September 1785, G. M. Ditchfield (ed.), *The Letters of Theophilus Lindsey (1723–1808)* (Woodbridge, 2007), p. 472.

[91] Conrad Wright, *The Unitarian Controversy: Essays on American Unitarian History* (Boston, 1994), p. 52.

Quakers were another group who quickly re-established connections which had never been totally interrupted. War and independence seem to have been irrelevant to them. They remained probably the most closely knit of all transatlantic communities, held together, as the Philadelphia Meeting put it, by 'the bands of Christian fellowship...long experienced and often livingly felt to subsist and flow between Friends here and those in the kingdom of Great Britain and its connections'.[92] The long-standing practices of transatlantic visits and of exchanging Epistles, which had still been spasmodically transmitted during the war, were restored. Thirteen American Friends immediately came over to Britain and asserted themselves in urging stricter discipline and greater activity on their British colleagues, above all in goading them into launching a campaign against the slave trade.[93] There were eight Americans at the London Yearly Meeting in 1787.[94] Some English Quakers found their American colleagues inclined to 'dictatorial meddlement' at Meetings where they made 'abrupt and sometimes rude' comments.[95] Americans also resumed tours throughout the British Isles. John Pemberton left a remarkable record of travelling the length and breadth of Britain and Ireland to witness and exhort.[96] Smaller numbers of British Friends crossed the ocean. Three were dispatched in 1785.[97] From Philadelphia they went to Virginia, Maryland, the Carolinas, and New England.[98] One of them, John Townshend, went on from New England to visit the Quaker communities of Nova Scotia, including those recently moved from Nantucket in order to carry on their whaling within the British imperial market. At Halifax the governor and his family attended his meeting at which 'the Gospel of life and salvation freely flow'd through my heart to the people'.[99]

Beyond the Rational Dissenters and the Quakers, it proved more difficult to re-establish transatlantic Dissenting connections. Indeed John Adams, in reporting on a lack of public enthusiasm for the United States in post-war London, concluded: 'I had almost said the friends of America are reduced to Dr Price and Dr Jebb.'[100] The vicissitudes of John Witherspoon in England and Scotland in 1784 exemplified these difficulties. The College of New Jersey had suffered severely in the war and hoped to revive the practice of fund-raising for American colleges in Britain. Against his own better judgement, Witherspoon allowed himself to be persuaded to go to Europe. He did not get a good reception and collected virtually no money. John Wesley commented that, since he had been 'the grand instrument of tearing away children from their parents to whom they were united by the most

---

[92] Meeting, 25–30 September 1786, Friends House, Epistles Received, 5, p. 262.

[93] Christopher L. Brown, *Moral Capital: Foundations of British Abolitionism* (Chapel Hill, NC, 2006), pp. 414–22.

[94] Ibid. p. 233.

[95] J. William Frost (ed.), *The Records and Recollections of James Jenkins* (New York, 1984), p. 183.

[96] W. H. [Hodgson], *The Life and Travels of John Pemberton* (London, 1844).

[97] Friends House, Minutes of Meetings for Sufferings, 37, pp. 193, 203.

[98] Their movements were reported in Friends House, Epistles Received, 5.

[99] John Townshend's Journal, 7 April–24 August 1786, Friends House, Temp MSS, 801.

[100] Letter to J. Jay, 30 August 1785, Charles F. Adams (ed.), *The Works of John Adams*, 10 vols. (Boston, 1850–6), VIII, p. 313.

sacred ties', he could hardly be surprised.[101] In the view of John Erskine and of all Witherspoon's friends who were consulted by Erskine, the venture was 'utterly imprudent'.[102] Initially alarmed at his appearing in Britain, the government was gratified by his failure. The Lord Justice Clerk of Scotland thought him 'a designing, turbulent and bad tempered man', who had been 'unnoticed' in Edinburgh, 'except by a few religious bigots'. He was 'a fool to expect any support for his plan for promoting education and literature in America'.[103] Other attempts to raise money, such as by Benjamin Rush on behalf the new Dickinson College in Pennsylvania or by the New England Baptists for their Rhode Island College, like Princeton, ravaged by war, produced little except books. Richard Price warned a Rhode Island supplicant that it was too soon after the war and that 'the Dissenting interest' was too impoverished to sustain a collection. 'The time has come', he told Ezra Stiles of Yale, 'when the Dissenters of England have more reason to look to America, than America has to look to them.'[104] This was a realistic assessment of the shift of power within dominations, as with the Methodists or the Quakers, from one of American dependence to one of at least equality. Abigail Adams found the English Dissenting clergy 'a very different set of men' from those in the United States. 'They are cramped, contemned, degraded, lacking that independant appearance and that consciousness of their own worth' of their American contemporaries.[105]

There is little to suggest that many people emigrated to America from Britain and Ireland immediately after the war either to escape religious persecution or to live in a land of religious freedom. Charles Nisbet of the Popular Party of the Church of Scotland, an opponent of the American War was, however, induced to cross the Atlantic to become the first president of Dickinson College. He was recruited by Benjamin Rush, who had been instrumental in bringing Witherspoon to New Jersey twenty years before. Nisbet was a close friend and admirer of Witherspoon and of very similar views. His reactions to the new America were, however, to be entirely different. Whereas Witherspoon signed the Declaration of Independence, Nisbet served Dickinson College for twenty years, but detested his sojourn at Carlisle in Pennsylvania. He lived there 'like a pelican in the wilderness'. Far from seeing America as God's chosen land, he believed that 'the Divine Providence has a controversy with the United States'. 'We have no men of learning or taste and of religious people fewest of all.' 'We are a weak, foolish and divided people.'[106] American democracy was giving power to 'a mob of bankrupts, fugitives

[101] Letter to B. Collins, 11 March 1784, Telford (ed.), *Letters of Wesley*, VII, p. 214.

[102] Letter of 5 February 1784, Ashbel Green, *The Life of the Revd John Witherspoon*, ed. Henry Lyttleton Savage (Princeton, NJ, 1973), p. 200. Other letters conveyed the same message, ibid. pp. 192–231.

[103] T. Miller to Sydney, 1 August 1784, TNA, HO 102/2, ff. 143–4.

[104] Price to H. Merchant 6 October 1783, to E. Stiles, 15 October 1784, Thomas and Peach (eds), *Price Correspondence*, II, pp. 199, 236.

[105] Letter to E. Smith, 29 August 1785, Butterfield et al. (eds), *Adams Family Correspondence*, VI, p. 316.

[106] James H. Morgan, *Dickinson College: The History of One Hundred and Fifty Years* (Carlisle, PA, 1933), pp. 63–6.

from justice, transported convicts and indented servants'.[107] On their own, Witherspoon and Nisbet can hardly be regarded as exemplars of different phases of Anglo-American relations. Nisbet's case does, however, seem to show that people who might have been disposed to be favourable to America would in fact have great difficulty in adjusting to the new religious order there which was being transformed by evangelical revivals. At the best of times American patterns of worship could prove to be disconcerting to learned Scottish ministers. Nisbet was most emphatically such a person. He was described as 'a kind of walking library'.[108] Even Witherspoon had found that his way of addressing mass congregations in Scotland in 'a calm rational manner' was not appreciated in America by 'a thin and negligent assembly, mostly composed of those who think themselves under no obligation to attend but when they please' and used to the 'loose and declaratory manner' adopted by their own preachers.[109] Scottish congregations were presumed to defer to their ministers; American congregations increasingly tended to challenge their authority. Thomas Coke, sent out as superintendent to the American Methodists found that congregations in Maryland in 1789 took matters into their own hands and would 'pray and praise aloud in a most astonishing manner'.[110] As revivals swept America at the end of the century, the gap between ministers from Britain and the potential members of their flocks could be very wide.

In time, however, transatlantic contacts were to multiply, less through institutionalized denominational links as in the past than by the coming together of like-minded individuals and groups. Under persecution some British radical Dissenters were forced to seek refuge in America in the 1790s, while American revivalists increasingly crossed the Atlantic to spread their messages in Britain and Ireland. Most prominent among these was the exotic Lorenzo 'Crazy' Dow with his flowing locks. He was an exponent of mass outdoor camp meetings, which appealed in Britain not only to a transformed popular Methodism splitting away from its established leadership but also to many of the rank and file of the old Dissenting denominations.[111] The new revivalists, however, operated in a very different Anglo-American world. The old denominational links had been shattered by the fratricidal war and the hold of established denominations over the religious life of the mass of Americans was being undermined.

[107] Letter to Earl of Buchan, 25 December 1787, John P. Kaminski and Gaspare Saladino (eds), *Documentary History of the Ratification of the Constitution: Commentaries Public and Private*, 6 vols. (Washington, DC, 1981–95), III, p. 89. Nisbet's correspondence is extensively cited in J. H. Smylie, 'Charles Nisbet: Second Thoughts on a Revolutionary Generation', *Pennsylvania Magazine of History and Biography*, XCVIII (1974), 189–205.
[108] J. Armstrong to Washington, 2 March 1787, W. W. Abbot et al. (eds), *The Papers of George Washington: Confederation Series*, 6 vols. (Charlottesville, VA, 1992–7), V, p. 67.
[109] Review of *Memoir of the Life and Writings of John Witherspoon*, by 'A Presbyterian of the West', *The Edinburgh Christian Instructor*, XXVIII (1829), 688–9.
[110] Wigger, *American Saint*, p. 167.
[111] W. R. Ward, *Religion and Society in England 1790–1850* (London, 1972), ch. 2; Richard Carwardine, *Trans-Atlantic Revivalism: Popular Evangelicalism in Britain and America* (Westport, CT, 1978).

Conclusion

I

The first half of the book was concerned with Anglo-American politics and with the failure of Britain and the American states to establish a working relationship in the early years after the war. No British minister was appointed to the United States and the embassy of John Adams to London from 1785 to 1788 was, not least in his own eyes, a failure. Unfinished business left over from the peace settlement, above all a commercial agreement, remained unfinished. Commercial relations were instead defined by unilateral British decrees, to some of which the Americans took the strongest exception, and the British also took unilateral action by retaining the fur-trade posts in retaliation for what they saw as the failure of the Americans to fulfil provisions of the treaty. There was to be no official adjustment of Anglo-American relations until 1794.

Americans found this situation intensely unsatisfactory. Few wanted anything remotely resembling reincorporation into the empire or even a 'special' relationship that would distinguish their dealings with Britain from those with other European powers. They wished, however, to do business with the British and they strongly felt that what they saw as hostile British actions were motivated by a deliberate intention to damage them. Not only did Americans want a working relationship with all countries, but they wished to be respected by all. The evidence that many craved the respect particularly of British opinion is overwhelming. With good reason, they felt that they were not respected. British governments evidently did not feel any incentive to cultivate good relations with them and their achievements and aspirations were consistently slighted in the British press and in the opinions relayed by Americans in Britain. Most Americans who tried to explain British attitudes towards them undoubtedly made matters worse by their inability to recognize change in Britain, their commitment to the republican critique, formed early in the eighteenth century and of little relevance to the age of the younger Pitt, and their obsession, characteristic of the period before the Revolution, with supposed plots against them.

American grievances certainly had some substance, even if their explanations for them were usually far-fetched. They were not the victims of plots inspired by the king, but the new America did indeed have some determined enemies, some of whom had suffered in their property and persons during the Revolution. Men such as William Knox, Thomas Irving, Charles Jenkinson, and Lord Sheffield, feared the economic rivalry of an independent America, especially at sea, and believed that measures to damage it and to restrain its growth were in Britain's interest. Knox even advocated a British guarantee of French and Spanish American colonies as a curb on American expansion.[1] Such men were able to exercise a disproportionate influence because of the disinclination of most British politicians to engage seriously with American issues after the war. In disengaging from any close concern with American affairs, British politicians were returning to what had been their attitude before the Revolution. The colonies had been greatly valued for their contribution to Britain's wealth and power, but the great mass of British politicians had given little attention to them. They had remained on the periphery of their interests. To protect her valuable stake in America, Britain had fought wars against foreign enemies. In 1775 a clear majority of opinion in Parliament evidently felt that there was no alternative to fighting to crush the revolt. The failure to achieve anything like a quick victory in America or to avert foreign intervention on America's behalf prompted a reassessment of what was at stake in what had become a secondary theatre in a great international war. Even before the making of peace, opinion was beginning to shift against empire in America. The cost of maintaining it would have been prohibitive, even if it had been practicable, and a beneficial trade probably did not depend on imperial rule, a conclusion soon to be vindicated by post-war developments. Realistically, Britain should cut its losses and concentrate on more profitable imperial projects. This it did.

The rebellion had thrust America into British politics. Peace took it out of them. Relations with independent America were not a major consideration in British diplomacy. Politicians had no reason to concern themselves any further with it. This also applied to most of those who had opposed the war. Once the war was over they too lost interest in America. Although large sections of British opinion wished to see the war ended, they expected it to end on terms that were as creditable as possible and did not involve what could be regarded as abject surrender to America. What were seen as undue concessions to America over the Quebec frontier, the fisheries, or the loyalists were genuinely unpopular. The good feelings towards Americans which may have been felt by opponents of the early stages of the war seem to have been seriously weakened by their French alliance and by their insistence on unconditional independence. The rancour generated by the peace continued for several years.

The tribulations that beset Lord Shelburne in trying to steer the terms of the peace between the American negotiators' unswerving pursuit of their aims and the hostility of the British public to any undue concessions show how fraught any attempt to put Anglo-American relations onto a new post-colonial footing would have been. In retrospect, since so many unofficial links were quickly restored, the failure of Anglo-American politics can be said to have mattered little. Nevertheless, the potential for breakdown and armed conflict was accumulating, as events in 1812 were ultimately to show. Difficult as it must have been to deal with Americans who were both inflexibly self-righteous and uncompromising in the pursuit of

---

[1] To W. Eden, 7 January 1786, WLCL, Knox MSS 7: 26.

objectives, including continental domination, which they equated with the good of humanity, blame for the failure to defuse tensions must rest largely with British ministers. Revolution and war had not changed the approach of British politicians to America. Relations with it were still judged, as they had been in the days of empire, primarily in terms of Britain's profit and loss. In as far as British opinion took account of the nature of American institutions and society, perceived deviations from British norms were deplored. An America that appeared to have lapsed into republican anarchy was to be dictated to on commercial matters, but otherwise ignored, at least until signs of what were regarded as improvements began to be detected after the enacting of the Constitution. Recognition that a different type of society within the British tradition had been evolving across the Atlantic over a long period, that Britain had a great interest in the continuing growth and prosperity of that society, and that the promotion of British interests required some flexibility of approach was very rare.

II

The second part of this book strongly suggests that the pre-Revolutionary British Atlantic world was able to survive the upheavals of war and of American independence. It was a world that functioned through the links that bound together families,[2] ethnic communities, or groups with common interests on both sides of the Atlantic. Where political developments had put obstacles in the way of continuing communication, they were being circumvented. In as far as the British imperial government and the new regimes in America tried to keep their peoples apart, they were generally unsuccessful. As a recent study has argued, although after American independence the 'Anglophones were never again to share a single state', they remained 'a transcontinental, transnational entity, an "Anglo-world"', based on 'transfers of things, thoughts, money and people between Britain and the new United States' which resumed immediately after the war.[3]

There are many examples of continuing transfers. War cut off opportunities for emigration, but a considerable number of those who had enlisted in the army seized their chance to become settlers in America. When transoceanic migration was resumed, the United States drew its European immigrants overwhelmingly from Britain and Ireland. The British consul in Philadelphia estimated that of nearly 26,000 immigrants that had come to Pennsylvania since the war by 1789, under 2,000 were German; the rest came from the British Isles.[4] People going to America tended to renew contacts with members of their own communities. The largest flow was from the north of Ireland, usually in the first instance to the port of

---

[2] See Sarah M. S. Pearsall, *Atlantic Families: Lives and Letters in the Later Eighteenth Century* (New York, 2008); Emma Rothschild, *The Inner Life of Empires: An Eighteenth-Century History* (Princeton, NJ, 2011).
[3] James Belich, *Replenishing the Earth: The Settler Revolution and the Rise of the Anglo-World 1783–1939* (Oxford, 2009), pp. 49, 56.
[4] P. Bond to Leeds, 10 November 1789, TNA, FO 4/8, f. 161.

Philadelphia, where their fellow Irishmen would care for them before passing some of them on to the Scots-Irish settlements in the interior. Highland Scots, scattered across the continent by war, began to reach back to bring over their fellow clans people from the Highlands. Movements of people between the United States and the British North American colonies continued after the great post-war emigrations of loyalists. Nova Scotia and New Brunswick maintained close links with New England as Upper Canada did with New York. Many of those who had fled to East Florida or the Bahamas seem to have returned to Georgia or the Carolinas or to have maintained their connections with them.

British and American merchants resumed a huge transatlantic trade with the ending of the war. Some mercantile connections, such as those of the Scots with Virginia, were badly damaged by the war, but others survived it and a multitude of new arrangements sprang up for distributing British manufactures and marketing American raw materials. Post-war regulations imposed new restrictions. American ships were now to be excluded from the British colonies and some states placed extra duties on British ships and British imports. There were, however, many ways round them. Ships and those who sailed them could assume British or American identities as might be needed to comply with what the regulations required. Even without an imperial link, British merchants and seafarers trading across the Atlantic and their American counterparts still constituted a single community of interest.

Common transatlantic values survived the sundering of imperial links. Britons and Americans still saw their rights as free peoples as embedded in their joint inheritance of the common law, much of which was adopted by the new states. Most Americans and British envisaged themselves as Protestant peoples. The war had meant that American Protestant denominations had to stand on their own feet without support from Britain and evangelical revivals were radically changing the religious landscape of the United States, turning it into one that was becoming distinctly American. In some cases, such as the Quakers and the Unitarians, close transatlantic denominational links revived with the peace. Others, notably the Anglicans and the Methodists, drifted apart. Americans still consumed great quantities of British goods. Their tastes were shaped by these imports. Most of the books that Americans read were either imported from Britain or were British books reprinted in America. The houses, furnishings, and entertainments of Americans who aspired to gentility were largely derived from British models. American authors, artists, and men of learning again sought recognition in Britain.

III

The continuing vitality of transatlantic Anglo-American links of many kinds and the strength of the ethnic or regional ties that still bound together communities, whether they happened to live within the American states or in the British empire, raise questions about the place of the federal republic or of the empire in the lives of the peoples over whom they claimed authority. Both the British empire and the United States of America had to compete with other loyalties that cut across their boundaries. A recent assessment has stressed the continuing dominance of local interests in the early republic and the strength of continuities with the colonial past. A 'weak American state' is said to have replaced a 'weak British state'.[5] The British imperial state was certainly more powerful than the American one, but, as this book has tried to show, there were strict limits on the extent to which it could impose its will on its subjects scattered across the world.

The Revolution had revealed beyond any doubt that there was an American leadership with a very strong sense both of a common identity that embraced all the thirteen colonies and of America's destiny to create a new empire in the North American continent. Institutions had been created that had given some practical effect to their aspirations. Effective collaboration was, however, hard to attain, even in the conduct of the war. In its closing stages, Robert Morris reflected on the extent and diversity of America. This made it virtually impossible for an enemy to subjugate it, but it made concerted action extremely difficult. The 'impulses of a sovereign mind' could not be communicated effectively 'to the remotest member of subjected power'. 'The inroads of the enemy create opposition, but when the inroad ceases, when the enemy retires, the storm subsides, each man returns to his domestic pursuits and employments and thinks no more of the scenes which have just passed before him.'[6] It was believed that initial resistance to Britain had been sustained by a great upsurge of popular zeal, but Washington spoke for many when he wrote in 1782: 'The spirit of freedom which at the commencement of this contest would have gladly sacrificed every thing to the attainment of its object has long since subsided and every selfish passion has taken its place.'[7]

In the years immediately after the ending of the war much of the American elite was to lament the pursuit of what they saw as narrow sectional interests by the states and the decline of public spirit and its replacement by a selfish scramble for material wealth. Such complaints were in part at least expressions of the difficulty that an aspiring leadership had in coming to terms with the challenge to their dominance brought about by the widening both of political participation and of opportunities for enrichment which were consequences of the war. Visions of an American future that did not include strong federal institutions were not necessarily any narrower or more self-interested than the visions of those who pressed for such institutions. Nevertheless, complaints about the weakening of support for a unified effort in the later years of the war, or about the lack of any consensus about national objectives after the war, had real substance. Colonial America had been a deeply divided society whose common aspirations had usually been expressed in British terms.

---

[5] Jack P. Greene, 'Colonial History and National History: Reflections on a Continuing Problem', *William and Mary Quarterly*, 3rd ser., LXIV (2007), 246. Greene's essay appears in a round table with six other contributions, not all of which support his conclusions, ibid. pp. 232–86. See also his earlier formulation of the 'strong private orientation of early American society' in 'The Limits of the American Revolution' in his *Understanding the American Revolution: Issues and Actors* (Charlottesville, VA, 1995), pp. 359–70.

[6] To B. Franklin, 27 November 1781, Leonard W. Labaree et al. (eds), *The Papers of Benjamin Franklin* (New Haven, CT, 1959–), XXXVI, p. 157.

[7] To J. Laurens, 10 July 1782, John C. Fitzpatrick (ed.), *The Writings of George Washington*, 39 vols. (Washington, DC, 1931–1944), XXIV, p. 421.

Early national America was also a deeply divided society onto which it was extremely difficult to engraft a new set of common American aspirations. The Constitution has been described as a roof whose supporting walls of national identity were yet to be built.[8] Success in the War of Independence had not been enough 'to supply the shared sentiments, symbols, and social explanations necessary for an integrative national identity'.[9] There were conflicting views as to what had been the aims and achievement of the Revolution which were to be central to the rivalry of Federalists and Republicans.[10]

The state apparatus of the British empire dwarfed anything as yet to be constructed in the United States, but its authority over the empire was constrained. The British Parliament still claimed sovereign authority over the whole empire and on occasions exercised it, as in the eventual abolition of the slave trade and of slavery, but it had renounced its power to tax colonies in 1778 and to legislate for Ireland in 1782. In the 1780s it was in general less inclined to use its imperial powers in assertive ways than it had been before the American Revolution. The bureaucratic institutions that managed imperial concerns had been weak and diffuse before the Revolution. There was some consolidation under Pitt in the 1780s, but responsibility was still divided and coordination remained difficult to achieve.

There was no significant strengthening of metropolitan authority in most colonies during the 1780s. In Ireland powers had been renounced, although the British administration was able to preserve much of its control by effective management of the Irish parliament. In the West Indies, Nova Scotia and New Brunswick, elected assemblies retained the powers that had given the pre-Revolution colonies a high degree of local self-government. Elected assemblies, albeit with attempts to create countervailing powers to them, replaced rule by governor and council in divided Quebec under the 1791 Canada Act. Only in India with the vesting of greater powers over the governments of the three presidencies in what amounted to a ministerially appointed Governor General had metropolitan control been effectively enhanced. Whether a wayward Governor General could be controlled from home was another matter.

In the new America, government at every level in principle depended on the consent of the governed, even though franchises in most states still required property qualifications. In practical ways, even if the machinery through which it was expressed was much less institutionalized, authority in the British empire also sought the consent of its subjects and could not easily ignore their demands. Even in India, although it was commonly assumed that British rule was despotic, the

---

[8] John M. Murrin, '"A Roof without Walls": The Dilemma of American National Identity' in Richard Beeman et al. (eds), *Beyond Confederation: Origins of the Constitution and American National Identity* (Chapel Hill, NC, 1987), pp. 333–48.

[9] Joyce Appleby, *Inheriting the Revolution: The First Generation of Americans* (Cambridge, MA, 2000), p. 240.

[10] See ibid. and David Waldstreicher, *In the Midst of Perpetual Fêtes: The Making of American Nationalism, 1776–1820* (Chapel Hill, NC, 1997).

exercise of imperial authority could be influenced by the governed.[11] Elsewhere, there were elected bodies and a vigorous and critical press—and resort to public petitioning, to lobbying the British Parliament and government, and sometimes to outright disorder. White populations throughout the empire mounted overt challenges to imperial authority in the 1780s as they had done in the 1760s and earlier. These varied in intensity from the support given by some of the Volunteers to movements for Irish parliamentary reform to the attempt to reverse what seemed to be rigged elections in New Brunswick or the protests against duties and new trade regulations in the West Indies. Even the whites of British India claimed their rights. Reincarnations of John Wilkes appeared from Nova Scotia to Calcutta.[12] British imperial authority had ridden out such challenges, which stopped well short of demands for independence and republican institutions, before the Revolution and it was to do so again in the 1780s.

The challenge of American republicanism, however, raised the stakes. Britain's rulers felt that they needed to assert their legitimacy against the universal rights of humanity which the Americans claimed to be championing. Strenuous efforts had been made, mostly by a multitude of self-selected protagonists of the virtues of the British constitution rather than by government propaganda, to exalt the rights and the ordered liberty enjoyed by the people of Britain against the spurious claims of the Americans, which were denounced as the slippery slope to anarchy and the tyranny of the mob. In Britain itself and even in Ireland, these efforts had been, up to a point, largely successful. Many in both countries opposed the war but very few advocated the adoption of republican principles. The response to the American Revolution proved to be a rehearsal for renewed attempts to mobilize opinion against the much more potent challenge of revolutionary France in favour of constitutional liberty through various loyalist and association movements.

IV

In the aftermath of the American Revolution there was much talk of trying to bring about distinctively British societies throughout the British empire, which would enjoy the benefits of the British constitution. Sir Guy Carleton and later William Grenville in his drafting of the 1791 legislation for Quebec emphasized the need for a strong royal executive, for a society based on hierarchy with a propertied elite exercising leadership, and for an influential established Church. All these would help to instil principles of order and social cohesion. Such principles can have had little relevance to the mass of the Anglophone population of British North America or the West Indies, even if they were recent refugees from the United States,

---

[11] The question of Indian 'consent' to and involvement in foreign rule is discussed in my *The Making and Unmaking of Empires: Britain, India and America c.1750–1783* (Oxford, 2005), pp. 263–70.

[12] For the Wilkes of Nova Scotia, see J. Parr to E. Nepean, 8 March 1788, TNA, CO 217/60, f. 173; for 'the Wilkes of India', see Alfred Spencer (ed.), *The Memoirs of William Hickey* 4 vols. (London, 1913–25), II. 182.

let alone for the French majority in Quebec. For British colonial populations before and after the Revolution the British constitution meant rights under the common law, not hierarchy. They had long traditions of contesting the executive power of governors, they resented the pretensions of local elites who had none of the prestige of British aristocrats, and the Church of England had no claims to pre-eminence over other Protestant sects whose adherents were more numerous. Many even of the upper-class loyalists saw themselves primarily as 'Americans', which they did not of course equate in the slightest with being republicans. Benjamin Marston, a 'Harvard-educated New Englander', who evidently had a strong sense of social hierarchy,[13] thought that offices in British North America should be filled by 'natives of America, who look on the country as their home, as the abiding place for themselves and their posterity'. He was writing from a Britain which 'Americans' used to call 'home, but it has become a very cold home to us in general. The original connections and attachments are long since worn out and dissolved.'[14]

Those who lived in the British Atlantic colonies of course accepted that they were British subjects, owing allegiance to the Crown of Great Britain. This distinguished them from those who lived in the United States, even though the distinction for many might be temporary, as they moved backwards and forwards across boundaries. But whether their sense of an overarching British identity was any stronger than the weak sense of American identity, which historians diagnose for the early years of the republic, seems doubtful. General Carleton's noble aspiration that the people of the colonies 'must have all our privileges, as far as circumstances may permit, so that we may have but one common interest, and become, as far as possible, one and the same people' probably remained no more than a noble aspiration.[15]

The strongest loyalties felt by the mass of those who lived both in British North America or the British Caribbean and in the United States in the aftermath of the Revolution were probably loyalty to the local communities among whom they lived; the enduring loyalties to individual colonies that became state loyalties in the new America; ethnic loyalties, such as those of the Highland Scots or the Scots-Irish on both sides of the ocean; or denominational loyalties, such as those that united Quakers everywhere, Presbyterians in Scotland, northern Ireland and America, or Congregationalists in New England and Nova Scotia.

Understanding of how the diversity of post-revolutionary British America eventually gave way outside French Quebec to a greater degree of conscious Britishness, distinct from an emerging American identity, seems at present to be tentative.[16] The influx of loyalists probably did not create new British societies; the mass of the

---

[13] For him, see Maya Jasanoff, *Liberty's Exiles: The Loss of America and the Remaking of the British Empire* (London, 2011), pp. 166–8.

[14] To E. Winslow, 17 March 1790, W. O. Raymond (ed.), *The Winslow Papers* (St John, NB, 1901), p. 377.

[15] To North, 5 October 1783, TNA, CO 5/111, ff. 21–2.

[16] See Nancy Christie's Introduction to the essays edited by her, *Transatlantic Subjects: Ideas, Institutions and Social Experience in Post-Revolutionary British North America* (Montreal and Kingston, 2008).

loyalists were too diverse and too American. In the West Indies, the wealthiest planters who had identified so closely with Britain and its values were increasingly becoming absentees. Other whites formed the upper tier of a Creole population rooted in the islands and often bitterly resentful of British attacks on the slave trade and on slavery.[17]

There is currently much interest in the concept of a 'British world' of which Canada eventually became a prominent member and in which the British West Indies were included. The British world is said to have been the product of 'mass migration from the British Isles' to '"neo-Britains" where migrants found that they could transfer into societies with familiar cultural values'.[18] Since the underlying conditions for creating neo-Britains hardly existed before the mid nineteenth century—migration from the British Isles into British North America cannot be described as 'mass' at least until the 1830s[19]—scholarship on the British world focuses on the period from the 1850s to the 1950s. British world studies in any period seem to have difficulty with the United States of America. Was it altogether separate from the British world or did it form part of an 'Anglo-world', which in some ways intersected with the British world? For the period of this book, however, if the concept of a British world overseas has any relevance, it would be entirely inappropriate to talk about one without the United States. The great bulk of people of British or Irish origin living overseas still lived in the United States. War and independence had not driven Britain and America apart in other ways. Economically and culturally, America was still tied to Britain. There can be no question but that the eastern United States, the remaining British Atlantic dependencies, and those parts of the British Isles which sent migrants across the Atlantic or traded extensively with America remained closely bound together into what can still be called a British Atlantic world. The ties would only weaken when the United States attracted immigrants on a large scale from beyond the British Isles, developed its own manufacturing capacity, and edged its way towards some sort of distinctly American national culture. Even then, many British and Irish migrants would continue to go to the United States, which would become the major source of cotton, Britain's most important imported raw material, and Britain and the United States would still share many tastes and values in common.

V

Any reader who has had the fortitude to persist to the end of this book can hardly fail to have noticed that the two themes that run through it—Anglo-American politics and the transatlantic links that made up the British Atlantic world—are

[17] For Barbados, the most self-consciously English of the islands, see David Lambert, *White Creole Culture, Politics and Identity during the Age of Abolition* (Cambridge, 2005).
[18] Carl Bridge and Kent Fedorowich, 'Mapping the British World', Bridge and Fedorowich (eds), *The British World: Diaspora, Culture and Identity* (London, 2003), p. 3.
[19] See table in Elizabeth Jane Errington, 'British Migration and British America 1783–1867' in Phillip Buckner (ed.), *Canada and the British Empire* (Oxford, 2008), p. 141.

presented as often being in conflict with one another. Politics nominally divided Britons and Americans. It put them on opposite sides in a war and kept their respective governments in a state of simmering ill feeling after the war. 'Ordinary' Britons and Americans, on the other hand, are shown as going about their businesses with little apparent regard to such divisions and perhaps with not much sense of difference. They traversed the American continent or crossed the Atlantic Ocean in search of land, employment, commercial profit, education, or spiritual fellowship. The book implies that they did so with little regard to politics except when political events disrupted their lives, most obviously during the war and its aftermath. Then some could take advantage of conflict and the change of regimes to win wealth and a new consequence in the world; most probably had to devise strategies to limit the damage while waiting for better times.

It would not be surprising if persevering readers found the implied assumption that politics was an unwelcome intrusion into the life of most participants in the British Atlantic world unconvincing. Were not great issues at stake? Were not 'ordinary' Britons or Americans also republicans or loyalists, strongly committed to their own interpretations of how liberty was to be sustained? Many Americans surely saw themselves both as defending the high degree of liberty which they believed they had already attained and as participating in the creation of a new order embodying ideals of freedom and equality never as yet realized in any other human society. The price of such noble objectives might be high, but many were clearly willing to pay it. In trying to suppress what they saw as the American insurgency, many American loyalists and British supporters of the war also claimed to be motivated by high principles. They were defending the British constitutional system with its proven capacity to combine national power with individual freedom against spurious claims that could only lead to anarchy or tyranny. Commitment to such values forced many to flee their homes.

There can be no doubt that, especially in the early years of the war, many in the British Atlantic world were passionately committed to political causes. People who migrated to America could hardly have done so with the expectation of fighting a war. When the war came, many, perhaps the majority, probably hoped to keep out of it and to avoid taking sides, but a good proportion became fervent partisans of one side or the other. Outside New England, recent immigrants may have been the staple of the Continental Army. One such was Job Johnson, who had gone from Ulster to Pennsylvania where he became a school master. The strength of his commitment to the patriot cause is clear. His health was ruined in campaigns against the Indians and ultimately at Yorktown, bringing him to an early death, but at the end of the war he could still 'bless God who has at last given us the victory and established our Independancy'.[20] Recent immigrants could also throw themselves wholeheartedly into the loyalist cause. The grandfather of Roger Bates, a settler in Upper Canada, came to America in the 1760s from Yorkshire. According to his grandson, he 'looked upon no form of government equal to the British

---

[20] Kerby A. Miller et al. (eds), *Irish Immigrants in the Land of Canaan: Letters and Memoirs from Colonial and Revolutionary America 1675–1815* (New York, 2003), pp. 569–71.

constitution founded on the principles laid down by the English barons at Runny-meade'. He fled to Canada in about 1780, 'determined never to side with the republicans'. There his 'indomitable courage and love for the British constitution' sustained him through 'great privations'.[21]

Yet for most people at most times, politics was probably a secondary consider-ation. The working of the British Atlantic world depended on free communication across the ocean. For those on the American side, Britain was the essential source of new immigrant labour, of the goods that made their lives comfortable, and of the cultural models by which they tried to live, as well as being the outlet for much of their produce and the source of credit that helped to lubricate their economic life. American needs opened opportunities for many people on the British and Irish side of the Atlantic to sell goods and services, or to lead new lives in a new world. Politics, and most especially war, tended to get in the way of free communication. British victory in the Seven Years War had opened up much new land, but thereafter British policies appeared to be aimed at restricting the growth of the colonies and curbing their freedom to take their own decisions. In the 1770s Britain made war on the colonies in defence of national interests in whose importance many British people were ceasing to believe by the end of the war. War brought most civilian transatlantic communication to an end. Immediately after the war, Britain generously subsidized new opportunities for settlement in Nova Scotia, Quebec, and the Bahamas, but her efforts at creating a new hierarchi-cal order in the remaining colonies and her attempts to curb inter-American trade and to discourage transatlantic migration would, had they been effective, have acted as checks on the growth of the British Atlantic world. The ambitions of the American political elite to curb the consumption of foreign imports and luxury and to stimulate self-sufficiency as well as excluding undesirable immigrants, such as slaves, convicts, and servants, had the same tendency but were even more ineffective. This book has tried to show that whatever British or American would-be policy-makers may have intended, the strength of the links holding together the British Atlantic world ensured its rapid recovery from the ultimate failure of politics that had led to a fratricidal war.

---

[21] 'Testimonial of Roger Bates', James L. Talmon (ed.), *Loyalist Narratives from Upper Canada* (Toronto, 1946), p. 30.

Bibliography

PRINCIPAL MANUSCRIPT SOURCES CITED

British Library
Add MS 20733 (John Almon Papers)
Add MSS 21705, 21821, 21874 (Frederick Haldimand Papers)
Add MS 33100 (Thomas Pelham Papers)
Add MSS 38192, 38219, 38310, 38343, 38346, 38349, 38375, 38380, 38388, 38391–2
    (Charles Jenkinson Papers)
Add MS 38716 (Lord Northington Letter Book)
Add MSS 59083, 59236, 59238, 59320 (William Grenville Papers)
Add MSS 61863–4, 61867, 61980 (Sheffield Park, Lord North Papers)
Add MSS 88906 (Bowood, Lord Shelburne Papers)

Friends House, London
Epistles Received, vol. 5
Minutes of Meetings for Sufferings
Temp MSS 301 (John Townshend's Journal)

Lambeth Palace Library
SPG Papers, 8

The National Archives
AO 12, 13 (Loyalist Claims—used for individual cases)
BT 6/20, 6/59, 6/84–5 (Board of Trade)
CO 5 (North America)
CO 5/560–1 (East Florida)
CO 23/25–6 (Bahamas)
CO 42/16–68, CO 43/10 (Canada)
CO 71/9 (Dominica)
CO 137/82–6 (Jamaica)
CO 188/3 (New Brunswick)
CO 217/56–61 (Nova Scotia)
CO 260/7 (St Vincent)
FO 4/2–9 (United States of America)
FO 27/9, 12 (France)
FO 97/157 (Richard Oswald Papers)
HO 42/1–4 (Home Office Domestic)
HO 48/1 (Law Officers' opinions)
HO 100/1–14 (Ireland)
HO 102/1–3 (Scotland)
PRO 30/8/323, 329, 343–4, 349 (William Pitt Papers)
PRO 30/55/70–86 (American Headquarters)
T 77 (East Florida Claims)
TS 11/985–90 (East Florida Claims)

WO/1 (War Office correspondence)
WO 28/4–10 (Canadian Headquarters)

National Archives of Scotland
CH 12/12 Episcopal Church of Scotland
GD 95/1/5 SSPCK Minutes

Rhodes House Library, Oxford
SPG Journals, vols. 23, 24

William L. Clements Library, Ann Arbor, Michigan
Knox MSS
Manchester MSS
Sackville-Germain MSS
Shelburne MSS
Sydney MSS

Unpublished Dissertations
W. S. Sorsby, 'The British Superintendency of the Mosquito Shore, 1749–1787', University of London PhD thesis, 1960.
Carole W. Troxler, 'The Migration of Carolina and Georgia Loyalists to Nova Scotia and New Brunswick', University of North Carolina PhD thesis, 1974.
James Vance, 'Constitutional Radicalism in Scotland and Ireland in the Era of the American Revolution, c.1760–1784', University of Aberdeen PhD thesis, 1998.

Index

Printed and bound by CPI Group (UK) Ltd, Croydon, CR0 4YY